THE
GOOD RETREAT
GUIDE

Stafford Whiteaker

RIDER

LONDON · SYDNEY · AUCKLAND · JOHANNESBURG

For Mary Bartholomew

1 3 5 7 9 10 8 6 4 2

First published in 1991 by Rider
Revised editions 1994, 1997

This edition published in 2001 by Rider, an imprint of
Ebury Press
Random House
20 Vauxhall Bridge Road
London SW1V 2SA

Random House Australia (Pty) Limited
20 Alfred Street
Milsons Point, Sydney
New South Wales 2061, Australia

Random House New Zealand Limited
18 Poland Road, Glenfield
Auckland 10, New Zealand

Random House South Africa (Pty) Limited
Endulini, 5A Jubilee Road
Parktown 2193, South Africa

The Random House Group Limited Reg. No. 954009

Papers used by Rider are natural, recyclable products made from wood grown in sustainable forests.

Layout and typesetting by Behram Kapadia

Printed and bound in Great Britain by Mackays of Chatham plc, Kent

A CIP catalogue record for this book is available from the British Library

ISBN 0-7126-0216-X

INTRODUCTION

What happens when one day you wake up and, in spite of the good job, the right relationship, even the children you always wanted, and all those many signs of a successful lifestyle, you start asking yourself: *Is this all there is to life?*

Such a question usually brings with it a sense of discomfort and unease. Some people cope by ignoring it or finding new roles or activities to boost their confidence, but many more today are accepting the challenge and searching for their own answers. This search can lead to an increased awareness of self that can be both exciting and rewarding. For, although the self is always with us, all too rarely do we take the time to look deep inside ourselves to discover this inner being that so dominates our nature. Yet everything we feel and do is filtered through our sense of self. Even sleep offers no escape. Call it self-awareness, self-identity or consciousness, the sense of self is intrinsic to being a human. Therefore, if you find yourself actively seeking this interior journey towards the true self, you have already begun the search for something more in life.

Whether you call it inner peace, spiritual hunger, the search for the sacred, or God, you will have joined millions of other men and women in the search for the spirit of themselves and the world around them. After decades of catering for the demands of our minds and bodies, the spiritual has truly risen to restake its claim in our well-being. There is now a new quest for spiritual meaning in the West. From stockbrokers to sportswomen, millions of people are embarking on a fresh search for the sacred in their lives. They want some answers to that question: *Is this all there is to life?*

Yet how can we begin to explore this question of our humanity until we have first found some peace and quiet, in a place where distractions of every kind are at a minimum? Our usual holidays cannot provide this kind of sanctuary. Most church services are filled with the business of ritual and sound. Even a quiet day alone at home is likely to end in the performing of some long-postponed domestic task. Many people feel today as if they are being swept along by a tide of events beyond their control without ever having a chance for a bit of peaceful living. There is no denying that the impact of the pace of the world, the economic imperative to succeed, and the demand to be goal-orientated, all help to erode people's sense of individuality and self. However, most people cannot simply drop out and go to live on some remote mountain because that would entail leaving behind the relationships and responsibilities that play an enriching part in their lives. So it is not surprising that more and more people are seeking special places where they can start their quest for the spiritual by temporarily withdrawing from their ordinary existence. This is why going on retreat has become the popular solution.

To cultivate an experience of the sacred we do not have to believe in a supernatural deity – what we do need to do is to develop an awareness of our lives that includes those elements and aspects that have become recognised as spiritual and that differ from the physical and mental aspects of ourselves. The poet T.S. Eliot summed it up this way:

> And the end of all our exploring
> Will be to arrive where we started
> And know the place for the first time
>   from 'Little Gidding'

This is the inner journey that going on a retreat will stimulate. The words *soul, sacred,* and *spiritual* will come to have new meaning.

So the primary reason for making a retreat is not just to get away from ordinary life. People go on retreats because they feel impelled more by reasons of the heart than of the mind to withdraw from the world in order to encounter the mystery of self and universe at the depth of human experience. The French writer Pascal observed that 'the heart has its reasons that reason does not know'. Drawn by inner needs that we only partially understand, we want to comprehend the universal in our lives. Here alone may lie the answer to that question: *Is this all there is to life?* For most people, this quest for the sacred is inspired by the simple need to connect their lives to something larger – that universal dimension often called *God*.

With respect to retreats, words like *soul, sacred,* and *spiritual* can readily join up with modern terms like *inner child, wisdom of the heart, sing out, eco-spirituality* and *wild explorer*. The range of different kinds of retreat is now huge, and retreat houses, monasteries and mind-body-spirit centres are adding new concepts and courses all the time. Accommodation is being upgraded continuously, especially with respect to en-suite facilities, in order to fulfill our modern expectations. While wanting some simplicity, most retreat guests are no longer willing to stay in rooms that fall too far below the standards found in a decent hotel. Staff at retreat houses and those offering spiritual guidance are becoming ever more professional, while counselling has slipped naturally into the offerings of many retreat houses, as have alternative healing therapies like reflexology, Reiki, T'ai-Chi, Qi Gong, aromatherapy, and various massage techniques. Meditation, whether Buddhist, Christian, or non-religious, continues to grow in popularity – as does the interest in yoga – and so many retreat centres routinely now offer those facilities. Retreats that bring together painting, pottery, embroidery or poetry with a spiritual dimension are widely available. Such is the demand for Buddhist retreats that leading centres have developed beginners' weekends for those without any prior experience.

All things considered, £45 per day seems to be the average cost of going on a retreat in Britain now, although you can still go on a private retreat for about £28 a day. Many centres have improved their programmes in order to provide more information about the retreats on offer and there has also been a notable increase in the number of relevant e-mail addresses and websites available. The number of places offering disabled facilities is on the up, as is the number of hermitages offering retreats. Most places now actively discourage mobiles and the use of notepads as well as tapes and radios.

There has been a recent trend towards marketing retreats as if they were some kind of special holiday – the *treat* in *retreat* being the central idea. These try to combine a pamper-yourself rest with a loosely spiritual element usually offered in the guise of an alternative healing technique. *The Good Retreat Guide* believes these endeavours miss the point and are inspired more by commercial interests than spiritual ones. It tries not to include them in its listings.

Retreats have taken their rightful place alongside all our other modern efforts to lead full and healthy lives in which we come to know our true selves. They are now so much a part of our everyday lives that they are regularly featured in the media. Like our sense of hope, our spiritual beliefs need nourishing from time to time. We need to have those spiritual experiences and reflections that make us think: *Yes, I remember now why I am here.* Going on a retreat is today's way of doing it.

Stafford Whiteaker

WHAT IS A RETREAT?

A retreat is a deliberate attempt to step outside our ordinary life. It is an inward exploration that lets our feelings open out and gives us access to both the light and dark corners of our deepest feelings and relationships. When we are able to reflect upon the discoveries we have made about ourselves, we grow in personal knowledge, opening ourselves to the adventure of living and to the manifest rewards of love. For most it will be a movement away from the ego and towards peace. For many, it will be an awakening to the presence of God in their lives.

Retreats are not a new phenomenon. All the world's great religions have found that men and women need at times to withdraw temporarily from daily living in order to nourish their spiritual life. Moses retreated to Mount Sinai. Jesus went into the desert. Buddhists annually make a retreat. Moslems go for a day of prayer and fasting within the mosque. The Hindu withdraws to the temple or wanders alone across the land.

A retreat is not an escape from reality. Silence and stillness are a very great challenge in this age of noise, diversion and aggression. Our lives are filled with preoccupations, distractions and sound. Even after a few hours of stillness, an inner consciousness opens up within ourselves, which is an unexpected and, for many people, a rather startling experience. Modern man has difficulty with silence and stillness.

In opening up your interior self, you may find a surprising void – an empty inner space you never knew existed. Suddenly, there are no radios, televisions, friends, children, pets or the constant background of human activity. There is no gossip, no grumbling, no meetings, no decisions, no interference in where you are inside yourself. You are faced with you alone. You begin to slip into a slower physical, mental and emotional gear and start to think differently. Taking stock of your deeper priorities is what it is about.

Happily, there is space and time on a retreat to dwell on this awareness of your deepest fears and feelings. In these moments your retreat truly begins for this new consciousness starts a meditation on self that is the giving of undivided attention to the spirit. Some have said that it is opening the door to God.

But going on retreat is not necessarily about having spiritual experiences. You might have one but most people don't. It is about refreshing yourself, relaxing, and taking a journey into the deeper self.

Reassessment about your life and relationships and values can happen. And why not? What other time have you ever had to do it?

It is not true that you have to be silent all the time on a retreat. Many retreats have little or no silence and there are retreat houses that can be noisy when fully booked. In any case, if you are desperate, there will be people at hand to help you. And if the combination of silence and stillness is too much, you may well find that a quiet physical activity such as walking, sewing, or painting is the best way to regain a sense of peace. That is why there are now so many kinds of retreats on offer.

WHO GOES ON RETREATS?

At a retreat centre you will meet people of all ages and from every kind of background – students, housewives, grandparents, businessmen and women, the millionaire celebrity and the unknown poor. It is a kind of spiritual club with membership open to all. A group retreat can be fun and a time of making new friends. Even on a private retreat you are likely to meet interesting people.

Having placed yourself amongst strangers at a retreat, you may meet people you like at once, those you do not want to know better and those who may make a nuisance of themselves – the kind of person who has some problem and cannot help talking about it to everyone they meet. You may also encounter another kind of person: someone who persists in hammering away about God and salvation or the greening of the planet or why vegetarianism or raw juice is the key to life. This is apt to annoy even the most virtuous and polite. If cornered by this sort of person, don't be embarrassed about cutting it short. You are there for another purpose, so excuse yourself without hesitation and go away at once to your room or for a walk. On the other hand, you may find it both charitable and instructive to *really listen* to what the person is saying – even if you do not believe a word of it.

DO YOU HAVE TO BE RELIGIOUS?

Men and women of all faiths and those of none go on retreat. You do not have to believe in God. You do not have to be a Christian or Buddhist to go on a retreat even in a monastery. The important factor is your positive decision to take this time for the nourishment and enrichment of your spiritual life. Access to places of the Islamic faith is a different matter and you must enquire first as to the position. You should also enquire first at places of Hindu worship and study. The Inter-Faith Network, for example, whose address is listed in the guide under *Helpful Addresses* may be able to assist you in these matters.

GOING ON RETREAT FOR THE FIRST TIME

If you have never been on retreat before, you will be venturing into unknown territory. How should you behave? What should you do? If you go to a monastery, everyone can seem pre-occupied. It can be confusing and strange. On top of that, you are faced in a group retreat with the possibility of having to talk about how you feel about God, about prayer and about yourself. It is a prospect that does not seem to stop people from going on retreat. Be like thousands before you and take courage, remembering that the people you meet on retreat are there for the same purpose as you – to deepen their spirituality. And you do not have to discuss any of your beliefs or feelings unless *you* want to.

FINDING A RETREAT

Having made the decision to go on retreat, here are four steps to finding the right one for you:

1. Select a place from this guide that strikes you as interesting in an area of the country where you might like to visit.
2. Write/telephone/fax or e-mail for more information and details of the retreat's programme.
3. Visit their website if they have one.
4. Book, giving the dates you would like to stay and explaining the retreat you want to do. Ask if you need to bring anything special such as towels, soap or special clothing and what time of arrival would be best. Many retreat places have separate facilties for men and women so it is always helpful to them if you make clear your gender.

You don't need to say anything more about yourself. Never mind your age, your beliefs or lack of them, or your circumstances, unless you are unemployed or a student, in which case mention those facts as you might pay less.

GOING ON RETREAT FOR PEOPLE WITH DISABILITIES

Unfortunately, many retreat centres and guest accommodation have not been updated to the national standard set for the disabled. Too many places still believe that a wheelchair ramp or a ground floor toilet is all that is needed. But change is slowly taking place and increasingly, whenever refurbishment or rebuilding takes place, retreat houses will include high standard accommodation and access for the disabled. However, even these facilities are often for independent people with disabilities and do not necessarily offer the kind of facilities necessary for those who need to be accompanied by a carer. The Pastoral Centre at Holton Lee in Dorset (see entry) is an exception to that and offers a retreat centre for people with disabilities and for carers. It is a beautifully designed modern complex of buildings with all facilities and a retreat programme to match. Residential courses are designed to meet physical, emotional and spiritual needs and to encompass a variety of workshops. Retreat themes for these may include *Take Time to Grow, Feminine Creativity, Living with Stress, Enneagram and Spirituality, Sexuality and Spirituality Workshop, Releasing Your Inner Dance, and Reflections on Advent.* Hopefully, the future will bring more such facilities so that the retreat movement is as truly inclusive as it ought to be.

Wherever possible the Guide tries to designate if a retreat centre has facilities for the disabled and if these are limited. You should always double-check before booking so that you are certain of exactly what is on offer.

DIFFERENT KINDS OF RETREATS

Most retreats aim towards self-discovery of an experiential nature. They fall into these main groups: conducted retreats, individually guided retreats, theme retreats, private retreats, awareness workshop retreats, day retreats, alternative therapies, healing retreats, shamanic and native spirituality retreats. The choices grow by the year and become ever more imaginative and exciting. No matter the theme or activity of the retreat or the spiritual tradition on which it is based, all of them share the aim of helping you deepen your inner awareness. Here are just a few of the many kinds of retreats usually on offer:

Beginners retreats are for those who are starting off for the first time. A number of retreat centres offer these. For the Christian and most mind-body-spirit retreats you usually need no prior experience. For Buddhist, yoga and others that use a particular system, such as types of meditation, you may need some previous practice and knowledge of techniques involved. Even in those cases, many retreat places are establishing basic beginner courses in their programmes because of demand.

Celtic Spirituality retreats. Recently there has been an emergence of retreats based on Celtic spirituality. The outstanding feature of this ancient Christian spiritual heritage is the overwhelming sense of the presence of God in the natural world. Rich in poems and songs, Celtic spirituality can bring an understanding of the depth of God's presence in his own creation. It is an ancient inheritance of Christian spirituality that has become newly appropriate in a time when we are concerned for the environment and the future of our planet.

Chardinian Spirituality retreats. Pierre Teilhard de Chardin (1881-1955) did not try to present an ordered way to spiritual progress although he was a Jesuit and follower of St Ignatius. Chardinian spirituality confronts the question of how to be in the world but not of it. It has a cosmic focus that eventually leads to a person's love of the world coinciding with her love for Christ. In order to do this, we reconcile a love of God with a love of the world but detach ourselves from all that impedes spiritual growth.

Contemplative retreats have the aim of being still and, through silence and intuitive prayer, to hold yourself open to God from the very core of your being. Contemplative prayer is not an intellectual exercise, yet it is demanding and searching, even painful on occasion – as the lives of numerous saints and holy men and women bear testimony. A convent or monastery devoted to a contemplative way of life is probably the best place for you if you want to make this kind of retreat. There you will find spiritual support by joining the community in their daily round of prayer and worship. Contemplation as a way of spiritual awareness is not confined to Christianity but is part of the practice of other faiths as well.

Dance retreats may be Christian, Native Spirituality or mind-body-spirit retreats. Sacred dancing is common to most spiritualities and helps release physical and emotional tensions and brings to the surface deep feelings and increased self awareness. The Sufis remind us to *dance with joy!* The Christian psalms tell us the same thing.

Day retreats can be very flexible. It might be a day for silence, a theme- or activity-centred day, a time for group discussion or talks, or for lessons in meditation technique. The day retreat is rather like a mini-retreat. It allows you to explore a number of different types of retreat during the year without taking a great deal of time away from your ordinary life.

Directed or Guided retreats are often based on the spiritual exercises of St Ignatius (see below) and can last for 6, 8 or 30 days. The Buddhist tradition offers directed retreats of several weeks, 30 days, six months and even up to three years. Any retreat that offers a spiritual director with guidance to the individual on his spiritual progress through a structured retreat routine may be said to be a directed or guided retreat.

Drop-in retreats are non-residential. The idea is that you live at home or stay elsewhere and 'drop in' to take part in the resident community's regular pattern of prayer or for a series of talks and other activities planned around a set programme. This is an increasingly popular type of retreat for those who have neither time nor resources to go away or whose commitments may prevent them from being away from home overnight. The idea of a drop-in retreat is a new idea for many Christians, but friends of a Buddhist centre or monastery often attend on such a basis.

Embroidery, calligraphy and painting retreats are theme retreats that focus on awakening personal creativity through a craft or other art form. Through this opening of new personal horizons an awareness of others may develop, together with a sense of creation beyond one's own efforts and personal world. There can be many other subjects as themes, such as pottery, poetry, music, gardening – the list is extensive.

Enneagram retreats. The Enneagram is a method intended to help you see yourself in the mirror of your mind, especially images of your personality that have become distorted by your basic attitudes to yourself. The Enneagram has a long history. It is reputed to have originated in Afghanistan some 200 years ago or perhaps in the early years of Christian influence in Persia. It then moved to the Indian subcontinent where it remained an oral tradition known to Sufi masters. Representing a journey into self, the purpose of the Enneagram is self-enlightenment. According to this system, there are nine types of human personality. These have a basic compulsion to behave in a certain way and this behaviour is maintained through a defence mechanism that avoids any change. For example, there are personality types who avoid at all cost anger or failure or weakness or conflict. The Enneagram technique leads to self-criticism which, in turn, leads to self-discovery. From there, we may gain a freedom from the negative aspects of self and this may open the way to deeper faith. Advocates of this spiritual exercise believe its careful study results in a new self-understanding and provides practical guidelines for healing.

Family retreats, held at places that have suitable facilities, give a family the experience of going on retreat together. These retreats need to be well planned and worked out so that each member of the family, from the youngest to the oldest, has a real chance to benefit from the experience. It would be difficult to find any convent, monastery or temple in which children would not be welcomed with love and joy – but many such places simply have no facilities for children. Like it or not, restless children and crying babes are a distraction for those at prayer and for anyone seeking interior stillness. So take your children to a place that clearly states they have facilities – then you can relax and so can everyone else. Buddhist centres and monasteries often have children's *Dahampasala*, which is a school study-session held each Sunday. Otherwise family retreats are often organised by larger Christian retreat and holiday centres which specialise in this type of event.

Gardening and prayer retreats. Most retreat houses have good gardens, and in this form of retreat some practical work is combined with the study of plants, trees and shrubs. Along with talks and time for rest and prayer, this kind of retreat works well in developing awareness of the world around you and can bring the benefit of working happily and productively with others – not something that many people today find true of their ordinary daily job.

Gay and lesbian retreats can address and be supportive of the problems gay and lesbian people may have in gaining access to established church life and to various spirituality groups. Such retreats often have themes that bear directly on living as a gay or lesbian person within society and which link into spiritual matters. It has to be said that the retreats for gays and lesbians are few and far between, no matter what the spiritual tradition. The Gay and Lesbian Christian Movement is trying to improve that situation (see *Helpful Addresses*).

Group retreats are for those in a group and they are usually led by someone who is experienced in such matters, who acts as a leader or facilitator. The group may be from a parish or consist of a number of people from different places coming together. Group retreats often have a theme or cover a particular topic or approach to spirituality. The retreat programme of the place will explain what these are, who is leading the retreat and any guest speakers who are coming.

Healing retreats may use prayer, meditation, chanting or the laying-on of hands. Inner healing and healing of the physical body through prayer and the laying-on of hands have become prominent features of many Christian ministries today. It is also often a feature of mind-body-spirit retreats and workshops. Healing may be concerned with a physical complaint or with the healing of the whole person in order to eliminate obstacles to personal and spiritual growth. It can help us realise our own potential as healers and reconcilers. For the Christian this always involves the inspirational power of the Holy Spirit. Although it sometimes can be for treating a specific illness, a healing retreat is usually for healing the whole person.

Healing therapy retreats make use of one or more of the many alternative healing therapies and techniques now available. Some may be more modern ones like aromatherapy or ancient practices like Ayurveda or herbal medicine. There are many healing therapies on offer today, including massage, reflexology, Shiatsu and Reiki. All are designed to relax the person and to bring about holistic healing.

Icon and Icon painting retreats are about creating and/or using a religious work of art as a form of prayer. It is an established Christian spiritual tradition, particularly in the Orthodox Church, and a very popular type of activity retreat. You do not have to be an artist to enjoy and benefit from such an experience. Similar to this, but in the Hindu tradition, is yantra painting, offered by a number of yoga centres.

Ignatian retreats are based on the spiritual exercises originated by the founder of the Jesuits, St Ignatius of Loyola, in the sixteenth century. A full retreat can last 30 days but shorter versions are available. The retreat director who is assigned to you and works with you on a one-to-one basis, provides different material from the Gospels for daily contemplative meditation. You then have an opportunity to discuss what response this has provoked within you. In the course of the retreat, you are led with some vigour to review your life in the light of Gospel teachings and to seek God's guidance for your future. Ignatian spirituality has been described as finding *God in all things*. It is a way of spirituality that is designed for anyone, whether Christian or not. The satisfaction of these exercises is found not in knowledge of the Gospels but in greater understanding of the most intimate truths of self and God.

Individually guided retreats are often structured around a particular system of spiritual exercises, such as those of St Ignatius, or based upon a defined form of meditation such as Vipassana, one of India's most ancient forms of meditation. Your guide acts as a kind of *soulmate* during your retreat.

Inner child retreats seek to bring you into contact with the most real and innocent part of yourself to renew and bring to life a greater sense of your true nature and inner being. This kind of retreat is enjoying enormous popularity today.

Insight retreats are especially good for people who have had no contact with a church or religion. It introduces them to a new vocabulary of spirituality and helps de-mystify religion. It is especially suitable for young men and women who are seeking access to forms of spirituality and the possible spiritual or religious paths they might take.

Journalling retreats introduce you to the concept and practice of keeping a journal as a spiritual exercise. In a busy life it is often hard to see where and how the spiritual dimension of ourselves or of God is at work in us. Keeping a daily journal by writing down what has happened helps us to remember and reflect. The aim is to become more sensitive to the content of your life and to see the continuity of your spirituality.

Meditation retreats. While all retreats are to a lesser or greater degree supposed to allow some time for individual meditation, there has been a growing demand for retreats specifically aimed at the study and practice of meditation. The Buddhist response to this has been excellent, creating many opportunities for learning how to meditate. In addition to weekly classes, most Buddhist centres and monasteries hold a monthly meditation retreat that is open to both beginners and the more experienced, enabling them to participate in what is considered to be an all-important practice of spirituality. In Christianity, meditation was long felt to be discursive, and the approach was to reflect in a devout way on some theme, often a biblical one. While this practice remains, there has been a world-wide revival of earlier Christian approaches to meditation which share much in common with those found in the religious traditions of the East.

Mind-Body-Spirit retreats. These retreats go under a number of different titles, such as *Soul Journeying, Whole Person retreat, Holistic Retreat, Awakening the Inner Self, and Awareness of the Inner Man/Woman*. The retreats are usually structured around rest, relaxation and inner discovery. There is a wide range of what may be offered. These may include drum workshops, voice and song workshops, Ayurveda workshops, Shamanism, and human-encounter groups. Almost all such centres have brochures that will detail what is involved in the workshop or retreat. It is often a good idea to telephone after you get the brochure and ask whatever questions you may have. This will help clarify terms and words that may be new to you. More and more traditional Christian monasteries are including such themes as well as some alternative therapies such as Reiki and massage in their programmes, so it is not just alternative spirituality centres that offer these types of retreat these days.

Mother and baby retreats offer that rare opportunity for a mother to have a little time to pray, to be alone, and share her feelings of spirituality with other mothers. It is a retreat designed for the mothers and not the babies, who are carefully looked after for much of the day. The nuns at Turvey Abbey (see entry) regularly offer these retreats during the year. The programme is for the mothers and babies to arrive about 9.45 am to a crèche. At 10 am coffee is served and everybody meets each other. Then there is a talk that focuses on spiritual dimensions of life and motherhood. At Turvey Abbey the topic is often *Motherhood and God*, followed by a group discussion. Then, there is time for prayer and meditation without interruptions. If there is a mid-day service of worship, such as Mass, the mothers can join in if they want. At lunch the mothers feed their babies, then go to their own lunch. In the afternoon, there is free time until about 2.15 pm when there is a reflective and prayerful session. After that, the mothers collect their babies and go home. It all makes for a great retreat idea that needs to be taken up by more retreat places.

Moving on and wisdom retreats are both especially for women in which the spirituality of ageing is considered. Various prayer, rituals, biblical or Buddhist meditations and exercises may be used.

Music and dance retreats. Music and dance are ancient aspects of religious worship and the praise of the sacred. The psalms call Christians to bring forth their songs, trumpets, lutes, harps and timbrels, and to dance. Don't worry if you can't sing very well or if you don't play a musical instrument or if you have never danced. That is not important. What is important are your good intentions, for music and dance retreats are a joyous encounter. Singing and dancing bring a gladness of heart that surprises and delights.

Myers-Briggs retreats. Isabel Myers-Briggs spent 40 years investigating personality types, building upon the research into personality done by Carl Jung. She set out eight qualities or characteristics found in each person. Myers-Briggs believed there were 16 personality types, all of which are either introverted or extroverted, and either perceiving or judging. By discovering which Myers-Briggs personality type you are, you select the form of spirituality that best suits you. The idea is that some personalities respond better and more easily to one way of spirituality than another. Here are two examples: an intuitive personality might do better with a spirituality of hope, whereas a person who is a thinking personality might do better with a spirituality centred on reason. Myers-Briggs and Enneagram retreats (see above) are very popular and a great many retreat centres offer them.

Nature and prayer and ecospirituality retreats both link care for the environment to your life and help you gain an increased awareness of the unity of all things in creation. Time is spent on observing flowers, birds and trees. These are active retreats, but ones in which stillness, meditation and prayer also play their part. They may well include *awareness walks* in which you concentrate on seeing things afresh and learn to appreciate colour, shape and texture in order to heighten your awareness of creation at work all around you. They may involve working in woodland, a meadow or an organic garden to focus you on the world and nature around you. This awareness of the inter-connection between all of creation is very much a part of Buddhist and mind-body-spirit approaches to spirituality. The Christian way focuses on it in Celtic and Creation spiritualities and in many of the psalms sung at Divine Office (see *Glossary*).

Open door retreats provide help to make a retreat in your own home while having the direction and support of a group. The idea is for a trained leader or a team of two religious or lay people to go to a private house or local church where a small group wishes to meet. The group meets for a few hours each week over a number of continuous weeks. The group members make a commitment to pray individually during their days back in their own home and to hold regular prayer meetings. The leader provides guidance, materials and talks which help all the members of the group in their meditation and reflection.

Preached retreats are traditional conducted religious Christian retreats that may be limited to a group from a parish or other organisation or may be open for anyone to join in. The retreat conductor may be a clerical, religious or lay person. Sometimes such retreats are led by a team rather than one person. Usually the retreat is planned around a series of daily talks, usually Bible-based, designed to inspire and to provide material for individual and group meditation and prayer. There can be opportunity for silence, but not always. Sharing together is a feature of these retreats.

Private retreats are those in which you go alone as an individual. It is usually a silent time in which you find solitude in order to reflect, rest and meditate. In many monasteries and retreat houses you may arrange to take your meals in your room or separately from others so that you can maintain this framework of silence.

Renewal retreats. Christian renewal means a new awareness of the presence of Christ, a deeper experience of the Holy Spirit and a clearer understanding for the committed Christian of his or her mission in the Church. If you think this kind of retreat is for you, then discuss the matter first, if you can, with your priest or minister.

Salesian Spirituality retreats. Francis de Sales (1567-1622) believed that a person need not enter a convent or monastery to develop a deep spirituality. In his famous work *Introduction to the Devout Life*, he suggested five steps for spiritual growth. These make a progression from a desire for holiness through the practice of virtue to methods for spiritual renewal. His methods are gentle and have always enjoyed wide appeal among people living ordinary lives.

Silent retreats are an adventure into stillness. There are some especially designed to provide you with techniques to help you lose your dependence on noise and distractions so that you are not upset the first time you experience this rare exposure to your innermost feelings. You can also just go on a personal retreat and remain in silence. Silence is one of the most powerful of all spiritual aids. A time of total silence for spiritual reasons is often called a *desert experience* because you have withdrawn from the world to a place that is barren like a desert. Here silence helps to focus you on your inner self. Then, in this empty interior landscape, inner realities may arise about yourself and your life.

Teresian Spirituality retreats. St Teresa of Avila (1515-82) wrote *The Interior Castle* in order to lead individuals from the beginnings of spiritual growth to the heights of mysticism. The steps she describes in this work constitute Teresian spirituality. These steps are viewed as mansions and we progress in our spiritual pilgrimage from one to the next. The seven mansions are those of self-knowledge, detachment, humility and aridity, affective prayer, the beginning of our union with God, the mystical experience or the prayer of quiet and, finally, the last mansion of peaceful union with God. Teresian spirituality is, at once, both logical and mystical.

Theme and activity retreats. In the last few years the growth in awareness of the intimate connection between mind, body and spirit has produced a wide range of courses and study retreats. These combine body and spiritual awareness in methods that spring from modern knowledge or that are based on rediscovering traditional forms of spiritual awakening. You enter an activity, such as painting or dance, through which you bring together your feelings, senses and intuition into a greater awareness of self, of others and of God. There are a great number of themes and activities available in this form of retreat, which is often called after the particular activity or theme; for example *Pottery and Prayer, Walking and Creation, Painting and the Inner Child, Clowning for God*.

Weekend retreats are the most popular form of retreat and are likely to run along the following lines. You arrive on Friday evening, settle your things in your room and go down to meet the retreat leader and the other guests. After supper you meet for a short talk about the weekend and are given a timetable. From that time onwards you will cease talking unless it is to the retreat conductor or unless a group discussion or shared prayer is held. During Saturday and Sunday, there will be religious ceremonies of some nature and probably a short address to the group on subjects that can help you meditate and pray. There will be times for walks, reading and just resting. It is all simple, easy and peaceful.

Yoga retreats employ body and breathing exercises to achieve greater physical balance and mental stillness as an aid to meditation and contemplation.

A TYPICAL DAY ON RETREAT

Nothing is obligatory on a retreat. When you arrive, you can expect to be welcomed and made to feel at home. Don't worry about what to do next – someone will tell you what the arrangements are for all the basics like meals.

A simple Christian day-retreat might be as follows: you arrive at your destination – say, a convent. The sister who is the guest mistress shows you to a quiet room where you meet a few other people who form a small group. Coffee is followed by a short introduction by one of the sisters or the retreat leader telling you about the place and the day's programme. From that moment until after lunch you and the others on retreat maintain silence. There will perhaps be a morning talk followed by worship or group prayer. You are not obliged to attend these if you choose not to. At lunch, you eat in silence while someone reads aloud from a spiritual work – or you may all talk, get acquainted and exchange views. Then there may be a walk alone through the garden or into the nearby countryside, followed by a talk from the retreat leader with a group discussion, ending on a sharing of thoughts and prayer.

A typical Buddhist day-retreat may include more silence and certainly more formal meditation times. But, again, you will be sharing with others in a new and gentle way.

At a mind-body-spirit centre the day may well include more active sessions and draw on the spiritual practices of Eastern or tribal cultures. If you want to have time to yourself, check in advance that no sound-orientated workshops like drumming, sacred dancing or chanting will be going on.

OBTAINING SPIRITUAL HELP

If you need to talk to someone about your life or your personal problems, many retreat places offer time for personal interviews of this nature. However, such talks should lead to some spiritual benefit. Those with over-riding emotional and psychological problems should seek help elsewhere unless this kind of counselling by professionally trained and qualified people is specifically offered. On the other hand, if you need to talk to someone about your spiritual life and could do with some guidance, most places of retreat will have someone who can help you. A directed or guided retreat, an Ignatian retreat or any retreat with a spiritual director or facilitator will usually offer opportunities for personal talks. Meditation, shared prayer, group discussions and directed reading are all ways of obtaining spiritual help.

STAYING IN A MONASTERY

The daily routine is different for monks and nuns who lead an active life, such as teaching or nursing, and for those religious who lead a contemplative life devoted to prayer and worship. Most people who have never stayed in a convent or monastery are afraid that somehow they will feel awkward and uncomfortable. Indeed, in a monastery or convent you *will* be sharing a different lifestyle. But once you understand the daily routine and discover that the monks or nuns are also ordinary men and women, you will start to relax. As a guest, you may expect to be received with warmth and affection. Everyone will try to make you feel comfortable as quickly as possible.

Buddhist monasteries are usually places of training for monks and nuns, although they often welcome guests. They are traditionally dependent on the generosity of their friends and visitors for all their material requirements, including food. Such places are traditionally kept as simple as possible.

Many Christian monasteries belong to *enclosed* orders, like that of the Carmel sisters. This means that the community members remain in their monastery separate from the world. There is usually a *parlour* or special room in which you may meet the nuns from time to time, but you will not mix with them.

Monasteries are busy places with a day divided by prayer and work. So if you have never been to one, do not expect to see the monks and nuns sitting around looking holy, for they follow an active and tough daily routine. Having said that, you are likely to be able to find someone for a little chat and, even when silence reigns, the atmosphere is usually cheerful.

Within the monastery the basics of life are in most ways like those of the outside world. Monks and nuns must eat and sleep. They have emotional ups and downs like the rest of us. There are health complaints and moans about changes that take place. The religious life is supposed to make you more human, not less, and even saints have been assailed with doubts. One of the most famous modern monks, Thomas Merton, expressed anxieties about his life in community until the end of his days. The famous priest-poet Gerard Manley Hopkins was never quite settled and happy. Yet no one could doubt the great personal spirituality of these men. So remember that monks and nuns are just as human as you are and that, like you, they too are seeking spiritual goals.

If you stay in a monastic guest house, you get up when you want to, and if you do not feel like attending any of the daily round of prayer or meditation or even the retreat programme if you are on one, no one is likely to demand that you do so. However, by joining the daily life of prayer and worship, you should find that it helps enormously to sustain and nourish you during your time there. If you stay inside a convent or monastery, be prepared for the bells. These let you know when it is time to pray or work or do whatever is next on the schedule. Christian monasteries, especially the contemplative ones, most often structure their life around what is called the Divine Office. The exact form may differ between, say the Roman Catholics and the Anglicans, but it is centred on the psalms from the Bible. While this may be done in private prayer, it is usually sung or chanted by the monastic community together at designated hours of the day and night.

CHRISTIAN SPIRITUALITY

Christianity is a religious faith based on the teachings of Jesus Christ, which had its origins in Judaism. Its believers hold that Jesus is the Messiah prophesied in the Old Testament. The belief of Christianity is based on the New Testament and the doctrines of the Trinity of God the Father, the Son, and the Holy Spirit, and the Incarnation of Christ and his resurrection from death. All are central to the faith. Christ's role is seen as that of redeemer of all humanity.

While there is a shared basic content in all Western Christian spirituality, the approaches to it may differ. For example, the approach of the twentieth-century philosopher and theologian, Pierre Teilhard de Chardin, is quite different from that of the sixteenth-century mystic, St Teresa of Avila. Yet both belong to our common Christian heritage. Included in the many ways of Western Christian spirituality is the rich treasury of Orthodox traditions on which we may draw.

The use of a particular spiritual approach in the form of exercises or meditations is common. There are also a number of popular techniques for discovering which way of spirituality might best suit your type of personality. Spiritual exercises are methods for spiritual growth. No matter how demanding, they are designed to help bring a change of heart. They are no shortcuts to sanctity, as many a nun and monk has found out. No matter what form they take, spiritual practices are essentially to be pursued in a spirit of prayer rather than as an intellectual exercise.

Today, such practices have come to mean every form of examination of conscience, meditation, contemplation and vocal and mental prayer. Such activities are designed to make the spirit (rather like the body in physical training) become ready and in shape. In this way, the spirit may become open to love and to the discovery of God's will. Some religious traditions might say it is the bringing to consciousness of the unity of all creation and of the eternal. These are ambitious tasks – but then, why not? Unlike the mind and body, the spirit goes forth with unlimited prospects. There are many Christian paths to spirituality, including the traditions of Anglican, English, Franciscan, Augustinian, Dominican and Benedictine spirituality – to name but a few. Some, such as Black spirituality and those from the Orthodox tradition, may be less familiar. The Charismatic Movement and Pentecostalism continue to foster a reawakening of the spirituality of the early Church and have developed an increasingly popular approach. Most people find after a while a particular way that seems to suit them. But for a Christian, Jesus Christ and Holy Scripture must be at the heart of it.

BUDDHIST SPIRITUALITY

The aim of Buddhism is to show us how to develop our capacity for awareness, love and energy to the point where we become 'enlightened' or fully awake to reality. Indeed, the word *Buddha* means *One who is awake*. Although Buddhists do not believe in a supreme creator, since they believe that the world rises and declines in an eternal and timeless cycle, like all the major religions, Buddhist philosophy still has worship that is central to its practice. There is a liturgy and scriptures that are chanted, physical acts of reverence and inner worship of contemplating the Buddha that is often compared to contemplative Christian prayer.

Buddhism began in India some 2,500 years ago and its teachings spread throughout Asia. There is no doctrine and no need to hold to any particular beliefs. It offers a practical path for a deeper under-standing of your life.

There are many different groups in Buddhism. The two major ones are Theravada and Mahayana. When you receive literature from a Buddhist centre, it will probably state which one is followed. The Theravada doctrine prevails in South-east Asia, including Sri Lanka, Burma, Thailand, Kampuchea and Laos. Mahayana doctrine predomi-nates further north in China, Tibet, Korea, Japan and Vietnam. There are sects and schools within these two major divisions so, in a sense, it is similar to Christianity in having many different groups and divisions around the world. Yet all spring from a single spiritual inspiration.

Much of the current interest in the West in Buddhism is due to its being non-exclusive and non-dogmatic. To be a Buddhist does not mean you have to wear strange robes or adopt Eastern customs or reject the cultural background of the West. Buddhism is often called a *way of harmony*, for the Buddha's teachings offer a set of tools with which to find inner peace and harmony by working with your own feelings and experiences of life. By learning to look closely and honest-ly at your thoughts, emotions and physical feelings, you come to a new perspective for understanding your frustrations and discontent. Then, you can start to deal effectively with those feelings. From such insights you may develop a joyful, kind and thoughtful attitude to others and to yourself. This should lead you onwards to a state of love and peace. This inner examination and insight is a direct method of transforming consciousness and is termed *meditation*.

MIND-BODY-SPIRIT SPIRITUALITY

It is easier to describe the mind-body-spirit spirituality movement than to define it, for it is a collection of all manner of ideas and practices aimed at personal growth. What is included at mind-body-spirit cen-tres ranges from past-life therapy, environmental concern, telepathy, healing and Shamanism, to the incorporation of elements from Eastern religions. For many mind-body-spirit enthusiasts it is simply choosing a way forward for self-discovery, self-help and the realisation of per-sonal growth. The majority of the ideas, techniques and approaches spring from well-established traditions of healing and self-discovery. The alternative approaches to health, healing and self-discovery that the mind-body-spirit movement has to offer are increasingly part of everyday living.

Mind-body-spirit spiritualities and practices embrace a wide range of thinking and include the work of prominent scientists whose dis-coveries – particularly in such disciplines as sub-atomic physics, psy-chology, parapsychology and geology – bring a new validity to the ancient teachings of Eastern spiritual traditions. They may also include astrology, rebirthing, work with crystals and paganism. The movement has no established dogma or leaders and is very much a phenomenon of our time. Christians may wish to make certain before attending a mind-body-spirit retreat that the course content or ideas put forward are not in their own judgement in conflict with their religious beliefs.

The retreats and workshops offered by mind-body-spirit centres offer an approach to self-growth that is helpful to many people who do not want to enter an established way as offered, for example, by

Buddhist or Christian spiritualities. The aspect that appeals to most people is the great emphasis placed on a holistic approach in treating mind, body and spirit as inseparable. This approach is hardly new, as it is part of all the major faiths. It is fair to say that the mind-body-spirit movement draws on some of the most ancient healing traditions in the world.

The criterion for including mind-body-spirit places of retreat in this guide has been that their approach is holistic, that there is a genuine interest in helping people and that the spirituality offered is of substance, such as that of the Native American Indian for example, or that it has become of interest to a large number of people. Mind-body-spirit centres do not share a common central basis of belief like established religious places, so you will find each place different from the other. Most places have very extensive programmes and will be happy to provide details. You may also find there is much personal sharing and discussion. If you want silence, ask if that is a feature of the retreat or workshop before you book.

WHAT IS PRAYER?

Each faith has its own tradition of prayer. The Christian prayer, the *Lord's Prayer*, and the opening prayer of the Koran, when God is praised and His guidance sought on the *Straight Path*, are examples of an outstanding and important single prayer to which all may turn. The number of books about prayer and the manuals on how to pray are legion, yet the question remains for most men and women: *How should I pray?*

If there were a single way to begin, perhaps the best might be the request: *Grant me a pure heart*. This involves surrender of self and the offering of your vulnerability and trust up to God. A pure heart brings forth charity, hope, trust, faith and reconciliation. Here, love may be discovered and we may hold fast to that which is best in ourselves and in others. Perfect love is not possible since we are humans and, therefore, fallible. But a pure and willing heart, prepared to view all things through love, is constantly possible for anyone. We might fail from time to time to hold ourselves in this state because we are so human, yet it returns and we can go on again. For those who have faith in God, divine love secretly informs the heart. Such faith makes prayer more instinctive than intellectual, and this prompting of the spirit may occur at any time and in any place. For the Christian, God is both the instigator and the object of such prayer.

WHAT IS MEDITATION?

Meditation is a stillness of body and a stillness of mind. There are many different meditation techniques to help you attain this state of being. They range from Insight or Vipassana Meditation practice from the Buddhist tradition to Christian meditation such as that set out by the monk Dom John Main (1926-82), which now enjoys a world-wide following among Christians.

Meditation begins by relaxing the body into a state of stillness, then the mind into inner silence. Many of the techniques that achieve this, start with a deliberate breathing pattern. (It is claimed that the breath is a bridge from the known to the unknown.) This approach is widely employed to marshal the body and mind and is used also in yoga, T'ai Chi and Shiatsu.

A single word or a phrase, sometimes called a *mantra*, is often used to help the regularity of your breathing. For example, in John Main's approach to meditation, the word *Maranatha* is repeated in a slow and rhythmical fashion. This word means *Come Lord* in Aramaic, the language Jesus himself spoke. It is used by both Saint Paul and Saint John in their writings.

Many people, including Christians, still believe that meditation is some strange mental state in which they may lose control of themselves. Nothing could be further from the truth, for the aim of meditation is not concerned with thinking but with *being*. In such a state of consciousness you are at peace. This peace could not exist if you felt insecure. Millions of men and women of all faiths and those of none find in meditation a method for reaching through deep, inner silence to an experience of self that leads to a more loving response to life.

SPIRITUAL DIRECTION
A spiritual director or guide is someone who helps you in your spiritual journey by being a good listener and by making suggestions for meditation, reading, study or prayer. They are often religious men and women, clergy or lay people who have had special training and experience in helping people with spiritual matters. If you ask in advance, there is usually someone at a Christian or Buddhist monastery with whom you can have a personal talk. If you go on a group retreat, it is likely it will involve sharing personal spiritual experiences and the retreat leader is usually prepared to help you.

YOGA TODAY
One of the most significant developments in European spirituality over the past few years, has been the wide-spread popularity and appeal of yoga. From local adult education classes in village halls to centres and organisations devoted exclusively to yoga, this ancient way to stillness, spiritual openness and better health has been adopted by people of all ages and from all walks of life.

Yoga is one of the six main schools of Hinduism, and yoga philosophy regards both spirit and matter as real and traces the whole of the physical universe to a single source. In modern practice, especially in the West, some elements of yoga are emphasised more than others. For example, Hatha Yoga, which is concerned with physical aspects – particularly with exercises and breathing, is often taught as a complete system of self-improvement. The calm and deliberate movements in yoga can lend themselves to deep relaxation and a peaceful harmony between mind and body. This can become a framework for prayer.

In addition to the yoga centres listed in this guide, you will find that many retreat centres offer yoga in their programmes for spiritual development.

HOW THE GUIDE IS ORGANISED
After the preface and introductory chapters, the guide is divided into sections: England, Wales, Scotland, Ireland, France, Spain, Yoga Centres, Open Centres, Helpful Addresses, Helpful Publications, Travel Organisations, Selected Reading and Glossary.

The section covering England is sub-divided according to geographical regions of the country such as, for example, South-east

England. In that region you will find the county and after it the name of the city, town or village where the retreat centre is located. Retreats in Wales and Scotland are listed first by the town or place, those in Ireland by county. After giving the name, address and telephone/fax/ e-mail/website of the retreat centre, the guide specifies the tradition to which it attaches; for example: *Roman Catholic, Ecumenical, Mind-Body-Spirit, Buddhist, Scottish Churches, Buddhist – Tibetan Tradition, Quaker,* etc. In the majority of cases, a short description will follow which tells you something about the place. After that, detailed information is given. When it is open and who is received. The number and kinds of rooms. Whether children are welcomed and whether it is possible to stay if you are disabled are noted if possible. What facilities are on offer and if any spiritual help is provided. Where you can and cannot go in the house, monastery or grounds. What kind of meals are served and whether or not vegetarians and special diets can be catered for. What special activities are available and where it is situated. How long you may stay. Finally, how to book, what the charges are and how to get there. Most places will send you a brochure about their activities and courses.

For France, the listing is by department with its number and then by city, town or village. For Spain, the listing is by place. Yoga Centres are listed by counties for Britain. Open Centres are listed by name of place.

HIGHLY RECOMMENDED PLACES OF RETREAT

Those places which it is felt can be highly recommended are marked at the start of the entry with a star symbol.

Reports welcomed: *The Good Retreat Guide* welcomes reports on places of retreat whether your opinion is favourable or not. There is a Report Form at the end of the guide or you may send an e-mail to 113364.3521@compuserve.com

There are two ways to go about getting enough – one is to continue to accumulate more and more. The other is to desire less.

G.K. CHESTERTON

ENGLAND

LONDON

Benedictine Centre for Spirituality
Bramley Road
London N14 4HE   Tel/Fax: 020 84492499
                    e-mail: benedictine_centre@compuserve.com

Roman Catholic

The Centre is above the Benedictine Parish Church of Christ the King and adjacent to the new monastery. You may join the monks at prayer for the Divine Office and at Mass each day. On offer as well is a full programme of retreats and events with residential courses on Benedictine monastic spirituality. There is a healing ministry for the sick, available to anyone, offering prayer and the laying on of hands. One of the monks, Br. Benedict Heron, has written a clear and informative book *Praying for Healing: The Challenge*, which explores the subject of Christian healing. It gives examples of testimonies to the healing power of prayer. There is a new monastery guest house which offers extra space for those guest retreatants who just want a B&B accommodation. When you go on retreat here the Community tries to welcome you into the daily Benedictine monastic life and so you are welcome to pray with the monks and to join them for the mid-day meal in the monastery. There are three Masses daily and lots of various Parish activities also going on – and Trent County Park is only a few miniutes walk away for some meditative time with Nature. The Community works to improve all the facilities on the site with new projects arising almost every year. The monastery itself is fairly new and full of light and a sense of privacy and space. **Highly Recommended.**

Open: All year. Receives men, women, young people, families, groups and non-retreatants.
Rooms: 6 singles, 5 doubles.
Facilities: Chapel. Prayer room. Conferences, garden, roof garden nearby park, library, guest lounge, payphone. French, Italian, German, Dutch languages available with monks.
Spiritual Help: Personal talks, meditation, directed study, prayer guidance, healing ministry. An Ecumenical Charismatic Prayer Group meets in the church. Both male and female spiritual directors available.
Guests Admitted to: Chapel. Prayer Room.
Meals: Self-catering. Enquire about what is provided and what you need to bring yourself.
Special Activities: Planned programme. Send for brochure.
Situation: On the edge of a North London suburb with walks near by and opposite a large country park in the green belt. Usually quiet but can be rather busy, especially in summer.

Maximum Stay: 2 weeks.
Bookings: Letter or telephone during office hours.
Charges: £25 full board, B&B £17. Quiet day rate also. B&B en-suite in guest house £25 per person per day.
Access: Piccadilly Line to Oakwood. Bus: 307 and 299. Car route M25 exit 24, A111.

Brahma Kumaris World Spiritual University
Global Co-operation House
65 Pound Lane
London NW10 2HH

Tel: 020 87273350
Fax: 020 87273351

Non-religious

Found in 1937 in Karachi, the Brahma Kumaris University is an international organisation working at all levels of society for positive change. The University carries out a wide range of educational programmes for the development of human and spiritual values through its 3,000 branches in 62 countries. It is a non-governmental organisation affiliated to the United Nations department of Public Information and recipient of seven UN Peace Messenger Awards. Courses, workshops, seminars and conferences covering a wide range of topics are on offer including self-development, stress-free living, self management, creating inner freedom, soul care, women's development, and meditation. Activities are held at all levels of the community to help people cope more positively with everyday living and to find greater harmony within themselves and their relationships. All courses, events and activities are free of charge. The University operates the **World Global Retreat Centre** at Nuneham Courtney near Oxford (see Oxfordshire entry) and **Inner Space**, an information Centre at 528 High Road, Wembley, Middlesex HA9 7BS, Tel: 020 89031911. Brochure of events and courses available.

Buddhapadipa Temple
14 Calonne Road
Wimbledon
London SW19 5HJ

Tel: 020 89461357
Fax: 020 89445788

Buddhist (Theravada)

This active Buddhist temple has up to eight monks in community. On offer are various forms of study and meditation retreats including one week's meditation course, meditation four days a week and there are meditation classes four evenings each week. A summer retreat is usually held in September. Chants which are usually in Pali can be followed by the use of an English/Pali book which is collected before entering the Uposatha Hall. Sometimes a monk may not be fluent in English so be patient when seeking information by telephone.

Open: Most of the year. Receives men, women.
Rooms: The temple itself has no facilities for guests but arrangements can be made elsewhere.
Facilities: Shrine room, study room. Sometimes part of garden.
Spiritual Help: One-day retreats, personal talks, meditation, directed study.
Guests Admitted to: Temple and most areas except Community private ones.
Meals: Everyone eats together. Thai/wholefood.
Special Activities: Telephone for information (See note above) or you may telephone the Lay Buddhist Association (Tel: 020 89467410/ 020 88702072) Thai festivals and New Year celebrations.
Situation: Urban.
Maximum Stay: For duration of meditation period, class or course only.
Bookings: Letter or telephone.
Charges: On request.
Access: London Underground and bus: regular service.

Community of the Word of God
90-92 Kenworthy Road
London E9 5RA   Tel: 020 89868511

Inter-denominational

The Community of the Word of God was founded in East London in 1972. The pattern of the Community's life is rather like that of a Christian family whose members seek to share the love of Christ and to encourage each other in their witness and work. Some follow secular occupations while others are home-based. The present Community is made up of a small group of women who form a small evangelical lay community living in two terraced houses with a third, Emmaus House, for the guests. Although in the inner city, Emmaus House offers a place for people who are looking to get away from their daily routine. Retreats which are usually traditional preached ones are organised during the year.

Open: All year except for Christmas and first week of January. Receives men, women, groups for day visits, and non-retreatants.
Rooms: 1 single, 1 double. A non-smoking house.
Facilities: Garden, small library, guest lounge.
Spiritual Help: Personal talks. Spiritual direction. Personal retreat direction.
Guests Admitted to: Chapel.
Meals: You may eat with the Community or alone in the guest house. DIY facilities are limited. Traditional, simple food. Vegetarians.
Special Activities: Retreats are organised during the year. Ask for details.
Situation: In a city.
Maximum Stay: 1 week.
Bookings: Letter or telephone – after 7pm.
Charges: Donation towards costs if possible.
Access: Train, bus and car all possible, but parking can be a problem.

Eagle's Wing Centre for Contemporary Shamanism
58 Westbere Road
London NW2 3RU   Tel: 020 74358174
                                   Internet: http://www.shamanism.co.uk

Mind-Body-Spirit (Shamanism, Native American Indian Spirituality)

This is a well-established and widely respected centre for information and courses on shamanism. Leo Rutherford, a leading and serious practitioner of this spiritual way for many years, who runs the Centre is well known and respected in his work. Chanting, drumming, dancing, instruction in the use of the medicine wheel, ceremony and celebration are all part of the Centre's teaching. *While there is no residential accommodation at the Centre*, there are a number of interesting day courses and workshops which explore these rich and ancient traditions of spirituality. These are held at various venues around the country with some abroad in Greece. Examples of what is on offer include *Shaman Dance, Sweat Lodge, Dance and Ceremony Weekend, Shaman Wisdom, Shaman Healing and Soul Retrieval,* and a trance-dance training group. **Highly Recommended.**

Open: According to programme. Receives men and women.
Rooms: Not at Centre but on courses elsewhere.
Special Activities: Send for brochure.
Bookings: Letter or telephone.
Charges: Planned programme of events and courses. See brochure.
Access: See individual events.

Ealing Abbey
Charlbury Grove
Ealing, London W5 2DY   Tel: 020 8622100

Roman Catholic

The monks serve a large parish so this is a busy place, well and truly integrated into the world at large. Yet guests are welcome to share in the liturgy and community prayer, which help sustain all the various activities of the Abbey.

Open: September to July. Both men, women, young people, families, groups, non-retreatants.
Rooms: 4 singles, 3 doubles.
Facilities: Chapel, garden, guest lounge.
Spiritual Help: Personal talks, directed study.
Guests Admitted to: Abbey church.
Meals: Meals eaten in the guest house. Traditional food.
Special Activities: Planned programme of events and regular retreats. Send for brochure.
Situation: Rather busy in a city.
Maximum Stay: 1 week.
Bookings: Letter.
Charges: By arrangement.
Access: Train: Ealing Broadway station 1 mile away. Bus: No. E2.

Greenspirit – Centre for Creation Spirituality
St James's Church
197 Piccadilly
London W1V 9LF

Tel: 020 72872741
e-mail: admin@greenspirit.org.uk
Website: www.greenspirit.org.uk

Judaeo-Christian Tradition

Creation spirituality finds support in the writings and life of some of the most distinguished religious thinkers and mystics over the last thousand years including Hildegard of Bingen, Meister Eckhart, Julian of Norwich, and St Francis. The Creation Spirituality movement is closely linked to ecological concerns and to a holistic view of living. Matthew Fox, a world leader in Creation Spirituality theology, has written a number of books which have had a significant influence in the development of this particular spirituality approach. These include *Original Blessing* and *The Coming of the Cosmic Christ*. The Centre does not offer retreats as such but there are various local groups and an annual programme of events, some national. Check out the website for further information on what may be currently available. Creation spirituality has had an international impact and it might offer you a new way of looking at your understanding of spirituality and God.

ICCS Retreats
St Giles Church (ICCS Oasis Days)
Cripplegate, Wood Street, Baribican
London EC2Y 8BJ

Tel: 020 77391500
Fax: 020 72519384

Christian

Quiet days for prayer and reflection are held on the *second Tuesday* of every month from 10am-4pm. At St Giles Church in the Barbican. Costs £15 for waged, £10 for unwaged which includes lunch and coffee plus hand-out materials. Send for annual programme with subjects of days. The programme currently has some of these in it: *What does the Lord Require of You, The Importance of Being Silent*, and *The God who Surprises*. If you can not get away for a few days retreat and can get to the Barbican, then try one of these days to nourish your spiritual life and take some time out to think about eternal values.

Glance at the sun. See the moon and stars. Gaze at the beauty of earth's greenings. Now, think.

HILDEGARD OF BINGEN

Kairos Centre
Mount Angelus Road
Roehampton, London SW15 4JA   Tel: 020 87884188
Fax: 020 87884198
e-mail: maryward@kairoscentre.demon.co.uk
Website: www.kairoscentre.demon.co.uk

Roman Catholic

Kairos is a Greek word meaning favourable time or graced moment. Retreats, conference facilities and various courses and meetings are on offer here at this centre located near beautiful Richmond Park and only a few miles from central London itself.

Open: Almost all year. Receives everyone.
Rooms: 7 singles, 8 doubles
Facilities: Disabled. Conferences, garden, park, library, guest lounge, TV, guest telephone.
Spiritual Help: Personal talks, group sharing, spiritual direction, personal retreat direction, meditation. Reflexology, Reiki.
Guests Admitted to: Unrestricted accesss. Chapel.
Meals: Everyone eats together. Traditional food. Vegetarians and special diets.
Special Activities: Planned programme. Send for information.
Situation: Calm and peaceful centre.
Maximum Stay: 1 month.
Bookings: Letter/tel/fax during office hours.
Charges: £30 full board per person per day.
Access: Rail/Underground, bus, car via M4 or A3.

London Buddhist Centre
51 Roman Road
London E2 0HU   Tel: 020 89811225
Fax: 020 89801960
e-mail: info@lbc.org.uk
Website: www.londonbuddhistcentre.com

Buddhist (FWBO)

The Friends of the Western Buddhist Order (FWBO) strive to put Buddhism's essential teachings into practice in the West, and the London Buddhist Centre is part of that world-wide movement. Buddhist practices and classes are offered as well as retreats for people at all levels of experience. The FWBO was established to communicate Buddhism to Westerners through a Western version idiom appropriate in the twenty-first century. The vision of the FWBO is to make the Buddha's teachings available to as many people as possible throughout the world. Evenings and lunch time classes available. **There are Gay Mens Retreats, Black Peoples Retreats, Family Retreats, and Parents and Childrens Retreats.**

Open: All year Monday-Friday 10am-5pm. Receives everyone.
Rooms: What is not available in London is available elsewhere on the

various types of retreats – discuss with the Centre. 25 singles and doubles. Dormitories and camping available on various retreats.
Facilities: Disabled, conferences, camping, library, guest lounge, guest telephone.
Spiritual Help: Personal talks, group sharing, spiritual direction, personal retreat direction, meditation, directed study.
Guests Admitted to: Shrine room and work of Community.
Meals: Everyone eats together. Wholefood, Vegetarian.
Special Activities: Programme of events. Brochure available and information on FWBO.
Situation: In a city, but other places outside London.
Maximum Stay: By arrangement.
Bookings: Letter/tel/fax – 10am-5pm.
Charges: Charges vary, but roughly at introductory level £40-£60 or £90. Longer retreats of a week plus might be 10 days at £168 waged, £108 concession.
Access: London Underground Bethnal Green and then a walk. Buses: Nos. 253 and 8.

London Buddhist Vihara
Dharmapala Building
The Avenue
Chiswick, London W4 4JU   Tel: 020 89959493

Buddhist (Theravada)

There is a resident community of monks at the Vihara and it is open daily from 9.00am to 9.00pm, but there is no resident accommodation. Evening classes explore a wide range of subjects: Bhavana (meditation) instruction and practice, Beginner's Buddhism, Dhamma study, Buddhist psychology, the Sinhala language and Pali, which is the language of the Buddhist Canon. A Buddhist discussion group meets twice a month in an informal atmosphere. There are monthly retreats and a children's Sunday school. The Vihara also caters for the needs of expatriate Buddhists from Asia – mainly Sri Lanka.

Open: All year. Receives everyone.
Rooms: None.
Facilities: Conferences, shrine room, garden, library, payphone, bookstall. Children welcomed.
Spiritual Help: Personal talks, meditation and directed study.
Guests Admitted to: Everywhere except monks' rooms.
Meals: Traditional food – monks eat separately, everyone else together.
Special Activities: See programme.
Situation: Quiet within the house.
Maximum Stay: 1 day.
Bookings: Letter or telephone.
Charges: By donation.
Access: London Underground or bus.

The Open Centre
Third Floor
188 Old Street
London EC1 9FR

Tel/Fax: 020 72511504
e-mail: info@opencentre.com
Website: www.opencentre.com

Mind-Body-Spirit

Now running for over twenty years, The Open Centre offers a programme to increase your awareness of yourself and others and to help you take a look at your relationships, your assumptions and your decisions about life and work. The key ideas are centred in therapy, movement, healing and growth. Courses may include primal integration, bio-energetics, and transactional analysis. There is a brochure available on request and, as a guide, prices range from £30-£35 per hour for individual sessions to intensives and residential courses at £110-£305.

Royal Foundation of St Katherine
2 Butchers Row
London E14 8DS

Fax: 020 77027603

Anglican

St Katherine serves people living in the area through teaching, spiritual ministry and social work. The retreats and conferences offered here in the past have been wide-ranging and interesting, but you must ask for the current programme.

Society of the Sacred Mission
90 Vassall Road
Kennington, London SW9 6JA

Tel: 020 75822040
Fax: 020 75826640
e-mail: ssmlondon@netscapeonline.co.uk

Anglican

Open: All year. Receives men, women, young people.
Rooms: 2 singles.
Facilities: Garden, library, TV.
Spiritual Help: Personal talks. Spiritual direction. Personal retreat direction. Meditation. Directed study.
Guests Admitted to: Unrestricted access.
Meals: Everyone eats together. Traditional/wholefood/vegetarian. Special diets.
Special Activities: None.
Situation: Reasonable quiet in a city.
Maximum Stay: 2-4 days.
Bookings: Letter/tel/fax – 8-9am
Charges: A donation suggested of £15 per night if affordable.
Access: Underground to Oval Station or Bus: 36, 185, 3, 59, 159, 133 to Vassall Road.

Spirit Horse Nomadic Circle
c/o 19 Holmwood Gardens
Finchley, London N3 3NS

Tel: 020 83463660

Mind-Body-Spirit

Nearly all events by the Spirit Horse Nomadic Circle are held in Powys, Wales in the summertime under canvas. The structured courses cover shaman practice, ceremony, meditation, sexuality (uninvited intimacy is not part of the process) and aspects of both Buddhism and Celtic mythology. What is offered here is an archaic, ceremonial environment, close to nature with a variety of different courses enabling a rediscovery of self through spiritual practices, healing, and mythology. The most influential sources used are Tibetan Buddhism, Celtic and Native American Indian traditions. Sweat lodge, stone medicine healing, story telling, Arabic dancing, song and voice work, Buddhist visionary instruction and much more can be on offer.

Open: Summer only. Receives everyone.
Rooms: Special tents.
Facilities: Conferences possible, camping.
Spiritual Help: Personal talks, group sharing, meditation, directed study.
Guests Admitted to: Unrestricted access.
Meals: Traditional food. Vegetarians catered for.
Special Activities: See brochure for programme.
Situation: In the countryside where it is peaceful.
Maximum Stay: 5-10 days.
Bookings: Letter.
Charges: In range of £125 to £400 for 3, 5, and 10 day courses.
Access: Car, sometimes via train.

St Peter's House
Sisters of St Andrew
308 Kennington Lane
London SE11 5HY

Tel: 020 75870087

Roman Catholic – Ecumenical

The Sisters run two retreat facilities, one here and the other in Kent (see that section). Quiet days and facilities are available for groups. Individuals come here for a silent or individually guided Ignatian retreat which is also much in silence. Contact the Sisters and discuss your retreat requirements as they try to suit each guest as much as is possible.

Open: Most of the year. Receives men, women, young people, groups for the day.
Rooms: 3 singles, 1 double.
Facilities: Small but nice garden, small library, guest lounge, direct dialling at cost.
Spiritual Help: Personal talks, personal retreat direction, spiritual accompaniment.

Guests Admitted to: Chapel.
Meals: DIY taken in room.
Special Activities: None.
Situation: In a city.
Maximum Stay: 8 days.
Bookings: Letter or telephone.
Charges: By donation.
Access: Underground, bus, car.

Society of St John the Evangelist
St Edward's House
22 Great College Street
London SW1P 3QA

Tel: 020 72229234
Fax: 020 77992641
e-mail: frpeterssteuk@talk21.com

Anglican

Run by an Anglican religious Community, guests stay with the Community and not separate. There is silence from 9.30pm until the same time next morning. A traditional monastic welcome here with regular conducted retreats, such as preached ones, and quiet days.

Open: All year except August. Receives men and women.
Rooms: 10 singles. No smoking, radios or mobile phones.
Facilities: Chapel, library, guest telephone, garden. Disabled possible, but ask for details.
Spiritual Help: Personal talks, meditation, spiritual direction, personal retreat direction, directed study. Guests do not have to attend religious services but may if they wish.
Guests Admitted to: Everywhere.
Meals: Everyone eats together. Food is simple and traditional. Vegetarians and special diets can be catered for but advance notice must be given.
Special Activities: Quiet days.
Situation: In a city. Rather busy, but near all London attractions if you have to have these on hand.
Maximum Stay: 14 days.
Bookings: Letter.
Charges: Ask for current rates.
Access: Underground to St James Park. Bus to Westminster Abbey.

St Saviour's Priory
18 Queensbridge Road
Haggerston
London E2 8NS

Tel: 020 77396775
Fax: 020 77391248

Anglican

There are no conducted retreats and groups are received only for the day facilities, but this is a good place for a private retreat, especially if you live in or near the Greater London area. Many such traditional Anglican convents as this one which do not offer any programmes but just a traditional private retreat have recently gained in popularity, especially among women with busy careers. St Saviour's may be booked up well in advance so do not be disappointed if there is no room for you when you want it. Most spiritualities claim patience as a virtue.

Open: Most of the year. Receives men, women, young people, families, groups for the day only.
Rooms: 6 singles. 2 doubles.
Facilities: Chapel. Garden.
Spiritual Help: Personal talks. Spiritual direction. Reiki. There is not always someone immediately available so appointments have to be arranged for this guidance and treatment.
Guests Admitted to: Chapel, garden.
Meals: Traditional. DIY available. If vegetarian you need to discuss it when booking.
Special Activities: None.
Situation: In a city.
Maximum Stay: 2 weeks.
Bookings: Letter/tel/fax – 10.30am-12.30pm and 6.30-8.30pm
Charges: Donations according to means – it costs the Community about £20-£25 per 24 hours per guest to give you an idea.
Access: Bus: No. 26, 48, 55. Car parking is difficult here.

**Swaminarayan Hindu Mission
and The Shri Swaminarayan Mandir
105-119 Brentfield Road, Neasden
London NW10 8JP**

Tel: 020 89652651
Fax: 020 89656313
Website: www.swaminarayan-baps.org

Hindu

The Swaminarayan Hindu Mission is a branch of the world-wide Bochasanwasi Akshar Purushottam Sanstha of India, which is a prominent and charitable Hindu organisation with a wide spectrum of activities including a medical college. It strives to promote social, moral, cultural, and spiritual values among all ages within society and has some 3,000 centres and 300 temples around the world. The London centre has now opened the largest traditional Hindu Mandir (Temple) in Europe and they welcome people from all faiths. The Mandir has transformed the north London district of Neasden. It took three years to build and employed 1,500 sculptors, 2,000 tonnes of marbles and 3,000 tonnes of limestone. Among those who have visited this temple with its nine shrines and marvelled at its design and craftsmanship have been the Prince of Wales, Diana Princess of Wales, the Duke of Edinburgh, and Tony Blair. Facilities include a community and social centre, cultural centre, school, sports and recreation facilities, library, health clinic and a programme of various activities for men, women, and families. There is a permanent exhibition on Hinduism and a video presentation on the construction of the Mandir. *This is a remarkable and marvellous place and worth the time you take to visit it.*

Open: All year from 9am to 6pm. *Please note dress code: Shorts, skirts and dresses above the knee are not permitted except when worn by children under 10 years.*

Tyburn Convent
8 Hyde Park Place
Bayswater Road
London W2 2LJ

Tel: 020 77237262
Website: www.tyburnconvent.org.com

Roman Catholic

Just opposite Hyde Park, Tyburn Convent is right in the heart of London. Amid the busy outside world the sisters preside over the perpetual exposition of the Blessed Sacrament – the chapel is open all day and retreat guests may go there at night. Near by was Tyburn's place of execution, which operated from 1196 to 1783 following the dissolution of the monasteries. Over a hundred officially recognised martyrs died there for their faith and the Convent's Martyrs' Altar is a replica of the Tyburn tree, erected in honour of the memory of its victims.
The Convent's website is one of the best – try it and go on a tour, look at the prrayer book and chapel. **Highly Recommended.**

Open: All year. Receives women who wish to make a private retreat and men only occasionally. Tyburn Convent is the National Shrine of the Martyrs of England and Wales so all are welcomed to visit the Crypt itself.
Rooms: 6 singles. Guests are usually expected to be in by 8.30pm when the Convent is locked.
Facilities: Chapel, small patio, library.
Spiritual Help: Retreatants are left to spend their time as they wish, but are welcome to share in the Divine Office, Mass and the Adoration of the Blessed Sacrament. If anyone feels the need, it can be arranged to talk with a sister.
Guests Admitted to: Chapel. Shrine room. A sister is available three times a day or by appointment to give individuals or groups a guided tour of the Martyrs' Crypt.
Meals: Everyone eats together in the guest house. Traditional food, with provision for vegetarian and special diets (within reason) by prior arrangement.
Special Activities: The perpetual exposition of the Blessed Sacrament in the chapel which is open to the public all day, a sung Divine Office, and the Shrine of the Martyrs.
Situation: Hyde Park is across the road but the Convent is in the very heart of busy London.
Maximum Stay: 5 days.
Bookings: Letter.
Charges: Usually arranged with the Guest Mistress.
Access: London Underground to Marble Arch. Central London buses. Parking difficult.

SOUTH WEST

BRISTOL

Clifton

Emmaus House
Clifton Hill
Clifton, Bristol BS8 4PD

Tel: 0117 9079950
Fax: 0117 9079952

Roman Catholic

Set in Clifton Village on the outskirts of Bristol, Emmaus House welcomes guests to workshops or simply to stay, have a meal and enjoy the view. Facilities are continuously upgraded and include award-winning gardens and food of a high standard. There are plenty of places to pray, an art room, and spiritual companionship available for those that want it. The Community here is noted for teaching the Enneagram in Helen Palmer's narrative tradition. It is an oasis in the midst of a busy world. **Highly Recommended.**

Open: All year except Christmas. Receives men, women, groups.
Rooms: 12 Singles, 12 double.
Facilities: Conference facilities including TV, video camera and most necessary equipment, a rather special small garden, library, payphone.
Spiritual Help: Spiritual direction. Personal retreat direction.
Guests Admitted to: Unrestricted access.
Meals: Taken in dining room. Traditional and whole food. Vegetarians and special diets.
Special Activities: Full programme of courses and retreats. Send for brochure.
Situation: In town. Amount of noise depends on group in house at any given time. Lovely views and pleasant neighbourhood.
Maximum Stay: 8-day retreat.
Bookings: Letter, telephone, fax.
Charges: Numerous courses and retreats from £20-£250.
Access: Train to Bristol Temple Meads. Bus: No. 8 from station to W. H. Smith in Clifton Down Road. Car: from north take M5, Exit 17, then A4018; from London take M4, Exit 20, then M5, Exit 19, followed by A369.

God in his mercy looks on you not for what you are, nor for what you have been, but for what you wish to be.

THE CLOUD OF UNKNOWING

CORNWALL

Helston

Trelowarren Christian Fellowship
Mawgan in Meneage
Helston, Cornwall TR12 6AD   Tel: 01326 221366
                                                  Fax: 01326 221834

Inter-Denominational

Located in an ancient manor-house buried in the heart of the countryside, the Fellowship is open to Christians of all denominations,
whether in groups or as individuals who want to spend time away
from it all. Healing, teaching and renewal conferences are held here,
and prayer, counselling and ministry in the power of the Holy Spirit are
available by arrangement. This is very much a place for those who are
already Christians and not for those who feel that the realisation of
their spirituality may be obtained through other faiths. It is a good
sanctuary of peace where you may deepen your spiritual awareness
and perhaps find a fuller understanding of the Christian Gospel.

Open: February – mid-December. Receives men, women, young
people, families, groups, non-retreatants and Christian religious.
Rooms: 1 single, 1 double, 8 twins, 2 family rooms.
Facilities: Conferences, garden, library, guest lounge, TV, payphone,
direct dialling. Children welcomed.
Spiritual Help: Personal talks, group sharing, directed study, spiritual
direction, prayer ministry.
Guests Admitted to: Chapel, work of the community.
Meals: Everyone eats together. Traditional food. Vegetarian and
special diets.
Special Activities: Planned programme of events including monthly
healing service. Send for brochure.
Situation: Very quiet.
Maximum Stay: 2 weeks.
Bookings: Letter or telephone – 9am-6pm.
Charges: By donation – guideline: £23 per day.
Access: Consult the brochure map which details travel arrangements.

Penberth

Shell Cottage
c/o Bridget Hugh-Jones
Penberth, St Buryan
Near Penzance, Cornwall TR19 6HJ   Tel: 01736 810659
                                                  Fax: 01736 810941

Anglican

Just a few yards from the water's edge and fishing boats, Shell Cottage
provides an unusual and rather idyllic location for a private or group

retreat, quiet days or simply space for rest and prayer. Although principally catering for those in ordained ministry, Shell Cottage is a place where all may come on retreat.

Open: All year. Receives men, women, and groups.
Rooms: 2 singles, 2 doubles.
Facilities: Guest lounge, payphone.
Spiritual Help: Anglican priest is available.
Guests Admitted to: Unrestricted access.
Meals: DIY facilities.
Special Activities: Regularly led Quiet Days.
Situation: Cottage is on the cliff overlooking a small fishing cove with sea views.
Maximum Stay: Open.
Bookings: Letter/tel/fax – best time evenings.
Charges: £10 per night per person. £3 for the day only.
Access: Train: Penzance Station. Car: not far from Land's End. Ask for details of route.

Penzance

CAER
Rosemerryn, Lamorna
Penzance, Cornwall TR19 6BN

Tel: 01736 810530
Fax: 01736 2840980
e-mail: connect@caer.co.uk
Website: www.caer.co.uk

Mind-Body-Spirit

This place has been going for some twenty years and offers a programme of innovative workshops for personal and spiritual development. Located on a Celtic site, some of the courses include *Midsummer Celebration, The Witches Womb, Soul Wave, The Mist of Avalon, Easter Regeneration.*

Open: All year. Receives everyone.
Rooms: 4 doubles, 4 dormitories.
Facilities: Garden, park. Guest lounge, guest telephone.
Spiritual Help: Group sharing. Workshops – see programme.
Guests Admitted to: Public visitors areas.
Meals: Everyone eats together. Vegetarian food. Special diets.
Special Activities: Planned programme. Send for colour brochure.
Situation: Very quiet located on Iron Age settlement. In the countryside.
Maximum Stay: Open.
Bookings: Letter/tel/fax anytime.
Charges: Workshops £40 per day inclusive.
Access: Ask for their map.

Stoke Climsland

Hampton Manor
Stoke Climsland
Cornwall PL17 8LX   Tel: 01579 370494

Inter-Denominational

Set in two acres of land in the Tamar Valley, Hampton Manor is a quaint old Victoria house which is now a place of Christian prayer, teaching and witness. All who are seeking a place of spiritual and physical refreshment are welcome. Morning and evening prayer is held in the chapel and there is a programme of quiet days as well as other retreats.

Open: All year except Christmas. Receives men, women, young people, families, groups for the day only, non-retreatants.
Rooms: 1 single, 3 doubles.
Facilities: Garden, library, guest lounge, TV, payphone, direct dialling. Children welcomed. Conference facilities for up to 35 people in separate building.
Spiritual Help: Personal talks, directed study, counselling.
Guests Admitted to: Unrestricted access everywhere. Chapel.
Meals: Everyone eats together. Traditional Food. Vegetarian and special diets catered.
Special Activities: Planned programme. Send for brochure.
Situation: Very quiet.
Maximum Stay: 2 weeks.
Bookings: Letter or telephone.
Charges: £25 per person full board. £35 double. £15 B&B single. Evening meal £5.
Access: Consult the brochure map which details travel arrangements with directions.

DEVON

Ashburton

The Ashburton Centre
79 East Street
Ashburton, Devon TQ13 7AL   Tel: 01364 652784
                                               Fax: 01364 653825
                    e-mail: stella@ashburtoncentre.freeserve.co.uk
                       Website: www.ashburtoncentre.co.uk

Inter-Denominational

The Ashburton Centre for Holistic Education and Training was founded in 1994 to provide personal development, spiritual, healing, environmental and related residential courses within a supportive Community. Guests join the Community during their stay so that a feeling of belonging and family is generated. The programme on offer covers a wide variety of modern approaches to spirituality, for example, meditation, Qi Gong, Shiatsu as spiritual practice, choice and transformation seminars, healing, yoga, and voice workshops. The centre is in the town, but there are many good country and woodland walks nearby. *The Centre is also a home of The Carers Trust offering a range of retreat breaks which are bursary funded for carers in the community and for professional carers such as nurses and social and health workers.*

Open: All year. Receives men, women, groups.
Rooms: 4 singles, 3 twin doubles, 2 three-bed rooms. No smoking. No outside shoes worn in the house.
Facilities: Garden, guest lounge, TV, payphone.
Spiritual Help: Meditation. Yoga, body exercises, T'ai Chai.
Guests Admitted to: Unrestricted access.
Meals: Everyone eats together. Wholefood vegetarian.
Special Activities: Planned programme. Send for brochure. Courses and holidays in France and Spain are offered and there are self-catering retreats possible.
Situation: In a small town adjoining Dartmoor National Park.
Maximum Stay: By arrangement.
Bookings: Letter, telephone, fax – 9am-6pm.
Charges: £25 B&B, weekend retreats about £115, weekend courses £155, holidays only from £345.
Access: Train: Newton Abbot mainline station is 10 minutes away. The Centre will collect you. Car route with easy access from M5.

Ashprington

The Barn
Lower Sharpham Barton
Ashprington
Totnes, Devon TQ9 7DX

Tel/fax: 01803 732661
e-mail: sharphambarn@dial.pipex.com
Website: www.sharpham-trust.org

Buddhist – Non-Denominational

The underlying purpose of The Barn, which has been going for some thirteen years, is to create a working retreat centre – a place where someone might come on retreat temporarily from the world at large, but also work on the land. The atmosphere is contemplative and there is much silence. During your stay here, you will be expected to be fully involved in the daily schedule of activities and to take your turn preparing vegetarian meals for everyone. One evening a week is devoted to discussing personal matters as well as broader issues that relate to the community's life together. You are encouraged to pursue those activities – such as Buddhist-study classes, yoga mornings, and listening to cassettes of Dharma talks – which support a contemplative way of life. The daily schedule includes four to five hours' work on the land and three 45-minute periods of group meditation. No previous experience of farm work is necessary. The Barn Community is based on the Buddhist meditation tradition but is non-denominational and does not require people to follow any prescribed methods of practice. **Highly Recommended.**

Open: All year. Receives men and women – you do not have to be a Buddhist, but some established background in meditation helps.
Rooms: 7 singles.
Facilities: Garden, library, payphone. Woodworking equipment is provided.
Spiritual Help: Personal talks when a teacher is available, group sharing and meditation. Personal retreat direction if required.
Guests Admitted to: Unrestricted access to all areas, including shrine room and work of the community, which consists of gardening, woodland maintenance, household care and upkeep, cooking, pre-serving, looking after poultry and other smallholding chores.
Meals: Everyone eats together. Meals are vegetarian. Special diets.
Special Activities: Daily schedule followed 6 days a week.
Situation: Very quiet and in the countryside. Beautiful location on the Sharpham Estate, on a hillside overlooking the River Dart – no roads visible.
Maximum Stay: 2 week *minimum* if possible – 6 months maximum.
Bookings: By letter or telephone, but you will be asked for some per-sonal details about your experience of retreats and meditation.
Charges: £90 week. Low income week £70. Unwaged week £65.
Access: By car is easiest, but enquire if you want to walk from the nearest place served by public transport.

Sharpham College for Buddhist Studies and Contemporary Inquiry
Ashprington
Totnes, Devon TQ9 7UT   Tel: 01803 732542
                                              Fax: 01803 732037
                              e-mail: college@sharpham-trust.org
                              e-mail: colinmoore@dial.pipex.com
Buddhist

Sharpham College for Buddhist Studies and Contemporary Enquiry occupies a beautiful English Palladian house with views stretching down to the River Dart. It is here that the Sharpham Trust strives to cre-ate a new way of education, aiming to achieve a balance between the practical and the spiritual. Although the approach is Buddhist, it does not adhere to any particular school. The Buddhist studies include Theravada, Indo-Tibetan Mahayana, Zen and Chinese Buddhism, plus Buddhist history, philosophy, and psychology, including courses such as *The Psychology of Awakening. Contemporary Enquiry* means studies on right livelihood, ecology and the environment, western philosophy and psychology, the new sciences, and arts and culture. The teachers come from a broad spectrum of backgrounds and have long-standing com-mitments to Buddhism. The college cannot accommodate short-term guests because the programme course students occupy all the living accommodation. Having said that, there is a programme of events as well which form day educational retreats. They are very interesting and have excellent teachers and speakers. Participants in the year and 3-month programmes need to be familiar with one of the Buddhist tra-ditions and an established meditation practice. If you are thinking of an in-depth study in Buddhism, this is a very good place to go.

Open: September to July for students. Closed January and August. Receives men, women.
Rooms: 10 singles. Silence until 10am.
Facilities: Garden, library, student lounge, TV, payphone. No smoking.
Spiritual Help: Personal talks, meditation, group sharing, directed study, personal retreat direction. Yoga, Chi Gung.
Guests Admitted to: Shrine room, work of community.
Meals: Everyone eats together. Meals consist of vegetarian whole food.
Special Activities: Send for programme brochure and information on the college.
Situation: A busy and active place.
Maximum Stay: The programmes are 3-months and a year, so short-term guests are not received.
Bookings: Letter.
Charges: Year programme fee is currently £5500. 3 month course £2200. Otherwise see programme brochure for cost of other courses.
Access: Car route best.

Buckfastleigh

Southgate Retreat Centre
Buckfast Abbey
Buckfastleigh
Devon TQ11 0EE   Tel: 01364 645521
e-mail: enquiries@buckfast.org.uk
Website: www.buckfast.org.uk

Roman Catholic

Getting onwards to a million people come to visit the Abbey, to walk through its grounds by the River Dart, and to admire the work of these monks whose history here has been so remarkable. The monastery was founded in AD1018. It experienced centuries of peace, followed by ruin when Henry VIII dissolved the monasteries and, finally, restoration in 1907, when the monks returned to rebuild their Abbey. The great church was finished in 1937, largely restored to its original form, and filled with beautiful artefacts from the enamelled and bejewelled Stations of the Cross to the glorious marble mosaic floor of the nave. The Lady Chapel has one of the most impressive stained glass windows of Christ in Europe, designed and made by one of the monks. It is justly famous. Just outside and down a nearby path, edged with pink cyclamen, stands the village of hives belonging to the Abbey's famous bees. Outside the silence of the monastic enclosure and the church, this is a top tourist attraction with shops, walks, and many thousands of visitors – a very busy place especially in the summer. There is a restaurant and even a separate modern shop selling the products made by religious of other Benedictine Communities in Europe. Still, this is a place for seeking God where the Rule of St Benedict remains in force and so you will find hospitality and sanctuary.

In the dark shadows of the church the voices of the choir at morning prayer bring awareness that you have left your ordinary life and are embarking on a new journey of the spirit.

Open: All year except early January. Receives men, women, groups.
Rooms: Singles and doubles.
Facilities: Disabled. Church. Large garden, guest lounge, library, payphone, direct dialling. Gift shop, book shop, Monastic products centre, and restaurant.
Spiritual Help: Personal talks.
Guests Admitted to: Church.
Meals: Taken in guest house. Traditional food. Vegetarians and special diets catered.
Special Activities: Some organised retreats. Ask for details.
Situation: Beautiful location, but many tourists around during the day.
Maximum Stay: 10 days.
Bookings: Letter.
Charges: Please enquire.
Access: Train: Newton Abbot station 11 miles away. Bus: Devon General No. 188 from Newton Abbot. Coach: National, Exeter – Plymouth. Car: via A38.

Combe Martin

The Wild Pear Centre
King Street
Combe Martin, Devon EX34 OAG   Tel/Fax: 0208 883086

Mind-Body-Spirit

The Wild Pear Centre is situated in the North Devon seaside village of Combe Martin, a gateway to Exmoor National Park. While no garden or grounds exist at the Centre you can treat the whole area like a wild garden on your doorstep. The Centre is available for both residential and non-residential use and hosts different workshops from yoga, meditation, bodywork, voicework, movement, dance to personal growth courses. *If you are interested in staying here then write in the first instance to Juliana Brown, 36 Womersley Road, Crouch End, London N89AN (Tel: 020 83417226)*

Open: All year for bookings. Receives everyone.
Rooms: 4-5 singles or doubles, depending how they are to be used.
Facilities: Guest hall and meeting room. Payphone.
Spiritual Help: None.
Guests Admitted to: Unrestricted access.
Meals: Everyone eats together. Wholefood/vegetarian food. Special diets. DIY facilities.
Special Activities: None.
Situation: Countryside. Quiet.
Maximum Stay: Short stays only.
Bookings: See above.
Charges: £15 per day self-catering. £30 per person per day for full board.
Access: Ask for travel information which is excellent.

Dunsford

The Sheldon Centre
Society of Mary and Martha
Sheldon, Dunsford, Exeter EX6 7LE   Tel/Fax: 01647 252752
e-mail: smm@sheldon.uk.com

Ecumenical Christian

This 15th century farm house and buildings were converted some years ago to provide modern facilities and equipment for retreats, quiet days, day conferences, celebrations and quality events drawn from a broad base of Christian traditions. It is run by a resident Community of lay men and women. Some retreats on offer might be on Celtic spirituality, individually guided ones, or a retreat of several days on some of the saints with a monk from Buckfast Abbey or a sister from the Community of St Francis acting as leaders. An atmosphere of peace and tranquillity prevails here.

Open: February – December. Closed January. Receives everyone.
Rooms: 6 singles, 8 doubles.
Facilities: Disabled – limited so please enquire. Conferences, garden, library, guest lounge, TV, payphone. Children welcomed at some of the events so do ask.
Spiritual Help: Personal retreat direction.
Guests Admitted to: Chapel.
Meals: It all depends on the event or retreat and what suits you. For example, those who come on a private retreat might want meals taken alone – if so ready-cooked meals can be provided. Meals can be taken with others or not as the mood suits, a very flexible arrangement. Traditional food. Vegetarians and special diets.
Special Activities: Planned programme. Send for brochure.
Situation: Usually quiet, beautiful views, 18 acres of fields and woods.
Maximum Stay: 1 week.
Bookings: Letter or tel/fax.
Charges: £23 per night accommodation, £11 per day food.
Access: Train station within 10 miles. Bus service poor. Car easiest. Ask for details.

Lynton

Lee Abbey Fellowship
Lynton
Devon EX35 6JJ   Tel: 01598 752621
Fax: 01598 752619
e-mail: relax@leeabbey.org.uk

Anglican – Inter-Denominational

Lee Abbey is a very large country estate in the Exmoor National Park. While Anglican in tradition, it is ecumenical in outlook. In addition to planned retreats, there are what they call *Breakaway* weeks or weekends for those who may wish to benefit from the accommodation and facilities without joining in an organised activity. The programme of events is quite extensive over the year with a wide choice of subjects.

Open: All year. Receives men, women, groups.
Rooms: For retreats all rooms are treated as singles but there are some 20 singles and 15 doubles with some en-suite plus other multiple combinations that add up to some 135 possible guests – a big place Lee Abbey.
Facilities: Disabled. Conferences, library, guest lounge, TV, payphone.
Spiritual Help: None.
Guests Admitted to: Access to house and grounds. Chapel.
Meals: Everyone eats together. Traditional food. Vegetarians and special diets.
Special Activities: A short programme of retreats, but individuals are welcome on their *Breakaway* retreats at other times. Send for details.
Situation: The house is set in a 260-acre coastal estate in the Exmoor National Park. Quiet surroundings.
Maximum Stay: By arrangement.
Bookings: Letter, telephone, fax.
Charges: £35 per night full board, standard low-season rate – see brochure.
Access: By car is easiest.

Monastery of Poor Clares
Lynton
Devon EX35 6BX

Tel: 01598 753373
Fax: 01598 753878

Roman Catholic

Those who wish to share the quiet, prayer and worship of the Franciscan way of life will find a warm welcome from the sisters whose convent in this small seaside resort is near many beauty spots on the edge of Exmoor. It is an ideal and simple place for a private retreat or for those who need a very peaceful and modest base. Lovely walks by the sea. Guests stay in self-catering facilities in their own accommodation which includes small kitchens. The doubles are really two self-contained small flats, one with dining room and bathroom and one with shower. As this is an enclosed Community of women, religious sisters who come as guests may eat with the Community in their refectory and two single rooms are set aside for such guests inside the private enclosure. *There is one single room for a woman guest inside as well – if you feel you might have a calling to this kind of spiritual life with God, then discuss it with the sisters and perhaps come and share a little in their life.* All guests are welcome to join the Community for Mass and the Divine Office. There will be some sisters available to meet guests who wish to see them for individual spiritual guidance or to be joined in accompaniment in prayer, but the sisters do not do spiritual direction as such. The Monastery of Poor Clares is a traditional monastic house with all the rich spiritual inheritance and daily life of prayer that this implies. It is a place to put aside your materialistic and personal comfort expectations for awhile at least and to get down to some serious time with God. **Highly Recommended.**

Open: Most of year except Christmas and Holy Week. Receives men, women, young people, non-retreatants, and religious on retreat.
Rooms: 2 doubles.
Facilities: Chapel, nearby beaches and moor for walking.
Spiritual Help: Personal talks by arrangement.
Guests Admitted to: Church. Choir.
Meals: Self-catering. DIY facilities. Meals served for religious sisters in the refectory.
Special Activities: None.
Situation: A delightful area in which to retreat from the world at large.
Maximum Stay: 2 weeks.
Bookings: Letter or telephone.
Charges: No fixed charge but a minimum donation of £5 per person is suggested to cover expenses. Most guests will want to dig deeper in their pockets than that and at least double the figure to £10 *minimum.*
Access: Car via A39. Train and buses to Barnstaple, which is about 18 miles distant.

Newton Abbot

Gaia House
West Ogwell, Newton Abbot
Devon TQ12 6DY

Tel: 01626 333613
Fax: 01626 352650
e-mail: gaiahouse@gn.apc.org
Website: www.ga.apc.org/gaiahouse

Buddhist

Gaia House was founded in 1984 to provide a setting for teaching and practice of ethics, meditation and wisdom learning. The Centre which is new and roomy is set in quiet countryside and offers a full programme with facilities for individual practice. The programme offers meditation retreats and personal retreats drawn from the Theravada and Mahayana traditions of Buddhism. Retreats cover such topics as *Breathing like a Buddha, Freedom of the Heart, Serenity, Wisdom, Compassion* and *Making Friends with Life.* The environment here is a silent one and there is opportunity to enjoy solitude. Work retreats are also available.

Open: All year. Receives men, women, young people. Families on Family Retreats once a year. Groups and non-retreatants only on a one-day retreat basis.
Rooms: Space for 20-30 people but no guarantee of a single room, some doubles, dormitory, hermitage wing for long retreats.
Facilities: Meditation room, park, garden, library, guest lounge, and payphone. Disabled: partial access only – ask before booking.
Spiritual Help: Meditation, personal talks, interviews with teacher of retreat.

Guests Admitted to: Unrestricted access.
Meals: Everyone eats together in house or in the garden or wherever it happens. All food is wholefood vegetarian and very good. Medical diets only catered.
Special Activities: Group and personal retreats offered. Send for detailed annual brochure.
Situation: Very quiet, in the countryside. Gaia is a silent house.
Maximum Stay: Not limited, depending on meditation experience.
Bookings: Letter.
Charges: About £12-20 per day.
Access: By car is easiest.

Plymouth

St Elizabeth's House
Sisters of Charity
Longbrook Street
Plympton St Maurice, Plymouth
Devon PL7 INL   Tel: 01752 336112

Anglican

St Elizabeth's House is set in a lovely garen surrounded by fields, and here you can have a traditional quiet private retreat visit. At present the Sisters hold two traditional retreats a year on their programme. There is no smoking, no pets and no alcohol and you go to your room by 10pm – exactly the kind of early-to-bed rule that a lot of tired and over-busy people need.

Open: All year. Receives men, women, groups and non-retreatants.
Rooms: 10 singles, 3 twin-doubles.
Facilities: Garden, library, guest lounge, TV, guest telephone.
Spiritual Help: Personal talks.
Guests Admitted to: Chapel. Choir.
Meals: Everyone eats together in guest house. Traditional food. Vegetarians and special diets.
Special Activities: 2 traditional retreats a year at present.
Situation: Quiet in countryside.
Maximum Stay: 1 week.
Bookings: Letter/tel/fax – 5.30-8.30pm
Charges: Residential £20 per day. £25 if retreat arranged. Quiet days with lunch £7.50. Just for the day £5.
Access: Train/Coach possible. Car: via A38.

Silence of the heart practised with wisdom will see a lofty depth and the ear of the silent mind will hear untold wonders.

HESYCHIUS OF JERUSALEM

Stoodleigh

Sacred Earth – Sacred Spirit
3 Rainbows, Stoodleigh
Devon EX16 9QQ   Tel: 01884 881406

Mind-Body-Spirit – Native American Spirituality Traditions

Small dynamic and supportive camps in spiritual discoveries and
adventures, held in area of natural beauty. Children may be brought
and they have their own activities area. Typical courses on offer are
*Rainbow Sweat Lodge and Vision Quest, Fly like an Eagle, Way of Peace, Self-
discovery and Transformation,* and *Shiatsu Practice Camp.* **No dogs. No
drugs.**

Open: April to Sept. Closed season Oct to March for camping. All
year in retreat hut. Receives men, women, young people for all
programmes and families and groups for camping
Rooms: Camping for 25. 1 retreat hut.
Facilities: Conferences, camping, garden, woodland, guest phone.
Children welcomed.
Spiritual Help: Personal talks, spiritual direction, meditation, direct-
ed study, one-to-one healing treatments using Medicine Wheel Way,
counselling, medicine-healing sweat lodge. Earth-wisdom-spirit
quests in wild woodland. Pipe ceremony.
Guests Admitted to: Unrestricted access.
Meals: Everyone eats together in the summer camps. Whole food.
Vegetarians. Retreat Hut is self-catering.
Special Activities: Planned programme for summer camps. *Send for
brochure and be sure to include a SAE.* Work on nature reserve, peace
pipe ceremonies. Sweat Lodge. Vision quests.
Situation: Very quiet in countryside.
Maximum Stay: 1 week.
Bookings: Letter with SAE or telephone.
Charges: Examples of charges: weekend camp £50, 4-day camp £65.
See brochure for various camp programme charges.
Access: Train to Tiverton Parkway, then taxi. Bus to Tiverton Town.
Car route via M5, J27.

Whitestone

The Beacon Centre
Cutteridge Farm
Whitestone, Exeter EX4 2HE   Tel/Fax: 01392 811203

Mind-Body-Spirit

Personal and planetary healing and transformation are the aims of the
centre. A variety of workshops, training courses, retreats and therapies
are on offer. The centre is part of a larger farm and there are a number
of buildings including several private apartments. The heart is a courtyard around which are the farmhouse, the centre, and the residences.

The centre has been running over ten years and the current programmes offer such courses as *Focusing and Experiential Listening, Gestalt Basics, Mindfulness Meditation for Health Care Workers, the Hakomi Method of Psychotherapy, Core Therapy Energetics,* and *Living Art Workshop.* The rooms are comfortable and many have en-suite facilities. On the other hand if you want to try a real hermit's existence, you can stay in the Retreat Hermitage down in the fields where there are no modern facilities – including no water. The resident directors are very welcoming and helpful and one is a working therapist. Group or private retreatants given a supportive space for spiritual growth.

Open: All year. Receives everyone.
Rooms: 10 doubles, camping site, retreat hermitage. The hermitage is away from the other facilities for a *back-to-nature* retreat – there is no water or indoor toilet facilities.
Facilities: Camping, garden, library, guest lounge, TV, payphone, direct dialling. There is a meditation sanctuary in the garden which is a quiet place for meditation and prayer.
Spiritual Help: Personal talks, group sharing, meditation. Counselling and healing.
Guests Admitted to: Unrestricted access to all areas except private residential areas.
Meals: Wholefood. Taken in guest house. There is also a DIY kitchen. Vegetarians and vegans catered for.
Special Activities: Daily schedule followed 6 days a week. Planned events each year.
Situation: Quiet, in the countryside. Traffic on the busy major road nearby can be heard but it is not too intrusive.
Maximum Stay: By arrangement when space is available.
Bookings: Letter or telephone
Charges: See programme.
Access: By car is easiest – 3 miles from Exeter. Train: Exeter St Davids and bus are possible. Ask for exact travel directions when booking.

Yelverton

Grimstone Manor
Yelverton, Devon PL20 7QY

Tel: 01822 854358
Fax: 01822 852318
e-mail: enquires@grimstonemanor.co.uk
Website: www.grimstonemanor.co.uk

Mind-Body-Spirit

Programmes are run throughout the year and space for personal and private retreats is not on offer here. You must join a specific group programme run either by the resident Community or visiting groups. Workshops have included *Healing Tao Retreat, Vortex Healing, Gestalt Workshop, Yoga – Sharing the Quest.* See website for current programme. There is a brochure available on travel there, what to bring and other basic information.

Open: All year except January. Open to men, women, families and groups, but it depends on which course you want to attend.
Rooms: Accommodation for up to 40 people. Bring towel, soap, slippers for the house. No pets. The brochure gives good details about your stay.
Facilities: Garden of some 30 acres with pond, swimming pool, sauna, Jacuzzi, guest phone 01822 854824.
Spiritual Help: Personal talks are offered depending on the course you are attending. Some Community members offer healing and massage. Group sharing.
Guests Admitted to: Group rooms.
Meals: Everyone eats together in the dining room doing their own washing up. Vegetarian food.
Special Activities: Planned programme. See website.
Situation: Very quiet in the countryside.
Maximum Stay: As long as the group is staying.
Bookings: Letter.
Charges: About £40 +VAT per day. Extra for single rooms about £8 per day. B&B over night about £20.
Access: Train to Plymouth. Bus to Horrabridge. Car route on map in brochure.

DORSET

Burton Bradstock

Othona Community House
Coast Road
Burton Bradstock
Bridport, Dorset DT6 4RN

Tel: 01308 897130
Fax: 01308 898205
e-mail: othona.bb@free4all.co.uk

Ecumenical – Christian Community Living

The Community live in a large stone house on an unspoiled stretch of heritage coast. They have a chapel and a separate arts and crafts building. The grounds are designated a site of special nature conservation interest and the beach is just a few minutes walk away. There is that good mixture here of a sense of community combined with stillness and peace. There is an extensive range of retreats and courses on offer. Some examples are *Introduction to the Enneagram, Simply Community, Encountering Creation* and a retreat on the *Changing Images of God*. There is another Community living in Essex (see that section).

Open: Most of year. Receives everyone.
Rooms: 3 singles, 7 doubles, 5 dormitories. No TV/radios.
Facilities: Disabled, 6 acre informal garden, library, payphone.
Children welcomed. Guests expected to join in a few daily chores like washing up or preparing some vegetables.
Spiritual Help: Spiritual help available varies with the programme course. Chapel services of an informal nature.

Guests Admitted to: Unrestricted access everywhere. Chapel. Work of community.

Meals: Everyone eats together. Whole food, home-cooked, local and home-grown produce where possible. Vegetarian.

Special Activities: Planned programme including work projects, concerts, music-making and a studio for arts and crafts including spinning and weaving. Send for brochure.

Situation: Quiet near a village, set in an area of outstanding natural beauty overlooking the sea.

Maximum Stay: By arrangement.

Bookings: Letter, telephone, fax, e-mail.

Charges: Usually about £44 for an adult for the weekend. Weekly rate available. Child reductions possible and concessions available.

Access: Car route easiest – but enquire as to train, taxi, bus service to Burton Bradstock.

Charmouth

Monkton Wyld Court
Charmouth, Bridport
Dorset DT6 6DQ

Tel: 01297 560342
Fax: 01297 560395
e-mail: monktonwyldcourt@btinternet.com

Mind-Body-Spirit/Holistic Education Centre

Eleven acres of grounds surround this large Victorian rectory that is situated in a secluded valley on the Devon-Dorset border where a green, healthy space is provided for people to hopefully find inner awareness. Monkton is a leading centre for holistic education run by a Community with their children and has wlecomed many visitors and enjoyed good media coverage of its activities from time to time. The emphasis is on encouraging personal and spiritual growth, combined with a firm commitment to ecology and green issues and self-sufficiency – for example, on the farm the cows are hand-milked. There are walks to the sea, peace for meditation and yet the comforting buzz of a Community with a family life. There are plenty of courses that reflect these approaches to the art of living. Courses in the programmes can be exciting and challenging and offer real potential for self-development and spiritual growth. Some examples include: *Non-Violent Communication, Affirming the Female Body, Celebrating Nature, Healing and Evolving Men's Sexuality* and *Women's Drumming*. Weekend retreats in peace with the Community itself can be done and there is T'ai Chi, devotional singing, a work camp, body-mind centring, stained glass making, drawing, circle and sacred dancing and chanting, shaman dancing, and Qi Gong as well. A broad and generous programme from which to chose a weekend retreat and prices seem reasonable for what is offered.

Open: Most of the year. Closed 4-7 April, 11-14 Sept and a week in January – this can change with each year so ask about current closure schedule when you contact them. Receives men, women, young people, families, groups, non-retreatants on a B&B basis. Religious should be a group booking and then Monkton Community will decide whether or not to receive the group.

Rooms: 3 doubles, 8 dormitories, barn. A single by arrangement.

Facilities: Conferences, possibility of camping, garden, library, guest lounge, crafts shop, arts and crafts facilities, meditation room, massage and healing room, guest phone. Children welcomed.

Spiritual Help: Through the courses and retreats on offer, meditation.

Guests Admitted to: Everywhere except Community living areas. Work of the community.

Meals: Everyone eats together. Vegetarian organic wholefood. Special diets catered. DIY facilities possible.

Special Activities: Planned programme of events. Send for excellent brochure.

Situation: Very quiet, in the countryside.

Maximum Stay: Dependent on course being attended.

Bookings: Letter. If you do telephone then call between 10.30am-1pm and 2.30-5pm.

Charges: From £15 per night B&B in the low season to £260 for a 5-day stay course.

Access: By train, station 3 miles away, take taxi. Car via A35.

East Holton

The Barn
Holton Lee
East Holton, Near Poole
Dorset BH16 6JN

Tel/Fax: 01202 631063
e-mail: holton@lds.co.uk
Website: www.lds.co.uk/holtonlee

Inter-Denominational

Lying between Poole and Wareham, **The Barn at Holton Lee is a centre for people with disabilities and for carers.** Here can be found relaxation, respite, care, retreats, education activities and courses. There is full personal care by staff and personal care assistance when needed. Everything is purpose built. The Barn provides residential accommodation for up to eight people and is comprehensively equipped for people with disabilities. The Pavilion is a multi-purpose building providing space for a wide variety of workshops and courses including pottery, painting, and sculpture. Gateway Cottage offers separate residential accommodation with its own meeting room. Farm Cottage provides a separate quiet building with facilities for counselling, spiritual direction, massage and two guest rooms. The programme on offer is short but interesting and may include such topics as *Enneagram and Spirituality, Living with Stress, Take Time to Grow,* and *Feminine Creativity.* **Highly Recommended.**

Open: All year. Receives men, women, young people (if under 16 must be accompanied by a guardian), families, small groups, non-retreatants

Rooms: 9 singles, 6 doubles. Modern, comfortable, clean and

designed for those with disabilities. Conferences, garden, camping, park, guest lounge, TV, guest telephone.
Facilities: Disabled. Small conferences, sometimes camping, garden, guest lounge, TV, payphone. Children welcomed. Guide dogs accepted.
Spiritual Help: Personal talks, meditation, directed study. Spiritiual direction and personal retreat direction. Reflexology. Aromatherapy.
Guests Admitted to: Unrestricted access everywhere. Chapel.
Meals: Everyone eats together. Self-catering also available. Traditional/vegetarian food. Special diets catered.
Special Activities: Planned programme of events. Send for brochure.
Situation: Quiet and in the countryside. 350 acres of beautiful land with paths to go on. Bird hide overlooking a pond.
Maximum Stay: 2 weeks.
Bookings: Letter or telephone.
Charges: Various rates – ask for tariff list.
Access: Train, bus, car all possible.

Gillingham

The Leela Centre
Foundation for Joyous Living
Thorngrove House, off Common Mead Lane
Gillingham, Dorset SP8 4RE   Tel: 01747 821221
                                      e-mail: info@osholeela.co.uk

Mind-Body-Spirit

Osho Leela is a commune of people welcoming all spiritual seekers and visitors for groups and celebration events who are disciples of Master Osho – but it is not necessary to be a follower of Osho to come here as a guest. The commune has a calendar of courses which may include dance, an energy ecstasy weekend, shaman gathering for women, a celebration of women as goddess, a men's group, cranio-sacral balancing training, chakra training, and a retreat on nature-art meditation.

Open: All year. Receives everyone.
Rooms: 40 bed spaces divided into singles, doubles and shared rooms, camping site with spaces for 23 caravans.
Facilities: Camping, caravan site, garden, library, guest lounge, TV, payphone, healing centre (aromatherapy massage.)
Spiritual Help: Personal talks, group sharing, meditation, directed study.
Guests Admitted to: Unrestricted access.
Meals: Everyone eats together. Whole food. Vegetarian. Special diets.
Special Activities: Planned programme. Working weekends. Evening classes. Music festival.
Situation: Quiet.
Maximum Stay: No limit.
Bookings: Letter/e-mail.
Charges: £22.50 per day to £70 per week on a working programme. Other weekends about £35-£165 all in.
Access: Train and Bus: To Gillingham. Car: M3/A303 West

Hilfield

Society of St Francis
The Friary
Hilfield, Dorchester
Dorset DT2 7BE

Tel: 01300 341345
Fax: 01300 341293

Anglican

It is up to each guest to decide how best to use his or her time at the Friary, but all are welcome to join the Community in chapel for prayer. Set in peaceful surroundings, this is a quiet place where you will find space for thinking things through. Many guests have busy and active careers, and find that the Friary is just the place they need for rest and reflection. Hospitality is offered to all, so you may find that the man at prayer next to you could equally well be a successful industrialist or a wayfarer who tramps the road. **Highly Recommended.**

Open: All year from Tuesdays to Saturdays, except August. Receives men, women, young people, groups, non-retreatants.
Rooms: 11 singles, 1 double.
Facilities: Disabled – ask what the arrangements are when booking. Chapel, oratory, choir, garden, library, a book and craft shop, guest lounge, payphone. Bring a towel.
Spiritual Help: Personal talks, meditation.
Guests Admitted to: Chapel, choir and work of the community.
Meals: Everyone eats together. Traditional food. Vegetarian and special diets with advance notice.
Special Activities: None.
Situation: Very quiet, in the countryside.
Maximum Stay: 5 nights.
Bookings: Letter or telephone.
Charges: By donation. £17.50 per person 24 hrs suggested.
Access: Train to Dorchester. Guests are met when possible. Car route easy.

Wimborne

Gaunts House
Wimborne
Dorset BH21 4JQ

Tel: 01202 841522
e-mail: courses@RGF-Gaunt.demon.co.uk

Non-Denominational – Spiritual

Part of the Gaunts estate and dedicated to the development of life on a spiritual basis. It offers space and help for spiritual and personal development with a supportive community, all set in beautiful park land. The facilities are wide ranging from a sanctuary to healing rooms. There are many different programmes on offer – for example during this past year there has been an *Easter Yoga Retreat* which included interfaith multicultural programmes, gospel choir, Sanskrit Mantra Chanting, Native American traditions, Druid Traditions, and Celtic Music.

Open: All year. Receives men, women, young people, families, and groups.
Rooms: Can accommodate up to 160 people at one time. Singles, doubles, camping, dormitories.
Facilities: Disabled. Conferences, camping, garden, library, guest lounge, TV, payphone. Children welcomed. No pets.
Spiritual Help: Personal talks, group sharing, meditation, support and advice. Therapies available on request.
Guests Admitted to: Unrestricted access to all areas including sanctuary, work of the community.
Meals: Vegetarian – guests can share the cooking. Food may be brought or purchased there. Provision for special diets if necessary.
Special Activities: Planned programme of events. Send for brochure issued twice yearly.
Situation: Very quiet in the countryside.
Maximum Stay: Unlimited.
Bookings: Letter or telephone.
Charges: These vary so ask for rates. An example would be a private retreat for two days at £75 or £175 for a week's stay.
Access: Train, bus, car all possible. Train to Poole. Bus to Wimborne, then taxi or telephone for a lift.

SOMERSET

Bath

Bainesbury House
Downside Abbey
Stratton on the Fosse
Bath and N.E. Somerset BA5 4RH   Tel: 01761 235161
                                             Fax: 01761 235124

Roman Catholic – Ecumenical

The retreat guest house, owned by Downside Abbey, is open to all Christian individuals and groups and is self-catering.

Open: All year. Receives everyone.
Rooms: 1 single and dormitories. Check when booking on exact arrangements.
Facilities: Abbey church, garden, park, library by arrangement, guest lounge, payphone. Children welcomed.
Spiritual Help: Groups usually look after their own programme. However, members of the monastic community are usually available to Roman Catholics for sacramental needs.
Guests Admitted to: Access to nearby Abbey church.
Meals: Self-catering.
Special Activities: No planned programme. Groups arrange their own.

Situation: Very quiet, near the village in the countryside, about 12 miles from Bath.
Maximum Stay: By arrangement.
Bookings: Letter, telephone, fax.
Charges: About £5 per person per night and about £4 students and unemployed.
Access: Train: to Bath Spa. Bus: from Bath Spa to Stratton on the Fosse. Car: via A367.

Downside Abbey
Stratton on the Fosse
Bath and N.E. Somerset BA5 4RH   Tel: 01761 232295

Roman Catholic

The home of a famous boys' public school with an abbey church of cathedral proportions. The community welcomes men who wish to share the monastic prayer and quiet or who may just want a peaceful private break. This is very much a hard-working place with a busy schedule, but the guest master is usually available for a personal talk and to help with spiritual guidance.

Open: All year except Christmas and mid-July to mid-August.
Receives men only.
Rooms: 10 singles.
Facilities: Abbey church, garden, library (by permission), guest lounge, TV, guest phone.
Spiritual Help: Personal talks, directed study.
Guests Admitted to: Chapel. Guests are not to enter the school area.
Meals: Everyone eats together. Traditional food. Vegetarians catered.
Special Activities: None.
Situation: Quiet, near the village, about 12 miles from Bath.
Maximum Stay: 1 week.
Bookings: Letter or telephone.
Charges: By donation.
Access: Train to Bath Spa. Bus from Bath Spa to Stratton on the Fosse. Car via A367.

Cleveden

Community of the Sisters of the Church
St Gabriel's
27a Dial Hill Road
Cleveden, Somerset BS21 7HL   Tel/Fax: 01275 872586

Anglican

A quiet house of prayer for anyone looking for time out from a busy life, direction in their lives or just a good break from routines. Silence is kept until late morning each day.

Open: All year.
Rooms: 4 singles.
Facilities: Garden, guest lounge, TV.
Spiritual Help: Personal talks, spiritual direction, personal retreat direction.
Guests Admitted to: Unrestricted access.
Meals: Taken in room. Vegetarian.
Special Activities: None.
Situation: Quiet overlooking Bristol Channel.
Maximum Stay: 10 days.
Bookings: Letter.
Charges: £20 per night.
Access: Train: Yatton and then collected. Bus and car good, ask for specifics.

Compton Durville

Community of St Francis
Compton Durville
South Petherton
Somerset TA13 5ES

Tel: 01460 240473
Fax: 01460 242360
e-mail: csp.compton@talk21.com

Anglican

The little hamlet of Compton Durville has the Community house, church, and guest facilities on either side of the entrance street like pretty stone guardians. The welcome and hospitality here is cheerful and very friendly. The main house is handsome inside and out, the garden walks remarkably peaceful and lovely, and the church intimate and light with a nice liturgy. The Community run a modest but good retreat programme and are trying to upgrade and improve their guest accommodation with each passing year.

Open: All year from Monday to after lunch on Sunday. Sometimes it is closed for short periods only. Receives everyone.
Rooms: 14 singles, 2 twin-doubles. Self-catering cottage for 6. Hermitage. The quality of the beds may vary so if you need a firm one, ask when you book.
Facilities: Conferences, large garden, library, guest lounge, TV, guest phone, direct dialling. Children welcomed by prior arrangement.
Spiritual Help: Personal talks by arrangement, chapel services, spiritual direction, personal retreat direction.
Guests Admitted to: Unrestricted access except to Community private areas. Work of community sometimes.
Meals: Everyone eats main meals together. Simple food. Vegetarian and special diets by prior arrangement.
Special Activities: Quiet Days. Individually guided retreats. Send for information.
Situation: Very quiet, in a small village.
Maximum Stay: Normally 6 days unless on an 8-day Ignatian retreat or in self-catering accommodation.

Bookings: Letter, telephone, fax.
Charges: £20 per day. Hermitage £10 per day. Cottage £200 per week.
Access: Train or by bus to local stations in Taunton and Yeovil where you can make arrangements to be picked up. Car route easy. Good directions brochure available.

Coursing Batch

Shambhala
Centre for Spiritual Growth and Healing
Coursing Batch, Glastonbury
Somerset BA6 8BH

Tel: 01458 831797
Fax: 01458 834751
e-mail: isisandargon@shambhala.co.uk
Website: www.shambhala.co.uk

Mind-Body-Spirit

Relaxing and healing breaks, spiritual growth experiences, regeneration and development, and physical and emotional healing – these are the core aims behind your stay at this truly alternative spirituality centre. It is located on the ancient sacred site of Glastonbury Tor with its acclaimed reputation. Indeed, there is a ley line straight down the middle of the separate hermitage in which Isis, the leader of Shambala, sleeps. There are massages, healing therapies, Reiki, a jacuzzi inside a small Oriental type building hidden away in the garden, and a wood-burning sauna. The centre does not occupy a lot of ground, yet once you walk through the gate and cross the crystal star set in the stones, the whole garden and house becomes a green sanctuary away from the world. You will find all sorts of people with widely differing spiritual beliefs staying here. Perhaps their concern is reincarnation or the lost civilisation of Atlantis or the counselling that comes through channelling with guardian angels. The accommodation is comfortable. There is a high degree of informality in the house and activities during the day are not usually structured into a programme. Before you book confirm exactly what is being included in your stay and what the total cost will be.

Open: All year. Receives everyone.
Rooms: 1 single, 3 doubles – 1 twin-bedded room.
Facilities: Sanctuary, sauna, jacuzzi, healing massage room, water garden, guest lounge, books, TV, payphone.
Spiritual Help: Spiritual healing, sanctuary for silence.
Guests Admitted to: Unrestricted access.
Meals: Everyone eats together. Vegetarian food.
Special Activities: Spiritual healing, awakening the inner self, deep tissue massage, neuro-muscular body work, Reiki, Secheim and Vortex Hands-on-Healing. See brochures and if you have questions then telephone and ask.
Situation: On the side of Glastonbury Tor.
Maximum Stay: By arrangement.
Bookings: Letter, telephone, fax, e-mail.
Charges: See the brochure. Prices are not cheap so find out what you are going to get for your money.

Access: Train: Castle Cary Station. Coach: Bath/Bristol. Car: On A361 between Shepton Mallett and Glastonbury. Be sure to follow the directions for parking.

Glastonbury

Berachah House
Well House Lane
Glastonbury, Somerset BA6 8BJ

Tel: 01458 8342214
e-mail: berachah.martin@ukonline.co.uk
Mind-Body-Spirit

Just ten minutes walk from Glastonbury High Street, this house was built on the site of the first known ashram in Britain and the former location of one of the most influential occultists of recent times, Violet Firth. Today, Berachah offers a programme of astrology, *aura soma* readings, and colour healing.

Open: All year. Receives everyone.
Rooms: 3 doubles.
Facilities: Garden, library, guest lounge, TV, phone.
Spiritual Help: Personal talks.
Guests Admitted to: Unrestricted access.
Meals: Guests eat together.
Special Activities: Planned programme.
Situation: Quiet.
Maximum Stay: By arrangement.
Bookings: Letter or tel/fax.
Charges: £25 single to £45 double en-suite. Therapies and readings separate rates. See brochure.
Access: Train: nearest station Castle Cary (15 miles). Bus, car to Glastonbury.

Abbey House
Chilkwell Street
Glastonbury
Somerset BA6 8BT

Tel: 01458 831112
Fax: 01458 831893
e-mail: abbeyhouse@easinet.co.uk

Anglican

This is the Bath and Wells Retreat and Conference House, which is set in the 40 acres of beautiful grounds of the old Benedictine Abbey in the town centre. A small resident staff manages the place. The great majority of the guests are sponsored by church groups but private retreatants are welcomed when there is room. Abbey House is booked a great deal in advance – apparently years in some cases which must make them the envy of many retreat centres elsewhere. While activities are mostly aimed at groups, there are plenty of silent and theme retreats which individuals might attend. The house is a silent house for part of the year and retreats are mostly silent ones.

Open: All year. Receives men, women, young people, families, groups.
Rooms: 18 singles and 9 twin-bedded rooms.
Facilities: Disabled. Conferences, garden, park, library, guest lounge, payphone.
Spiritual Help: Personal talks.
Guests Admitted to: Unrestricted access most of the time except when a group is resident then it may be restricted.
Meals: Traditional simple food. Vegetarian and special diets.
Special Activities: Planned programme. See brochure.
Situation: In town but quiet.
Maximum Stay: By arrangement.
Bookings: Letter or telephone/fax, daytime hours.
Charges: £58-70 per weekend per person. £100-120 Mon-Fri per person full board.
Access: Train: nearest railway station is Castle Cary (15 miles). Bus: Badgerline No. 376 travels hourly at 5 minutes to the hour from Bristol coach station; National Express coach runs daily from London Victoria to Bristol.

Tordown Healing Centre
5 Ashwell Lane
Glastonbury, Somerset BA6 8BG

Tel: 01458 832287
Fax: 01458 831100
e-mail: torangel@aol.com

Mind-Body-Spirit

A quiet place for a bed and breakfast type retreat with really good view from some of the bedrooms. A helpful place for those wishing some peace and rest

Open: All year. Receives everyone.
Rooms: 2 singles, 5 doubles. This is a no smoking house.
Facilities: Garden, park, library, guest lounge, TV, payphone. Children welcomed. Pets by prior arrangement.
Spiritual Help: Personal talks, personal retreat direction. Meditation.
Guests Admitted to: Unrestricted access.
Meals: Taken in guest house. Vegetarian food.
Special Activities: No planned programme. Activities include Reiki teaching, healing, and sessions concentrating on higher self-awareness.
Situation: Quiet.
Maximum Stay: 1 month.
Bookings: Letter or telephone.
Charges: From £18 B&B per person per day but maximum of £30 per person per day.
Access: Train to Castle Cary then taxi. Bus to Glastonbury town hall. Car route off A301 to Frome.

Langport

St Gilda's Christian Centre
The Hill
Langport, Somerset TA10 9QF   Tel: 01458 250496
                                               Fax: 01458 251293

Inter-Denominational

A big white 18th century house in the middle of Langport which has
been called *The Light on the Hill*. There is a very good library, a fine light
chapel, and in the five acre garden there is a seasonal-use swimming
pool. The retreat programme is not overly ambitious and it includes
quiet days, a retreat for beginners, preached retreats and some on
prayer and nature and prayer and painting.

Open: All year, except over Christmas. Receives everyone.
Rooms: 4 singles, 19 doubles, 2 dormitories.
Facilities: Disabled. Conferences, garden, park of 5 acres with
summertime swimming pool, library, guest lounge, TV, payphone.
Children welcomed.
Spiritual Help: Personal talks.
Guests Admitted to: Unrestricted access.
Meals: Everyone eats together. Traditional food. Vegetarians and spe-
cial diets catered.
Special Activities: Planned programme of events. Send for informa-
tion.
Situation: Quiet, in a large village.
Maximum Stay: 2 weeks.
Bookings: Letter, telephone, fax.
Charges: Rates vary according to what accommodation you are in
and what is going on – so ask when you book.
Access: Train, bus and car all possible – ask for directions. It is about a
mile walk from South Petherton and only 2 miles by car from the
A303.

Radstock

Ammerdown Centre
Bath
Bath and N.E. Somerset BA5 5SW   Tel: 01761 433709
                                               Fax: 01761 433094

Ecumenical

Ammerdown, now operating for over twenty-five years, offers one of
the most extensive ranges of retreats and courses on offer anywhere.
Some of the courses on offer may include *A Taste of Buddhism, A Taste of
Hinduism, Prayer Weekend, Circle Dancing, Dreams, The Four Faces of the
Moon, Art of Living Healing Breath Workshop,* and *The Beatitudes and
Colour.* In addition to rooms, they provide people who wish to get away
from it all with the accommodation for being alone for a prayer retreat.
Study, personal growth, ecumenical dialogue, interfaith dialogue,

Christian ethics, Christian Jewish Bible study, meditation skills, and group development are just a few of the aims of the courses. The Centre occupies various attractive old buildings in and around the stable-block of Ammerdown House, the private residence of Lord Hylton and his family. Some of the park lands and gardens are open to residents. While predominantly Christian, the governing body represents other religious communities. For example, one of the governors has been the well-known Rabbi Lionel Blue. The Ammerdown Centre is an open Christian Community dedicated to peace, reconciliation and renewal. It makes provision within a secure, welcoming and prayerful atmos-phere with respect for all regardless of beliefs. There is plenty on offer both for the first-time private retreatant and for those who attend reli-gious retreats regularly. Those who conduct the courses are experi-enced and informed and include such people as Dr Karen Jankulak from the University of Wales at Lampeter and Rabbi Mark Solomon from Leo Beck College in London. **Highly Recommended.**

Open: All year except Christmas. Receives men, women, young people, groups, non-retreatants.
Rooms: 30 singles, 8 doubles, 5 family rooms. Two self-catering flats. A *Peace Cottage* sleeping 13 people.
Facilities: Disabled – 2 ground-floor singles, loop system. Conference rooms, garden, park, library, guest lounge, TV, payphone. Chapel, prayer room, religious bookshop, craft shop, walks in woodland and parkland. Various games such as badminton.
Spiritual Help: Personal talks, group sharing, meditation, directed study, spiritual dirtection, personal retreat direction. Community prayer twice a day.
Guests Admitted to: Unrestricted access. Chapel.
Meals: Everyone eats together. DIY facilities. Traditional food. Vegetarian and special diets.
Special Activities: A very extensive programme. See brochure.
Situation: Very quiet, in the countryside.
Maximum Stay: By arrangement.
Bookings: Letter or telephone – 9am-5pm.
Charges: By donations – suggested rate for private stay £30 and courses cost anywhere from £75 to £260 but most falling into the lower rate. There are day courses at £6. Each course is priced so con-sult the programme for the current year.
Access: Train: to Bath Spa. Buses: to Radstock. Car: Centre is just off A362.

Queen Camel

Self-Realisation Meditation Healing Centre
Laurel Lane, Queen Camel
Near Yeovil, Somerset BA22 7NU

Tel: 01935 850266
Fax: 01935 850234
e-mail: info@selfrealizationcentres.org
Website: www.selfrealizationcentres.org

Mind-Body-Spirit – Non-Denominational

The Centre is a charitable trust run by a team of counsellors and healers living and working together as a family and using the guidance of yoga, meditation, and healing self-development in their work and courses. Meditation is a central feature of the centre – a 17th century house with extensive grounds of some 3½ acres and offering plenty of space and facilities, including a therapy pool. Near the River Cam and open countryside. The ancient spiritual centres of Glastonbury and Wells are within easy reach. Many people who come here on their first experience of a retreat away from their ordinary life, have been pleased with the comfort and thoughtfulness of the resident Community and the facilities. **Highly Recommended.**

Open: All year. Receives men, women, young people, groups, non-retreatants.
Rooms: 5 singles, 4 doubles, dormitories, hermitage.
Facilities: Meditation room, garden and 3 acres, library, guest lounges, payphone.
Spiritual Help: Personal talks, groups sharing on courses, meditation, directed study, personal retreat direction.
Guests Admitted to: Unrestricted access.
Meals: Meals taken together, guest house and at times DIY. Whole food, vegetarian, organic when possible. Special diets.
Special Activities: Planned programme, so send for the brochure.
Situation: Very quiet, in the village. Within easy reach of Glastonbury, Wells, Bath, Bristol and Yeovil.
Maximum Stay: By arrangement.
Bookings: Letter or telephone.
Charges: £32.50 per day full board. Therapy charges are extra – see brochure.
Access: Car: via A303. Collecting service from the nearest train station.

Street

Creative Arts Retreat Movement
182 High Street
Street, Somerset BA16 ONH

Painting, calligraphy, embroidery, creative writing, poetry, pottery, music and art appreciation are all creative retreats under the umbrella of this organisation. Each retreat has a chaplain and a tutor who coordinate all the various elements. On the retreat the spiritual is focused on during times of worship and there can be a daily Eucharist, Night Prayer, meditation or a talk. The retreats are held at centres throughout Britain, many listed elsewhere in this guide. Sometimes retreats are on offer which are overseas in such attractive places as Bruges in Belgium. The Creative Arts Retreat Movement is a clever and timely idea that has much appeal and the programme brochure is an excellent starting point for those thinking about going on such a retreat. There are some 40 tutors and 40 chaplains now involved who give their services free and the membership is almost a thousand. For those less financially able, there is the possibility of a bursary fund toward costs. Officers of the organisation do change from time to time, therefore **there is not a**

telephone number. All enquiries should be by letter in the first instance for this reason. Chairman of the Movement, Preb. Geoffrey Sunderland, says: *Whatever inspires you to take a retreat, I hope you find it an imaginative and peaceful experience.*

Taunton

Amitabha Buddhist Centre
St Audries House
West Quantoxhead, Taunton
Somerset TA4 4DS

Tel: 01984 633200
Fax: 01984 633807
e-mail: buddha@amitabha.net

Buddhist – New Kadampa Tradition

Meditation retreats in beautiful Somerset sums this place up. The setting is lovely, the surrounding woods glorious in the autumn and the programme includes various meditation courses including those for beginners. Also there are courses on relationship building and introductions to Buddhist thought. The centre is home to a large Community of ordained and lay Buddhist practitioners, families and others wanting this way of life.

Open: Most of year. Men and women.
Rooms: Both singles and doubles are available.
Facilities: Camping, garden, park, library, guest lounge, guest telephone.
Spiritual Help: Spiritual direction. Meditation. Directed study.
Guests Admitted to: Unrestricted access.
Meals: Everyone eats together. Vegetarian food. Special diets.
Special Activities: Programme of courses. Brochure available.
Situation: Quiet in countryside.
Maximum Stay: 1 month.
Bookings: Letter/tel/fax/e-mail.
Charges: Single £24 per night. Twin room £20 per person per night. Dormitory £15 per night. Prices include three meals.
Access: Train: Taunton. Bus: No. 28 from Taunton. Car: A39.

Winford

Winford Manor Retreat
Winford, Bristol
N. Somerset, BS18 8DW

Tel: 01275 472262
Fax: 01275 472065

Ecumenical

The Order at Winford Manor Retreat was founded in 1980, taking its title from the words of Christ – *I am the Alpha and the Omega, the first and the last.* The Manor has gone from strength to strength over the years and guests are welcomed at all times, either to attend courses and retreats or to find space for rest and reflection and to join the community of lay and religious men and women in the rhythm of a life of prayer. Courses may include retreats to enhance insight through the study of calligraphy, contemplative dance, Christian and Buddhist spirituality, or taking new and scientific concepts of God. Creativity is encouraged. There are also traditional courses on contemplative prayer and meditation. The Prior and Founder, Canon Peter Spink, has written a number of thought-provoking spirituality books, and Winford Manor Retreat has produced a series of cassettes and offers a correspondence course to help participants develop their own perceptions and insights. In short, Winford Manor Retreat offers silence in which to reflect and studies in which to expand and develop consciousness of the spirit. A good location for those who may not want their first retreat to be in a church setting that is overwhelmingly traditional. Indeed here is a place where you will be taken seriously if you ask why God is referred to as masculine – and you will get a considered answer. *The Omega Offices* which are used as a daily liturgy are delightful. If you are invited to join in a little circle dancing with the others in the chapel as part of the service, do participate as it is easy and very much an act of praying together. When you join in, recall that King David in the Old Testament *danced* for joy before the altar of the Lord God. Winford Manor Retreat may help you feel the presence of the Universal and Cosmic Christ perhaps more than many other places of Christian religious or church life. **Highly Recommended.**

Open: All year. Receives everyone.
Rooms: 13 singles, 14 twin-doubles, self-contained flat which is self-catering. Cottage.
Facilities: Disabled, conferences, garden, park, excellent library, very spacious and comfortable guest lounge, payphone, direct dialling. Children welcomed.
Spiritual Help: Personal talks and personal retreat direction, group sharing, meditation, directed study. Social and spiritual rehabilitation, counselling, spiritual direction.
Guests Admitted to: Chapel, shrine room, work of the community.
Meals: Everyone eats together. International food, well prepared and presented with provision for vegetarians.
Special Activities: Planned programme of events. Send for information. Meditation techniques, yoga, reflexology, massage, aromatherapy, assistance in recovery programmes, respite care and counselling.
Situation: Quiet, in the countryside. An old house standing in 7 acres of wooded grounds.
Maximum Stay: None.
Bookings: Letter or Tel/fax – 9am-5pm weekdays.
Charges: From £20 B&B per night to £37.50 up per night in an en-suite room.
Access: Train: Bristol Temple Meads station 7 miles away.
Buses: Central Bristol Bus Station. Car: via A38 from Bristol to Exeter Road.

WILTSHIRE

Heddington

**International Meditation Centre
Splatts House
Heddington, Calne
Wiltshire SN11 0PE**

Tel: 01380 850238
Fax: 01380 850833
e-mail: imc.uk@virgin.net
Website: www.webcom.com/imcuk/

Buddhist – Theravada

The International Meditation Centre, founded by the Sayagyi U Ba Khin Memorial Trust, provides for the instruction and practice of Theravada Buddhist Vipassana meditation, guided by disciples who have practised and taught meditation for more than forty years. Ten-day residential courses are held each month. The meditation practice is of the Buddhist traditon of the Eightfold Noble Path which divides into three parts: morality, concentration and wisdom. The Light of the Dhamma Pagoda, focal point of the meditation centre, is very beautiful and inspiring. Many people have come here for the 10-day courses with good results. Splatts House is a handsome red brick building where the practice of meditation is done to directly experience the truth of oneself – this includes *Noble Silence* which means *no unnecessary talking.* The daily timetable here for the retreats begins with 4.30am meditation and goes through to 9pm with rest periods, meals and teachings along with periods of meditation in the Hall.

Open: All year for 10-day retreats. Receives men, women, young people.
Rooms: 2 singles, 2 doubles, dormitories.
Facilities: Light of the Dhamma Pagoda. Garden. Disabled possible.
Spiritual Help: Meditation. Students observe noble silence but may speak with their teacher and the staff at any time.
Guests Admitted to: Access to most areas. Meditation Hall. Residential areas.
Meals: Everyone eats together. Vegetarian food. Special diets will be accommodated as far as possible.
Special Activities: Daily schedule of meditation practice. Planned schedule for the courses. Send for brochure.
Situation: Quiet on edge of a village.
Maximum Stay: 10 days.
Bookings: Letter, telephone, fax, e-mail.
Charges: £170 for 10-day retreat (£17 per day). No charges for the teaching.
Access: Rail, bus, and car all possible. Train from Paddington to Chippenham. See brochure with map.

Salisbury

Sarum College
19 The Close
Salisbury, Wilts. SP1 2EE   Tel: 01722 424800
                                                 Fax: 01722 338508

Inter-Denominational

Sarum College is an ecumenical institution being developed as a new
and innovative resource for all the churches in England and Wales. It
occupies historic buildings, directly opposite the great Salisbury
Cathedral. There are extensive facilities ranging from an excellent theological library to a book shop. Already in operation is a flourishing
Institute for Christian Spirituality which offers courses in spiritual
direction, retreats and workshops here and around the country. There
is also an **Institute for Liturgy and Mission** which is up and running.
The programme offers a good range of retreats and courses including
events organised by the Marian Study Centre and the Centre for
Creation Spirituality (see London section).

Open: All year. Receives everyone.
Rooms: 30 singles, 10 doubles.
Facilities: Garden, guest lounge, library, TV, payphone. Children
welcomed.
Spiritual Help: Personal talks, group sharing, meditation.
Guests Admitted to: Mostly everywhere.
Meals: Everyone eats together. Traditional food. Vegetarian and
special diets catered.
Special Activities: Planned programme. Send for brochure.
Situation: Rather busy in a Cathedral close.
Maximum Stay: By arrangement.
Bookings: Letter, telephone, fax.
Charges: £30 per day full board.
Access: Centre of Salisbury. Access by train, bus, car.

Warminster

St Denys Retreat Centre
2 Church Street
Warminster
Wilts. BA12 8PG   Tel: 01985 214824

Anglican

This is a big brick and stone house set right on the street. The
Community offers individual retreats in the Ignatian tradition as well
as 'walk-into-quietness days' when a team of sisters welcome you to a
day retreat in the centre. Well organised and friendly with the aim of
helping people to *be* rather than *do*.

Open: All year except Christmas and first 2 weeks of January.

Receives men, women, young people, groups and non-retreatants when there is space.

Rooms: 16 singles, 6 doubles.

Facilities: Disabled – one-person ground floor room, no lifts. Small conferences, chapel, garden, 2 guest lounges, dining room, payphone.

Spiritual Help: Individually guided retreats, mainly Ignatian type. Personal retreat direction. Spiritual direction.

Guests Admitted to: Access to most areas. Chapel.

Meals: Everyone eats together. Traditional and simple food. Vegetarian. Special diets can be catered with advance notification.

Special Activities: Planned programme. Send for brochure.

Situation: Quiet, in the town. Old fashioned garden, listed building.

Maximum Stay: 2 weeks unless doing the 30-day retreat.

Bookings: Letter or telephone.

Charges: It varies but about £29 per 24 hours.

Access: Train: Portsmouth – Cardiff line. Bus: from Salisbury, Bath or Trowbridge. Car: via B3414, off A36. Good maps in brochure and leaflet.

The Lord is my shepherd;
there is nothing I shall want.
Fresh and green are the pastures
where he gives me repose.

PSALM 23

SOUTH AND SOUTH EAST

BERKSHIRE

Ascot

Ascot Priory
Ascot
Berks. SL5 8RT   Tel: 01344 885685

Anglican

Open: All year. Receives men, women, young people, groups.
Rooms: 22 singles, 2 doubles.
Facilities: Disabled – facilities are planned so please ask what is available. Conferences, camping, park, guest lounge, TV, payphone.
Spiritual Help: Group sharing.
Guests Admitted to: Chapel.
Meals: Self-catering.
Special Activities: None.
Situation: Very quiet, in the countryside.
Maximum Stay: By arrangement.
Bookings: Letter.
Charges: Ask for current charges.
Access: Rail and bus both possible. Send for detailed instructions.

Kintbury

St Cassian's Centre
Kintbury
Berks. RG17 9SR   Tel: 01488 658267

Roman Catholic

The De La Salle Brothers run this centre for young people. Thousands come here to participate in the various group events. The retreats are almost entirely offered to groups from schools, and individual retreats are not taken. However, each year there are usually three family weekends in summer and there is a self-catering cottage which sleeps eight and is sometimes available for quiet breaks or private retreats.

Open: Most of year. Receives young people in school years 10, 11 and Sixth Form. There are family weekends.
Rooms: 5 singles, 29 doubles. Self-catering cottage.
Facilities: Conferences, garden, guest lounges, payphone.

Spiritual Help: Personal talks, group sharing.
Guests Admitted to: Unrestricted access.
Meals: Everyone eats together.
Special Activities: Planned programme of group events for young people, mainly schools.
Situation: Very quiet, in the countryside.
Maximum Stay: According to programme.
Bookings: Letter.
Charges: Ask for rates.
Access: Train to Kintbury. Car via A4.

Reading

Douai Abbey
Upper Woolhampton
Reading
Berks. RG7 5TQ   Tel: 0118 9715342
                                                       Fax: 0118 9715203
                                          e-mail: douaiabby@aol.com

Roman Catholic

One of the most famous monasteries and a place for men to make a private retreat in an atmosphere of Community life and prayer. A traditional monastic place in the countryside and yet not far from London, Reading or Oxford. In addition to facilities in the monastery for men and the retreat house for everyone else, there is a Pastoral Programme which organises the retreats, conferences, and events and a retreat house for both men and women (see below).

Open: All year except Christmas, Easter and mid-July to mid-August. Receives men.
Rooms: 15 singles.
Facilities: Chapel. Choir.
Spiritual Help: Personal talks.
Guests Admitted to: Chapel, choir.
Meals: Everyone eats together. Traditional food. Vegetarians.
Special Activities: Planned retreats – see below.
Situation: Quiet and in the countryside.
Maximum Stay: A few days usually. Otherwise by arrangement with guest master.
Bookings: Letter, telephone, fax, *e-mail is best.*
Charges: By arrangement.
Access: Train: Midgham 1½ miles. Bus: No. 102. Car: via M4, Exit 1. Ask for brochure with map.

Douai Abbey – Guest Accommodation and Pastoral Programme
Upper Woolhampton
Reading
Berks. RG7 5TH   **Guest Accommodation:** Tel: 0118 9715342
                Pastoral Programme Enquiries: Tel: 0118 9715333

Fax: 0118 9715203
e-mail: douaiabby@aol.com
Web Site: http://members.aol.com/douaiweb

Roman Catholic

There is a guest accommodation available at the monastery (see above) and you may join the monks in the chapel and for the daily schedule of prayers. There is a Pastoral Programme which offers a variety of spiritual and educational opportunities in the areas of theology, ministry and spirituality. For example, one series of lectures is on the English saints from St Bede to St Hugh of Lincoln. The arrangements for guests on a private visit and those attending a Pastoral Programme event are different, so do ask for details when you contact them.

Open: Most of year except Christmas, Easter, mid-July to mid-August. Receives men, women, young people, groups, non-retreatants.
Rooms: 17 singles. 5 doubles. Hostel. Various combinations of accommodation depending on whether you are attending a programme event or are on a visit. It is informal, self-catering and small rooms, even camping is possible. Do ask what is on offer when you contact the guest master or programme director.
Facilities: Conferences, chapel, garden, library, guest lounge, payphone. Children welcome.
Spiritual Help: Meditation, directed study and sharing in the daily round of prayer in a planned event stay. Organised retreats.
Guests Admitted to: Chapel, choir.
Meals: Everyone eats together on programme events in the guest house. Traditional food. Vegetarians and special diets. Otherwise self-catering.
Special Activities: Planned programme. Send for brochure.
Situation: Quiet and in the countryside.
Maximum Stay: 2 weeks.
Bookings: Letter, telephone, fax, e-mail best.
Charges: Suggested fee of £35 per day.
Access: Train: Midgham 1½ miles. Bus: No. 102. Car: via M4, Exit 1. Good map in brochure.

Speen

**Elmore Abbey
Church Lane
Speen, Newbury
Berks. RG13 ISA**   Tel: 01635 33080

Anglican

This is a distinguished Anglican abbey with a new and beautiful church with oak columns that seem like trees in a woodland. The little cloister courtyard at the entrance could not be prettier or more charming. All the refurbishment, rebuilding and designing have been done with obvious care and considerable talent. Everywhere is elegant and peaceful and so too seem the Community of monks who live here. There is a large oblate membership who come often and they have first priority on the guest accommodation.

Open: All year except over Christmas. Receives men, women, and those for day retreats.
Rooms: 6 singles.
Facilities: Chapel. Garden, library with permission.
Spiritual Help: Personal talks, individual guidance given if on a private retreat, but not guided retreats.
Guests Admitted to: Chapel, some work of Community.
Meals: Everyone eats together. Traditional food. Vegetarians catered.
Special Activities: None.
Situation: Quiet, in the countryside.
Maximum Stay: By arrangement.
Bookings: Letter.
Charges: On application.
Access: By train to Newbury or by car.

Thatcham

Cold Ash Centre
The Ridge
Cold Ash, Thatcham
Berks. RG18 9HU

Tel: 01635 865353
Fax: 01635 866621
e-mail: fmmmcac@aol.com

Roman Catholic – Inter-Denominational

The planned programme of retreats here run by the Franciscan Missionaries of Mary is short but good, offering both preached and directed retreats. There are pleasant warm rooms and fine views in this very large building. A popular place so you may need to book up well in advance.

Open: All year except August. Receives men, women, young people, groups.
Rooms: 28 singles, 3 doubles.
Facilities: Disabled. Conferences, garden, small library, coffee rooms, guest lounges, TV, payphone, direct dialling. Take towel, soap, and soft shoes for indoor use.
Spiritual Help: Spiritual direction, personal retreat direction.
Guests Admitted to: Chapel, church, oratory.
Meals: Taken in the guest house. Traditional and vegetarian food. Special diets.
Special Activities: Planned programme of events, preached retreats, bio-spiritual focusing retreats and workshops, massage retreats. Send for brochure.
Situation: Quiet, in the countryside.
Maximum Stay: 1 month.
Bookings: Letter.

Charges: Currently about £27 full board per person.
Access: Train: Thatcham. Bus: Newbury or Reading. Car: Centre is 4 miles from Newbury. Map available if requested.

HAMPSHIRE

Alton

**Abbey of Our Lady and St John
Alton, Hants GU34 4AP**   Tel: 01420 562145/563575

Anglican

The Abbey is a place where you may find stillness and, hopefully, that reflection which may lead to worship and prayer with the Community. Benedictine hospitality helps provide a very wide range of retreats tailored to a retreatant's needs.

Open: Most of the year. Receives everyone.
Rooms: 15 singles. One self-catering flat for two.
Facilities: Disabled – limited but more being built so ask what is available. Conferences, garden, guest lounge, TV, payphone. Children welcomed.
Spiritual Help: Personal talks, group sharing, meditation, directed study, spiritual counsel, personal guided retreats.
Guests Admitted to: Chapel, sometimes work of Community.
Meals: Everyone eats together in refectory. Good traditional food. Vegetarians and special diets catered.
Special Activities: Planned programme including theme retreats, private retreat *desert days* a feature. Send for brochure.
Situation: Quiet in the countryside.
Maximum Stay: 1 week.
Bookings: Letter or telephone.
Charges: On application.
Access: Train: Alton, then No. 208 bus. Car: Abbey is off A339.

Basingstoke

**Malshanger Estate
Newfound, Basingstoke
Hants**

Anglican – Ecumenical

Do not call or write to the estate, as it is used by several church groups in London (such as Holy Trinity, Brompton, and All Souls, Langham Place) for group events and for 'Land-Mark Retreats', and you must apply through them. *Contact St Mark's Church, Battersea Rise, London SW11 1EJ in first instance.* Malshanger itself is a large country house in a private estate of over 3,000 acres. Retreats are usually of a renewal and inspirational nature.

Bordon

Acorn Christian Healing Trust
Whitehill Chase
High Street, Bordon
Hants GU35 0AP
                                    Tel: 01420 478121
                                    Fax: 01420 478122

Ecumenical

A Christian resource centre set in a large 19th century hunting lodge within 6 acres of gardens and woodlands, the Acorn Christian Healing Trust exists as a teaching resource on Christian healing and medicine to churches and society at large. There is an extensive programme of teaching, training and retreats. Typical themes are *Christ, Stress and Glory, Family Dynamics, Beginning a Healing Ministry in the Church, Bible Retreat, Myers Briggs Weekend, Ignatian Weekend* and *Angels and Miracles.* The chapel is especially attractive with much light and seating arrangements around the alter.

Open: For the programme. Receives men, women, groups, religious.
Rooms: 5 singles. 3 doubles. 10 twin.
Facilities: Disabled. Chapel. Conferences, garden, library, large lounge, book shop, payphone.
Spiritual Help: Personal talks, group sharing.
Guests Admitted to: Unrestricted access. Chapel.
Meals: Everyone eats together in refectory. Traditional food. Vegetarians and special diets.
Special Activities: Planned programme. Send for brochure.
Situation: In a small town but rural area.
Maximum Stay: 1 week.
Bookings: Letter.
Charges: Various rates ranging from £70 for a weekend to self-catering at about £15 per 24 hours.
Access: Car route easy. Train possible as there is a rail-bus link. Good map in brochure.

Bramdean

Krishnamurti Centre
Brockwood Park
Bramdean, Hants. SO24 0LQ
                              Tel: 01962 771748
                              Fax: 01962 771875
                    e-mail: info@brockwood.org.uk

Non-Religious

Krishnamurti, who was born in India and died in the United States in 1986, was a universal man whose major contribution to 20th century thought, many say, was in questioning the basis upon which we make our judgements and that this misinterpretation of our reality causes much unhappiness. He believed truth to be a pathless land. The centre is intended for the serious study of his teachings. It is for people who would like for a few days to be in a quiet environment where they can devote their full attention to his teachings and the implications for their own lives. No seminars or lectures are offered but there is an excellent library on his work with video and audio tapes and other records.

Open: All year. Receives men, women. Day guests by arrangement.
Rooms: 20 singles.
Facilities: Disabled – one room. Garden, park, library, guest lounge, quiet room, payphone.
Spiritual Help: None.
Guests Admitted to: Unrestricted access.
Meals: Taken in dining room. Vegetarian food.
Special Activities: None, but brochures about the centre are available.
Situation: Very quiet in the countryside.
Maximum Stay: 2 weeks with a minimum stay suggested of 3 nights.
Bookings: Letter, telephone, fax, e-mail.
Charges: £44 per night inclusive of everything. Suggest guests stay three nights. A 2-night stay £95. Day guests £15–£20 meals included. Concessions for students and unemployed.
Access: A detailed information sheet is available on request giving directions to Brockwood Park.

Southampton

The Cenacle
48 Victoria Road, Netley Abbey
Southampton SO31 5DQ

Tel: 02380 453718
Fax: 02380 453718
e-mail: cenacle.netley@virgin.net

Roman Catholic

Open: All year except Christmas and New Year. Receives men and women.
Rooms: 6 singles.
Facilities: Garden, library, guest lounge.
Spiritual Help: Personal talks, spiritual direction, personal retreat direction. Massage. Reiki.
Guests Admitted to: Unrestricted access. Chapel.
Meals: Everyone eats together. Traditional food. Vegetarians and special diets.
Special Activities: None.
Situation: Quiet in a village.
Maximum Stay: 30 days.
Bookings: Letter/tel/fax.
Charges: £30 per person per 24 hours.
Access: Train and car possible. Ask for instructions.

Wickham

Park Place Pastoral Centre
Winchester Road, Wickham
Fareham, Hants PO17 5HA

Tel: 01329 833043
Fax: 01329 832226
e-mail: parkplacec@aol.com

Roman Catholic

There is lots of room here, including a youth wing with self-catering. All of it is situated in some 18 acres of grounds, overlooking open countryside. The Centre is fairly booked up by parish groups because they are geared to group bookings – but it is a good place for a family to go on retreat. Individuals of any denomination are welcome who wish to spend time on a retreat here with or without guidance.

Open: All year except August. Receives men, women, young people in Youth Wing which is self-catering, families, groups, religious, non-retreatants for study purposes. *Mainly receives group bookings.*
Rooms: 50 singles, 15 dormitories.
Facilities: Disabled possible in ground floor room. Conferences, garden, book shop, payphone.
Spiritual Help: Meditation, Christian Meditation, Yoga.
Guests Admitted to: Chapel, church, choir.
Meals: Everyone eats together. Traditional food. Vegetarians, special diets.
Special Activities: Planned programme of events. Send for brochure.
Situation: Very quiet, in a village and countryside.
Maximum Stay: 5 days.
Bookings: Letter/fax or telephone – morning hours.
Charges: From £34 to £41 per person per day full board.
Access: Train: Fareham. Buses from Southampton, Winchester, then Fareham. Car: via M3 and M27 – see brochure.

Old Alresford

Old Alresford Place
Winchester Diocesan Retreat and Conference Centre
Old Alresford
Hants SO24 9DH

Tel/Fax: 01962 732518
e-mail: old.alresford.place@dail.pipex.com

Anglican – Inter-Denominational

A Georgian complex set in extensive grounds in Old Alresford – the birthplace of the Mothers' Union. Run as a diocesan retreat, conference and training centre, the whole place is tastefully decorated and furnished, the library and meeting rooms light and airy. The team who run the house provide good food and are happy to help with any queries. All the bedrooms are warm and each has a wash basin.

Open: All year except Christmas period. Receives men, women, young people, families, groups, non-retreatants.
Rooms: 25 bedrooms accommodating 47 people. Hermitage. Barn. Camping. Hostel. Caravans possible.
Facilities: Chapel. Conferences, small area for camping, 5 acre garden, car parking, library, guest lounge, payphone. Children welcomed.
Spiritual Help: Discuss what your needs are when you book.
Guests Admitted to: Unrestricted access. Chapel.
Meals: Meals taken in dining room. Traditional food. Vegetarian and special diets.
Special Activities: Planned programme of events. Send for brochure.
Situation: Quiet in the village and countryside.
Maximum Stay: 2 weeks.
Bookings: Letter or telephone – 9-5pm weekdays.
Charges: £44 per person per 24 hrs.
Access: Train: Alton or Winchester. Bus: from Alton. Car: via A31, then B3046.

KENT

Addington

The Seekers Trust
Centre for Prayer and Healing
Addington Park, Addington
West Malling, Kent ME19 5BL

Tel: 01732 843589
Fax: 01732 842867

Inter-Denominational

Addington Park is a large place set in some 37 acres of woodlands and gardens. Here the Seekers Trust operate a centre of prayer for healing, spiritual guidance and protection with prayer chapels, a healing sanctuary, and prayer help for anyone, regardless of their beliefs, for which there is no charge. A programme of events is also run and brochures on the Seekers Trust, their work, and the annual events programme are all available by request.

Open: All year. Receives everyone.
Rooms: 4 singles, 3 doubles. These are in the form of guest flats. No smoking.
Facilities: Disabled if self-sufficient or accompanied. Conferences, garden, park, library, payphone.
Spiritual Help: Personal talks, meditation. Prayer and healing ministry. Two open healing days a week. Otherwise healing by request.
Guests Admitted to: Unrestricted access except residents' quarters. Quiet in the Cloisters is requested.
Meals: Guests prepare their own food.
Special Activities: Prayer and healing. Groups for yoga meditation, T'ai Chi, Feng Shui, Circle Dancing. Send for brochure
Situation: Quiet.
Maximum Stay: 3 weeks.

Bookings: Letter or telephone – 9-5pm
Charges: Single flats £82 per week. Double flats £135 per week.
Minimum stay: 3 nights – £42 single/£75 double.
Access: Train: Victoria Station to Borough Green, taxi to Addington.
Local map on request if coming by car.

Canterbury

Centre Space
3 Alcroft Grange, Tyler Hill
Canterbury CT2 9NN   Tel: 01227 462038

Inter-Faith – Christian based

Silent and shared retreats here with meals alone or in company. Music, painting, calligraphy, healing therapies, inner growth courses, sacred dancing and day conferences are all possible as well as the private personal retreat. There is a quiet room, woodland and that special place – a Hermit Hut.

Open: All year. Receives everyone.
Rooms: 4 singles. 2 doubles. Camping. Carvans. Hermit hut.
Facilities: Conferences, camping, garden, library, guest lounge, TV, guest telephone, woodland nearby.
Spiritual Help: Personal talks. Group sharing. Spiritual direction. Personal retreat direction. Meditation. Yoga. Spinal touch therapy.
Guests Admitted to: Almost everywhere.
Meals: Everyone eats together. Wholefood, organic. Vegetarian and special diets. DIY facilities.
Special Activities: Planned events. Send for information.
Situation: Very quiet in the countryside.
Maximum Stay: Open.
Bookings: Letter, tel, fax – best time mornings.
Charges: £15–£20 B&B. Half-Board £25–£30. Non-residential day rate £10.
Access: Train: easy – taxi from station. Coach and bus possible also. Car: easy.

Edenbridge

Sisters of St Andrew
Eden Hall, Stick Hill
Edenbridge, Kent TN8 5NN   Tel: 01342 850604/388

Roman Catholic – Ecumenical

Quiet days and facilities are available for groups. Individuals come here for a silent or individually guided retreat which is also much in silence. They live in a part of the house reserved for that purpose.

Open: All year. Receives men, women, young people, groups for the day, non-retreatants.

Rooms: 5 singles, 3 double.
Facilities: Chapel. Conferences, camping, garden, National Trust walk in the grounds, library, direct dialling possible at cost.
Spiritual Help: Personal talks, group sharing, meditation.
Guests Admitted to: Chapel, work in garden.
Meals: Self-catering possible. Ask what the current meal arrangements are when you enquire.
Special Activities: None.
Situation: Quiet in countryside.
Maximum Stay: 2 weeks.
Bookings: Letter or telephone.
Charges: By donation.
Access: Train to Edenbridge or Edenbridge Town. Car is easiest.

Maidstone

The Friars
Aylesford Priory
Aylesford, Kent ME20 7BX

Tel: 01622 717272
Fax: 01622 715575
e-mail: friarsprior@hotmail.com

Roman Catholic – Inter-Denominational

The Carmelite Friars say that hope is a source of joy and that joy is a source of strength. At Aylesford they offer an open door to everyone seeking spiritual renewal. The Marian Shrine is a special feature. The retreat programme is a solid one. Here are some examples you might find on offer: inner child retreat, a singles weekend for those who live their baptismal calling as a single person, looking at different Carmelite themes for modern people, Holy Week and Lenten retreats, and an introduction to the spirituality of St John of the Cross.

Open: All year. Receives everyone.
Rooms: 27 singles, 38 doubles.
Facilities: Disabled. Conferences, guest lounge, payphone. Children welcome.
Spiritual Help: Personal talks. Spiritual direction. Personal retreat direction.
Guests Admitted to: Chapel.
Meals: Guests eat together. Traditional food. Vegetarian and special diets.
Special Activities: Planned programme of events. Send for brochure.
Situation: Rather busy in a village.
Maximum Stay: 2 weeks.
Bookings: Letter or telephone.
Charges: There is a rate sheet available which details all the various different combinations – but examples would be £30.75 per person per day in a single room for an adult guest to £18.50 per night B&B. Meal prices are separate and run about £6.20 for lunch and £4.70 for a light supper. Senior citizen special rates and some for children too.
Access: Train, coach, car all possible. Map and directions in brochure.

Ramsgate

St Augustine's Abbey
Ramsgate, Kent CT11 9PA

Tel: 01843 593045
Fax: 01843 582732

Roman Catholic

The guest house was once the home of Augustus Pugin, leader of the Gothic Revival and he built the Abbey church. Men are welcomed into the monastic ambience and to share the life of quiet and prayer here – but the Community does do parochial work and run a school which is not on site. You will be expected at Mass and the Evening Office and Compline. If guests learn about living in harmony with others, then the Community's aims will have been achieved. *Religious vocation discernment and advice is available.* There is silence in the cloister here and mobile phones and radios are not allowed – after all you are getting away from it all.

Open: All year except Christmas period. Receives men *over 22 years of age* individually and in groups.
Rooms: 8 singles. 8 doubles.
Facilities: Garden, library by permission, guest lounge, use of Community phone system.
Spiritual Help: Personal talks, spiritual direction, personal retreat direction, meditation. *Religious vocation discernment and advice.*
Guests Admitted to: Chapel and access to most parts of the Abbey. Some work of Community, usually manual chores.
Meals: Everyone eats together. Traditional simple food. Vegetarian and special diets.
Special Activities: None.
Situation: Near a busy road – but also next to the sea.
Maximum Stay: 2 weeks for the first visit. Then by arrangement.
Bookings: Letter. Telephone 10am-6pm
Charges: By donation of between £15-£20 per day full board.
Access: Train: Ramsgate, then taxi. Bus: from Ramsgate. Car: M2-A299-A253.

Speldhurst

Centre of New Directions
White Lodge
Stockland Green Road
Speldhurst, Kent TN3 0TT

Tel: 01892 863166
Fax: 01892 861330
e-mail: enqueries@white-lodge-fsnet.co.uk

Mind-Body-Spirit

Open: Only at certain times – you need to ask. Receives everyone.
Rooms: 1 single, 2 doubles.
Facilities: Camping, garden, library, guest lounge, payphone.
Spiritual Help: None except aromatherapy by arrangement.

Guests Admitted to: Unrestricted access.
Meals: Bed and Breakfast only – Vegetarian.
Special Activities: None.
Situation: Quiet in countryside.
Maximum Stay: By arrangement.
Bookings: Letter/telephone 9am-3pm
Charges: £20 per person per night B&B.
Access: Train: Tonbridge, then taxi. Car route supplied when you book.

Ramsgate

Saint Mildred's Abbey
Minster, Ramsgate, Kent CT12 4HF   Tel: 01843 821254

Roman Catholic

A graceful place of mainly stone with some remains visible of the first monastery. The Crypt is Norman. Guests are received in the spring and summer either as individuals or in groups There is room for some forty guests. Simple food and about £14 per day per person full board.

Tunbridge Wells

Burrswood Chapel House
Groombridge
Tunbridge Wells, Kent TN3 9BR
                                        Tel: 01892 863637
                                        Fax: 01892 863632
                              e-mail: admin@burrswood.org.uk

Inter-Denominational Christian with the Anglican Church

The retreat house is Chapel House and it is part of a large Christian centre for health care and ministry which includes a medical centre, hospital, guest accommodation and a resident Community. The facilities here are modern and very pleasant. The house was recently refurbished and it is very comfortable with a welcoming and homey atmosphere. All rooms have en-suite bath or shower, telephones and TV. A private chapel is at hand for private prayer and there is a full-time guest hostess to enable guests to make the most of their stay. There is a country house feel to the place and you are invited to explore the beautiful surrounding areas of places open to the public such as Chartwell and Sissinghurst Gardens. A pool and tennis are also available as well as the services for an extra small charge of a physiotherapist and the use of the hydrotherapy pool. It is a good place to come for both tranquillity and for healthy activity. The church is impressive. Burrswood, founded in 1948 as a healing centre for Christian health care and ministry, is a unique partnership between medicine and Christianity – a place of healing. **Highly Recommended.**

Open: All year. Receives everyone.
Rooms: 10 singles, 3 doubles.

Facilities: Disabled. Conferences, garden, park, library, guest lounge, hydrotherapy pool, book shop, TV, guest telephones in each bedroom.
Spiritual Help: Spiritual direction. Personal retreat direction. Personal talks with Chaplain by request. Healing service with laying on of hands, daily Eucharist, Evening prayers.
Guests Admitted to: Unrestricted access except for Hospital Wing. Chapel. Church. Oratory.
Meals: Taken in dining room. Traditional food. Vegetarian and special diets.
Special Activities: None but brochures available about the guest house and Burrswood.
Situation: Quiet and in the countryside.
Maximum Stay: As arranged.
Bookings: Letter, telephone, fax.
Charges: Single from £36 per night. Doubles £54. B&B, half-board and full board available.
Access: Train to Tunbridge Wells, then bus 290 or taxi. Car route access from A264, then B2110.

West Kingsdown

Stacklands Retreat House
School Lane
West Kingsdown, Kent TN15 6AN   Tel: 01474 852247

Anglican – Ecumenical

The first purpose-built retreat house in England, Stacklands is an Anglican centre for the study and giving of retreats according to the spiritual exercises of St Ignatius Loyola. It also is concerned with training retreat conductors and there is also a programme of preached, open, and other retreats on offer. It is a quiet place with many acres of grounds in which to wander in order to enhance the atmosphere of solitude and silence.

Open: All year except Christmas and New Year. Receives men, women, young people, groups.
Rooms: 21 singles.
Facilities: Disabled – limited. Conferences, garden, library, guest lounge, direct-dialling telephone.
Spiritual Help: Spiritual direction. Personal retreat direction.
Guests Admitted to: Chapel.
Meals: Everyone eats together. Traditional food. Vegetarian and special diets. Optional self-catering for day visitors only.
Special Activities: Planned programme of events. Brochure available.
Situation: Quiet and in the countryside.
Maximum Stay: 10 days.
Bookings: By letter or telephone.
Charges: £30 per 24 hours full board.
Access: Train: from Victoria to Swanley. Car: via A20.

West Wickham

Emmaus Centre
Layhams Road
West Wickham, Kent BR4 9HH

Tel: 020 87772000
Fax: 020 87762022

Roman Catholic – Ecumenical

Run by a religious community and a lay team, this rather large centre manages to be very homely and offers good-sized, well-equipped rooms. There are two chapels – one grand and one more modest. Good walks can be taken in the nearby woods. There is a small flat for silent private retreats. The Centre is a popular place for organisations to hold annual retreats and meetings. There are a number of art-related retreats on offer, such as ones with patchwork, painting, and pottery. All denominations welcome.

Open: All year except over Christmas period. Receives men, women, groups, and non-retreatants.
Rooms: 9 singles, 32 doubles.
Facilities: Disabled. Conferences, 2 chapels, garden, library, guest lounge, payphone.
Spiritual Help: Spiritual direction. Personal talks. Personal retreat direction.
Guests Admitted to: Chapel and all retreat-house facilities.
Meals: Everyone eats together. Traditional/vegetarian food. Special diets.
Special Activities: Planned programme of events. Send for brochure.
Situation: Quiet, on the edge of the countryside – good walks.
Maximum Stay: By arrangement.
Bookings: Letter, telephone, fax.
Charges: £15 B&B. Ignatian Retreats £36 per day. Retreat Weekend £64. Day Group £14 per person with lunch. Conference rates available.
Access: Train: Hayes, Bromley South or East Croydon. Bus: No. 119. Car: Centre is near A232.

Whitstable

Convent of Our Lady of Mercy
Northwood Road
Tankerton, Whitstable
Kent CT5 2EY

Tel: 01227 272649

Roman Catholic

Open: Most of year except August and December. Receives women.
Rooms: 4 singles.
Facilities: Disabled – limited so do enquire. Garden, library.
Spiritual Help: Individually guided retreats only.
Guests Admitted to: Chapel.
Meals: Taken in guest house. Traditional food.

Special Activities: None.
Situation: Quiet near the seashore.
Maximum Stay: As arranged.
Bookings: Letter.
Charges: About £20 per night.
Access: Train or car.

MIDDLESEX

Edgware

St Mary at the Cross Convent
Priory Field Drive
Edgware, Middlesex HA8 9PZ

Tel: 020 89587868
Fax: 020 89581920

Anglican

The atmosphere of peace which enfolds the visitor to this convent will come as a surprise in this otherwise rushed and busy suburb of Edgware. The provision of care has long been the mission of this Community and today they welcome guests who want a retreat in tranquillity not far from the heart of London.

Open: All year except Holy Week and Christmas. Receives men, women, young people, groups.
Rooms: Singles, hermitage.
Facilities: Conferences, garden, guest lounge, TV, payphone. Children welcomed.
Spiritual Help: Personal talks, sharing in the Divine Office, meditation, direct study by arrangement.
Guests Admitted to: Unrestricted access. Chapel, work of Community.
Meals: Everyone eats together. Traditional food. Vegetarians and special diets catered.
Special Activities: None. There is an excellent brochure available about the place.
Situation: Quiet.
Maximum Stay: 2 weeks.
Bookings: Letter.
Charges: By arrangement but inexpensive.
Access: By London Underground, bus or car.

Harrow on the Hill

St Mary's Church House
Church Hill
Harrow, Middlesex HA1 3HL

Tel: 020 84228409

Anglican

St Mary's Church House, a Victorian annexe, has been renovated and made into a small conference centre providing self-catering accommodation for up to 12 people. It has a quiet atmosphere away from busy life, yet it is within easy reach of central London. *It is for groups of 6–12 only* and stands adjacent to St Mary's Church and the vicarage.

Open: All year except August. Receives men, women, young people, groups.
Rooms: 1 room for 4 and another for 2.
Facilities: Small conferences, guest lounge, library, TV and payphone.
Spiritual Help: None.
Guests Admitted to: Unrestricted access.
Meals: Self-catering only. Well-equipped kitchen.
Special Activities: None.
Situation: In an area of character amidst the vast suburban sprawl of West London. Next door is the 900-year-old Church of St Mary, while beyond the churchyard are woods.
Maximum Stay: By arrangement.
Bookings: Letter, tel/fax.
Charges: Ask what is expected when you book. Usually very reasonable.
Access: By London Underground, bus or car.

Osterley

Osterley Retreats
112 Thornbury Road
Osterley, Middlesex TW7 4NN
Tel: 020 85683821
Fax: 020 88476227
e-mail: Osterley.Retreats@btinternet.com
Website: www.CampionHouse.org.uk

Roman Catholic

Campion House is situated in very spacious grounds just outside London. It is best known for the number of priests who started here. Now it combines this training with the work of a full-time centre of Ignatian Spirituality. There are Ignatian 4, 8, and 30-day retreats and various other retreats and workshops on offer including art ones.

Open: All year except Christmas holidays. Receives men, women, groups, religious.
Rooms: 40 singles.
Facilities: Garden, park, guest lounge, payphone.
Spiritual Help: Personal talks, group sharing, meditation.
Guests Admitted to: Chapel.
Meals: Everyone eats together. Traditional food. Vegetarian and special diets catered.
Special Activities: Varied programme of retreats and workshops. Send for brochure.
Situation: Close to Central London and Heathrow Airport with a large park and nearby banks and shops.
Maximum Stay: 1 month.

Bookings: Letter or telephone.
Charges: About £30 per night full board. Ask for current year's charges.
Access: London Underground, bus or car.

Pinner

The Grail Centre
125 Waxwell Lane
Pinner, Middlesex HA5 3ER

Tel: 020 8660505
Fax: 020 8866140
e-mail: grailcentre@compuserve.com

Roman Catholic

Just 25 minutes from Baker Street Underground Station, the Grail Centre stands in some 10 acres of grounds. It offers small cedar-wood chalets set in the woods where you can experience 'poustinia', which in Russian means 'a place apart'. Here you can live in silence, reflection and prayer like a hermit. Lunch is eaten either with the Community or taken away. You prepare your own breakfast and supper with the food provided. There is an extensive programme of events and courses, one of which is a family week, which provides a good opportunity for adults to be together and the children to be cared for. Everyone of whatever faith, or of none, is welcomed.

Open: Most of the year. Receives men, women, young people, groups, non-retreatants.
Rooms: 5 singles, 15 doubles, hermitage chalets – one for winter, six for summer.
Facilities: Conferences, large garden, library, guest lounge, payphone.
Spiritual Help: Personal talks, meditation, limited spiritual direction, aromatherapy, healing, limited counselling.
Guests Admitted to: Chapel and work of the community.
Meals: Everyone eats together (see above). Traditional food. Vegetarian and special diets catered. DIY in hermitages.
Special Activities: Planned programme of events. Send for brochure.
Situation: Quiet, on edge of London in a town.
Maximum Stay: Receives individual guests between group events so enquire.
Bookings: Letter or telephone.
Charges: Send for details as there are various charges.
Access: London Underground Baker Street to Pinner. Bus: from Harrow.

God is beauty.

SAINT FRANCIS OF ASSISI

Teddington

The Eden Centre
252 Kingston Road
Teddington, Middlesex TW11 9JQ

Tel: 020 89774034
Fax: 020 89777747
e-mail: teddington@welcome100.freeserve.co.uk

Roman Catholic

The Eden Centre is about a mile from Kingston on Thames with its beautiful riverside walks. Easy access to Bushy Park with its lakes and nature life as well as Hampton Court with its extensive grounds. A team here at the Eden Centre offer preached, directed and private retreats with quiet days, spiritual accompaniment, and counselling if wished.

Open: All year. Receives men, women, groups, non-retreatants.
Rooms: 17 singles. Non-smoking house.
Facilities: Conferences, garden, park, library, guest lounge, TV, guest phone.
Spiritual Help: Personal talks, group sharing, meditation, spiritual direction, personal retreat direction.
Guests Admitted to: Unrestricted access.
Meals: Guest dining room. Wholefood. Vegetarian and special diets.
Special Activities: Planned programme of events. Send for brochure.
Situation: Rather busy – just beside Bushy Park and Hampton Court Palace.
Maximum Stay: 8 days.
Bookings: Letter or telephone – 9am-5pm.
Charges: £30 per person per 24 hours.
Access: Train, bus, car all possible. Details in brochure.

SURREY

Camberley

Tekels Park Guest House
The Guest House
Tekels Park, Camberley
Surrey GU15 2LF

Tel: 01276 23159
Fax: 01276 27014
E-mail: Ghouse.tekels@btclick.com

Mind-Body-Spirit

The Park is owned by the Theosophical Society in England and the programme on offer may include these kinds of events: *Mayan Mysteries, the Sacred Circle, New Aspects of Space and Time, The Rebirthing Experience,* and *Dancing the Sevenfold Energies of Life.* Tekels is a wooded estate set in over 50 acres of secluded woods and fields which form a wildlife sanctuary within 35 miles of London. The Guest House has earned a reputation for serving excellent vegetarian food.

Open: All year. Receives men, women, young people, groups, religious, non-retreatants.
Rooms: Both singles and doubles are available.
Facilities: Camping, garden, park, library, guest lounge, TV, payphone.
Spiritual Help: Personal talks, group sharing, meditation, directed study. Healing courses available.
Guests Admitted to: Unrestricted access.
Meals: Guests eat together. Vegetarian and whole food. Special diets catered.
Special Activities: Some events. Send for brochure.
Situation: Very quiet in the countryside with spacious grounds.
Maximum Stay: By arrangement.
Bookings: Letter or telephone.
Charges: Enquire when sending for information.
Access: By rail or car.

Cheam

Ruth White Yoga Centre
99 College Road
Epsom, Surrey   Tel: 0208 6440309
                                               Fax: 0208 2875318
                              Website: www.ruthwhiteyoga.com

Mind-Body-Spirit – Yoga

Retreats are usually at weekends but there are also 4-day breaks and a summer holiday. You book at the above address where you can obtain details of the programme on offer.

Open: Closed season at Christmas and Easter. Enquire as to opening schedule. Receives everyone.
Rooms: None.
Facilities: Disabled. Conferences. Camping. Garden. Guest lounge. TV, guest telephone.
Spiritual Help: Meditation, yoga breathing and postures.
Guests Admitted to: Access to whatever are the guest areas.
Meals: Guests eat together. Wholefood, vegetarian.
Special Activities: Planned programme of events. Send for brochure. Guest groups received.
Situation: Quiet in a town.
Maximum Stay: Per programme event.
Bookings: Letter, telephone, fax.
Charges: Specific for each event and venue so ask when you book.
Access: Will provide a map.

Chobham

Brook Place Ecumenical Centre
Bagshot Road
Chobham, Woking
Surrey GU24 8SJ   Tel/Fax: 01276 857561

Ecumenical

There is a Tithe Barn here for large groups and a garden cottage for 2-4 people. Set in its own grounds with a lake and a hermitage hut. Daily ecumenical prayers.

Open: All year except Christmas season. Receives groups for day events and individuals for quiet days.
Rooms: Doubles available.
Facilities: Garden, guest lounge, payphone.
Spiritual Help: None.
Guests Admitted to: Chapel.
Meals: Guests eat together. Traditional food. Vegetarian and special diets catered.
Special Activities: None.
Situation: Quiet, in the countryside.
Maximum Stay: With group or by day.
Bookings: Letter, telephone, fax.
Charges: Ask for sheet which details charges.
Access: By rail plus taxi or car route.

Dormansland

Claridge House
Dormans Road
Dormansland, Near Lingfield
Surrey RH7 6QH
                                              Tel: 01342 832150
                                              Fax: 01342 836730

Quaker – Ecumenical

A Quaker centre of healing, rest and renewal, run by the Society of Friends Fellowship of Healing and open to everyone. There are facilities for group conferences, retreats and private visits and a programme of courses on offer. These may include such things as a walkers week, self-healing, exploring fine arts, massage, silent retreats. The centre itself is an old Victorian house in a small village, standing in its own two acres of lovely gardens. Peace and the time to recover yourself in this place.

Open: All year except first week of January. Receives men, women, young people, groups, non-retreatants.
Rooms: 3 singles, 9 doubles.
Facilities: Disabled. Quiet room. Conferences, garden, library, guest lounge, guest phone.

Spiritual Help: Personal talks. Spiritual healing. Counselling.
Workshops on related subjects. Quaker meeting and twice weekly
quiet time.
Guests Admitted to: Unrestricted access. Quiet room.
Meals: Everyone eats together. Vegetarian and special diets.
Special Activities: Planned programme of events. Send for brochure.
Situation: Quiet in a village in the countryside.
Maximum Stay: 2 weeks.
Bookings: Letter or telephone – best time 9am-6pm
Charges: Ask for tariff leaflet.
Access: Rail: Victoria Station. Car: M25/A22/B2029

East Molesey

House of Prayer
35 Seymour Road
East Molesey, Surrey KT8 0PA   Tel: 0208 9412313

Ecumenical

Many people appreciate the space and freedom available here – and at
only 17 miles from London, it is convenient to get to. A spacious and
comfortable house for rest and relaxation with a Community who offer
a daily rhythm of prayer. Self-organised groups are often going on here
but over-night stays and individual retreats can be arranged.
Hermitages are avilable for silence and solitude. There is a modest but
good programme of events on offer which largely centre around prayer
and include celebrations for Advent and Lent and study of the
Enneagram system. The Community especially welcomes those who
may need a retreat during an important transitional stage in their lives.

Open: All year except July. Receives men, women, young people,
families, groups.
Rooms: 5 singles. 1 double. Hermitages, each furnished with living
and praying area, provide seclusion, silence and prayer, available for
a day or longer. Self-catering facilities.
Facilities: Garden, library, guest lounge, direct dialling. Prayer room.
No smoking. No tape recorders.
Spiritual Help: Spiritual direction. Meditation. Personal retreat
direction.
Guests Admitted to: Unrestricted access everywhere.
Meals: DIY facilities. Vegetarian and special diets.
Special Activities: Planned programme of events. Send for brochure.
Counselling.
Situation: Quiet.
Maximum Stay: 30-day retreat.
Bookings: Letter or telephone.
Charges: £20 full board per day. Day rates, B&B and other charges
available. A weekend retreat is about £55 full board. Fees for spiritual
direction/counselling negotiable.
Access: Train: To Hampton Court. Car: A3/M25.

Goldalming

Ladywell Retreat Centre
Ladywell Convent
Ashstead Lane
Godalming, Surrey GU7 IST   Tel: 01483 428083

Roman Catholic

Near to Ladywell is an ancient shrine on one of the main old pilgrim
routes to Canterbury. Guests who only want a holiday and are not prepared to make an effort to use the contemplative environment to seek
peace through prayer, should try another place. Individually directed
retreats and on-going spiritual direction are available to help each person along this path, combined with the community's notable spirit of
hospitality. The retreat centre itself is in a wing of the main building
with a small oratory and prayer room.

Open: Most of year. Receives men, women, young people, groups.
Rooms: 29 singles, 5 doubles.
Facilities: Disabled – limited. Conferences, garden, library, guest
lounge, TV, payphone.
Spiritual Help: Personal talks, meditation.
Guests Admitted to: Chapel, choir.
Meals: Guests eat together. Traditional food. Vegetarian and special
diets catered.
Special Activities: Planned programme of events. Send for brochure.
Situation: Quiet, in the countryside, with spacious grounds and gar-
dens.
Maximum Stay: 8-day retreat.
Bookings: Letter or telephone.
Charges: Around £25 plus per day full board.
Access: By rail or car.

Tuesley Retreat
Tuesley Manor
Goldalming, Surrey GU7 IUD   Tel: 01483 417281
                                        Fax: 01483 420415

Roman Catholic – Ecumenical

Tuesley Retreat is based around a large restored barn with a dining and
sitting area, a group room, a kitchen for self-catering, garden, a covered
and heated swimming pool, a chapel and a choice of rural walks. The
manor estate itself is set in 13 acres of countryside. This is a non-residential retreat place and charges are negotiable for both individuals
and groups – but in range of £60-£100 per day. As to accommodation,
they can provide you with some recommended local B&B places.

Guildford

Cultural Country Retreats
Orchard Cottage
Broadstreet Common
Guildford, Surrey GU3 3BN   Tel: 01483 562007

Cultural Country Retreats organise and run retreats in centres up and down the country, drawing together many kinds of expertise. It is a concept of short breaks designed to provide a cultural and rural backdrop against which men and women may hopefully deepen their faith. The retreats are based in carefully selected retreat houses and small hotels throughout Britain. At each retreat there is an experienced Retreat Director and opportunities are given to explore the need for peace and spirituality. The retreats are limited to no more than twenty persons and they can range from eight up to that number. Many well-known people have favourably commented on this organisation, some of them authors like Laurens van der Post and Gerard W. Hughes. Brochure available.

New Malden

Inigo Enterprises New International Centre
Links View
Traps Lane, New Malden
Surrey KT3 4RY   Tel: 020 89491670
                         e-mail: inigonewmalden@cs.com
                         Website: www.jesuit.co.uk

Christian – Ecumenical

A Jesuit priest founded and runs Inigo Enterprises as an organisation for communicating Ignatian spirituality. There are workshops, retreats of various duration at different venues, introductory days and talks. Current offerings include the life and spiritual exercises of St Ignatius reflected in the light of the French writer Rene Girard, the centering techniques of Anthony De Mello, journalling in the style of Ira Progoff, and integration with Celtic spirituality approaches. Write for programme information to the Secretary at the above address. There are tapes, books and course materials also available.

Richmond

St Michael's Convent
56 Ham Common
Richmond
Surrey TW10 7JH   Tel: 020 89408711/89482502
                         Fax: 020 83322927
                         e-mail: valerie.csc@which.net

Anglican

St Michael's Convent where the Community of the Sisters of the Church live is a smart place on Ham Common in Richmond, with the park near by for walks and a large garden in which to sit. Founded in 1870, the Community of the Sisters of the Church is an international body of women within the Anglican Communion. Here the sisters are committed to a life of prayer and worship, community service, and their outreach work includes hospitality, informal education, and leading retreats and workshops at which they have earned a deserved reputation. The Community has a special interest in the idea of prayer and the clown, running *clown* workshops as part of its extensive and interesting retreat and workshop programme. It may also include circle dancing, Enneagram work, Taizé and Iona music, prayer through dance, Myers-Briggs work, and a look at Mary of Nazareth as a model for contemporary women and men. There are opportunities for women 18-30 to live with the community and experience a life of prayer and fellowship. **Highly Recommended.**

Open: Almost all year. Receives men, women, families, groups, non-retreatants.
Rooms: 11 singles, 3 doubles.
Facilities: Disabled – *limited but there is a loop system for the deaf in chapel and conference areas, lift by request, so do ask what is possible.* Conferences, garden, library, guest lounge, payphone.
Spiritual Help: Personal talks, spiritual direction, personal retreat direction. Some reflexology is offered. Eucharist most days.
Guests Admitted to: Chapel. Help in the garden welcomed.
Meals: Everyone eats *silently* together. Traditional food. Vegetarian and special diets.
Special Activities: Planned programme of events. Send for brochure.
Situation: Quiet, but only 8 miles from Heathrow. Situated in a suburban area near Richmond Park, with access to the Thames.
Maximum Stay: 1 week or by arrangement.
Bookings: Letter or telephone.
Charges: £25 per day donation if possible. £4-£10 for quiet days.
Access: By rail, bus or car – all easy.

Woking

St Columba's House
Maybury Hill
Woking
Surrey GU22 8AB

Tel: 01483 766498
Fax: 01483 740441
e-mail: retreats@st.columba.org.uk

Anglican – Ecumenical

St Columba's welcomes men and women of all faiths or none and provides a common ground for ecumenical discussion and prayer. There is an interest here in the relationship between art and spirituality. Recently refurbished in 1998, this is a pleasant and comfortable place in pleasant surrounding with home style meals. There is a garden prayer

walk and a collection of contemporary paintings.The retreat programme is an interesting one with courses like *The Spirituality of
Childhood, Introductionn to Christian Zen, Circle Dancing*, and *Eight Day
Individually Guided Retreat*. The chapel is modern, light, and impressive
in its simplicity.

Open: All year. Receives men, women, young people, groups, non-
retreatants.
Rooms: 25 singles, 1 double. No smoking.
Facilities: Disabled. Conferences, garden, library, guest lounge, TV,
payphone, direct dialling.
Spiritual Help: Personal talks, group sharing, spiritual direction,
personal retreat direction, meditation. Sacramental ministry.
Guests Admitted to: Chapel.
Meals: Everyone eats together. Traditional food. Vegetarian and
special diets. DIY suite.
Special Activities: Planned programme of events. Send for brochure.
Weekly house quiet day each Monday. Open to all. £5 and bring your
own lunch, starts 10am, ends at 4pm. Liturgical education. Specialist
facilities for business and corporate quiet days. Aromatherapy.
Situation: Very quiet, in the countryside. Retreat house is within the
grounds of the convent.
Maximum Stay: 1-2 weeks
Bookings: Letter, telephone, fax, e-mail. 9.30–12 noon Mon-Fri.
Charges: £36 per day full board.
Access: Train from Waterloo station to Woking (1 mile from house),
then taxi. Car: via Maybury Hill off the B382 – avoid entering Woking
town.

SUSSEX (EAST)

Brighton

**St Benedict's
1 Manor Road
Kemp Town, Brighton
E. Sussex BN2 5EA**

Tel: 01273 674140
Fax: 01273 680527
e-mail: generalate@graceandcompassion.co.uk

Roman Catholic

A retreat establishment run by the Grace and Compassion sisters – so
you know all will be comfortable and the welcome warm.

Open: All year. Receives everyone.
Rooms: 7 singles, 9 doubles, 2 self-catering single flats, 1 self-con-
tained self-catering flat with 3 bedrooms – sleeps 6. Hermitage.
Facilities: Conference room, garden, park, library, guest lounges, TV,
payphone. Children welcomed. Pets allowed by permission.
Spiritual Help: Personal talks, meditation.
Guests Admitted to: Chapel, choir, work of Community.

Meals: Taken in dining room of guest house. Traditional/vegetarian food. Special diets.
Special Activities: None.
Situation: Quiet on edge of town, near the seashore.
Maximum Stay: 1 week.
Bookings: Letter or telephone/fax.
Charges: Daily rate from £18 per person B&B to £30 full board.
Access: Train to Brighton, then No. 7 bus. Coach from Victoria Station, London. Car via A23.

Forest Row

Emerson College
Forest Row
East Sussex RH18 5JX

Tel: 01342 822238
Fax: 01342 826055
e-mail: mail@emerson.org.uk
Website: www.emerson.org.uk

Interdenominational – Rudolf Steiner tradition

The College is named after the American philosopher Ralph Waldo Emerson, who believed in building a harmonious relationship between nature and the human imagination. The educational philosopher Rudolph Steiner translated this into practical methods for achieving spiritual development, and Emerson College is one of several establishments which recognise Emerson's work. Weekend workshops and full-time courses are offered – subjects range from *How the Body Speaks, The Music of what happens – Stories from the Celtic World, Wisdom of Plants, Holy Darkness, The Great Goddess and the Green Man,* and *Singing and Movement.* There is a Christmas retreat and a new studio has been built for the visual arts programme. Emerson is an opportunity to spend some quiet days away from it all in beautiful countryside not far from London – and find stimulus for self-discovery.

Open: All year. Receives men and women. *Only 15 retreat guests at a time.*
Rooms: 52 singles, 3 doubles. Summer camping.
Facilities: Camping, garden, library, guest lounge, guest phone and fax.
Spiritual Help: Personal talks. Group sharing. Directed study.
Guests Admitted to: Unrestricted access. Work of Community.
Meals: Everyone eats together. Wholefood, vegetarian, organic. Special diets.
Special Activities: Planned programme with excellent brochures available.
Situation: Very quiet, outskirts of village next to a biodynamic farm and within walking distance of Ashdown Forest.
Maximum Stay: For retreat only.
Bookings: Letter or telephone/fax during business office hours.
Charges: £50 per day fully inclusive for a minimum stay of 3 nights. See brochuirtes for cost of various educational and other programmes.
Access: Train to East Grinstead and then by taxi. Enquire as to best car route.

Hove

The Monastery of Christ the Saviour
23 Cambridge Road
Hove, East Sussex BN3 1DE   Tel: 01273 726698

Anglican

Founded in 1985 in a run-down area of Hove, these members of the Community of the Servants of the Will of God, live a corporate life of silence, work, and prayer, providing a foundation for the renewal of the local church. Daily worship is held in the parish church and the monks are engaged as well in teaching and spiritual direction. The house itself is a large 19th century one, formerly used as flats which have been renovated as a monastery to include guest accommodation.

Open: Most of the year. Receives men and women.
Rooms: 2 singles.
Facilities: Library.
Spiritual Help: Personal talks.
Guests Admitted to: Chapel.
Meals: Everyone eats together. Traditional food, mainly vegetarian.
Special Activities: None.
Situation: Reasonably quiet in a town.
Maximum Stay: By arrangement.
Bookings: By letter or telephone.
Charges: Donation of £15 per day as a guide.
Access: By rail or bus to Brighton/Hove.

Waldron

Monastery of the Visitation
Waldron
Heathfield, East Sussex TN21 0RX   (Letter only)

Roman Catholic

The sisters are called to be a praying presence in the world and they offer an environment of stillness, prayer and spiritual renewal to those women who wish to share their lives for a time. Retreatants are asked to stay within the enclosure throughout their stay. This is a place for silence.

Open: After Easter to end October. Receives women over 18 years and women religious only.
Rooms: 3 singles at top of house so there are stairs to climb.
Facilities: Garden, small number of books, direct-dialling.
Spiritual Help: Personal talks with retreat Mistress.
Guests Admitted to: Unrestricted access. Choir (retreatants area), work in the garden.
Meals: Everyone eats together. Very plain food. Vegetarian catered if kept simple – no complicated diets.

Special Activities: None.
Situation: Very quiet – set in the countryside in 50 acres of parkland with beautiful views over South Downs.
Maximum Stay: 8 days.
Bookings: Letter addressed to *Retreat Mistress*.
Charges: On request.
Access: By rail to 8 miles away, then take taxi. Car route easiest.

SUSSEX (WEST)

Arundel

Convent of Poor Clares
Crossbush
Arundel, West Sussex BN18 9PJ   Tel: 01903 882536/883125

Roman Catholic

Here is a traditional convent with all the gentleness and space to pray that one could want. The surrounding countryside is beautiful with the South Downs at hand and the sea but four miles away. The Community have a small guest house where people are welcome to stay for a private retreat or just to rest and be quiet. While there is no garden for guests, there is a small patio and places to sit outside. A comfortable sitting room with television is also available. The accommodation is modest but the welcome warm. Guest are always invited to join the Community for Mass and Divine Office if they should wish to do so. There is no charge for accommodation and meals, only donations but these donations do provide one of the few sources of income for the Community. The dove of peace is one of the little signs of this prayful Community. **Highly Recommended.**

Open: All year except 1 November to 8 December. Receives men, women, families in the caravans on site, groups up to 8.
Rooms: 4 singles, 2 double. 2 large caravans.
Facilities: Guest lounge, TV, payphone.
Spiritual Help: Personal talks, spiritual direction, personal retreat direction.
Guests Admitted to: Chapel. Church.
Meals: Taken in guest house in your room. Traditional, simple, vegetarian food. Caravan guests DIY.
Special Activities: None.
Situation: House is quiet but on a busy road. Lovely countryside with good walks near by. Few miles from the coast.
Maximum Stay: 2 weeks.
Bookings: Letter or telephone.
Charges: By donation, suggested rate £10–£20 a day which is very modest indeed.
Access: Train: Arundel station 5 minutes away. No easy buses. Car via A27.

Crawley

Grace and Compassion Convent
Paddockhurst Road
Turners Hil
Crawley
West Sussex RH10 4GZ   Tel: 01342 715672

Roman Catholic

Open: All year. Receives men, women, young people and non-retreatants.
Rooms: 1 double (or single).
Facilities: Small garden, library, guest lounge, TV, guest telephone. Children by special arrangement.
Spiritual Help: None.
Guests Admitted to: Chapel. Choir.
Meals: Everyone eats together, or can eat alone if this is preferred. Traditional/wholefood. Vegetarian.
Special Activities: None.
Situation: In the countryside but rather busy.
Maximum Stay: By arrangement.
Bookings: Letter or telephone – best time 10am–12.30pm.
Charges: £25 full board per person.
Access: Train to Three Bridges. No bus. Car route from Crawley.

Crawley

Monastery of the Holy Trinity
Crawley Down
Crawley
West Sussex RH10 4LH   Tel: 01342 712074

Anglican

This is an enclosed contemplative order for men. Guests are asked to respect the timetable and silence of the monks' daily life. Within the Christian vision of life, the Community here offer traditional liturgy and prayer from a perspective common to both the Christian East and West. For all guests, both the committed and uncommitted, the Community offers a place of natural beauty, silence and peace to facilitate openess and stillness. This is not a suitable retreat place for those who are under psychological stress or feel that they could not handle silence and lack of conversation. Having said that, this is a fine place to share in the liturgical and contemplative life of a monastic Community. **Highly Recommended.**

Open: All year except for certain days or weeks which are concerned with holy days so you need to ask during the current year. Receives men and women. Groups only for the day.
Rooms: 6 singles.
Facilities: Garden, library, guest telephone.

Spiritual Help: Personal talks, personal retreat direction, spiritual direction, participation in the Divine Office and group prayer including the Jesus Prayer.

Guests Admitted to: Chapel, grounds of monastery except monastic enclosure, work of the community.

Meals: Everyone eats together. Wholefood with provision for vegetarians.

Special Activities: None.

Situation: Very quiet, in the midst of 60 acres of woodland.

Maximum Stay: 1 week.

Bookings: Letter or telephone – best times 9.45-11.45am and 2-5pm.

Charges: Donation guide: £15 per day.

Access: Ask for travel instructions when booking.

Worth Abbey Centre for Spirituality
Paddockhurst Road
Turners Hill, Crawley
West Sussex RH10 4SB

Tel: 01342 710318
Fax: 01324 710311
e-mail: spirituality@worth.org.uk
Website: www.worth.org.uk

Roman Catholic

This Community of monks places their main emphasis on the experience of Benedictine hospitality and spirituality. They are committed to a collaborative ministry in the service of the Church and the community in the south-east of England. The Community places a strong emphasis on ecumenism. The setting is beautiful and quiet can be found. Guest accommodation has been recently expanded and updated and there is a programme on offer.

Open: All year except July and August. Receives everyone.

Rooms: 10 doubles, 2 dormitories. Singles in monastery for men. Camping site.

Facilities: Disabled. Conferences, camping, garden, guest lounge, payphone. Children welcomed.

Spiritual Help: Personal talks, group sharing, spiritual direction, personal retreat direction, meditation. T'ai Chi, Yoga.

Guests Admitted to: Chapel, church, choir.

Meals: Guest house. Traditional, simple food. Vegetarian and special diets.

Special Activities: Planned programme. Ask for information about what may be on offer. Guests are welcome to attend Divine Office as well as Mass.

Situation: In the countryside, with beautiful grounds.

Maximum Stay: 7 days.

Bookings: Letter.

Charges: £20 per night. £75-£110 for courses and programme retreats depending on length of time.

Access: Train from Victoria station to Three Bridges. Car via M23, Exit 10 to East Grinstead.

East Grinstead

Neale House Conference Centre
Moat Road
East Grinstead
West Sussex RH19 3LB   Tel: 01342 312552

Anglican

Neale House offers a centre from which to explore the Sussex countryside and there are plenty of things to do locally. It is usual for groups
who have arranged their own special retreat programme to come to
stay, but special help on spiritual matters can be arranged for individuals who wish to stay.

Open: Weekends lasting from Friday supper to Sunday tea-time.
Receives men, women, young people, families, groups, non-
retreatants. Closed August and Christmas.
Rooms: 5 singles, 9 doubles, 6 dormitories.
Facilities: Disabled. Conferences, newly designed garden, park nearby,
books to read, guest lounge, TV, payphone. Children welcomed.
Spiritual Help: Personal talks.
Guests Admitted to: Unrestricted access. Chapel.
Meals: Everyone eats together. Traditional food. Vegetarian and
special diets catered.
Special Activities: None.
Situation: In a town, close to Sussex countryside.
Maximum Stay: 4 days.
Bookings: Letter or telephone.
Charges: On application.
Access: By rail to East Grinstead then a 10-minute walk. Car: A22

St Margaret's Convent
St John's Road
East Grinstead, West Sussex RH19 3LE   Tel: 01342 323497
                                              Fax: 01342 328505

Anglican

There are two guest houses for retreatants here. One is St John's House
which is a few minutes walk from the convent. The other is St Michael's
which is adjacent to the convent and is intended for those wanting to
make a silent retreat and for those who are too infirm to go to the other
guest house. Silence is kept in St Michael's.

Open: All year. Receives men and women.
Rooms: 12 singles, 2 doubles – 6 of these are in guest house and 6 in
the retreat house.
Facilities: Garden, library, guest lounge, TV, payphone. Park
nextdoor.
Spiritual Help: Personal talks. Spiritual direction. Personal retreat
direction if previously arranged when you book.

Guests Admitted to: Chapel. Oratory. Refectory, library, and garden and rooms in guest and retreat houses.
Meals: Everyone eats together. Traditional food. Vegetarian.
Special Activities: None.
Situation: Quiet in a town. Countryside nearby.
Maximum Stay: 2 weeks.
Bookings: Letter or telephone – 6-7pm
Charges: By donation in the range of £17.50 per 24 hours.
Access: Train and car directions in leaflet.

Hassocks

Priory of Our Lady
Sayers Common
Hassocks
West Sussex BN6 9HT

Tel: 01273 832901

Roman Catholic

One heart and one soul in God sums up the way of life of this flourishing Augustinian monastic community. All men and women of good faith, whether Christian, Buddhist, Hindu or Jew, are welcomed by the sisters at their delightful modern priory set at the end of a drive that is edged with daffodils in the spring. The Roman Catholic Community has strong links with the Church of England. There is a retreat centre in a separate house for guests and a simpler but good programme ranging from a weekend on awareness of the invisible and the meaning of prayer, an adventure in painting and prayer, redemption made meaningful in the 21st century to praying with the psalms. **Highly recommended.**

Open: All year except mid-August to mid-September. Receives men, women, young people, families, groups, non-retreatants. Facilities are not really suitable for young children.
Rooms: 4 singles, 14 doubles, 1 room with 4 beds. Sometimes it is possible to camp. No smoking inside. No pets. Silence of individuals and groups must be respected.
Facilities: Disabled – limited but ask them for exact facility details. Conferences, garden, library, guest lounge, TV, payphone.
Spiritual Help: Personal talks, spiritual direction, personal retreat direction. Guests are welcome at Divine Office and Mass with the Community.
Guests Admitted to: Church, choir. Occasionally work of Community
Meals: Taken in guest house. Traditional food. Vegetarians catered.
Special Activities: Planned programme of events. Send for brochure.
Situation: Quiet and in the countryside.
Maximum Stay: 1 week.
Bookings: Letter or telephone.
Charges: £22 per day per person.
Access: By bus, which stops at Sayers Common, or by car. Rather complicated so ask for direction when you book and know what transport you will be using.

ISLE OF WIGHT

Ryde

Abbey of Our Lady of Quarr
Ryde
Isle of Wight PO33 4ES   Tel: 01983 882420
                                              Fax: 01983 884402
                            e-mail: 106440.3427@compusrve.com
Roman Catholic

Here you may share for a few days in the life of a Benedictine monastic community, following their daily life of prayer and work. The purpose of your visit should be to enter fully into this place of silence and recollection in order to dedicate time to the things of God. The daily Mass is at the heart of the monastic day.

Open: All year. Receives men and women.
Rooms: 10 male singles, 5 female singles.
Facilities: Chapel, garden, park, guest lounge, library, payphone.
Spiritual Help: Personal talks, meditation. Opportunities exist to discuss spiritual matters with one of the Guest Masters.
Guests Admitted to: Chapel, refectory, monastery grounds, and to share in community work.
Meals: Men usually eat in refectory. Women in the guest house which is self-catering. Traditional food. Vegetarians catered for.
Special Activities: None.
Situation: Near sea, farm and countryside, woodlands.
Maximum Stay: 10 days.
Bookings: Letter, fax, e-mail.
Charges: Donation.
Access: Ferry to Ryde from Portsmouth.

The Garth Retreat
St Cecilia's Abbey
Ryde
Isle of Wight PO33 1LH   Tel/Fax: 01983 562602
                        Website: www.stceciliasabbey.org.uk

Roman Catholic

Divine Office is sung in Gregorian chant by this Benedictine community of nuns. Many people find great serenity and rest in this peaceful, modal music and in the tranquil rhythm of the liturgy and psalmody. Moreover, the Abbey itself is a very quiet place near the sea. The Garth, adjacent to the monastery, offers guest accommodation to those wishing to spend some days in an atmosphere of prayer and recollection.

Open: Most of the year. Receives women and married couples.
Rooms: 2 singles, 3 doubles.
Facilities: Small garden.

Spiritual Help: Personal talks possible.
Guests Admitted to: External chapel of the Abbey church.
Meals: Self-catering only.
Special Activities: None.
Situation: Quiet, on the outskirts of a seaside town.
Maximum Stay: 1 week.
Bookings: Letter with SAE if possible. Tel/Fax – 10.30am-6.30pm
Charges: No fixed charge – donations accepted.
Access: By ferry. Taxi from landing stage if required.

THE CHANNEL ISLANDS

Guernsey

Les Cotils Christian Retreat and Conference Centre
Les Cotils L'Hyureuse
St Peter Port, Guernsey
Channel Islands GYI 100

Tel: 01481 727793
Fax: 01481 701062
e-mail: lescotils@aol.com

Christian – Inter-Denominational

A grand white place on a hill with glorious views to the port and sea.
In 12 acres, it offers first class comfort, pretty furnished rooms and a
coffee shop and tea room. This is retreating in luxury. For those on
retreat peace and quiet is possible even if other non-retreatant guests
are staying – there is an active management policy to try and maintain
this balance.

Open: All year. Receives everyone.
Rooms: 7 singles, 10 doubles, 2 family or large rooms.
Facilities: Disabled. Conferences, garden, park, library, 3 guest
lounges, TV, guest telephones.
Spiritual Help: Personal talks. Group sharing and spiritual direction
and directed study on retreats. Morning and evening prayer.
Guests Admitted to: All public rooms.
Meals: Everyone eats together. Traditional and vegetarian food.
Special diets.
Special Activities: Special programme – they are expanding their
programme so ask to see current brochure.
Situation: Situated above the port in a large garden and park with
great views.
Maximum Stay: Open.
Bookings: Letter/tel/fax/e-mail.
Charges: There are varied individual and group and conferences
rates, but a standard B&B with full English breakfast £26 per night.
Half-board £33 per night per person.
Access: Any south coast airport or ferry port.

EAST AND EAST ANGLIA

Biggleswade

Yoga for Health Foundation
Ickwell Bury
Biggleswade
Beds. SG18 9EF   Tel: 01767 627271

Mind-Body-Spirit – Non-religious

This is a special place for caring retreats for those who have health problems and disabilities of various kinds as well as the fit and healthy – no division is made between the fit and the severly disabled, everyone is well-regarded and given loving care by the staff. The Foundation, a charity operating in many parts of the world, is in what must be the last unspoiled bit of this commuter-belt county. A 17th-century grand manor and farm, it is surrounded by park land and you drive up a sweeping entrance raod. There are fine gardens, and a fishing lake left over from the Middle Ages when an abbey occupied the site. Inside the house, all is given over to creating a family sense of place and an atmosphere that is busy, caring and helpful. The food is excellent with much that is home-produced. There are nursing staff and the place is well equipped for the disabled. Yoga training and other healing treatments are available. This is a place where people share and grow in strength together. The health benefits of regular yoga practice, particularly for those suffering from stress, are well established. On any visit here you are likely to encounter people who will praise the improvements in their lives that stays here have brought them. **Highly Recommended.**

Open: All year except over Christmas. Receives men, women, young people, families, groups, non-retreatants.
Rooms: 15 doubles – subject to supplement for a single. Dormitories, caravans and camping by prior arrangement only.
Facilities: Excellent for disabled, meditation room, small conferences, camping by arrangement, garden, library, guest lounge, payphone. Pets by prior agreement. Children welcomed.
Spiritual Help: Personal talks, group sharing, meditation, directed study. *Full range of yoga activities for both able-bodied and disabled guests.*
Guests Admitted to: Unrestricted access. Work of resident Community by arrangement.
Meals: Everyone eats together. Vegetarian wholefood only. Special diets possible.
Special Activities: Send for programme of events, which includes a

10-day Family Festival of Yoga.
Situation: Peaceful, in countryside and village.
Maximum Stay: 3-4 weeks.
Bookings: Letter or telephone.
Charges: £275 per person per week all in. Rates for shorter stays.
Access: Train to Biggleswade then by taxi. Buses: coach to Bedford.
Local bus runs twice a day. Car: via A1 to Biggleswade.

Turvey

Monastery of Christ Our Saviour
Abbey Mews
Turvey
Beds. MK43 8DH

Tel: 01234 881211
Fax: 01234 881742
e-mail: abbey.mews@which.net

Roman Catholic

This is one of two Benedictine communities at Turvey who worship in common and work in close co-operation. The monks' guest house has been converted from a stone barn. The rooms are spacious and comfortable with lots of books to read, an easy chair in every room and a guest kitchen. This can be a busy place but it is one where personal silence is very much respected. If you are on a private retreat, you will be left in peace to get on with it. As it is a small community, help in the garden is usually welcomed. The life here is deliberately kept simple – organic gardening, tomato growing, and producing pottery are some of the specialities of the monks. Attached to the monastery is the Turvey Centre for Group Therapy. Its main activity is to provide courses, both for beginners and professionals. These are run in conjunction with Oxford Brookes University. The courses take place over weekends with the students being resident at the monastery or nearby. For a private retreat try to go when the course is not having its weekend. *Although the Community is small in numbers, it is big in talents and if you want to experience what monastic life is about, then this is one of the best places to do it. Nothing is grand, everything is real – a peaceful place of prayer and seeking God.* **Highly Recommended.**

Open: All year except Christmas and Easter seasons. Receives men, women, young people, groups can have accommodation arranged if there are not enough rooms available within the guest house.
Rooms: 3 singles, 1 double. A silent, peaceful guest house.
Facilities: Small meetings, garden, library, fields in which to walk, guest lounge, kitchen, payphone.
Spiritual Help: None but try going to the Divine Office as the singing, praise, and prayers can give great spiritual help.
Guests Admitted to: Chapel: you can join in with the monastic choir in the Divine Office – if you have not done so before, Turvey makes it easy with books and clear instructions. Some work in the garden possible if you want to do it.
Meals: Taken in the guest house. Self-catering with some meals provided. Provision for vegetarians if requested.

Special Activities: None.
Situation: The village has a lot of traffic, but the guest house and gardens are quiet – and the walled vegetable garden is not just for food, it also has wild places and hide-aways for all manner of natural wildlife. Insects, butterflies, surprises abound.
Maximum Stay: By agreement.
Bookings: Letter is best.
Charges: Enquire when booking.
Access: Train: to Bedford or Northampton, then by local bus – not frequent however. Car: via M1, Exit 14 to Olney.

Priory of Our Lady of Peace
Turvey Abbey
Turvey
Beds. MK43 8DE

Tel: 01234 881432
Fax: 01234 881538

Roman Catholic

Although the Abbey is next to a busy road, the sisters have created an oasis of peace in this picturesque stone village by the River Ouse. They are a lively and hard working Community who warmly welcome their guests and put them immediately at ease. The modern guest house is warm and the bedrooms are well-appointed with very good beds. They also sometimes utilise the adjoining guest house of the monks (see this section) which is equally comfortable. There is a garden in which to sit, while the grounds offer good walks through Abbey Park and beyond to open fields – you may pass the nuns' goats who are friendly, very productive, and managed with great care and affection. Guests do not have to join the daily offices of prayer but the beautifully sung liturgy helps immeasurably in the quietening of mind and body and in the opening of the heart. The chapel is modern, full of light and simply decorated by work of the Community who are famous for the quality of the design and execution of their projects Their series of posters based on Scripture are justly popular as is the embroidery work on the church vestments they make. The meals are excellent and served either in the small guest dining room or in a beautiful stone carriage house attached to the chapel. The programme of events is very popular and run with efficiency and much good humour. The Icon Painting and Prayer retreat is one of the best of its kind available. **There is an annual summer event for men and women under forty to join both Communities in a week of living the Benedictine monastic life**. If you are at all interested in how the religious contemplative life in community can be successfully lived today, then here is a good place to visit. You do not need to be a Catholic to come here. The Community are here for all those seeking God – that is seeking to find meaning for their life and spiritual journey. So people of every faith or none are welcomed. **Highly Recommended.**

Open: All year, except Christmas and Easter week periods. Receives men, women, young people, groups, religious.
Rooms: 6 singles, 3 doubles. No mobile phones. Silence expected from 9pm-9am.

Facilities: Small conferences, garden, library, guest lounge, payphone. There are day retreats some for mothers with young children.

Spiritual Help: Guests are welcome to join in the Divine Office and are provided with books which are easy to follow even if you never have attended such a service before. From time to time introductory talks are given to help people participate more deeply. Daily Mass. Personal talks, meditation, spiritual direction, personal retreat direction.

Guests Admitted to: Chapel, Divine Office, the library, occasionally work of the community, .

Meals: Meals are taken in a guest house. Food is more or less traditional with some wholefood dishes. With advance notice, provision can be made for vegetarian and for special diets which are not too complicated.

Special Activities: Planned programme of events. Examples of events include *Calligraphy and Prayer, Hearing the Word Within, Monastic Experience Week, Icon Painting*. Send for brochure.

Situation: In the village near countryside with fields to the rear and side.

Maximum Stay: 3 nights and by arrangement.

Bookings: Preferably by letter.

Charges: Private retreats £25 per 24 hours. Retreat weekends £57 inclusive. Days are £8.50. Ask for information on individual visits.

Access: Train: to Bedford or Northampton and then bus to Turvey – the buses are not frequent. Car: via A428.

CAMBRIDGESHIRE

Buckden

St Claret Centre
The Towers
Buckden, Cambs. PE18 9TA

Tel: 01480 810344
Fax: 01480 811918

Roman Catholic

Formerly a palace, this centre at Buckden Towers is a famous historic place. Today, the owners are the Claretian Missionaries, a religious Community. They run a large rural parish, organise retreats and youth activities, welcoming visitors from all over the world. There is a church and two chapels. The accommodation ranges from dormitories for youth to self-contained apartments in the gate house. There is a good colour brochure about the place and one on the programme, which is mainly Catholic in nature, available on request.

Open: Open all year. Receives everyone.

Rooms: Plenty of room here ranging from 6 self-contained apartments and 9 doubles to youth dormitories in the Great Tower.

Facilities: Disabled. Conferences, camping, garden, park, TV in some accommodation. Children welcomed.

Spiritual Help: Directed study.

Guests Admitted to: Chapel.
Meals: Self-catering.
Special Activities: Planned programme. Send for brochure.
Situation: Quiet in the countryside.
Maximum Stay: By arrangement.
Bookings: Letter, telephone, fax.
Charges: Rates on request.
Access: Good map in the brochure with details.

Ely

Bishop Woodford House
Barton Road
Ely, Cambs. CB7 4DX   Tel: 01353 663039
                                                     Fax: 01353 665305
                          e-mail: bpwoodford@e-l-y.freeserve.co.uk

Anglican

A 1973 purpose-built modern place with lawns, and easy to find in the
grounds of an old theological college. The chapel is large and traditional and there are plans to update in time the whole place – this is
needed as many of the beds could do with replacing. The plans to have
en-suite twin rooms for the disabled sounds good as does the idea that
there will be lots of singles with en-suite facilities. There is a bookshop
and a bar and the staff here are welcoming and helpful. Five minutes
walk from the Cathedral, the river and the town.

Open: All year. Receives all.
Rooms: 32 singles.
Facilities: Disabled – ground floor bedrooms and toilet. Conferences,
chapel, garden, library, guest lounge, TV, payphone. Children wel-
comed.
Spiritual Help: None
Guests Admitted to: Unrestricted access.
Meals: Everyone eats together. Traditional food. Vegetarian and
special diets.
Special Activities: Some planned events. Send for brochure.
Situation: In a town and next to a school – quiet in the school holidays
and at night.
Maximum Stay: 7 nights.
Bookings: Letter or telephone/fax.
Charges: From £35 for full board per 24 hours.
Access: By rail, bus to Ely. Car: A10

Compassion is aroused when we realise we are One with all life
                                      THROSSEL HOLE BUDDHIST PRIORY

Horseheath

Mill Green House
Mill Green
Horseheath, Cambs. CB1 6QZ

Tel: 01799 584937
Fax: 01799 584390
e-mail: walkermgh@compuserve.com

Inter-Denominational

Mill Green House is an old 16th century house which is available for all who wish to have time and quiet in which to pray, read and wait upon God. It is a family house but with the children mostly away. Individual counselling, day retreats and opportunities for individuals to be alone and for groups to do their own programme are on offer.

Open: All year except August. Receives men, women, young people, groups on a day basis, and non-retreatants, religious.
Rooms: 2 double. Dormitories.
Facilities: Conferences, garden, chapel/library, guest lounge, guest phone.
Spiritual Help: Personal talks, group sharing, spiritual direction, personal retreat direction, counselling, meditation.
Guests Admitted to: Chapel. Church.
Meals: Everyone eats together. Traditional simple food. Vegetarian.
Special Activities: Planned programme. Send for brochure.
Situation: Quiet in the countryside.
Maximum Stay: 1 week.
Bookings: Letter, fax or telephone 9am-4pm.
Charges: £17.50 B&B. £2.50 simple lunch. £5 supper. Donations extra for spiritual direction/retreat giving from £15-£50.
Access: Train possible. Car route easy. Good map in brochure.

Rumwood
Cardinal's Green
Horseheath, Cambs. CB1 6QX

Tel: 01223 891729
Fax: 01223 892596
e-mail: Robin/MaryEllis@Rumwood.demon.co.uk

Mind-Body-Spirit

Rumwood is a large Colt-type wooden house, very warm and nicely furnished with various extensions made over the last few years – for example, a summer house and sauna. The sitting room has a wonderful fire and there is an amazingly designed open stone fire as well. Carpeted throughout, it is a place where much thoughtfulness has gone into making people feel comfortable and relaxed. People come here then to rest and to release tension and stress. On offer are several healing therapies including Thai healing massage, Bach Flower Remedies, lifestyle analysis, Reiki, and herbal nutrition. *Thought Healing Therapy* is a major interest of the owners and one is a Reiki Master. Information is available on both these healing approaches. One speciality course is on peacemaking between men and women.

Open: All year mainly on weekends. Closed for Christmas. Receives men and women.
Rooms: 1 single, 1 double.
Facilities: Garden, guest telephone. Bring soft shoes for indoors and a swim towel if you want to use the sauna.
Spiritual Help: Personal talks.
Guests Admitted to: Unrestricted access.
Meals: Everyone eats together. Simple wholefood. Vegetarian and vegan.
Special Activities: Special programme. Send for brochure.
Situation: Quiet in a small village.
Maximum Stay: 3–4 days.
Bookings: Telephone.
Charges: There are special rates. See brochure.
Access: Train, bus, national coach, and car route all possible.

Huntingdon

St Francis House
Community of the Resurrection
Hemingford Grey
Huntingdon, Cambs. PE18 9BJ   Tel: 01480 462185

Anglican

Renovated a few years ago, St Francis House is designed for retreatants and the aim is to maintain a peaceful atmosphere at all times. Although the house is in the village, there is a large garden and you can walk beside the nearby river and through the meadows. There are open retreats and those for groups and quiet days. A simple and elegant chapel is available and rooms are quiet and comfortable. Beautifully kept garden with roses and chestnut trees can be seen from the bedrooms. Every effort is made by the Warden here to ensure your peace and comfort. **Highly Recommended.**

Open: All year except August, Christmas, and Easter. Receives men, women, groups.
Rooms: 17 singles, 3 doubles.
Facilities: Disabled – limited, chapel, garden, large cheerful sitting room, pleasant dining room, library, payphone.
Spiritual Help: Peaceful atmosphere and retreatants may talk personally with the retreat conductor when on a retreat.
Guests Admitted to: Unrestricted access. Chapel
Meals: Everyone eats together. Traditional food. Vegetarians and special diets catered.
Special Activities: Planned retreats. Send for brochure.
Situation: Quiet, in a village.
Maximum Stay: 5 days.
Bookings: Letter or telephone – 9am-6pm.
Charges: Depends on length of stay and the retreat so ask for special leaflet giving details. These range from about £10 for the day to £80 for Mon-Fri stays.
Access: Car: via A604.

ESSEX

Boreham

The Barn
Diocesan Pastoral Centre
New Hall, Boreham
Chelmsford, Essex CM3 3HT

Tel: 01245 451760
Fax: 01245 464348

Roman Catholic – Ecumenical

Do not have second thoughts when you come up the drive to New Hall and think with all the big buildings it will lack warmth and peace – nothing could be further from the truth. The centre itself is a 250-year-old converted barn, adjoining New Hall. It is alongside a small lake, surrounded by lawns, trees and shrubs and beyond is a big field. Country walks abound although you are not far from the busy roads. The hospitality is excellent here and the conversion with its own chapel offers small sitting rooms, comfortable and modern bedrooms and plenty of space for prayer and silence. It is very well-equipped, fresh, neat, and warm. The programme of retreats includes *Clowning and Prayer, Prayer and Clay, Music for Advent* and a day of reflection – *The Spirit of the Lord is Upon Me.*

Open: All year except for Christmas, Easter and August. Receives men, women, young people, groups.
Rooms: 7 singles, 4 twin-doubles.
Facilities: Disabled – limited. Conferences, camping, garden, park, library, guest lounge, TV and payphone. No smoking.
Spiritual Help: Personal talks, personal retreat direction, meditation, group leaderships for days of prayer and recollection. The centre is attached to a religious Community whose regular prayer services all are welcome to attend.
Guests Admitted to: Chapel.
Meals: Cafeteria or in guest house – it varies. DIY facilities available. Traditional food. Vegetarian and special diets.
Special Activities: Planned programme. Send for information.
Situation: Quiet, in the countryside.
Maximum Stay: 7-10 days.
Bookings: Letter or telephone.
Charges: Donations – suggested rate £22 full board per person per day, £14 per person self-catering.
Access: Train and coaches to Chelmsford, local buses.

We can never know God until we first know clearly our own soul.

JULIAN OF NORWICH

Bradwell-on-Sea

Othona Community
East Hall Farm
East End Road, Bradwell-on-Sea
Essex CMO 7PN

Tel: 01621 776564
e-mail: OthonaCommunity@Bradwell-on-Sea.freeserve.co.uk
Website: www.nodeknot.demon.co.uk/othona.htm

Ecumenical

This place is in the far reaches of the Essex estuary which stretches right out into the North Sea. You drive and drive and the lanes get narrower and you find a farm and then – surprise! Here in the middle of nowhere is the Othona Community. A new building, purpose built, centrally heated, and only open a few years provides lots of space for visitors. The new dormitories and rooms in the new building are not quite completed as far as decoration goes but they are comfortable enough. There is a disabled room available and school groups and families can visit here too. Hidden here and there are tiny hermitages without loos or electricity for those that may want a real *desert* spiritual experience. A site of special scientific interest is here because of the abundant birds and it is a well-known spot for bird watching enthusiasts. An almost haunting scene of birds, busy people, silence, peace and wilderness. This is one of two Othona Communities, the other is in Dorset (see that section). Founded by Canon Norman Motley in 1946, the Othona Community is a deeply British concept and aims to explore and experience the meaning of fellowship of the Holy Spirit and to promote unity among all Christians. There is an excellent brochure available about the movement if you send for it. Up to 100 people for a conference or 28 guests staying overnight can be accommodated here. The setting being so close to a site of special scientific interest and a nature reserve and close to the sea makes this a very special retreat place for those who are keen on nature and wildlife. The Community has use of the 7th century chapel of St Ceed which dates from AD645. It sits on a windswept and grassy rise on the edge of the sea. Empty of all furnishings and built of deeply weathered stones, it is one of Britain's very oldest places of prayer. Access for disabled. Charges are reasonable. Send for details.

Open: All year. Receives everyone.
Rooms: Lots of rooms – singles, doubles, dormitories, tents available, barn, hermitages – and everything slowly being rebuilt or upgraded.
Facilities: Disabled. Conferences, camping, garden, park, guest lounge, guest telephone.
Spiritual Help: Depends on programme course. The Community works closely with the local churches.
Guests Admitted to: Everywhere except Community private rooms.
Meals: Everyone eats together. Simple, wholefood. Vegetarian and special diets. DIY facilities available.
Special Activities: Planned programme – send for brochure.
Situation: Quiet and remote with its own beach, fields, orchards, woodlands and ancient chapel.

Maximum Stay: 3 weeks.
Bookings: Letter/tel/fax/e-mail.
Charges: Prorgamme events £15 per day per person. Children and concessionary rates available.
Access: Bus, train and car are possible – *you need to ask for specific instructions.*

Pleshey

Chelmsford Diocesan Retreat House
The Street
Pleshey, Chelmsford
Essex CM3 1HA

Tel: 01245 237251
Fax: 01245 237594
e-mail: retreathouse.pleshey@virgin.net

Anglican – Inter-Denominational

The House of Retreat is mostly used by parish groups; individuals are welcome when there is room. A good range of weekend courses are available, ranging from an introduction to the John Main method of meditation, to instruction about how to breathe and use the body most effectively when you have embarked on the journey of prayer. It has been called *the new Jerusalem just off the M25.*

Open: Most of the year. Receives men, women, young people, groups.
Rooms: 22 singles.
Facilities: Disabled. Garden, library, day conferences, guest lounge, guest telephone.
Spiritual Help: Personal talks, personal retreat direction, directed study, spiritual direction.
Guests Admitted to: Chapel. Church.
Meals: Everyone eats together. Traditional simple food. Vegetarian. Special diets – on limited basis.
Special Activities: Myers Briggs retreats, open retreats, quiet days, course for spiritual directors – send for the brochure.
Situation: Quiet in historic Essex village in countryside village.
Maximum Stay: 7 days.
Bookings: Letter, tel/fax – 9.30am-12.30pm.
Charges: £37 per day full board, Groups of 13-22 people Fri-Sun £74 each, Mon-Thurs £103 each, Mon-Fri £140 each.
Access: Train/bus: to Chelmsford. Car: via M11.

Stansted

The Arthur Findlay College
Stansted Hall
Stansted, Essex CM24 8UD

Tel: 01279 813636
Fax: 01279 816025
e-mail: afc@snu,org.uk
Website: www.snu.org.uk

Spiritualist

The Arthur Findlay College for the Advancement of Psychic and Spiritual Science has been going since 1964. The seven principles of Spiritualism are: the Fatherhood of God, the Brotherhood of Man, the Communion of Spirits and the Ministry of Angels, the Continuous Existence of the Human Soul, Personal Responsibility, Compensation and Retribution hereafter for all good and evil deeds done on earth, and the Eternal Progress open to every Human Soul. The College runs an extensive series of courses and programmes and you need to send for their brochure to really get any idea of the range available and the various costs involved. Some examples might be as follows: *Crystal Enlightenment, Dance of the Spirits, Psychic Art Weekend, Spiritualist Healing Mediumship, Your Inner Spirit,* and *Investigating the Paranormal.*

Open: All year according to programme.
Rooms: 14 singles, 2 doubles plus other rooms available. No smoking.
Facilities: Disabled – limited. Conferences, garden, library, guest lounge, TV, payphone.
Spiritual Help: Personal talks, group sharing, spiritual direction, personal retreat direction, meditation, directed study. Many other ways available such as acupuncture, aromatherapy, massage, aura soma. Spiritual healing, private spiritual sittings/readings.
Guests Admitted to: Unrestricted access.
Meals: Everyone eats together. Traditional/Vegetarian food. Special diets.
Special Activities: Planned programme – brochures available each year.
Situation: Set in 15 acres of parkland and woods.
Maximum Stay: Not limited.
Bookings: Letter/tel/fax.
Charges: Day visits from £30. Residential from £106 to £350. Therapies from £8. Spiritualist sittings £25. No charge for healing.
Access: Easy access to airport and motorways.

HERTFORDSHIRE

Buntingford

Country Churches Day Retreats
The Rectory
Warren Lane
Cottered, Buntingford
Herts. SG9 9QA   Tel: 01763 281218

Anglican

What is on offer here are strictly day retreats. Organised by an Anglican vicar trained in the Ignation Exercises, the space for day retreats is offered in the quiet villages which she serves. In the main church there is a Lady chapel and both individuals and groups are welcomed. For those who are active or want a meditative personal retreat with nature, there are specially designed faith and nature trails between the churches – a clever idea that should appeal to many people. The fees for the day are between £5 and £20 – or an hour's gardening. You can be picked up at the train station. Easy to get to by car and impossible by bus. A very pleasant, gentle and appealing kind of retreat and rather English in style.

Hemel Hempstead

Amaravati Buddhist Centre
Great Gaddesden
Hemel Hempstead
Herts. HP1 3BZ   Tel: 01442 843239

Buddhist

This is a Community of Buddhist monks and nuns of the Theravada tradition, but people of any or of no formal religious affiliation are welcomed. In fact from time to time, you may well meet nuns and monks from other faiths visiting here and, certainly, people who are new to Buddhism. Retreats are held in separate facilities away from the often busy life of the Armarvati religious Community itself. Accommodation is basic in the dormitories, so bring a warm sleeping-bag, a blanket for use during meditation, and a towel and soap. Pack heavy socks or slippers too, as no shoes are worn indoors. There is a full calendar of events, talks and long and short retreats, so have a look at the programmes. It is possible by arrangement and at their discretion for you to stay with the monastic Community for a time, but you must participate fully in their daily routine of meditation, meals and work.

Open: April to December for planned retreats. Receives men, women, teenagers for a special annual retreat, families, groups for organised retreats, religious.
Rooms: 9 singles, 6 doubles but for those with special needs such as the sick or elderly. Most accommodation is in dormitories, but the sexes are separated.
Facilities: Disabled with their own facilities. Field, payphone in monastery.
Spiritual Help: Personal talks on the retreats, otherwise evening talks. Guided meditation.
Guests Admitted to: Shrine room, work of the Community, all daily routine.
Meals: Everyone eats together; rice-based Asian food.
Special Activities: Festivals, retreats, workshops, courses, long retreats. Send for programmes.
Situation: Quiet.
Maximum Stay: Weekend or 10 days.
Bookings: Letter.
Charges: About £6 per day of retreat for food and room. Donations at end of the retreat toward running costs.
Access: By car is easiest, but *please drive very slowly and carefully as the lanes to the Centre are narrow.*

LINCOLNSHIRE

Lincoln

Edward King House
The Old Palace
Lincoln LN2 1PU

Tel: 01522 528778
Fax: 01522 527308
e-mail: ekh@oden.org.uk

Anglican

Once the residence of the Bishops of Lincoln, this beautiful and historic house is set in the area of the Cathedral and next to the Old Palace. A programme of open events is on offer which includes a journey of the senses and a pilgrimage around the Cathedral as a path of holiness.

Open: All year except Christmas. Receives everyone.
Rooms: 5 singles, 11 doubles.
Facilities: Disabled. Conferences, garden, library, guest lounge, TV, payphone. Children welcomed.
Spiritual Help: Personal talks. Spiritual direction.
Guests Admitted to: Unrestricted access.
Meals: Meals other than for groups of 6 or more are limited to breakfast for guests.
Special Activities: Planned events. Send for brochure.
Situation: In the city.
Maximum Stay: By arrangement.
Bookings: Letter or telephone.
Charges: B&B £18.50-£21. Full board for groups runs about £34 per person per day.
Access: Train, coach, car to Lincoln.

Market Rasen

The Calyx Trust
Redhurst, Holton-cum-Beckering
Market Rasen, Lincolnshire LN8 5NG

Tel: 01673 857927

Non-Religious

This is a self-supporting trust which is non-religious and formed to offer people a space in which to reflect, recuperate and find some stress-free time. The house, Redhurst, is set in a garden with orchard, heated pool and little wood on the edge of a village in farmlands.

Open: All year. Receives everyone.
Rooms: 2 singles, 2 doubles. Camping possible for families. No smoking.
Facilities: Disabled. Garden, library.
Spiritual Help: None.

Guests Admitted to: Unrestricted access.
Meals: Everyone eats together. Traditional food, some organic and garden produce.Vegetarian and special diets.
Special Activities: None.
Situation: Very quiet in a village in the countryside.
Maximum Stay: 21 days.
Bookings: Letter or telephone.
Charges: Donations only. Guidelines £15-£20 per night B&B for example.
Access: Train: Lincoln to Market Rasen. Bus and Coach possible – ask for details. Car: Map provided with brochures.

Woodhall Spa

Time Away
Station House
Stixwold, Woodhall Spa
Lincs. LN10 5HW
Tel: 01526 352548
e-mail: timeaway@stixwold.surfaid.org

Anglican – Non-Religious

There are no chapel, daily offices or programme of retreats here and many guests come for non-religious reasons. Having said that, Time Away, does offer itself for individuals to come on a private retreat and the house is sufficiently rural to enable quiet to be enjoyed. The village church is at hand for prayer and worship. Groups of up to 12 may come for quiet days.

Open: All year. Receives everyone.
Rooms: 4 singles. 4 doubles.
Facilities: No specific facilities for the disabled but two rooms are on the ground floor so do enquire. Garden, library, guest lounge which is very light, TV, direct dialling phone. Children welcomed. Pets by arrangement.
Spiritual Help: Personal talks. Village church nearby.
Guests Admitted to: Unrestricted access.
Meals: Everyone eats together or taken in room. Traditional food. Vegetarian and special diets.
Special Activities: None.
Situation: Very quiet in the countryside.
Maximum Stay: By arrangement.
Bookings: Letter or telephone.
Charges: Quiet day with lunch and refreshments £13.50 Full board £30 per person per day.
Access: Train and bus possible – see brochure. Pick up from station can be arranged. Car route.

NORFOLK

Bowthorpe

Bowthorpe Community Trust
I St Michael's Cottages
Bowthorpe Hall Road
Bowthorpe, Norwich
Norfolk NR5 9AA   Tel: 01603 746380

Ecumenical

The Trust offers short-stay accommodation set up through the combined sponsorship of Anglican, Baptist, Methodist, Quaker, Roman Catholic and United Reform churches. Near by is a woodcraft workshop for the disadvantaged. A small sitting room, a selection of devotional books and a prayer and study room with all meals provided make this one of the more cosy places to stay. The Walsingham shrines are only an hour's drive away.

Open: All year. Receives men, women and non-retreatants.
Rooms: 1 single, 1 double.
Facilities: Garden, guest lounge, TV, phone, direct dialling.
Spiritual Help: Personal talks.
Guests Admitted to: Most areas.
Meals: Everyone eats together. Traditional food with provision possible for vegetarians. No special diets.
Special Activities: None.
Situation: Quiet in town.
Maximum Stay: 2 weeks.
Bookings: Letter.
Charges: Day and weekly rate – ask for leaflet.
Access: Train: from Norwich to Thorpe. Car: via A47.

Bungay

The Community of All Hallows
Ditchingham
Bungay (Suffolk)
Norfolk NR35 2DZ   Tel: 01986 892840

Anglican

The Anglican Community of All Hallows run a number of establishments in addition to this house. **Holy Cross House** is the guest wing of the convent for those seeking to share in the worship of the Community. **St Mary's Lodge** is a silent house for reflection and prayer. **The Gate House** is a small self-contained house on the ground of All Hallows with accommodation for three people. **St Gabriel's** is a huge complex now being completely rebuilt with all modern facilities – a big investment by the Community in the future. **St Raphael's** is for guests who wish to self-cater and are happy with dormitory accommodation.

See this section for details about **St Michael's House** which has its own chapel. There is a happy atmosphere here and group retreatants often return on an individual basis. Open retreats of various kinds are held, bearing such titles as *Beginners, Light out of Darkness, Julian and Healing, Pottery and Prayer, Celtic Retreat* while Advent and summer courses are available for residential groups.

As to **All Hallows House** itself – well, it can hardly be faulted for hospitality, comfort, nice food, pleasant sitting room – even Luke the dog makes you feel right at home. There are several brochures available about the various facilities in all these places and about the retreats on offer. Do not be confused about where this place is situated. It is in Norfolk but the postal address puts it in Suffolk because of the Bungay address. It is about 12 miles from Norwich. The Community here really do work hard to make going on retreat a comfortable and spiritual event. The choice of accommodation is wide and the church and domestic arrangements among the best. **Highly Recommended.**

Open: All year. Receives men, women, young people, families, groups, non-retreatants.
Rooms: 3 singles, 3 doubles and then more with so many facilities.
Facilities: Chapel, prayer room, garden, 47 acres of grounds, guest lounge, library, TV, guest phone. Children welcome. Pets by prior arrangement.
Spiritual Help: Personal talks, group sharing, meditation.
Guests Admitted to: Convent grounds, the garden and chapel.
Meals: Meals taken in guest house. Traditional food. Vegetarian and self-catering catered.
Special Activities: Retreat programme in some of the other properties (see above). Send for details.
Situation: Quiet and in the countryside.
Maximum Stay: 3 weeks.
Bookings: By letter or telephone.
Charges: By donation. Guide lines: £22 for 24 hours.
Access: Car is easiest but coach from Victoria Station to Bungay, train to Norwich, and local buses offer possibilities. Discuss when you book if you are not coming by car.

St Michael's House
All Hallows Convent
Ditchingham
Bungay (Suffolk)
Norfolk NR35 2DT   Tel: 01986 892749

Anglican

Open: Most of year. Receives men, women, young people, families, groups, non-retreatants.
Rooms: Singles, doubles, dormitories.
Facilities: Conferences, chapel, garden, library, guest lounge, payphone. Children welcome.
Spiritual Help: Personal talks, direct study, spiritual direction possible.

Guests Admitted to: Convent chapel and gardens.
Meals: Everyone eats together. Traditional food. Vegetarian and special diets catered.
Special Activities: Planned programme of events. Send for brochures.
Situation: Quiet.
Maximum Stay: 2 weeks.
Bookings: Letter or telephone.
Charges: From £21 full board per day.
Access: See entry for All Hallows House.

Norwich

Community of the Sacred Passion
All Hallows
Rouen Road, Norwich
Norfolk NR1 1QT   Tel: 01603 624738

Anglican

Though it is on a busy street, All Hallows House has a peaceful atmosphere inside. St Julian's Church is next door and contains a chapel that is built on the site of the cell of the 14th-century mystic Julian of Norwich. Her *Revelations of Divine Love* is a classic English Christian mystical work and can be obtained at all good bookshops. Reading her book, then coming here for a retreat built around some of her writings might prove a worthwhile spiritual journey.

Open: All year. Receives men, women, groups, and non-retreatants.
Rooms: 2 singles, 2 doubles.
Facilities: Chapel, garden, small library, Julian Library next door, guest lounge, TV.
Spiritual Help: None.
Guests Admitted to: Chapel.
Meals: Everyone eats together. Traditional food. Vegetarian and special diets on request.
Special Activities: None.
Situation: In the town, a busy location.
Maximum Stay: 2 weeks.
Bookings: Letter or telephone.
Charges: By donation – usually £10-£15 per night.
Access: By rail, bus or car to Norwich.

Surlingham

Padmaloka Buddhist Retreat Centre for Men
Lesingham House
Surlingham, Norwich
Norfolk NR14 7AL
                              Tel: 01508 538112
                              Fax: 01508 538076
                  e-mail: Padmaloka@compuserve.com

Buddhist

A Buddhist retreat centre for men only, run by the Friends of the Western Buddhist Order. Here, no time is wasted in getting you into stillness and simplicity, and the study of what may be the fastest growing spiritual tradition in the West. In addition to meditation and other related classes, you can discover how to make spiritual practice work in your career through talks by men who have achieved it. They may be managing directors of successful companies or even medical school lecturers – but all have developed what Buddhists term, 'Right Livelihood'. Bring a sleeping-bag, towel, soap, and old clothes and shoes for the work periods that everyone does during the day. For meditation wear loose clothes. There is much here that will prove meaningful to modern men who are burdened with career and personal responsibilities and are searching for balance and spiritual nourishment in their lives. The teaching is soundly based on the Buddhist way of life and principles. Padmaloka is a centre for the ordination of men but others may join but first you must go to some introductory meditation courses at one of the FWBO centres. All this will be explained to you in the various brochures which are available. On open retreats the main thing here is to introduce men to meditation, Buddhist rituals and to discuss central Buddhist themes including the life story of the Buddha, Buddhist insight and what spiritual friendship really means. Fellowship and friendship and harmony among men is the aim. Many men are seriously challenged to look again at their present lifestyles and values when they have made a Buddhist commitment at Padmaloka. Facilities are modern and handsome with comfortable rooms. Disabled men can come too and there is a garden and a small delightful courtyard. A happy, peaceful and justly famous place with a gracious atmosphere. **Highly Recommended.**

Open: All year. Receives men only to spend a set period of time up to 2 weeks on retreat.
Rooms: Dormitories – bring your own towel and sleeping-bag. The term *dormitories* needs a bit of unpacking here – this is not prep-school stuff because the dormitories are like a double room but with bunks and they are modern and perfectly adequate.
Facilities: Disabled, garden, library, guest lounge and guest telephone.
Spiritual Help: Personal talks, spiritual direction, meditation, directed study, yoga, T'ai-Chi, Buddhist devotional practice (Puja).
Guests Admitted to: Unrestricted access except to Ordination Team and Support Team accommodation areas. Shrine room. Work of Community.
Meals: Everyone eats together. Vegetarian/Vegan food.
Special Activities: Planned programme. Send for brochure.
Situation: Quiet, in a village and countryside.
Maximum Stay: 2 weeks.
Bookings: Letter.
Charges: £24 per person per night – concession £21 per night.
Access: By rail to Norwich then by taxi or bus. Bus to Surlingham village drops you at the gate.

Sutton

St Fursey's Orthodox Christian Community
111 Neville Road
Sutton,
Stralham,
Norwich NR12 9RR   Tel: 01692 583394/580552

Orthodox Christian – British Antiochian Orthodox Deanery

Open: Mostly all year. Receives everyone.
Rooms: 1 single, 1 double.
Facilities: Garden, library, guest lounge, TV.
Spiritual Help: Personal talks. Spiritual direction. Personal retreat direction.
Guests Admitted to: Guest areas and chapel.
Meals: Everyone eats together. Orthodox fasting discipline is practiced here and the food is vegan on certain days. Discuss meals when you ask for information.
Special Activities: Daily services, visits to other Orthodox churches, pilgrimages and other visits arranged, weekly bible study.
Situation: Village.
Maximum Stay: 5 days.
Bookings: Letter.
Charges: Donations only.
Access: Rail is possible but car is easiest. Ask for details of route.

Walsingham

Shrine of Our Lady of Walsingham
Knight Street
Walsingham, Norfolk NR22 6BW   Tel: 01328 820239
Fax: 01328 820990
e-mail: accom.olw@netcom.co.uk

Anglican

Walsingham Shrine is an ancient place of Christian pilgrimage and this is a famous, busy pilgrimage centre. This means that you will not find facilities for silence or for spiritual guidance. To go on a pilgrimage to a holy place is a long-established religious practice of most major world faiths. It can, and ought to, be regarded as a kind of retreat, especially as the pilgrim hopes for a deepening of personal spirituality. Before starting out, read about the history of Walsingham so that you may understand what has drawn Christians there over the centuries. This should put meaning into what might otherwise simply be a visit to another *monument*. The Centre is a pleasant place to stay from which to visit either this Anglican shrine or the Roman Catholic one situated a mile away. Both continue to attract many thousands of people every year.

Open: 1 Feb to 8 Dec. Closed 9 Dec-31 Jan. Receives everyone.
Rooms: 50 singles. 75 doubles.

Facilities: Disabled. Conferences, garden, library, guest lounge, TV, payphone. Children welcome.

Spiritual Help: No facilities for silence and spiritual direction only on request. There is a Shrine priest who can help with spiritual programmes.

Guests Admitted to: Chapel. Shrine room. Work of Community.

Meals: Everyone eats together. Traditional simple food. Vegetarian and special diets.

Special Activities: Each weekend there is a programme organised by the parish groups attending. This usually includes Stations of the Cross, Procession and Benediction.

Situation: Rather busy in the village.

Maximum Stay: By arrangement.

Bookings: Letter preferred.

Charges: The charges are based on various lengths of stay but an example would be £29.75 full board for one night up to £297.50 full board for 10 nights. Half-board and child rates are availble. Children under 5 are free. As to meals, the cost currently is £19.95 for B&B and lunch/supper charge of £4.90.

Access: By car is easiest but public transportation is possible. Ask for best routes.

Sue Ryder Retreat House
Walsingham
Norfolk NR22 6AA

Tel: 01328 820622
Fax: 01328 820505

Inter-Denominational

Facilities are offered here for groups and individuals to make private retreats and there are no spiritual programmes or direction available. Groups usually have their own facilitator. The staff concentrate on providing for the practical needs of visitors.

Open: All year. Receives all.

Rooms: 8 singles, 9 doubles, dormitories, hermitage.

Facilities: Disabled good including one bedroom en-suite. Conferences, small garden, guest lounge, TV, payphone. Children welcomed.

Spiritual Help: None.

Guests Admitted to: Chapel.

Meals: Taken in guest house. Traditional food. Vegetarians and special diets catered.

Special Activities: None.

Situation: Quiet in the countryside.

Maximum Stay: None.

Bookings: Letter, telephone, fax.

Charges: Ask for rates.

Access: Car route easiest.

SUFFOLK

Beccles

Ringsfield Hall
Ringsfield
Beccles, Suffolk NE34 8JR   Tel: 01502 713020
e-mail: info@ringsfield-hall.freeserve.co.uk
Website: www.ringsfield-hall.freeserve.co.uk

Inter-Denominational

Run by a trained nurse and counsellor with theological training and a former Baptist minister, this is a large brick house with a programme which includes an Easter Retreat and retreats for mature women. There are also facilities and courses for young people and children and a separate cottage for a group booking.

Open: Open all year for self-catering, otherwise for programme. Receives all.
Rooms: 2 singles, 2 doubles, dormitories, hermitage planned.
Facilities: Conferences, garden, park, library, guest lounge, TV, guest telephone. Games facilities, tennis court, nature trails, playing fields. Children welcome.
Spiritual Help: Personal talks. Spiritual direction. Personal retreat direction. Directed study. Eclectic counselling.
Guests Admitted to: Unrestricted access.
Meals: Everyone eats together. Simple food. Vegetarian and special diets. DIY facilities.
Special Activities: Plannned programme. Brochure available.
Situation: Quiet in the countryside in 14 acres of grounds.
Maximum Stay: 1 week.
Bookings: Letter, telephone, fax.
Charges: Self-catering £6.50 week days, £7.50 weekends. £24 per night up to £73 for 4 nights stay with catering.
Access: Car route easiest.

Broadwater

Niggles House
Broadwater, Near Framlingham
Suffolk IP13 9LS   Tel: 01728 723800

Russian Orthodox

People of all spiritual traditions are invited to stay here for short periods to enjoy some peace and to renew their sense of God's love for them. The two foundation stones of the residents are the biblical way of contemplation as taught by the Fellowship of Contemplative Prayer (see *Helpful Addresses* section) and the Russian Orthodox Church. Throughout the year there is a series of quiet days and various events of a religious nature. For those seeking solitude, there is a hermitage in the garden. A weekly timetable gives structure to your stay here.

Open: All year except Christmas. Receives men, women, young people, groups and non-retreatants for the day only.
Rooms: 2 singles, 1 double, hermitage.
Facilities: Disabled possible as all on one level. Wheelchair available if needed. Chapel, garden, library, guest lounge.
Spiritual Help: Personal talks, meditation through contemplative prayer.
Guests Admitted to: Chapel, garden.
Meals: Everyone eats together. Wholefood. Vegetarian and special diets catered.
Special Activities: Planned programme. Send for brochure.
Situation: Quiet in the countryside, open views.
Maximum Stay: 1 week.
Bookings: Letter.
Charges: About £20 full board per day. Otherwise see brochure for rates.
Access: Train with pick up from Wickham Market Station. Car route via A12 or A14, signed to Framlingham.

Bury St Edmunds

Hengrave Hall Centre
Bury St Edmunds
Suffolk IP28 6LZ

Tel: 01284 701561
Fax: 01284 702950
e-mail: co-ordinator@hengravehallcentre.org.uk
Website: www.hengravehallcentre.org.uk

Ecumenical

Hengrave Hall is a Tudor mansion set in its own grounds of some 45 acres and is the home today of an ecumenical Community of Christians living, working and worshipping together. Membership is drawn from any of the Christian churches. It is a Community devoted to reconciliation. Charges for guests are kept to a minimum – so your help with domestic tasks after such things as meals will be most welcomed. The programme offers a range of retreats including a quiet day reflecting on the topic, *Is Religion Bad for your Health?*

Open: All year except Christmas, Easter. Receives everyone.
Rooms: 13 singles, 11 doubles, dormitories, barn, camping site.
Facilities: Disabled good. Conferences, camping, garden with Prayer Walk, library, group TV, payphone. Children welcome. No pets.
Spiritual Help: Personal talks.
Guests Admitted to: Unrestricted access. Chapel.
Meals: Everyone eats together. Food is simple and plain. Vegetarian and special diets catered.
Special Activities: Planned programme of events. Send for information.
Situation: Quiet in a village near countryside.

Maximum Stay: 1 week.
Bookings: Letter.
Charges: On application.
Access: Train or bus to Bury St Edmunds and then by taxi. Car route easy.

Clare

Clare Priory
Clare, Sudbury
Suffolk CO10 8NX

Tel: 01787 277326
Fax: 01787 278688
e-mail: clare.priory@virgin.net

Set in eight acres of secluded gardens beside a river, Clare Priory remains behind its walls in the same solitude and quiet that it has enjoyed for centuries. Now it is a place to share the daily routine of the Augustian friars and the lay community. Private or guided retreats for individuals and groups are available. Also quiet days, away days, theme weekends. Chapel and library. Telephone the Secretary Monday to Friday 9.30am-1pm and find out what is currently on offer at this lovely monastic retreat in Suffolk.

Great Ashfield

Water Hall Retreat Centre
Great Ashfield
Bury St Edmunds
Suffolk IP31 3HP

Tel: 01819 811225 (All enquiries)

Buddhist

Water Hall, a simple farmhouse with dormitories, is run by the London Buddhist Centre specifically for retreats. These are usually in the form of introductory weekend retreats for adults wishing to learn meditation as well as attending more advanced classes. Classes are taken by full-time practising Buddhists who are members of the Friends of the Western Buddhist Order. There are also courses about Buddhism where you can learn who the Buddha was, what he taught and what relevance his teaching has for us in the West today. There are short courses, summer retreats, and gay men's retreats. You book through the London Buddhist Centre (see London section).

Open: During organised group retreats. Receives everyone depending on kind of retreat.
Rooms: Dormitories.
Facilities: Disabled – limited.
Spiritual Help: Meditation, directed study.
Guests Admitted to: Unrestricted access.
Meals: Everyone eats together. Vegetarian.
Special Activities: There is a special programme of planned events – see brochure.

Situation: Very quiet, in the village and countryside. No passing traffic.
Maximum Stay: 10 days.
Bookings: By letter or telephone.
Charges: See brochure as charges depend on course.
Access: By rail to Bury St Edmunds, or by car.

Newmarket

The Old Stable House Centre
3 Sussex Lodge
Fordham Road, Newmarket
Suffolk CB8 7AF

Tel/fax: 01638 667190

Roman Catholic – Inter-faith

Very close to Newmarket Heath, this former stable offers a warm, comfortable environment with as much freedom as possible for individuals and groups to work on their personal and spiritual development. The atmosphere is informal and homelike. The focus of the workshops is holistic and creation centred. The idea has been to create an environment which supports your inner journey, encourages growth toward wholeness, challenges you to be open and aware, brings out your creativity and allows you to feel comfortable with your true self – a tall order but goals always worth striving for if you want to unify yourself and not feel life is fragmented. Events range from *Dreams and the Inner Journey, Spring Meditation, Sacred Body: Sacred World* to a *Mid-Winter Advent Retreat*. Open to all who are committed to healing, growth and the desire to increase their spiritual awareness. **Highly Recommended.**

Open: All year except Christmas and Easter weeks. Receives men, women, young people over 14, families with children over 14, groups, non-retreatants.
Rooms: 4 singles, 4 doubles, 1 dormitory.
Facilities: Disabled. Conferences – limited, library, garden, guest lounge, payphone, direct dialling. *Children welcomed but over 14 years of age.*
Spiritual Help: Retreats and workshops designed to meet the needs of individual groups. Group sharing, directed study, meditation, and spiritual guidance. Acupuncture. Reiki healing.
Guests Admitted to: Unrestricted access. Chapel. Church.
Meals: Self-catering except for scheduled events. Food when catered is wholefood/vegetarian and organic where possible.
Special Activities: Planned programme of events. Send for brochure.
Situation: Quiet, with a small woodland area and paddock. 12 miles from Cambridge.
Maximum Stay: 8 days.
Bookings: Letter or telephone.
Charges: Suggested donations list available on request. There is a small bursary fund for people on low income.
Access: Train: Newmarket station 5 minutes away. Local buses. Car: via A45. Excellent map available when you book.

CENTRAL ENGLAND

BIRMINGHAM

Woodbrooke Quaker Study Centre
1046 Bristol Road
Birmingham B29 6LJ

Tel: 0121 4725171
Fax: 0121 4725173
e-mail: enquiries@woodbrooke.org.uk
Website: www.woodbrooke.org.uk

Quaker

Woodbrooke welcomes all of any faith or none and runs a programme of courses in addition to retreat facilities with a twice daily meeting for worhsip and is set in ten acres of organically managed grounds – an oasis in the city.

Open: All year. Receives everyone.
Rooms: Up to 70 singles and doubles.
Facilities: Disabled – limited. Conferences, gardens, park, library, guest lounge, TV, guest telephone.
Spiritual Help: Spiritual direction. Meditation. Directed study.
Guests Admitted to: Public rooms plus meeting room, silent room.
Meals: Everyone eats together. Vegetarian and special diets catered.
Special Activities: Planned programme. Send for information.
Situation: Quiet in city.
Maximum Stay: By arrangement.
Bookings: Letter/telephone.
Charges: See programme or ask for charges when you telephone.
Access: Train to Birmingham New Street. Bus: No. 61/62. Car: A38 6 miles from M42.

BUCKINGHAMSHIRE

Chesham

Little Grove
Grove Lane, Chesham
Bucks. HP5 3QQ

Tel: 01494 782720
e-mail: bookings@cortijo-romero.co.uk
Website: www.Cortijo-Romero.co.uk

Mind-Body-Spirit

Run by the same people who operate Cortijo Romero in Spain (see Spain section), Little Grove is close to London but quiet in the Bucks' countryside and situated in two acres of fields. The type of courses run at Little Grove include topics like holistic massage, psycho-drama, sacred dancing, African drumming and those with titles like *Moving with the Landscape, Finding Your Voice,* and *Hidden Talents.* The aim of all the courses and events is personal growth.

Open: All year. receives men, women, young people, families, groups, non-retreatants.
Rooms: Single and double rooms available.
Facilities: Disabled. Conferences, camping, garden, guest lounge, payphone, direct dialling. Children are welcome to certain types of events so check first if it is suitable.
Spiritual Help: This varies according to what course you attend.
Guests Admitted to: Mostly everywhere.
Meals: Taken in guest house. DIY facilities. Wholefood. Vegetarian and special diets.
Special Activities: Planned programme of events. Send for brochures.
Situation: Quiet.
Maximum Stay: None.
Bookings: Letter or telephone
Charges: See brochures or for individual enquiries please telephone.
Access: Train, bus and car all reasonable routes.

Milton Keynes

Society of the Sacred Mission Priory
1 Linford Lane, Willen
Milton Keynes, Bucks. MK15 9DC   Tel: 01908 663749

Anglican

This is a small Community of older women who want guests to enjoy their Community home and so you will get a warm welcome. Other members of the Community and different associates live nearby and the whole Community join forces in the two local churches for services and worship. There is morning prayer, mid-day office and Evensong in the parish church, and Compline in the house chapel.

Open: All year. Receives men and women.
Rooms: 1 single, 1 double. Silence maintained 9pm-9am next morning. No mobiles/radios/tapes.
Facilities: Garden, library, TV.
Spiritual Help: None.
Guests Admitted to: Unrestricted access. Chapel. Church.
Meals: Everyone eats together/taken in room. Traditional food. Vegetarian.
Special Activities: None.
Situation: Quiet.
Maximum Stay: 10 days in first instance.
Bookings: Letter.
Charges: Donations usually – but ask please when booking.
Access: Easiest by car.

Stoke Poges

The Quiet Garden Trust
Stoke Park Farm
Park Road
Stoke Poges, Bucks SL2 4PG

Tel: 01753 643050
Fax: 01753 643081
e-mail: quiet.garden@ukonline.co.uk
Website: www. Ukonline.co.uk/members/quiet.garden

Ecumenical

The Quiet Garden Trust movement began in 1992 and was the vision of Revd Philip D. Roderick. The trust encourages provision of local venues where there is an opportunity to set aside time for rest and prayer. A quiet garden comes into being when someone opens their home and garden for occasional days of stillness and reflection. It may also be in a retreat centre or local church. Another development has been to offer quiet spaces in cities to give space and opportunities for prayer, learning about Christian life, hospitality and healing. Send for information and a list of quiet gardens across the world.

DERBYSHIRE

Alfreton

Community of the Prince of Peace
Baptist Monastery
4 Church Street
Riddings, Alfreton
Derbyshire DE55 4BW

Tel: 01773 603533
e-mail: commpp@ukonline.co.uk

Baptist

The Community of the Prince of Peace is **a new Baptist Religious Community** serving the church which was founded in 1997. The Community is listed as a Baptist organisation in the Baptist Union Directory and it is a member of the ecumenical Conference of Religious. The monastery itself is an attractive Victorian house in two acres of grounds in a quiet location with nice views over parkland. Close to the M1 it is easily accessible.

Open: All year except on Sunday and Monday afternoons. Receives men and women and small groups for reflection, rest and retreat.
Rooms: 1 single, 3 doubles. Self-contained flat with 2 bedrooms. No smoking. Bring own soap and towel.
Facilities: Sitting room, dining room, library, garden. Chapel.
Spiritual Help: Personal talks, personal retreat direction, and spiritual direction if requested.
Guests Admitted to: Almost everywhere. Chapel.
Meals: Taken with Community in silence. DIY for breakfast and

refreshments. Plain food. Vegetarians and special diets if notice given.
Special Activities: None as such but all are welcome to share in
Community Prayers.
Situation: Quiet in a small town.
Maximum Stay: By arrangement.
Bookings: Letter or telephone.
Charges: No fixed charge but donation guidelines of £25 per person
per night full board and £10 for a quiet day with lunch and a room.
Access: Car: M1/ J26 and J28

Belper

Community of St Lawrence
Field Lane, Belper
Derbyshire DE5 1DD   Tel: 01773 822585

Anglican

Open: All year. Receives everyone.
Rooms: 24 singles, 7 doubles.
Facilities: Conferences for small groups, guest lounge, library, garden,
TV and payphone.
Spiritual Help: Personal talks if requested.
Guests Admitted to: Chapel.
Meals: Everyone eats together. Plain food. Vegetarians and special
diets catered for.
Special Activities: No planned programme of events as most groups
bring their own spiritual director.
Situation: Quiet in a small town.
Maximum Stay: By arrangement.
Bookings: Letter or telephone.
Charges: About £25 per 24 hours.
Access: Train: to Belper, then short walk. Bus: Derby to Belper.
Car: A6.

Horsley Woodhouse

Sozein Trust
The Old Vicarage
Church Lane,
Horsley Woodhouse
Derbyshire DE7 6BB   Tel: 01332 780598

Ecumenical – Anglican Sacraments

Sozein is a New Testament verb signifying the setting free, making safe
and healing of the individual or the community. It refers to God's work
on behalf of us all. This defines the purpose and the work carried out
at the Old Vicarage by the Rev. Neil Broadbent. Healing services, group
prayer, the offering of a quiet healing environment and the laying on of
hands are some of the activities here. The Sozein Trust is a Churches

Ministry of Healing Trust. Special activities include courses on *Christian Spirituality, Christian Mystics,* and *Prayer and Contemplative Practice.*

Open: Open by arrangement – but closed for Christmas, Holy Week. Receives men, women, and young people, families and groups for the day only. Non-retreatants for quiet days or counselling.
Rooms: 1 single, 1 double.
Facilities: Disabled welcomed on a day basis visit – but toilet facilities are not suitable for wheelchairs. Chapel. Garden, library, TV, guest telephone, direct dialling.
Spiritual Help: Personal talks, spiritual direction, personal retreat direction, prayer, Anglican Sacraments.
Guests Admitted to: A family house. Prayer room, library, kitchen access.
Meals: Taken together as part of family. Traditional food. Vegetarians by prior arrangement.
Special Activities: Retreats are individually tailored so discussion is necessary before hand.
Situation: Quiet in the countryside with hills in background.
Maximum Stay: 1 week.
Bookings: Letter or telephone 9am-noon Mon-Fri.
Charges: By donation – suggested about £15-£20+ per day.
Access: Bus, car routes possible, but train plus bus coming from Derby. See leaflet.

Morley

Morley Retreat and Conference House
Church Lane
Morley, Ilkeston
Derbyshire DE7 6DE   Tel: 01332 831293
                                          Fax: 01332 834944
                    e-mail: Wardens@morleyretreat.fsnet.co.uk

Anglican

Modern accommodation has been built for guests next to the old Morley Rectory. There is a good programme of retreat and house events, ranging from quiet days to a weekend devoted to silent prayer called, appropriately, 'Listening to God'. The house is a former Georgian rectory set in its own five acres of grounds amid rich farmlands. There is a large meeting room with a log fire in winter, two smaller sitting rooms, a chapel – and even a bar. Accommodation is both in the main house and in an annexe.

Open: Most of the year. Receives men, women, young people, and groups.
Rooms: 24 singles, 7 doubles. *Ask what you need to bring.*
Facilities: Chapel, conferences, garden, 5 acre park, library, guest lounge, TV and payphone.
Spiritual Help: Personal talks.

Guests Admitted to: Unrestricted access.
Meals: Everyone eats together. Traditional food. Vegetarian and special diets.
Special Activities: Planned events which include walking and other craft holidays. Send for brochure.
Situation: Very quiet, in the countryside, with a walled garden and 14th-century parish church, set in the midst of 5 acres of grounds.
Maximum Stay: By arrangement.
Bookings: Letter or telephone.
Charges: £32 for 24 hrs.
Access: Train: to Derby, but there are no local bus services. Car: via M1, Exit 25, followed by A52, A61 and A608.

Whaley Bridge

Community of the King of Love
Whaley Hall
Reservoir Road
Whaley Bridge, High Peak
Derbyshire SK23 7BL

Tel: 01663 732495
e-mail: the guardiansckl@compuserve.com
Website: www.whaleyhallckl.org.uk

Christian Ecumenical

This gritstone house was built in 1853 for a mill-owner and is now run as a retreat centre. The Community is ecumenical and composed of both men and women. A pleasant and welcoming place.

Open: All year. Receives everyone.
Rooms: 4 singles, 13 twin-doubles.
Facilities: Conferences, guest lounge, library, garden, TV and guest phone. Chapel.
Spiritual Help: Personal talks, spiritual direction, personal retreat direction.
Guests Admitted to: Unrestricted access.
Meals: Everyone eats together. Traditional food. Vegetarian and special diets.
Special Activities: Planned programme of events.
Situation: Quiet in a small town.
Maximum Stay: By arrangement – usually only short stays.
Bookings: Letter or telephone.
Charges: £42 for 24hrs, £80 for 48 hrs. Longer stays negotiable.
Access: Train: Whaley Bridge. Car: A6.

Let all guests that come be received like Christ.
RULE OF SAINT BENEDICT

GLOUCESTERSHIRE

Cranham

Prinknash Abbey and St Peter's Grange
Cranham
Gloucester GL4 8EX   Tel: 01452 812455

Roman Catholic

The monastery sits on its hill looking rather stark and modern, but
inside all is warm, comfortable, and purpose-built. Men retreatants are
received here in separate guest accommodation. Men, women, young
people, families and groups can all come and stay at St Peter's Grange,
the monks main guest house which is very comfortable. The chapel is
at the side of the monastery and gives the impression of going 'downstairs', but the liturgy is inspiring and there is a reassuring modesty in
the simplicity of the place. You may attend the daily round of services
and there is usually some work to do if you feel you want to contribute
in that way. St Peter's Grange is a distinguished place of mainly Tudor
buildings and was originally a monastic property connected with
Gloucester Cathedral. It was used as the monastery by the present community of monks until they built the new Abbey in the 1970s. St Peter's
Grange is about a mile away but within the estate and connected by a
long drive which is a pleasant walk to the chapel. The Grange is a mellow pile of stone set against a hill with a small quiet garden entrance.
Inside, most of the panelling and other antique features have been
retained. This includes a remarkably beautiful decorated chapel and
choir. The following information applies to St Peter's Grange.

Open: Most of the year. Receives men, women, young people, families,
groups.
Rooms: 5 singles, 2 doubles. Dormitories
Facilities: Estate grounds, library, garden, guest lounge, TV, pay-
phone.
Guests Admitted to: Grounds, church, chapel.
Spiritual Help: None.
Meals: Everyone eats together. Traditional food. Vegetarian and
special diets with notice.
Special Activities: Pentecost and Advent led retreats each year.
Situation: On a great hill with sweeping views across the Cotswold
countryside and the Malvern Hills.
Maximum Stay: Monday to Friday.
Bookings: Letter.
Charges: Donations around £22.50 B&B, £30 full board.
Access: Train: Stroud from London or if coming from the North, then
take train to Cheltenham. Bus: Available usually – ask for details. Car:
M5 then A46.

Newnham

The Old Vicarage
Newnham, Gloucester GL14 1EL
Tel: 01594 510282
e-mail: all@nickandmays.fsnet

Inter-Denominational – Christian

A retreat in a home, offering sensitivity and understanding to people with eating disorders, crafts through which you may seek God, and acceptance of people exploring who they are.

Open: All year. Accepts everyone.
Rooms: 1 single, 3 doubles.
Facilities: Garden, library, guest lounge, guest telephone.
Spiritual Help: Group sharing. Spiritual direction. Counselling by appointment.
Guests Admitted to: Public rooms and garden.
Meals: Everyone eats together. Traditional, wholefood, vegetarian. Special diets.
Special Activities: None.
Situation: Very quiet and walking distance to river.
Maximum Stay: 5 days.
Bookings: Letter/telephone/fax.
Charges: £25 B&B £10 dinner £5 lunch. £5 craft sessions. £50 per day for any courses held.
Access: Ask for details as train and bus possible.

Nympsfield

Nympsfield in the Cotswolds
Marist Convent
Nympsfield, Stonehouse
Glos. GL10 3TY
Tel: 01453 860228

Roman Catholic

All people of every spiritual persuasion or none are welcome in this delightfully named convent tucked away in the beautiful Cotswolds. Situated half-way between Bristol and Cheltenham or Gloucester, Nympsfield is a village of great antiquity containing many charming stone houses. There is much of historic interest all around the place. There is a chapel and prayer room in the convent and guest accommodation has specially equipped kitchens for self-catering. The beds are new and firm. Non-residential hospitality is on offer as well. Rooms are simply but nicely furnished. There is a kind and warm welcome here from the Community who are flexible and accommodating. Plenty of peace and room to roam at Nympsfield. *Gentleness* is the key word here. **Highly Recommended**.

Open: All year. Receives everyone.
Rooms: 4 singles, 13 doubles. More can be accommodated if necessary.

Facilities: Conferences, garden, park, library, guest lounge, TV, pay-phone, direct dialling.
Spiritual Help: Spiritual direction. Groups usually bring their own spiritual director.
Guests Admitted to: Chapel and all areas not private to the Community.
Meals: Taken in guest house together. DIY kitchens. Meals can be provided if needed. Vegetarians and special diets.
Special Activities: None – but there is a brochure about the centre.
Situation: Quiet in a village.
Maximum Stay: 1 week.
Bookings: Letter or telephone.
Charges: £14 a day for self-catering, £25 a day for full board. 6-day retreats £160.
Access: Train and car routes. Ask for travel directions if taking train.

Randwick

More Hall Convent
Randwick
Stroud
Glos. GL6 6EP
Tel: 01453 764486
e-mail: rosemarie@boddington.co.uk

Roman Catholic

Open: All year. Receives men, women, young people, and non-retreatants.
Rooms: 3 singles.
Facilities: Garden, library, guest lounge, camping, TV, payphone.
Spiritual Help: Personal talks. Silence from 8pm-9am. Join Community in prayers.
Guests Admitted to: Chapel and sometimes help with the work of the community which is care of the elderly.
Meals: Everyone eats together. Traditional food.
Special Activities: None.
Situation: Quiet and in the countryside.
Maximum Stay: 2 weeks.
Bookings: Letter.
Charges: About £20 per day.
Access: Train: to Stroud then by bus or taxi 2 miles to convent. Car route easy.

Stroud

Hawkwood College
Painswick Old Road
Stroud, Gloucester GL6 7LE
Tel: 01453 759034
Fax: 01453 764607
e-mail: hawkwoodcollege@cs.com

Anthroposophical – Rudolf Steiner Tradition

Situated at the head of a small Cotswold Valley, Hawkwood provides a beautiful setting for a retreat, adult education courses and conferences. The facilities are centred around a 19th-century manor house with fields and woodlands.

Open: All year. Receives everyone.
Rooms: 14 singles, 17 doubles.
Facilities: Disabled. Conferences, garden, library, guest lounge, TV, guest telephone.
Spiritual Help: Spiritual direction, meditation, courses in Ayurveda, Kinesiology, yoga.
Guests Admitted to: Public areas.
Meals: Everyone eats together. Traditional, wholefood. Vegetarian and special diets.
Special Activities: Planned events. Send for brochure.
Situation: 42 acre estate with cotswold valley views.
Maximum Stay: Open.
Bookings: Letter/tel/fax.
Charges: Around £100 per person per weekend. Prices can vary.
Access: Train possible – enquire. Car: easy.

HEREFORDSHIRE

Harewood End

Vipassana Trust
Dhamma Dipa
Harewood End
Hereford HR2 8NG

Tel: 01989 730234
Fax: 01989 730450
e-mail: dhammadipa@compuserve.com

Non-Religious

Vipassana means 'to see things as they really are'. It is a way of self-purification by self-observation and is one of India's most ancient meditation techniques. It is grounded in reality of self and there is no visualisation, verbalisation or mantras involved but careful observation of the body and self. Today in India over 600 Roman Catholic nuns, for example, use the Vipassana techniques and there is an increasing demand for it around the world whether Eastern or Western cultures are involved. The Trust offers courses in the tradition of Sayagyi U Ba Khin as taught by S.N. Goenka. You need to give all your effort on these courses, observing the rules of the house and taking your study seriously. The daily timetable which all are urged to follow starts at 4am and goes on until 9.30pm. Noble silence reigns here and there is complete segregation of men and women and this includes married couples and partners. It is really best if you are a married couple to come at different times because the retreats are intensive and demand full personal attention of each partner. The silence is important so if you have a problem with this and are a chatterbox, self-adjustment will be necessary. One of the reasons for silence between students is to keep yourself focused and not be distracted – you can talk to your teacher on a one-to-one basis however and there may be group discussions. People come here to meditate, serve on courses or to help with improvement of the property which is set in 22 acres of gentle rolling countryside near the cathedral city of Hereford. There are local practising Vipassana groups in London, Bedfordshire, Bristol, Liverpool, Suffolk, Sussex, Devon and Wales. A newsletter is published three times a year giving details of short and long courses throughout Europe with addresses of Vipassana centres around the world. A serious retreat centre with established programmes and the basic accommodation and peaceful setting for those looking for increased self-awareness and development. **Highly Recommended**.

Open: All year. Receives men, women and young people for specific courses.
Rooms: A few singles are available. 15 doubles, 3 dormitories. *Men and women are segregated and restricted to their own areas.* The rooms for men are basic but beds and central heating are good. The toilet/shower block is modern and clean. Women's quarters are slightly more comfortable.
Facilities: All the facilities are basic and divided into those for men and those for women. There is a garden. A new building programme is underway and a Meditation Hall has recently been completed which can hold 120 guests. The new building plan looks to establish an ideal and modern facility for Vipassana practice and retreats in this beautiful part of England.
Spiritual Help: Meditation. Teachers are available to guide students and answer questions about technique.
Guests Admitted to: Almost everywhere, but *male and female guests have designated and separate areas.*
Meals: Men and women eat separately. The food is vegetarian. Special diet arrangements only for specific medical reason. *There is a morning and a mid-day meal and that is it with only fruit consumed until the next morning – most people find this no problem. It keeps you alert and attentive.*
Special Activities: Very specific courses are on offer. Send for information which fully explains what is on offer and how the courses are run.
Situation: Quiet in the countryside.
Maximum Stay: None but there is a minimum stay unless it is specifically a 3-day course. 11 days minimum for beginners.
Bookings: Letter, telephone, fax, e-mail requesting *application form which must be completed.*
Charges: Voluntary donations only, according to what people wish to give.
Access: Sent with booking information. Train, bus and car all possible – but the centre is located up a long lane.

Hereford

Belmont Abbey
Hereford HR2 9RZ

Tel: 01432 277388

Roman Catholic

The Community at Belmont Abbey offers very modern and comfortable guest facilities in Hedley Lodge guest house and a full programme of courses with such titles as *Plainsong and Prayer, Jesus as a Man of Prayer, Not Angles but Angels*, and workshops on human development and spiritual growth, Christian architecture and music, and calligraphy and prayer. Some of the course leaders are very well-known such as Abbot Alan Rees and Dom Henry Wansbrough. Retreats at Belmont centre around the Divine Office of prayer with the monks, but this leaves ample time for private prayer, spiritual guidance and rest. The facility is an unusual mixture of monastic and modern living environments. It mostly works but some people on retreat may find the ordinary activities taking place here, for example wedding parties, not quite in keeping with their expectations. Perhaps such things serve to remind us that our spiritual life is not a thing apart from us and that it goes on in the midst of our ordinary living which should be joyous – just like a wedding feast. The garden fronting the abbey is splendid and there are places to walk and sit in perfect solitude. **Highly Recommended**.

Open: All year. Receives men, women, young people, families, groups and non-retreatants.
Rooms: 9 singles, 9 doubles – 8 with en-suite facilities. All rather luxurious and up-market to get you comfortable and relaxed. No piped music and any compromise between the hotel-type accommodation offered and those for retreatants falls always on the side of monastic hospitality.
Facilities: Disabled – limited to day visitors because there is no lift to the accommodation at this time. Conferences, park, library, TV, payphone, direct dialling. Abbey shop. Children welcomed. Small oratory which is always open and warm. There is an extended choir for guests to take part.
Spiritual Help: Personal talks, sharing in Divine Office.
Guests Admitted to: Chapel, choir.
Meals: Eaten in guest house. Buffet lunch and a good solid supper are served. Traditional food. Vegetarian and special diets.
Special Activities: Planned programme of events. Send for information.
Situation: Close to beautiful countryside, River Wye, Welsh mountains.
Maximum Stay: None.
Bookings: By letter/tel/fax/e-mail.
Charges: Varied scale – apply for details.
Access: Hereford is easily reached by rail, bus or car.

Ross-on-Wye

St Joseph's Retreat Centre
Courtfield
Ross-on-Wye, Herefordshire HR9 6JJ

Tel: 01594 860215
Fax: 01594 860221

Roman Catholic

This location in the beautiful Wye Valley seems ideal for relaxation, rest and reflection for the day, weekend or longer. There is a lovely church dating from 1875 attached to Courtfield and a priest available, if needed, for spiritual direction and retreats. A rather famous house in its day and owned now by the Mill Hill Missionaries.

Open: All year. Receives everyone but limited for those not on retreat.
Rooms: 22 singles, 9 doubles.
Facilities: Conferences, garden, park, guest lounge, guest telephone.
Spiritual Help: Personal talks, group sharing, spiritual direction, personal retreat direction, meditation.
Guests Admitted to: Unrestricted access. Chapel. Church.
Meals: Everyone eats together. Tradition, wholefood. Vegetarian and special diets.
Special Activities: None.
Situation: In an area of outstanding natural beauty.
Maximum Stay: Indefinite.
Bookings: Letter/tel/fax during office hours.
Charges: Donation £30 a day full board.
Access: Train: Hereford or Gloucester. Bus from Ross. Car: M50/A40.

LEICESTERSHIRE

Coalville

Mount St Bernard Abbey
Coalville
Leicester LE67 5UL   Tel: 01530 832298
                                           Fax: 01530 814608

Roman Catholic

Built of local stone, the buildings are simple, not over-ornate, and in keeping with the Cistercian traditions. In the fine and very large granite church, Latin Mass is sung once a month and the vernacular Mass daily. Rooms are clean, comfortable, and have good new beds. The Abbey has a large working pottery, as well as carpentry and printing shops. Meals are very traditional. Located in the middle of the famous Quorn Hunt country, the Abbey offers good walking over hill, pasture and moor. Create your own retreat here, using a Bible and a devotional book as the monks are not available for guided retreats. This monastery is a very popular place and you may find it hard to get accommodation except by booking well in advance. The more you look after yourself, the better it will be for this overstretched but welcoming Community of monks. It is a place, after all, for prayer and seeking God. So if you go to Mount St Bernard Abbey just get on with it.

Open: All year except one month to mid-January, first week of June and September. Closed Christmas period. Receives men, women, young people, families, groups.
Rooms: The Guest House accommodation is reserved for relatives and friends of the monks and for retreatant guests. The main guest

house provides rooms for two married couples and up to 9 male guests in single rooms. The Lodge provides single and double rooms for 7-10 women. There is one downstairs en-suite room adapted for the disabled. The church has ramp access and loop system.

Facilities: *No chapel in guest house.* Well stocked library, guest lounge, payphone, direct dialling.
Spiritual Help: None.
Guests Admitted to: Chapel.
Meals: Taken in guest house. Plain food with provision for vegetarians if required. You can talk during the meals if you want.
Special Activities: None. There is a small leaflet available about the Abbey guest arrangements.
Situation: 150-acre estate in hills of Charnwood Forest with commanding views of Soar river-valley.
Maximum Stay: 5 days.
Bookings: Letter or telephone.
Charges: Donation average about £20 per day.
Access: Train: Loughborough, then by taxi. Car: M1, Exit 23.

East Norton

Launde Abbey
East Norton
Leics. LE7 9XB

Tel: 01572 717254
Fax: 01572 717454
e-mail: Launde@leicester.anglican.org
Website: www. Launde.org.uk

Anglican – Ecumenical

This is a huge red-brick house built by Thomas Cromwell in 1540 on the site of an early Augustinian priory. It retains today the comfort and charm of a distinguished private country mansion with a cheerful drawing room fire, a panelled dining-room and games room. A beautiful chapel, still intact from the 15th century, is the jewel of Launde Abbey. You might be given a room in either the house, a small annexe or in the refurbished Georgian stable-block, which overlooks a large pond. All this is set in 350 acres of parkland. Everyone is welcome here. **Highly Recommended.**

Open: All year except Christmas to mid-January. Receives men, women, young people, families, groups and non-retreatants which includes charities, cultural and educational groups for conferences.
Rooms: All in various buildings. 14 singles, 22 doubles. Hermitage.
Facilities: Disabled, conferences, chapel, good size garden, park, library, guest lounge, TV and payphone. Children welcomed.
Spiritual Help: Personal talks, spiritual direction, personal retreat direction. Opportunity to join in regular worship with resident Community.
Guests Admitted to: Unrestricted access. Chapel.
Meals: Everyone eats together in an oak-panelled room. Traditional food. Vegetarian and special diets. *Sticky toffee pudding is a speciality here.*

Special Activities: Planned programme of events. 8 and 5-day retreats, calligraphy and prayer, and praying through playing retreat are some of the course topics offered here. Send for the brochure.
Situation: Very quiet, in the countryside.
Maximum Stay: 8 days.
Bookings: Letter or telephone – 9am-5pm week days.
Charges: £38 per person per 24 hours. Course prices vary from a quiet day at £14.50 to £260 for an 8-day Ignatian retreat with spiritual directors.
Access: Very close to Leicester. Train: to Oakham, 6 miles away. Bus: No. 147 to Leicester. Car: via A47 from Leicester.

Theddingworth

Hothorpe Hall Christian Conference Centre
Theddingworth
Leics. LEA 6QX   Tel: 01858 880257
                                          e-mail: office@hothorpe.co.uk
                                          Website: www.hothorpe.co.uk

Inter-Denominational

A grand big house looking out over grass and fields and specialising as a conference centre in offering a wide range of facilities for Christian, Charity and Disability organisations. Most of the guests are Christian groups or individuals. Hothorpe Hall is not a retreat centre as such but many people come here for quiet days. There are no less than nine rooms for the disabled here.

Open: All year except Christmas week. Receives everyone.
Rooms: 3 singles, 48 doubles, 6 family rooms.
Facilities: Disabled. Conferences, garden, library, guest lounge, TV, payphone. Children welcomed.
Spiritual Help: None.
Guests Admitted to: Chapel. Guest areas.
Meals: Everyone eats together. Wide selection of food with provision for vegetarians. Special diets possible.
Special Activities: None.
Situation: In the countryside.
Maximum Stay: No restriction.
Bookings: Letter or telephone.
Charges: Ask for rates.
Access: Train to Market Harborough. Car route easy.

Peace does not dwell in outward things, but within the soul.
                                                          FENELON

NORTHAMPTONSHIRE

Ecton

Ecton House
Church Way
Ecton, Northants NN6 OQE

Tel: 01604 406442
Fax: 01604 787052

Anglican

The spiritual heart of Ecton House is the Chapel which is used for corporate worship and private prayer. This old house has welcomed many guests over the years, not least William Hogarth who came to sketch and relax and Benjamin Franklin to seek out his ancestors. It is a good setting for a retreat and a rest. The programme on offer includes Franciscan and Holy Week retreats and sometimes retreats for widowed, separated or divorced people.

Open: All year. Receives men, women, young people, families, groups, non-retreatants.
Rooms: 25 singles, 1 double.
Facilities: Chapel. Conferences, garden, library, guest lounge, TV, payphone.
Spiritual Help: Chapel, personal talks by prior arrangement.
Guests Admitted to: Chapel, guest areas.
Meals: Everyone eats together. Traditional food. Vegetarians and special diets catered for.
Special Activities: Planned retreats. Send for brochure.
Situation: Quiet in a village.
Maximum Stay: By arrangement.
Bookings: Letter, telephone or fax.
Charges: About £30 full board for 24 hours.
Access: Train: Northampton or Wellingborough. Bus: Ecton from either Northampton or Wellingborough. Car route: M1 Junction 15.

OXFORDSHIRE

Boars Hill

Carmelite Priory
Boars Hill
Oxford OX1 5HB

Tel: 01865 730183

Roman Catholic

Boars Hill is an ideal location for this centre run by the Teresian Discalced Carmel Friars. The Centre, where a lot of new building has been done to offer even better facilities, stands in its own 17 acres of woodland. It aims to provide courses on prayer and spirituality, special attention being given to the teaching on prayer of the great Carmelite writers such as St Teresa of Avila, St John of the Cross and St Teresa of Lisieux. There is an annual 'vocation' weekend open to all young men interested in the religious life and the Carmelites in particular. The programme of planned retreats and events is an exciting, intelligent and full one. **Highly Recommended.**

Open: All year except Christmas and New Year. Receives men, women, young people, families, groups.
Rooms: 15 singles, 14 doubles.
Facilities: Disabled. Chapel, garden, park, payphone.
Spiritual Help: Personal talks, group sharing, meditation, directed study.
Guests Admitted to: Unrestricted access.
Meals: Everyone eats together. Traditional food. Vegetarian and special diets catered.
Special Activities: Planned programme. Send for brochure.
Situation: Very quiet, in the countryside.
Maximum Stay: 1 week.
Bookings: By telephone but confirm by letter with a deposit.
Charges: Voluntary offering.
Access: Train to Oxford (5 miles away), then by taxi. Car via A34 – send for a map as route is a little complicated.

Burford

Priory of Our Lady
Burford
Oxon. OX8 4SQ   Tel: 0993 823605

Anglican

Pretty Burford, with its stone houses, antique shops, tourists and air of new money and material success, is also the home of a Community of Anglican Benedictine monks and nuns. The Community has vitality and is growing in the number of both men and women who want to try the contemplative life here. The guest house is a late 16th century house in its own gardens within the Priory grounds. The bedrooms are well-equipped and there is an oratory. Not so easy to get to by public transportation but once there, you will find a proper warm Benedictine welcome and an atmosphere in which you may pray, study and reflect. Try not to be tempted out into Burford with its many little shops, entertaining as it all might seem. This may seem a test of your desire to withdraw from the world for a little while, but the monastery and its prevailing atmosphere of spiritual calm will help you. Most people who come here want space, silence and a place just to be quiet, and the Priory atmosphere is conducive to this with its transparency and caring in a non-intrusive manner. Many moments of profound spiritual sharing between complete strangers occur because they have met here at the deep level of their common humanity. **Highly Recommended.**

Open: All year except 2 weeks in October plus Christmas and Easter. Receives men, women, young people, groups.

Rooms: 4 singles, 4 doubles.
Facilities: Chapel, gardens, park woods, library, guest lounge and payphone. Children welcome in the retreat house. *Not suitable for wheelchairs.*
Spiritual Help: Personal talks, directed study, individually guided retreats, non-resident groups.
Guests Admitted to: Chapel, choir and work of the Community.
Meals: Everyone eats together. Wholefood. Vegetarians catered for. DIY facilities in guest house.
Special Activities: None.
Situation: Quiet on the village edge – splendid views of Windrush Valley but Burford is a busy place, particularly in summer.
Maximum Stay: 6 nights.
Bookings: Letter.
Charges: No formal charge but donation invited. Guideline is £27 per day and £10 for a pastoral session.
Access: Buses from Oxford or Cheltenham. Easiest by car from A40.

Charney Bassett

Charney Manor
Charney Bassett
Nr. Wantage
Oxon. OX12 0EJ

Tel: 01235 868206
Fax: 01235 868882
e-mail: charneymanor@quaker.org.uk

Quaker

The Manor is a Grade 1 listed house and one of the oldest inhabited buildings in the Vale of the White Horse. It is well-maintained, very clean and has a country-home feeling with an old-fashioned sitting room. The rooms are neat, modern and reasonably up-to-date and meals are professionally prepared. There are Quakers living here, so a warm welcome awaits all guests. Quakers say: *Each person is unique, precious, a child of God.* Short courses and retreats on offer include exploring of radical faithfulness and Quaker marriage, spiritual music, calligraphy and meditation and an exploration of masculine spirituality from a Quaker-Christian perspective. *Plans have been made to make new disabled accommodation that is up to today's expectations.*

Many of those who have come here say they came away feeling uplifted at sharing troubles and with renewed hopes for the future.

Open: All year. Receives men, women, young people, families, groups and non-retreatants.
Rooms: 11 singles, 12 doubles, barn, self-catering cottage, *The Gilletts*, in the grounds. 2 en-suite rooms. Camping possible for 2 or 3 guests.
Facilities: Conferences, garden to walk in with places to sit, library, guest lounge, TV, payphone, direct dialling. Craft and workshops. Camping. Small Anglican church almost in the garden – Sunday services. Children welcomed.
Spiritual Help: None

Guests Admitted to: Unrestricted access everywhere.
Meals: Everyone eats together. Traditional food. Vegetarian and special diets.
Special Activities: Planned programme of retreats and events. Send for brochure.
Situation: Very quiet, in the countryside.
Maximum Stay: 1 week.
Bookings: Letter, tel/fax. You should send a confirming letter/fax after telephoning.
Charges: About £44.50 per 24 hours. See room and conference rate sheet.
Access: Train: to Didcot Parkway, then by taxi. Car route easy.

Fernham

St Gabriel's Retreat House
St Mary's Priory
Fernham, Faringdon
Oxon. SN7 7PP　　　　　　　　　　　Tel: 01367 240133

Roman Catholic

St Gabriel's is a Scandinavian chalet in the grounds set in the Valley of the White Horse. The retreat house, which is surrounded by farmland and beautiful views, is modern and simple but very comfortable. As it is a separate accommodation with limited space, all the guests are usually on retreat here. Nearby there are several sites of historical interest.

Open: All year except first fortnight of August. Receives men, women, young people, groups.
Rooms: 4 doubles.
Facilities: Garden, guest lounge, payphone.
Spiritual Help: Personal talks if requested.
Guests Admitted to: Chapel.
Meals: Taken in the guest house – DIY with food provided in well-stocked cupboards and a freezer. The kitchen is clean and modern. Special diets are advised to bring their own food. Self-catering available.
Special Activities: Participation in daily Mass and the Divine Office.
Situation: Very quiet, in the Vale of the White Horse, with unbroken views over Downs.
Maximum Stay: 7 days.
Bookings: Letter.
Charges: By donation.
Access: Train: to Oxford or Swindon. Bus: No. 66 or 66A Oxford/Swindon. Car: via A420 – take turning signposts to Fernham and White Horse Hill.

Nuneham Courtney

**Global Retreat Centre
Nuneham Park, Nuneham Courtney
Oxon. OX44 9PG**

Tel: 01865 343551
Fax:01865 343576

Non-religious

The Brahma Kumaris World Spiritual University (see entry in London) operate this Centre in a magnificent Palladian Villa built by the Earl of Harcourt in 1756. George II called it, 'The most enjoyable place I know.' and Queen Victoria wrote after her visit, 'This is a most lovely place, with pleasure grounds in the style of Claremont.' About 15 minutes drive from Oxford, the house is situated by the River Thames in 60 acres of land and gardens. The Centre is staffed by teachers of meditation who are experienced in creating an atmosphere of peace and spirituality. As well as regular retreats lasting from one day to one week, a variety of seminars, workshops, and courses offer a range of opportunities to learn meditation, develop personal skills, and explore the common values essential to world harmony. These sessions include *Knowing the Self – Exploring and Developing Meditation, Our External Relationship with God,* and *Spirituality in Daily Life.* January and February are normally quiet months for programmes.

Open: All year. Receives men, women, young people, families, groups and non-retreatants only by prior arrangement. The building is open to the public during certain weekends of the year.
Rooms: 8 singles, 20 doubles.
Facilities: Disabled. Conferences, garden, park, guest lounge and payphone.
Spiritual Help: Group sharing, meditation, directed study, personal retreat direction.
Guests Admitted to: Unrestricted access.
Meals: Everyone eats together. Vegetarian food. *No alcohol is allowed.*
Special Activities: Planned programme of events. Guests are expected to attend the scheduled programme. Ask for information.
Situation: Very quiet in its own parkland surrounded by countryside.
Maximum Stay: 3 days.
Bookings: Letter, telephone or fax.
Charges: No charges are made but donations are welcome.
Access: Train: to Oxford. Car: M40 or from Oxford.

Sutton Courtenay

**The Abbey
Sutton Courtenay
Oxon. OX14 4AF**

Tel: 01235 847401
Fax: 01235 847608
e-mail: Admin@theabbeysc.demon.co.uk

Inter-faith – Christian Traditions

Now here is a *very* special place. The Abbey seeks to offer space, peace and support for individuals and groups who want to be still and find closer connection with the sacred dimension of life and with God. The Abbey with its charming inner courtyard, flowers and surrounding meadow-like areas has been going for a number of years and the Community here is engaged in projects ranging from the dynamics of unemployment to the complementary relationship of men and women working in the ministry. The current Community here is very small but dynamic, young, full of cheer and thoughtful. The programme of events is designed to encourage personal, social and ecological trans-formation and nourishment of our inner lives. There are many courses on offer at the Abbey, including *Qi Gong* and the *Tree of Life*, Tibetan healing exercises, the mysteries that lead us to Easter, music as the bridge of the soul, prayer retreats, and a retreat on *Sacred Economics: Spirit, Money, and Peace.* This latter retreat asks some important questions such as: Can money be a commodity of spirit? *If you are between 18–25 taking time out before going on in your education, the Abbey Community is willing to discuss you joining them for three months to a year to experience their life and work. Even if you are older than this, you might like to talk to them about possibilities.* **Highly Recommended.**

Open: All year but sometimes closed for Community needs. Receives men, women, young people, and groups by arrangement.
Rooms: 3 singles and 1 twin in Abbey plus 4 singles and 5 twins in modern guest house. Camping possible.
Facilities: Conferences, camping, 4 acre garden, library with Gandhi archive, payphone.
Spiritual Help: Please enquire.
Guests Admitted to: Unrestricted access except Community members' rooms. Work of the community.
Meals: Vegetarian food. Can be taken alone or with the Community. Self-catering in guest house.
Special Activities: Planned programme. Send for brochure. Courses on crafts and sculpture. *Green lectures. Gandhi school of non-violence pro-gramme has been offered most years.* There is often a weekly ecumenical Eucharist.
Situation: Surrounded by 4 acres of wooded grounds, the Abbey is of archaeological important because of the underlying Roman and Saxon remains. Location is quiet, in a village.
Maximum Stay: 1 week.
Bookings: Letter or telephone.
Charges: £18.50 B&B. Full board £35 per day. Longer Community Lifestyle Retreats £70 per week.
Access: Train: to Didcot Parkway, 3 miles away. Bus: No. 32 from Oxford runs every half an hour. Car: via A34.

Wallingford

Braziers Park
Ipsden near Wallingford
Oxon OX10 6AN

Tel/fax: 01491 680221
e-mail: admin@braziers.org.uk

Non-Religious – Evolutionist

Braziers Park is a residential adult college deep in the south Oxfordshire countryside. The programme is broad but centres mainly on the arts. It is not necessary to attend a course to stay here and you can use the space and time for a private retreat and rest.

Open: All year except Christmas period. Receives men and women.
Rooms: 10 singles, 4 doubles.
Facilities: Conferences, camping, garden, park, library, guest lounge, guest telephone.
Spiritual Help: Personal talks. You may become temporary members of the Brazier Community if you like.
Guests Admitted to: Unrestricted access.
Meals: Everyone eats together. Traditional plus vegetarian. Special diets.
Special Activities: Planned programme. Brochure available.
Situation: Countryside.
Maximum Stay: 2 weeks.
Bookings: Letter/tel/fax.
Charges: Weekend £75 up. Courses in range £75-£100
Access: Car.

Wantage

St Mary's Convent
Wantage, Oxon OX12 9DJ   Tel: 01235 760170
                    e-mail: guestwing@csmvsagehost/co.uk

Anglican

Open: All year except 2 weeks in February. Receives everyone.
Rooms: 12 singles, 1 double. Silence is maintained in the guest area.
Facilities: Disabled. Garden, library, guest lounge, guest telephone.
Spiritual Help: Personal talks. Spiritual direction. Personal retreat direction. Aromatherapy. Massage.
Guests Admitted to: Chapel.
Meals: Taken in guest house. Traditional food. Vegetarians and special diets.
Special Activities: None.
Situation: Quiet in a town.
Maximum Stay: 8 days.
Bookings: Letter/telephone.
Charges: £20 full board per day.
Access: Information provided when you book.

SHROPSHIRE

Clunbury

The Llan Retreat House
Witchen, Clunbury
Craven Arms, Shropshire SY7 0HN

Tel: 01588 660417
e-mail: LlanT-P@beeb.net

Anglican – Ecumenical

This may well be the dream retreat place of most people – it is set in a magnificent part of England just on the edge of Wales, the views are stunning, the gardens lovely and well-designed, the facilities are up-to-the-minute, comfortable, tastefully furnished, and quiet and the chapel an inspiring place of prayer and holy celebration. If this makes you want to say, *Wow!* – then go ahead because this is an *idyllic* retreat house. Just 8 miles west of Craven Arms and not far from the attractive Georgian town of Ludlow, Llan Retreat House is a converted 17th century range of barns. The building includes a Great Hall with seating for about 20 people, a library, quiet rooms, dining room and the chapel where worship is offered daily. The accommodation offers room for up to 14 people and is suitable for individuals, groups, and parish conferences and retreats. There is a self-contained wing for individuals, clergy couples and small families. All facilities are self-catering or can be full board whichever is right for you or your group. The costs have been kept as low as possible. If all this were not enough, the retreat house is run by a married couple, both of whom are active Anglican priests and who continue with this retreat house to serve God, the Church and people with enthusiasm, intelligence and kindness. Their home is adjacent to but separate from the retreat house so everyone has plenty of privacy. **Highly Recommended.**

Open: Most of the year except Christmas and Easter.
Rooms: 2 singles, 6 doubles. (see above)
Facilities: Disabled. Small conferences, gardens, library, guest lounge, TV. (see above)
Spiritual Help: Personal talks. Spiritual direction. Daily Divine Office and the Eucharist in the Chapel. 2 priests available.
Guests Admitted to: Mostly unrestricted access. Chapel.
Meals: Everyone eats together. Traditional, simple food – organic where possible. Vegetarians and special diets by prior arrangement.
Special Activities: None.
Situation: On a working farm, high on a hill in the Welsh Mountains – quiet and beautiful.
Maximum Stay: 1 week.
Bookings: Letter/telephone.
Charges: On application – brochure available – but ranging anywhere from £30 self-catering a day to £60 full board from Friday dinner to Sunday lunch.
Access: By car is easiest. Map on request.

Ellesmere

The Grange
Ellesmere
Shropshire SYI2 9DE

Tel: 01691 623495
Fax: 01691 623227
e-mail: grange@medpress.demon.co.uk

Interfaith

A lovely short drive hedged with cherry trees and magnolias and spring daffs brings you to this mellow, comfy and welcoming old country house. Rooted in Christianity but open to all faiths, the Grange has recently changed management from the older generation of the family to the younger one – an exciting time at the Grange with new things happening but many of the older traditions carried on. The new approach takes the idea of offering a Country House Retreat with the slogan: *Here is the house, let's use it for peace and quiet!* So traditional bed and breakfast accommodation for a peaceful stay as well as a programme of courses comprise the offering here. For older women there is a weekend to reflect, reassess and search for new personal potential within the security of a small group. Indeed one of the main concerns here has long been to explore and celebrate the second half of life for women. Craft courses are being developed with the theme that these can be spiritual adventures for personal development and not just pastimes. There is also a Natural Therapy Centre with various therapies on offer like psychotherapy, osteopathy, aromatherapy, reflexology, nutritional advice, and Reiki healing. The garden has a labyrinth based on the one in Chartres Cathedral and this garden plus woodland and pasture gives a guest over 10 acres in which to wander. Peace, harmony and kindness are to be found here.

Open: March to November inclusive. Receives men, women, young people, groups, and non-retreatants.
Rooms: 4 singles, 11 doubles. Most rooms have en-suite and tea/coffee facilities.
Facilities: Disabled. Conferences, meditation, garden, park, small library, guest lounge, TV, guest telephone, direct dialling.
Spiritual Help: None.
Guests Admitted to: Access everywhere except private family rooms.
Meals: Everyone eats together. Traditional food. Vegetarian and special diets.
Special Activities: The aim of the courses is to promote inner understanding and spirituality The aim of the house is also to offer non-retreatants a place for stillness and enjoyment. Send for information.
Situation: Quiet about 10-minutes walk from a small town.
Maximum Stay: 5 days.
Bookings: Letter or telephone.
Charges: £140 weekend. B&B £30 per person per night.
Access: Train: to Shrewsbury, 17 miles away. Infrequent buses. Car: via A528 from Ellesmere.

Ludlow

Bishop Mascall Centre
Lower Galdeford
Ludlow, Shropshire SY8 1R2

Tel: 01584 813882
Fax: 01584 877945

Anglican – Inter-Denominational

About 5 minutes walk from the Ludlow railway station, this centre has been going for some years and caters for groups and others who arrange their own retreats or programmes. The staff will help in such arrangements if you need it. In recent years Ludlow, a pretty and busy Georgian town, has been *discovered* by tourists and the national press. Now there are all manner of smart and interesting shops and cafes, including a specialist art bookshop run by a knowledgable and helpful American woman in pretty Quality Square. Ludlow also boasts no less than three Michelin star restaurants.

Open: All year. Receives everyone.
Rooms: 16 singles. 4 doubles, 2 dormitories.
Facilities: Disabled. Conferences, library, guest lounge, TV, guest telephone.
Spiritual Help: None.
Guests Admitted to: Unrestricted access everywhere.
Meals: Everyone eats together. Traditional food. Vegetarian and special diets.
Special Activities: None.
Situation: Former church school set in town.
Maximum Stay: By arrangement.
Bookings: Letter/telephone.
Charges: 3 rates available up to £30 per person per day in a single, full board.
Access: Train and car easy.

Rowley

Retreat Cottage
Charles and Sylvia Ruxton
New Place, Rowley
Near Westbury, Shropshire SY8 9RY

Tel: 01743 891636
Fax: 01743 891507
e-mail: sylviaruxton@btinternet.com

Christian

A simple old retreat cottage is on offer here. It is attached to the main house and guests may use it to find rest and peace. The owners are especially interested in guests who may not have been on retreat before and they are willing to be helpful and offer guidance if it is wanted. There is a Quiet Room for morning prayer each day. Children including babies are welcomed here – even well-behaved dogs downstairs in the cottage. No smoking and no mobile phones.

Open: Most of year. Receives everyone except groups.
Rooms: 2 doubles.
Facilities: Garden, guest lounge.
Spiritual Help: Personal talks, personal retreat direction. Therapeutic masssage.
Guests Admitted to: Guest areas and Quiet Room.
Meals: DIY facilities. The Retreat Cottage has its own kitchen but a single guest is welcome to join in the family evening meal.
Special Activities: None.
Situation: Very quiet on hillside with lovely views.
Maximum Stay: 7 nights.
Bookings: Letter/telephone.
Charges: Donations £15 per night suggested. £20 if evening meal included with family. Massage £10 a session.
Access: You need to ask as train and bus are possible. Car probably easiest.

Whitchurch

Taraloka Buddhist Retreat Centre for Women
Bettisfield, Whitchurch
Shropshire SY12 2LD
Tel: 01948 710646
e-mail: taraloka@compuserve.com

Buddhist

Situated peacefully on the plains of the Welsh borderlands, this Buddhist women's community acts as a focal point for women throughout the world from various walks of life. It provides inspiration and affords a glimpse of new spiritual and personal vistas for all who come. Taraloka is one of the few retreat centres specifically run by women for women and it has developed a kind and gentle space in which all women may find relaxation and be well supported in their spiritual journey. Over the last fourteen years the Centre has established clear and simple methods of teaching meditation and Buddhism through its yearly programme. The retreats run from complete beginners to committed practising Buddhists. Guests come only on one of the retreats or events in the published programme. Those with no experience of meditation and Buddhism can come for an introductory course weekend. The programme teaches Buddhist meditation and study within the context of the Friends of the Western Buddhist Order. It is done with careful guidance. The retreat centre is separate from the Community house, but some of the facilities are shared. All teachers are well qualified both in Buddhist teaching and in their specialist subject, such as music. Other features are yoga weekends, spiritual life and motherhood, and retreats designed for older women. The facilities are modern, light and airy. They have been converted from farm buildings and most of the work was done by women. There is a garden, views, a pond and flowers – in the early spring white magnolias are in bloom. The place is high on a hill and you can go for a walk in safety. Everywhere shines out with cleanliness and there is an art room for those who want to paint and make things. Taroloka has made a solitary suite for a private retreat with a bedroom, small kitchen and conservatory which could make you want to stay forever it is so delightful. On the other hand the dormitories are large and light and sometimes it is good to stay there and get to know a selection of other people you might not ordinarily meet, this too can be a very spiritual experience. A place of peace, self-discovery and transformation – and you do not have to believe in anything you do not believe in to take a retreat here. **Highly Recommended**.

Open: *Specific programme of retreats for women – no other guests received.*
Rooms: 3 singles, 2 doubles, 2 dormitories.
Facilities: Disabled. Shrine room. Guest lounge, camping, garden.
Spiritual Help: Personal talks, group sharing, meditation, directed study, personal retreat direction, spiritual direction.
Guests Admitted to: Shrine room.
Meals: Taken in guest house. Wholefood/vegetarian food. Special diets.
Special Activities: Planned events only available. Send for brochure.
Situation: Very quiet, in the countryside with beautiful country walks – near the Shropshire Union Canal. Nearby is a peat moss of special scientific interest.
Maximum Stay: For the duration of the retreat.
Bookings: Letter or telephone.
Charges: £85 per person for weekend, £50 per person concession basis.
Access: Map and details are provided with booking confirmation.

STAFFORDSHIRE

Stone

Shallowford House
Lichfield Diocesan Retreat and Conference Centre
Norton Bridge, Stone
Staffs. ST16 0NZ

Tel: 01785 760233
Fax: 01785 760390
e-mail: warden@shallowfordhouse.freeserve.co.uk

Anglican

Open: All year. Receives men, women, young people, families, groups, and non-retreatants.
Rooms: 14 singles, 11 doubles.
Facilities: Disabled. Conferences, garden, library, guest lounge, TV and payphone. Children welcome.
Spiritual Help: Personal talks, meditation, directed study available by arrangement prior to visiting.
Guests Admitted to: Unrestricted.
Meals: Everyone eats together. Traditional cooking. Vegetarian, special diets
Special Activities: Planned programme of events. Send for brochure.
Situation: Quiet and in the countryside.

Maximum Stay: By arrangement.
Bookings: By letter or telephone.
Charges: These depend on course and retreat – but examples are a weekend retreat for £75 with others between £69 to £170 and up to £210.
Access: Train: to Norton Bridge. No buses.

WARWICKSHIRE

Leamington Spa

Offa House
Offchurch
Leamington Spa
War. CV33 9AS

Tel: 01926 423309
Fax: 01926 330350

Anglican

The Coventry Diocesan Retreat House and Conference Centre is situated in an old Georgian vicarage, with a large garden. The house has been organised in such a way that all visitors are helped to feel that this is their own *special place*, and the staff try to be as non-intrusive as possible. Small programme but offering both Julian and Cursillo retreats.

Open: All year. Receives men, women, young people, families, groups and non-retreatants.
Rooms: 16 singles, 8 doubles, hermitage.
Facilities: Disabled. Conferences, chapel, garden, library, guest lounge, TV and payphone. Children welcomed.
Spiritual Help: Personal talks, directed study.
Guests Admitted to: Chapel.
Meals: Everyone eats together. Traditional. Vegetarian and special diets catered for.
Special Activities: Planned programme of events. Send for brochure.
Situation: Quiet, in the village and countryside.
Maximum Stay: 30 days for guided retreats.
Bookings: Letter, telephone or fax.
Charges: Ask for rates for guests applying individually. Residential and non-residential rates possible.
Access: Rail, bus, car and airport links are all excellent.

When a man surrenders all desires that come to the heart and by the grace of God finds the joy of God, then his soul has indeed found peace.

THE BHAGAVAD GITA

WORCESTERSHIRE

Chadwick

Community for Reconciliation
Barnes Close
Chadwick, Bromsgrove
Worcs. B61 0RA

Tel: 01562 710231
Fax: 01562 710213
e-mail: cfrbookings@aol.com

Ecumenical

Enjoying close links with the United Reform Church through founder members, prayer and financial support, the Community here has developed ecumenically in its team, membership and patterns of work. Barnes Close is a group of buildings situated on the southern slopes of Waseley Hill with five acres of grounds, near a country park. There are fine views of the Malvern Hills and beyond toward the Cotswolds. Accommodation is modern and some rooms are en-suite. There are plenty of extra facilities such as a coffee bar, conservatory and games room. If you want a silent retreat then you should discuss this first when you contact the Community here.

Open: All year. Receives everyone.
Rooms: 4 singles, 1 double, 2 dormitories.
Facilities: *Disabled – 3 rooms are available.* Conferences, garden, park, reading room, guest lounge, TV, games room, conservatory, coffee bar, payphone. Guide dogs only permitted. Children welcomed. There is a smoking room – otherwise no smoking.
Spiritual Help: Community prayers, individual counselling with pastoral leader is possible by arrangement.
Guests Admitted to: Almost everywhere in public rooms and Upper Room plus Chapel.
Meals: Everyone eats together. Traditional/vegetarian food is home-cooked. Special diets.
Special Activities: Planned programme – send for details.
Situation: Quiet in the countryside.
Maximum Stay: 2 weeks or by arrangement.
Bookings: Letter or telephone.
Charges: Ask for current charges.
Access: Train 6 miles away at Longbridge, then by taxi. Bus to Rubery, then taxi. Car route easy. Close to Bromsgrove and Birmingham.

Cropthorne

Holland House
Retreat, Conference and Laity Centre
Cropthorne, Pershore
Worcs. WR10 3NB

Tel: 01386 860330
Fax: 01386 861208
e-mail: laycentre@surfaid.org

Ecumenical

Holland House was set up to help people who are trying to relate their prayer life more closely to the world around them. It is a big old 17th-century place, with lots of thatch and gardens laid out by Lutyens. There is a new chapel and a modern conference and bedroom wing. The house is close to the village church, and although not far from busy roads, it is quiet. In addition to retreat courses, there are non-residential and quiet days. Titles of some of the events offered include: *Painting and Prayer, Millennium Men, Myers-Briggs, Retreat on the Streets,* and *Modern Theological Approaches. Come let us Play* as an introduction to playfulness and prayer sounds like serious spiritual fun.

Open: All year except Christmas and the week after Easter. Receives men, women, young people, families, groups and non-retreatants.
Rooms: 18 singles, 6 doubles.
Facilities: Garden, library, guest lounge and payphone. Children welcome.
Spiritual Help: Group sharing on certain courses.
Guests Admitted to: Unrestricted access. Chapel.
Meals: Everyone eats together. Traditional food. Vegetarian and special diets.
Special Activities: Planned programme of events. Send for the brochure.
Situation: Quiet, in the village and countryside.
Maximum Stay: 1 month.
Bookings: Letter or telephone.
Charges: £35-£45 per 24 hours.
Access: Train: to Evesham, 3½ miles away. Buses: from Evesham. Car: via M5, Exit 7, then A44.

Shrawley

Society of St Francis
Glasshampton Monastery
Shrawley
Worcs. WR6 6TQ   Tel: 01299 896345

Anglican

Up a road beyond cultivated fields or other houses, Glasshampton sits waiting for you. If you take the bus here you will have a good long walk to get there and this may well be a perfect meditation time before commencing your retreat. The monastery is well-established and was built from the stable blocks of a once very grand house which burned down years ago. It is a simple place with a certain elegance about it – homey and silent, yet charming and welcoming. The guest rooms are modern and pleasant and there is a library. The Guest Master Br. Raymond will welcome you warmly and make certain you are comfortable. One member of the Community, Br. Ramon, is famous for his many books on spirituality. This is a serious place for a private retreat.

Open: All year except. Receives men, women, young people, groups for the day, non-retreatants.
Rooms: 5 singles, 1 hermitage.
Facilities: Garden, library, guest lounge, guest telephone, direct dialling.
Spiritual Help: Personal talks, meditation.
Guests Admitted to: Chapel, choir, work of Community.
Meals: Everyone eats together. Traditional food/Vegetarian.
Special Activities: None.
Situation: Quiet and peaceful, in the countryside.
Maximum Stay: 7 days.
Bookings: Letter or telephone.
Charges: No fixed charge, suggest £15 donation per day.
Access: Car, bus, train all possible.

West Malvern

Runnings Park
Croft Bank
West Malvern, Worcs. WR14 4DU   Tel: 01684 573868
Fax: 01684 892047
e-mail: info@runningspark.co.uk

Mind-Body-Spirit

Built about 100 years ago by Lady Howard de Walden as a model dairy farm, Runnings Park has been converted to an hotel and rest centre with an emphasis on health, relaxation and self-development. The place has all modern comforts and the programme is a continuous one. Meditation, channelling, healing and Celtic spirituality, and taking control of your destiny are topics which give a good idea of what to expect. Some group courses have titles like *Planetary Alignment, Exploring the Chakras of the Hills, Crop Circle Phenomenon*, and *Power of Myths*. Massage, aromatherapy, reflexology, floatation, counselling, hypnotherapy, nutritional therapy and healing are all on offer. Facilities are considerable, comfortable, large and airy. Spectacular views, a sauna and pool are available to all. Food is developing toward the organic and the rooms are what you would expect in a hotel. The atmosphere is quietly busy and even with larger groups in residence there is space and peace to be found here.

Open: All year except at Christmas. Receives men, women, groups – but there are no family rooms.
Rooms: 18 singles, 8 doubles.
Facilities: Conferences, park, TV, telephones in all bedrooms, direct dialling.
Spiritual Help: Personal talks, self-development courses. Some counselling. Health and relaxation centre on site. Various therapies available.
Guests Admitted to: Unrestricted access.
Meals: Dining room/restaurant. Tell them you are a vegetarian when you book.

Special Activities: Send for brochure.
Situation: Very quiet in countryside.
Maximum Stay: Open.
Bookings: Letter, telephone or fax.
Charges: These vary considerably as various treatments are available like reflexology as well as the course costs and the room costs, so do check it out when you are asking for information. Current examples: £29 B&B per person, therapies from £12.50 a session.
Access: Train and car route possible.

Worcester

St Mary's House
Stanbrook Abbey
Callow End, Worcester
Worcs. WR2 4TD

Tel: 01905 830307
e-mail: warden@stmarysstanbrook.org.uk

Roman Catholic

St Mary's is the guest house of Stanbrook Abbey, one of the best-known Benedictine women's religious communities in Britain with an international reputation for literary, musical and artistic work. Its influence can be seen and heard in the liturgical arrangements of many other monastic communities. The sisters are enclosed which means you do not meet many of them, but the welcome is very warm and friendly. This is a grand monastery with an enclosed walled area for the Community that is one of the biggest remaining in Europe. The church is grand too and the Divine Office is sung in Latin and English with some handsome voices to be heard. Rooms at St Mary's are modern, comfortable and pleasant. There is a simple, elegant oratory in the house and a big library open to all. The guest kitchen and dining room are excellent and just outside a little garden full of flowers. The Community is considering whether to become active in doing some retreats – at the moment they do have some retreats at St Mary's run by others than from their Community. If they should decide to add this activity to their already full contemplative life at Stanbrook, we are all in for a real treat for these are talented women with many personal and spiritual gifts. A classic Christian place for making a private retreat where the rich monastic choir provides a good framework for your stay. **Highly Recommended.**

Open: All year except 2 weeks at Christmas and in August. Receives men, women, young people, groups.
Rooms: 10 singles, 4 doubles.
Facilities: Disabled, garden, library, guest lounge.
Spiritual Help: Personal talks. Guests are welcome to attend Divine Office in the church.
Guests Admitted to: Extern chapel and guest house facilities.
Meals: Eaten in the guest house. Traditional food. Vegetarian and special diets catered for.
Special Activities: None.

Situation: Quiet and in the village.
Maximum Stay: 2 weeks.
Bookings: Preferably by letter.
Charges: £21 fuil board 2 nights or more.
Access: Train: to Worcester Shrub Hill or Foregate Street, then by taxi. Buses are very infrequent. Car: via M5, Exit 8, then take Malvern Road.

It is better to be silent and real than to talk and be unreal.
SAINT IGNATIUS OF ANTIOCH

NORTHERN ENGLAND

CHESHIRE

Chester

The Retreat House
11 Abbey Square
Chester, Cheshire CH1 2HU   Tel: 01244 321801

Anglican – Inter-Denominational

After 43 years the Community of the Holy Name here have ceased to run the house. It will continue as a retreat house but with a warden.

Open: All year except August. Receives men, women, groups and non-retreatants.
Rooms: 27 singles, 2 doubles.
Facilities: Conferences, chapel, garden, library, guest lounge, guest phone.
Spiritual Help: Personal talks, meditation, spiritual direction, help with making a first retreat, quiet days or part of a day.
Guests Admitted to: Unrestricted access.
Meals: Everyone eats together. Traditional food. Vegetarian and special diets.
Special Activities: Planned programme of events. Send for brochure.
Situation: In the city square, by the cathedral.
Maximum Stay: 1 week.
Bookings: Letter or telephone.
Charges: £27 for 24 hours, £50 per weekend but this could change with the new arrangements so do check when booking.
Access: By rail, bus or car to Chester.

Crewe

Wistaston Hall
89 Broughton Lane
Crewe
Cheshire CW2 8JS   Tel: 01270 568653
                    Fax: 01270 650776

Roman Catholic

This is a 200-year old country house, set in six acres of garden and peaceful countryside. The Centre is staffed by Oblate Fathers and some forty guests can be accommodated. The aim is to enable those who come here to wind down from the stresses and strains of modern living and to enter into a deeper experience of prayer and reflection in the presence of Christ. Much effort goes into making guests feel comfortable with professional catering for meals, and log fires in the winter months.

Open: All year except Christmas, August. Receives men, women, young people, groups.
Rooms: 2 singles, 18 doubles, some en-suite.
Facilities: Disabled – some ground floor rooms. Conferences, chapel, large garden, library, guest lounge, TV, payphone. Children welcomed.
Spiritual Help: Personal talks, group sharing, meditation, directed study.
Guests Admitted to: Unrestricted access to all areas, including chapel.
Meals: Everyone eats together. Traditional wholefood. Vegetarian, vegan diets catered.
Special Activities: Planned programme of events from time to time. *Autumn Venture, Advent Retreats, Touched by God* are some of the courses on offer.
Situation: Very quiet, in the village.
Maximum Stay: Usually a week or length of course.
Bookings: Letter or telephone.
Charges: Day rate, non-residential £18, residential day rate £30, weekend £58, reduced prices for students, unwaged and senior citizens.
Access: Train: to Crewe, then 5 minutes by taxi to Centre. Car: via M6.

Malpas

St Joseph's Retreat and Conference Centre
Tilston Road
Malpas
Cheshire SY14 7DD   Tel: 01948 860055
                                   e-mail: scjmalpas@aol.com

Roman Catholic – Ecumenical

Run by the Sacred Heart Fathers, there are Enneagram and Myers-Briggs workshops as well as courses on Celtic spirituality and weekends devoted to relaxation. A large and rambling old building with a modern wing and all amenities in a pretty village.

Open: All year except Christmas. Receives men, women, religious, groups.
Rooms: 38 singles and 3 doubles are available. Hermitages and a small gate lodge.
Facilities: Disabled. Conferences, garden, park, library, guest lounge, TV, payphone.
Spiritual Help: Personal talks, group sharing, meditation, directed study, Sacrament of Reconciliation, Eucharist.
Guests Admitted to: Chapel.
Meals: Taken in dining room. Traditional food. Vegetarian and special diets catered.
Special Activities: Planned programme. Send for brochure.

Situation: Quiet in a small village.
Maximum Stay: By arrangement.
Bookings: Letter or telephone.
Charges: Varies for individual retreats – contact centre for rates.
Access: Train: Whitchurch. Bus: National coach to Chester. Car: A41 between Chester and Whitchurch.

Warrington

Tumble Trust
7 Grammar School Road
Warrington, Cheshire WA4 1JN   Tel: 01925 635662

Roman Catholic

Tumble Trust, now ten years old, runs retreats at different venues throughout the country. It takes its main inspiration from the Christian contemplative tradition. It is also good fun with an emphasis on community and shared spiritual journeys. There is an annual programme of retreats, all of which may concentrate on a theme – for example relaxation and spirituality. Send for brochure. All inclusive prices for weekends currently range from £55 to £70 with a cost for a week's retreat about £165. *Relax, enlighten, encourage* and *sustain* are bywords for Tumble Trust retreats so new perspectives can be gained.

CUMBRIA

Ambleside

Rydal Hall
Carlisle Diocesan Retreat and Conference Centre
Ambleside
Cumbria LA22 9LX   Tel: 01539 432050
                                         Fax: 01539 434887
                                 e-mail: rydalhall@aol.com
                    Website: http://users.aol.com/rydalhall32050

Anglican – Ecumenical

There is a relaxed atmosphere in this big Georgian house set in the heart of the Lake District, in a 30-acre estate with waterfalls and formal gardens. It is mainly used by groups, but individuals are welcomed and there is no pressure to join in any activities that may be taking place.

Open: All year. Receives everyone.
Rooms: 10 singles, 15 twin-bedded, 3 triples, dormitories, barn, camping.
Facilities: Disabled. Conferences, camping, garden, park, library, guest lounge, TV, payphone. Children welcome.
Spiritual Help: Personal talks, group sharing, spiritual direction,

personal retreat direction, meditation, directed study.
Guests Admitted to: Unrestricted access.
Meals: Everyone eats together. Traditional food. Vegetarian and special diets.
Special Activities: Planned programme of events. Send for the brochure.
Situation: Quiet.
Maximum Stay: No limits applied.
Bookings: Letter or telephone/fax – 9am-5pm.
Charges: £41 per person per day full board.
Access: Train: to Windermere. Bus: Ambleside. Car: via M6, Exit 40 from north, Exit 36 from south, then A591.

Greystoke

Friends Fellowship of Healing
Lattendales
Berrier Road, Greystoke
Penrith, Cumbria CA11 0UE   Tel: 01768 483229

Quaker – Interfaith

A lovely old stone house with gardens and a peaceful atmosphere. Worship in the manner of the Religious Society of Friends is held each morning. The Fellowship is run in accordance with the principles of the Society of Friends (Quakers) but is open to all, irrespective of religious beliefs. The house is situated on the edge of Lakeland National Park, with easy access to the Lake District, Scotland and the North Pennines and set in its own 17 acres. The accommodation is comfortable, clean and pleasant. The function of Lattendales is to provide a sanctuary for all who feel in need of rest whether it is spiritual, mental, or physical. There is a good if small range of retreats on offer here. Self-catering is possible in the two independent flats.

Open: March – November. Receives men, women, young people, families, groups and non-retreatants.
Rooms: 6 twin-bedded rooms, 1 double, 5 singles, all with hot and cold water. One on ground floor. 2 separate flats.
Facilities: Quiet room. Disabled facilities are limited but check out if what is available is okay for you. Conferences, garden, library, guest lounge, payphone. Children welcomed.
Spiritual Help: Group sharing, meditation.
Guests Admitted to: Unrestricted access.
Meals: Taken in the guest house. Traditional food, with provision for vegetarian and special diets.
Special Activities: Planned programme of events. Send for brochure.
Situation: Quiet in the village and countryside just outside Lakeland National Park.
Maximum Stay: By arrangement.
Bookings: Letter or telephone.
Charges: Available on application. Leaflet available.
Access: To reach Lattendales by car leave the M6/A66 at junction 40,

A592 to Penrith and after station it is signposted. See brochure which has a good map.

Ulverston

Manjushri Buddhist Centre
Conishead Priory
Ulverston, Cumbria LA12 9QQ   Tel: 01229 584029
                                        e-mail: ino@manjushri.org.uk

Buddhist – New Kadampa Mahayana Tradition

The Centre is based on the shores of Morecambe Bay, surrounded by gardens and woodlands. It is an ideal setting for the courses which are teachings and meditation led by Gen-la Samden Gyatso, the principal teacher here. There is a general programme and a foundation one with teacher training courses.

Open: During courses. March – November. Receives men and women – residential and non-residential possible.
Rooms: Singles and doubles. Dormitory.
Facilities: Rooms and meditation/teaching rooms.
Spiritual Help: Meditation.
Guests Admitted to: Unrestricted access.
Meals: Taken together.
Special Activities: Planned programme of events. Send for brochure.
Situation: Quiet in countryside.
Maximum Stay: By arrangement.
Bookings: Letter or telephone.
Charges: Single £140 full board, double/twin £120 per person full board, dormitory £84 for full board during course.
Access: The brochure gives details by train and car and includes a small map.

DURHAM

Consett

Minsteracres Retreat Centre
Consett
Durham DH8 9RT
                                        Tel: 01434 673248
                                        Fax: 01434 673540
                                        e-mail: mwhite8684@aol.com

Roman Catholic – Ecumenical

Huge trees line the way to this property which was built in 1775. Once a family house, then a monastery it is now run as a retreat and prayer centre by a Community. There is a main house with different and comfortable meeting rooms and a good size library plus a retreat house and a youth centre. The setting is in Northumberland's rolling hills.

Open: Feb to mid-Dec, closed January. Receives everyone.
Rooms: 17 singles, 27 doubles.
Facilities: Disabled. Conferences, camping, garden, park. Library, guest lounge, TV, guest phone. Children welcomed. There is a 36 bed fully self-sufficient Youth Centre which provides self-catering accommodation.
Spiritual Help: Personal retreat direction, spiritual direction, meditation.
Guests Admitted to: Unrestricted access.
Meals: Everyone eats together. Traditional food. Vegetarian and special diets.
Special Activities: Planned retreats and events. Send for brochure.
Situation: A little busy but in the countryside in sixty acres of grounds with lots of walks and super views.
Maximum Stay: 1 week.
Bookings: Letter or tel/fax 9am-5pm.
Charges: Average rate about £25 for night full board.
Access: Car route best. Enquire as to train and local bus.

HUMBERSIDE

Pocklington

Madhyamaka Buddhist Centre
Kilnwick Percy Hall
Pocklington
Humberside YO42 1UF

Tel: 01759 304863
Fax: 01759 305962
e-mail: Info@madhyamaka.org

Buddhist

The Centre is located in a very large and beautiful Georgian country mansion built in 1784. Its aim is to preserve and promote the teachings and traditions of Buddhism. There is a large Community here, ranging in age from 20 to 70 years, who regard this as their home. Some are ordained and all of them work and study together. Many are Buddhist teachers. There are group discussions, weekend and day courses throughout the year, plus a summer school. Other centres are in Bath, Buxton, and Ulverston. Some of the retreat courses have great titles – such as *The Hitch-hikers Guide to the Mind* and *Stop the Week* – but make no mistake Madhyamaka Buddhist Centre is a serious spirituality place. Courses on offer for beginners and those who are able to do more in-depth teachings.

Open: All year. Receives men, women, families, groups, non-retreatants.
Rooms: Doubles, dormitories, camping.
Facilities: Shrine room, camping, garden, library, guest lounge, payphone. Children welcomed. No smoking or alcohol.
Spiritual Help: Meditation, directed study, spiritual direction.
Guests Admitted to: Unrestricted access. Shrine room. Work of Community.

Meals: Everyone eats together. Wholefood, vegetarian. No special diets.
Special Activities: There is a special programme, including working holidays. Send for brochure – and ask about their other centres in Bath, Buxton, and Ulverston.
Situation: Quiet, in the countryside.
Maximum Stay: Open.
Bookings: Letter, telephone, fax, e-mail. Best time to phone 2pm-5pm Mon-Fri.
Charges: There are various charges but they are modest. Ask for rate details.
Access: Train, bus, car all possible. York is 16 km away. Ask for directions when you book – a small map is in the brochure.

LANCASHIRE

Blackburn

Whalley Abbey
Blackburn Diocesan Retreat House
Whalley, Clitheroe
Lancs. BB6 9SS

Tel: 01254 828400
Fax: 01254 828401

Anglican

Here is a comfortable and gracefully furnished house within the grounds of a once great Cistercian abbey steeped in history. It attracts many visitors each year. The programme of events includes quiet day and weekend retreats plus art courses, senior citizen holidays, and book, craft, and Oxfam. This can be a busy place.

Open: All year except Christmas and New Year. Receives everyone.
Rooms: 6 singles, 15 twin-doubles. No radios/tape recorders in rooms.
Facilities: Conferences, garden, library, guest lounge, TV, payphone, gift shop, coffee shop, guided tours. Children welcome.
Spiritual Help: None.
Guests Admitted to: Unrestricted access.
Meals: Everyone eats together. Traditional food. Vegetarian and special diets. DIY facilities.
Special Activities: Planned programme. Send for brochure.
Situation: Quiet and peaceful environment, with beautiful tranquil gardens where there is the ruin of a 14th century Cistercian abbey.
Maximum Stay: By arrangement.
Bookings: By letter/tel/fax – 8-4.30 Mon-Sat
Charges: £15 day only. £66 weekend full board. Group rates from £41–£87 p.p. B&B £26 per person per night.
Access: Train to Blackburn. Bus to Whalley. Car via A59 to Whalley.

Carnforth

Monastery of Our Lady of Hyning
Warton
Carnforth
Lancs. LA5 9SE   Tel: 01524 732684

Roman Catholic

Particularly suitable for private retreats and day retreats, the Monastery
is set in private grounds. In some rooms cheerful fires greet you in
winter, while there is a peaceful and welcoming atmosphere everywhere. A barn has been converted into a church where guests may join
the sisters in their daily schedule of prayer.

Open: All year except for mid-July to late August. Receives everyone.
Rooms: 8 singles, 1 double, 14 twins.
Facilities: Conference room, garden, library, guest telephone.
Spiritual Help: Personal talks, one to one retreats by arrangement.
Guests Admitted to: Chapel, choir.
Meals: Large dining-room and small dining-room serving mainly
traditional food. Vegetarian and special diets catered for.
Special Activities: Groups and individuals welcomed for day retreats,
one to one retreats by arrangement, programme of events. Send for
information.
Situation: Quiet and in the countryside.
Maximum Stay: By arrangement.
Bookings: Letter or telephone.
Charges: Ask for the tariff.
Access: Train to Carnforth. Some local buses pass the gate. Car via
M6, Exit 35, and A6.

LIVERPOOL

Liverpool

The Cenacle
7 Lance Lane
Liverpool L15 6TW   Tel: 01517 222271

Roman Catholic

The Sisters of the Cenacle offer individually directed retreats and a programme of various retreats and events. If you wish to come for a quiet
time or a day of prayer and reflection, contact the sisters' retreat team.

Open: All year, except July, August. Receives men, women, groups *for
the day only.*
Rooms: Non-residential.
Facilities: Garden, library, payphone.
Spiritual Help: Spiritual direction, personal retreat direction,
meditation.

Guests Admitted to: Everywhere.
Meals: Everyone eats together. Traditional food.
Special Activities: Day retreats and workshops. Leaflet available.
Situation: In city but quiet.
Maximum Stay: As arranged.
Bookings: Letter or telephone.
Charges: £12 per day 10am-4pm
Access: Train to Lime St station, then bus. Car: via M62.

GREATER MANCHESTER

Stockport

Shalom Spirituality Centre
I Adswood Lane West
Cale Green, Stockport SK3 8HT

Tel: 01612 927270
Fax: 01612 927470

Roman Catholic

Here, a small Community of sisters have undertaken a new adventure in caring and community in what was once a Noviciate House. This developing centre for spirituality work aims to provide day group retreats and various ways of experiencing the benefits of stillness, silence, solitude and the Good News of Christian spirituality. This is done through Scripture, dialogue, silence, symbol, music, hand massage, and reflexology. So far it all seems to be working and visitors come for a day retreat or event. The welcome is warm and friendly. The gardens, while on a corner between roads, are surprisingly peaceful and the whole place has an atmosphere of sanctuary from the busy world just outside the door. This place shows what can be achieved in providing a small and simple oasis of Christian peace in the middle of a densely populated and busy urban setting.

Open: Most of year except August and December. Receives men, women, young people, groups, non-retreatants.
Rooms: No guest rooms. Guests only come for the day.
Facilities: Chapel, quiet room. Conferences, garden, guest lounge, TV.
Spiritual Help: Spiritual direction, group sharing, meditation, Taizé Prayer.
Guests Admitted to: All guest areas, chapel, quiet room.
Meals: Meals taken in the house, usually together. Traditional food and plain. Vegetarians and special diets.
Special Activities: Individually or group-directed retreats. *Care for those who care for others. Hand massage for relaxation. Music meditation. Taizé prayers.* Spiritual direction if requested. As for details of any planned events.
Situation: Although in a busy place, it is quiet in the house.
Maximum Stay: 1 day.
Bookings: Letter/telephone/fax.
Charges: On application.
Access: Train, bus, and car all possible. There is parking at the house, but ask for detailed travel directions when you plan a visit.

MERSEYSIDE

Prescot

Loyola Hall Spirituality Centre
Warrington Road
Rainhill, Prescot
Merseyside L35 6NZ

Tel: 01514 264137
Fax: 01514 310115
e-mail: Loyola@clara.net

Roman Catholic – Ecumenical

This is a Jesuit retreat centre and that usually means some hard work on prayer, personal introspection, and spiritual growth if you want to undertake an individually guided retreat. In addition to this form of retreat, there are preached ones, days of prayer and reflection, guided prayer weeks, theme retreats on icons and the Enneagram, women's retreats, and special courses for those who work with young adults. The Centre itself is set in a park and consists of a combination of older buildings and functional new ones. The facilities are modern and excellent. The Centre has a special programme aimed at the 18-30 age groups. The colour brochures available are exceptionally well designed and informative.

Open: All year except Christmas week. Receives men, women, young people, groups, non-retreatants.
Rooms: 45 singles, 4 doubles plus dormitories. All the bedrooms will be en-suite eventually.
Facilities: Disabled – lift and loop system provided. Conferences, garden, park, library, guest lounge, payphone. Prayer rooms available.
Spiritual Help: Personal talks, group sharing on some retreats, meditation, directed study. Individually guided retreats in the tradition of St Ignatius of Loyola. Courses on spiritual direction, prayer guidance. Massage and aromatherapy. Art room. Exercise equipment to get you going – and a jacuzzi to wind you down.
Guests Admitted to: Unrestricted access.
Meals: Eaten in the guest dining rooms. Traditional food. Vegetarian and special diets.
Special Activities: Planned programme of events, including conferences, courses on spiritual direction, lecture programme, parish retreats. Send for brochures.
Situation: Quiet, in a village.
Maximum Stay: Up to 30 days depending on programme course undertaken plus a stay of 3 months if you are doing that retreat.
Bookings: Letter, telephone, fax, e-mail.
Charges: See brochures, lower prices usually available for students and unemployed. Current range £30 per night and £19 for students and registered unwaged. The retreat courses vary in prices from about £120 to £270 and the longer ones can run to £2300 for an 11-week training course.
Access: Train to Rainhill. Bus 106, 10A, 61. Car: via M62, Exit 7 to Prescot.

NORTHUMBERLAND

Alnmouth

The Friary of St Francis
Alnmouth, Alnwick
Northumberland, NE6 3NJ

Tel: 01665 830213
Fax: 01665 830580
e-mail: ssf@almouthfriary.fsnet.co.uk

Anglican

The Friary is situated on the coastline with beautiful Northumberland scenery and the Scottish borderlands near by. The Community here offer support and accommodation for those who need a retreat of a religious nature but also those who may want just a quiet break with a few days of peace and reflection.

Open: All year. No guests on Sunday evenings. Closed certain times of year. Receives men, women, young people, groups, non-retreatants.
Rooms: 12 singles.
Facilities: Disabled – a room for one person. Garden, library, guest lounge, TV, payphone. *No smoking.*
Spiritual Help: Personal talks if needed but this is a small Community with a full and busy schedule so such talks can not always be done immediately.
Guests Admitted to: Chapel, work of the Community.
Meals: Everyone eats together unless on silent retreat, then you can eat separately. Simple, traditional food. Vegetarian. Breakfast is a silent meal but you can talk at other times.
Special Activities: Planned programme of events. Send for leaflet.
Situation: Edge of village, beside the sea with great views.
Maximum Stay: Monday to Sunday afternoon.
Bookings: Letter addressed to *Guest Brother*.
Charges: By donation which is expected to be realistic – about £18-£22 per 24 hrs per person.
Access: Train to Alnmouth, 1 mile away. Bus from Alnmouth to the Friary. Car via A1. Ask for leaflet with directions map.

Berwick Upon Tweed

Marygate House
Holy Island of Lindisfarne
Berwick Upon Tweed
Northumberland TD15 2SD

Tel/Fax: 01289 389246
e-mail: ian@marygate.freeserve.co.uk

Inter-Denominational

Marygate House is situated on an island which is famous in Christian history and even today a place of pilgrimage and tourism for this very reason. The centre is very quiet in winter but busy and popular in the summer. There are two houses that form the centre. One is Marygate House which is the home of the small Community who run the place. This house accommodates up to 22 people for religious, educational or cultural purposes. The other house, Cambridge House, is for private retreats, study time or for a few days of peace and quiet. Please note that there is no medical care on Holy Island and that life on the island is dominated by the coming and going of the tides. It is safe only to cross the causeway for a period of about 6 hours twice in every 24. The Community has prayers in the Crypt at Marygate House each morning and also silent prayer there on Sunday evenings. Marygate House and Cambridge House are a world away from the one most of us know. *Love at first sight* is a common reaction of many guests. **Highly Recommended.**

Open: January 4 to December 15. Receives everyone except children as it is a place for adult quiet retreats in the houses here.
Rooms: 5 singles, 3 doubles. Dormitories. Altogether about 30 beds available. Bring your own towels, warm windproof clothes are suggested.
Facilities: Disabled. Conferences, garden, library, guest lounge, guest telephone. Pets are welcome but not to come into the kitchen. **There is a new annexe to Cambridge House for those who require wheelchair access or who have difficulty with stairs. No medical care on the island.**
Spiritual Help: Personal talks. Group sharing. Spiritual direction. Personal retreat direction. Directed study. Quiet place set aside for prayer and there are regular prayer times. Local RC and Anglican churches.
Guests Admitted to: Unrestricted access.
Meals: Everyone eats together. Traditional, wholefood, simple food. Vegetarians and special diets.
Special Activities: None.
Situation: An island accessed by car when tide is low.
Maximum Stay: 2 weeks.
Bookings: Letter/tel/fax – best mornings and then 5.30-6.30pm
Charges: Donations only – suggested amount £20 per day.
Access: Train: Berwick upon Tweed. Bus: to Beal. Car: A1, 7 miles south of Berwick upon Tweed

---

Community of Aidan and Hilda
The Open Gate
Marygate, Holy Island of Lindisfarne
Berwick upon Tweed TD15 2JZ

Tel: 01289 389222
Fax: 01289 389378
e-mail: theopengate@ndo.co.uk
Website: www. theopengate.org.uk

Inter-Denominational

The Open Gate is a cottage reteat house in a place of ancient spiritual history. There are various events, and retreats both private and group are possible. A booklet *Give Yourself a Retreat on Holy Island* has been produced to help people making a self-directed individual retreat here.

Open: All year except first 2 weeks of January. Receives everyone.
Rooms: Single and double rooms available.
Facilities: Library, guest lounge.
Spiritual Help: Personal talks. Spiritual direction. Personal retreat direction. Directed study. There are local church services available on the island and there is a chapel here.
Guests Admitted to: Unrestricted access.
Meals: *No meals are served here.* There are 4 hotels within 250 yeards of The Open Gate.
Special Activities: A leaflet detailing some events is available.
Situation: Quiet.
Maximum Stay: Open.
Bookings: Letter/tel/fax/e-mail.
Charges: £27 B&B each in double. £32 B&B in single.
Access: Train: Berwick upon Tweed. Car route easiest.

Carrshield

**Throssel Hole Buddhist Abbey
Carrshield, Hexham
Northumberland, NE47 8AL**
Tel: 01434 345204
Fax: 01434 345216

Buddhist

Since the time of Buddha many schools of Buddhism have developed. This monastery, centre of the Soto Zen School of Buddhism, practises Serene Reflection Meditation tradition which is Japanese Soto Zen, Chinese Ts'ao Tung. Here men and women have equal status and recognition and train together in the Buddhist priesthood. A lay programme is available in which all may participate. A variety of services for lay Buddhists is available, including naming ceremonies for children; cemetery plot and memorial services; and spiritual counselling by letter or telephone. There is a quarterly journal and a mail-order service offering books, taped lectures, meditation benches and cushions. The monks run retreats and make public talks outside the monastery. There are sub-priories in Reading and Telford staffed by monks and associated groups of lay people meeting together in 21 cities in Britain plus four in Europe. There is a sister monastery, Shasta Abbey, in California. If you are interested in any of these monasteries or groups, write for information.

Open: All year except for pre-published periods. Receives men and women over 18 years. Families only received on specific weekends. Group educational visits from schools and colleges by arrangement. Non-retreatants taken for tours of the monastery by appointment.
Rooms: Dormitories – men and women are housed separately.
Facilities: Disabled – limited. Garden, park, library, common room, payphone. Children are welcomed but for specific events – discuss this with the guest master.
Spiritual Help: Spiritual direction. Meditation. Classes led by senior monk – private spiritual guidance on request. Full instruction given in meditation. Guidance is also given for private study and reflection.

Guests Admitted to: The ceremony hall, lay common-room, ceremonies with monks, and work of Community.
Meals: Taken together whenever possible. Vegetarian food.
Special Activities: Special programme, public talks, group evenings, day retreats, long retreats. Send for brochures.
Situation: Very quiet in the countryside. Designated area of outstanding natural beauty.
Maximum Stay: By arrangement with guest master.
Bookings: Letter or tel/fax – 9-11.15am and 2-4.45pm.
Charges: For a stay of a month or longer £13 per night. Suggested donations: weekend retreats £50, other retreats £20 per night.
Access: Train: from Newcastle, or Carlisle to Hexham. Then taxi. Bus: from Newcastle to Hexham and Allendale. Car: via M6 or A1 to Bishop Auckland.

Riding Mill

Shepherds Dene Retreat House and Conference Centre
Riding Mill
Northumberland, NE44 6AF   Tel: 01434 682212
                                            Fax: 01434 682311
                      e-mail: sheperds_dene@newcastle.anglican.org
Anglican

Open: All year. Receives everyone – *but almost all are groups, and individuals only from time to time at present.*
Rooms: 7 singles, 12 double.
Facilities: Conferences, garden, TV, payphone. Children welcomed. Pets by arrangement.
Spiritual Help: None.
Guests Admitted to: Chapel.
Meals: Everyone eats together. Traditional and wholefood. Vegetarians and special diets catered.
Special Activities: A few open events otherwise they organise group retreats.
Situation: Quiet, in the countryside.
Maximum Stay: By arrangement.
Bookings: Letter or telephone.
Charges: £21.45 B&B £7.90 Lunch. Evening meal £8.
Access: Train station 1¼ miles away. Bus stop ¾ miles away. Car route easiest, but ask for details of other travel arrangements.

WEST MIDLANDS

Solihull

Fellowship of Contemplative Prayer
202 Ralph Road
Solihull, West Midlands B90 3LE   Tel/Fax: 0121 7456522

Inter-Denominational

The Fellowship of Contemplative Prayer is a loose-knit association of individuals and groups who follow the way of prayer taught by the founder, Robert Coulson, which is called *The Prayer of Stillness*. Central administration is minimal and groups and retreats are largely self-run. There are various publications available and various retreats offered around the country. An annual newsletter gives details of Fellowship contacts and retreats held in the U.K. and Ireland. Membership and details are available on request.

YORKSHIRE (SOUTH)

Sheffield

Whirlow Grange Diocesan Conference Centre
Eccleshall Road South
Sheffield S11 9PZ   Tel: 0114 2363173
                                           Fax: 0114 2620717

Anglican

The Centre occupies a grey-stone house on a rise on the outskirts of Sheffield, near Peak District beauty spots. The place is rather institutional, but it has comfortable rooms and facilities. There are healing seminars, sacred-dance group weekends and Franciscan directed retreats.

Open: All year. Receives men, women, young people, families, groups, non-retreatants.
Rooms: 20 singles, 10 twin-bedded rooms.
Facilities: Disabled, conferences, garden, bookstall, library, guest lounge, TV, payphone. Children welcomed.
Spiritual Help: Personal talks, group sharing, meditation, directed study.
Guests Admitted to: Unrestricted access, chapel.
Meals: Taken in guest house. Traditional food. Vegetarian and special diets catered.
Special Activities: Planned programme of events. Send for brochure.
Situation: Quiet and on the outskirts of the city. Peak District National Park within easy reach.
Maximum Stay: Open.
Bookings: Letter, telephone, fax.
Charges: On application.
Access: By rail, bus or car (via A625).

Unstone Grange
Crow Lane
Unstone, Sheffield S18 5AL   Tel/Fax: 01246 412344

Mind-Body-Spirit

A Victorian country house set in five acres and run by a local charity with the aim of catering for community and youth groups of all types.

The hope is that such groups will use Unstone to access and express their creative spirit, be it through dance, drama, craft work, writing, painting. music, meditation, body work, healing or any other of the various activities which increase self-awareness and inner growth. The view taken here is very much holistic and devoted to the idea of personal creative growth. The guiding principle is *Unity in Diversity*.

Open: All year. Receives everyone.
Facilities: Conferences, camping, garden, guest lounges, small library, payphone. Children welcomed. Pets by permission.
Spiritual Help: Re-birthing, relaxation massage, reflexology, Reiki. Sweat Lodge ceremonies.
Guests Admitted to: Unrestricted access.
Meals: Taken in house or self-catering. Wholefood, vegetarian, vegan, organic.
Special Activities: Programme. Brochure/newsletter available.
Situation: Quiet in the countryside.
Maximum Stay: Open.
Bookings: Letter, telephone.
Charges: From £11 per person per night self-catered to £36 board and room. Therapies by arrangement. Enquire what may be included when booking.
Access: Train or car.

YORKSHIRE (NORTH)

Ampleforth

Ampleforth Abbey and The Grange
Ampleforth
N.Yorks. YO6 4EN   Tel: 01439 766889
                                        Fax: 01439 766755
                          e-mail: pastoral@ampleforth.org.uk

Roman Catholic

Ampleforth has several sites – the Guesthouse, the Grange, Archway, Central Building and Park House, all adding up to some 60 beds. The facilities at this large and busy monastery are excellent. There are sometimes single rooms in the monastery for men but for staying in the monastery write to the guest master there. The course and retreat programme is extensive and thoroughly Roman Catholic in nature. It ranges from celebrating Christianity and Lent retreats to unfolding God's Word through scripture studies and a look at C.S. Lewis. Anyone interested in living the monastic life and seeking God by prayer and apostolic work in the Community is welcome to stay and an e-mail to laurence@ampleforth.org.uk will get you started in that direction. A very well-known and popular place to go on retreat.

Open: All year except Christmas and 2 weeks in August. Receives everyone.
Rooms: 27 singles, 8 twin-doubles.

Facilities: Disabled. Church, choir, chapel, conferences, guest lounge, payphone, plenty of places to walk. Bookshop.
Spiritual Help: None – but see programme.
Guests Admitted to: Chapel, choir, work of Community.
Meals: Served in guest house. Traditional food. Vegetarian and special diets.
Special Activities: Full programme – ask for details.
Situation: Quiet, in the countryside.
Maximum Stay: 4 days.
Bookings: Letter or telephone.
Charges: Monastery by donation, Grange £35 full board, £28 B&B plus lunch/supper, £21 B&B. The charges at Ampleforth are variable and are given in the programme brochure.
Access: Train and coach: to York, 23 miles away. Bus: ask about local public transport when you book. Car: via B1363 from York. Ask for travel directions leaflet.

Kettlewell

**Scargill House
Kettlewell, Skipton
N.Yorks. BD23 5HU**

Tel: 01756 760234
Fax: 01756 760499
e-mail: info@scargillhouse.co.uk
Website:www.scargillhouse.co.uk

Anglican – Inter-Denominational

The Scargill Community is a group of Christian men and women from all walks of life who come together for a few years to live and work and worship together. The amenities in this large establishment are modern and well-considered with comfort and peacefulness in mind. The location of the house and building is lovely. A busy place as some 90 guests can be accommodated – but silence can be found here in the chapel, the quiet room, and in the extensive grounds.

Open: All year with a few weeks of closure in January, July and September and Christmas week. Receives everyone.
Rooms: 16 singles, 20 doubles, 13 cabins accomodating guests in bunk beds, 2 family rooms.
Facilities: Disabled – *limited*. Chapel. Conferences, garden, park, library, guest lounges, payphone. Children welcomed.
Spiritual Help: Personal talks, group sharing, preached retreats with individual talks.
Guests Admitted to: Chapel, house and grounds.
Meals: Everyone eats together. Traditional simple food.
Special Activities: Planned programme. Send for information.
Situation: Quiet in the countryside in the Yorkshire Dales National Park.
Maximum Stay: By arrangement.
Bookings: Letter, telephone, fax.
Charges: See programme for charges on courses, but private

retreatants pay £21-27 B&B, £40 full board. 20% discount if you stay in the bunk bed accommodation.

Access: Train: nearest station is 15 miles away but there are arrangements with local taxi company so ask for details when you book. Car route easy.

Kirkby Fleetham

Kirkby Fleetham Hall
Kirkby Fleetham, Northallerton
N. Yorks. DL7 0SU   Tel/Fax: 01609 748747

Mind-Body-Spirit

A big and rather elegant English house as you approach, but inside all is devoted to the art of living in peace and well being. The range of courses on offer covers yoga, regression therapy or soul drama as it is now called, the art of loving in peace, Shiatsu, and neuro-linguistic programming.

Open: March–October. Receives men, women, groups, non-retreatants.
Rooms: Doubles but singles available for a supplementary charge.
Facilities: Garden, guest lounge, TV, payphone.
Spiritual Help: None, but a therapy centre is being planned.
Guests Admitted to: Guest areas.
Meals: Everyone eats together. Vegetarian wholefood. Special diets catered.
Special Activities: Planned events – send for brochure.
Situation: Very quiet in the countryside.
Maximum Stay: By arrangement.
Bookings: Letter.
Charges: See programme brochure.
Access: Train to Northallerton which in 8 miles away. Bus service limited. Car route easiest.

Scarborough

Highbank Wholistic Hotel
5 Givendale Road
Scarborough, Yorkshire YO12 GLE   Tel: 01723 365265

Mind-Body-Spirit

Open: All year. Receives all.
Rooms: 1 single, 4 doubles. 1 dormitory.
Facilities: Garden, library, guest lounge, TV, guest telephone.
Spiritual Help: Personal talks. Meditation. Aromatherapy. Creative visualisation. Bereavement counselling.
Guests Admitted to: Unrestricted access.
Meals: Taken in guest house. Traditional/vegetarian/organic foods. Special diets.

Special Activities: None.
Situation: Quiet in town close to sea and parks.
Maximum Stay: None.
Bookings: Letter/tel/fax.
Charges: From £19 B&B. Therapies from £20. Ask for other rates.
Access: Train, Bus, Car all possible. Ask for their directions.

Wydale Hall and Emmaus Centre
Brompton by Sawdon
Scarborough
N. Yorks. YO13 9DG

Tel: 01723 859270
Fax: 01723 859702

Anglican – Inter-Denominational

An old house set in 14 acres with formal gardens with good views to the Yorkshire Wolds. Quiet Christian hospitality is on offer here with the purpose of trying to create a place where people can unwind, rest and perhaps draw nearer to God. The retreats and one-day workshops cover a wide range from assertiveness skills and stress management to a Creative Arts Retreat Movement painting and prayer retreat.

Open: January 9 to December 28. Receives men, women, young people, families, groups, non-retreatants.
Rooms: 10 singles. 17 doubles (7 rooms en-suite).
Facilities: Disabled. Chapel, conferences, garden, library, guest lounge, bookstall, TV, payphone, direct dialling. Children welcome. Guide dogs only. Self-catering in the Emmaus Centre.
Spiritual Help: Personal talks possible.
Guests Admitted to: Unrestricted access except staff areas.
Meals: Everyone eats together. Traditional food. Vegetarian and special diets.
Special Activities: Programme of events. Send for brochure.
Situation: Quiet and in the countryside.
Maximum Stay: By arrangement.
Bookings: Letter, telephone, fax.
Charges: Send for details as there are a number of rate charges
Access: Train: to Scarborough. Buses: from Scarborough. Car: Wydale Hall is 1 mile north of A170.

Skipton

Parcevall Hall
Appletreewick
Skipton
N. Yorks. BD23 6DG

Tel: 01756 720213

Anglican – Ecumenical

This is an Elizabethan manor house with grand views in a super setting whose interior is filled with oak and atmosphere. Legends and history abound, and the nine acres of garden are said to have been admired by the late Queen Mary. A traditional place for either a private retreat or participation in the programme of events which includes many parish group retreats but also retreats like the *Spirituality of Julian of Norwich, Painting and Prayer*, and *Spring Walkers Weekend Retreat*.

Open: All year except Christmas period. Receives everyone.
Rooms: 7 singles, 10 doubles.
Facilities: Conferences, garden, library, guest lounge, TV, payphone.
Spiritual Help: Personal talks. Spiritual direction, personal retreat direction.
Guests Admitted to: Chapel.
Meals: Everyone eats together. Traditional food with provision for vegetarian and special diets by prior arrangement only.
Special Activities: Programme of events. Send for brochure.
Situation: Very quiet, in the countryside.
Maximum Stay: 1 week.
Bookings: By letter.
Charges: Currently £38.50 full board per 24 hrs.
Access: By car or train to Skipton, then by taxi.

Thirsk

Holy Rood House and Community
Centre for Health and Pastoral Care
10 Sowerby Road
Sowerby, Thirsk
N. Yorks. YO7 1HX

Tel: 01845 522580
Fax: 01845 527300
e-mail: holyroodhouse@centrethirsk.fsnet.co.uk
Website: www.holyroodhouse.freeuk.com

Ecumenical

Holy Rood House is run by the North of England Christian Healing Trust and all are welcome to visit. The healing approach is holistic and a safe place is offered where guests can begin the healing process and discover new inner resources and strengths. It is a place for prayer, fun, reflection, exploration and discovery. Some of the retreats and courses on offer include *Sexuality and Spirituality, Women's Spirituality, Celebrating Our Bodies, Art and Spirituality, Women and Healing*. All ages may enjoy this oasis of peace and tranquillity where a gentle Christian ethos forms the background to all activities and therapies. Holy Rood House is a member of the British Association of Counselling and the National Association of Christian Communities and Network. **Highly Recommended.**

Open: All year except August. Receives everyone.
Rooms: 6 to 7 singles, 8 doubles.
Facilities: Disabled ground floor room and chair lift to first floor. Chapel. Conferences, garden, library, guest lounge, TV, payphone, direct dialling. Children and pets welcomed. Aromatherapy, massage, art therapy, professional counselling.

Spiritual Help: Personal talks, group sharing, meditation, directed study, counselling, ministry of healing, personal retreat direction, spiritual direction.

Guests Admitted to: Unrestricted access. Chapel. Work of community.

Meals: Everyone eats together. Good wholefood cooking with provision for vegetarians if required. DIY food in August if you visit then. Special diets.

Special Activities: Planned programme of events and courses. Send for brochure. Counselling, psychotherapy, creative arts, massage and body therapies. There is no nursing here and no treatment offered to those with mental health problems who may create an unsafe environment for others.

Situation: Quiet and in the village.

Maximum Stay: 3 weeks.

Bookings: Letter or telephone.

Charges: Please enquire when booking but £32.50 for 24 hour stay is the current recommended rate. Donation basis for having therapy.

Access: Good train and coach connection. Train to Thirsk 1½ miles away. Bus to Thirsk, then 10-minute walk. Car via A61 to B1448, or A19 and A168.

Whitby

Sneaton Castle Centre
Whitby, N. Yorkshire YO21 3QN

Tel: 01947 600051
Fax: 01947 603490
e-mail: holden@freeserve.co.uk
Website: www.sneatoncastle.co.uk

Anglican

A peaceful and picturesque location providing Christian venues for conferences, B&B, music workshops, and retreats. A big place with room for over a 100 guests.

Open: All year but Christmas week. Receives everyone.

Rooms: 40 singles, 30 doubles. Non-smoking.

Facilities: Disabled. Conferences, garden, guest lounge, TV, payphone.

Spiritual Help: Personal talks if needed.

Guests Admitted to: Public rooms and Chapel.

Meals: Everyone eats together. Vegetarian and special diets.

Special Activities: Currently none but ask as a programme is being considered.

Situation: On the edge of a fishing town and near the moors and national park.

Maximum Stay: None.

Bookings: Letter/tel/fax.

Charges: B&B £18 to £29 full board per person. En-suite facilities add £7.

Access: Train: Middlesborough. Bus: Whitby. Car: motorway.

St Hilda's Priory
Sneaton Castle
Whitby, N. Yorkshire YO21 3QN

Tel: 01947 602079
Fax: 01947 820854
e-mail: ohppriorywhitby@btinternet.com

Anglican

The Priory itself is not a retreat house as such. Guests come for a quiet retreat on an individual basis and there is no structured programme other than the daily pattern of worship.

Open: Open all year except 3 weeks in August. Recieves men and women.
Rooms: 6 singles. 2 doubles.
Facilities: Disabled. Garden, library, guest lounge, use of telephone if needed.
Spiritual Help: Personal talks, personal retreat direction.
Guests Admitted to: Chapel. Refectory.
Meals: Main meals taken together. DIY facilities. Vegetarian and special diets.
Special Activities: None.
Situation: In the countryside, edge of town and near national park.
Maximum Stay: 1 week.
Bookings: Letter.
Charges: Donations, suggested at £25 per day full board, £10-£15 per day self-catering.
Access: Train: Train to Scarborough via York. Bus: to Whitby. Coach: Coastliner. Car: From Teeside A171. From York A169.

St Oswald's Pastoral Centre
Woodlands Drive
Sleights, Whitby
N. Yorks. YO21 1RY

Tel: 01947 810496
Fax: 01947 810750
e-mail: ohpstos@globalnet.co.uk

Anglican

The sisters welcome guests to conducted retreats, individually guided retreats, and for private quiet time for rest and study. The facilities for guests are in a small complex of buildings set in beautiful Yorkshire surroundings.

Open: All year except Christmas and August. Receives men, women, young people, groups, non-retreatants.
Rooms: 8 singles, 4 doubles.
Facilities: Garden, library, guest lounge, TV, payphone.
Spiritual Help: Personal talks, meditation, group sharing, directed study.
Guests Admitted to: Unrestricted access except to community quarters. Chapel.
Meals: Everyone eats together. Traditional simple food. Vegetarian

and special diets catered within reason.
Special Activities: Planned programme of events. Send for the brochure.
Situation: Very quiet, in the countryside near to the moors.
Maximum Stay: 1 week.
Bookings: Letter or telephone/fax – mornings and then 2-6pm best.
Charges: By donation. Guidelines available so ask when booking.
Access: There is a leaflet available which gives full information.

York

St Bede's Pastoral Centre
21 Blossom Street
York YO24 1AQ

Tel: 01904 464900
Fax: 01904 464967
e-mail: stbedes@freenetname.co.uk
Website: www.stbedes.org.uk

Roman Catholic

St Bede's was founded in 1987 as a joint venture by the Middlesborough Diocese and the Ampleforth monks. It is a base for ecumenical work right in the heart of York and next door to the historic Bar Convent which has modern comfortable accommodation on a B&B basis (Tel: 01904 629359). St Bede's is a lovely place with a museum, cafe, shop, and gallery around a central courtyard. There is a pretty small garden at the rear which is very pleasant. There are events, exhibitions and talks throughout the year. There are Julian meetings, Bible study, and prayer and reflection courses. A friendly and welcoming place in the heart of a great and hospitable city.

Open: All year except Christmas. Receives everyone.
Rooms: Accommodation for about 20 people in singles and doubles.
Facilities: Chapel. Disabled. Conferences, garden, library, 2 guest lounges, TV, payphone, museum, shop, exhibition hall, cafe. Children welcomed.
Spiritual Help: Spiritual direction, personal retreat direction, meditation.
Guests Admitted to: Chapel and areas open to the public.
Meals: Food at the Bar Convent Cafe next door.
Special Activities: Programme of events and courses. Send for brochure.
Situation: Busy and in the city, but once inside quite peaceful.
Maximum Stay: Day only at St Bede's, otherwise B&B at Bar Convent.
Bookings: Letter or telephone.
Charges: Ask for current charges for B&B at Bar Convent.
Access: By rail, bus or car to York then walk.

YORKSHIRE (WEST)

Hepworth

**Foster Place Retreat House
Hepworth, Near Holmfirth
West Yorkshire HD7 1TN**   Tel: 01484 688680

Inter-Denominational

Foster Place has as its aim the provision of what people may need in order to recover a sense of well-being and stillness. For this reason there are a selection of types of retreating here – quiet days, group retreats, and various spiritual days such as *Preparing for Holy Week*. One of the most important kinds of retreat is also available which is the *guided retreat* where an individual is taken through their time on retreat by a spiritual guide – there is talking, guidance, reflection, perhaps readings. No previous retreat expereince is needed for this. **There is no overnight accommodation here.** The place itself is a homely 300-year-old stone dwelling with a maze of rooms and an extensive library.

Open: Daily. Receives everyone.
Rooms: None
Facilities: Garden, library.
Spiritual Help: Personal talks, group sharing, spiritual direction, personal retreat direction, meditation.
Guests Admitted to: Unrestricted.
Meals: Everyone eats together. Wholefood. Vegetarian.
Special Activities: Planned programme. Send for brochure.
Situation: Very quiet in countryside.
Maximum Stay: Not applicable.
Bookings: Letter/tel.
Charges: See brochure – Weekend retreat £40 – a series of weekends (5) is about £200 which is what you are asked to sign up for at the moment. This includes tuition and course materials and lunch.
Access: Ask for directions.

Ilkley

**Briery Retreat Centre
38 Victoria Avenue
Ilkley, W. Yorks. LS29 9BW**   Tel: 01943 607287
                                                 Fax: 01943 604449
                                                 e-mail: srscp@aol.com

Roman Catholic

The Briery Retreat Team are Sisters of the Cross and Passion and their programme is firmly spiritually based in such traditions as the Rosary, preached retreats, and transformation retreats. Individuals and small groups may make a retreat by joining some of the Parish groups on a weekend if they want. Directed and private retreats are also available.

Open: All year except Easter Week and over Christmas and New Year. Receives men, women, young people over 18, groups.
Rooms: 23 single, 4 doubles.
Facilities: Disabled – limited facilities. Conferences, garden, guest lounge, TV, payphone.
Spiritual Help: Personal talks, meditation, spiritual direction, group sharing, personal retreat direction.
Guests Admitted to: Unrestricted access.
Meals: Everyone eats together. Traditional food.
Special Activities: Planned programme of events. Send for the brochure.
Situation: 10-minutes walk from Ilkley town but in countryside and surrounded by Ilkley Moor.
Maximum Stay: 10 days.
Bookings: Letter or telephone.
Charges: Suggested offerings about £28 full board per day to retreats ranging from £60 to a 6-day one at £170. Day groups can have coffee, lunch and tea for £12.
Access: Train, bus, car all possible.

Leeds

Hinsley Hall
Diocese of Leeds Pastoral Centre
62 Headingley Lane
Leeds LS6 2BX

Tel: 0113 2618000
Fax: 0113 2242406

Roman Catholic

A rather grand place with any number of comfortable, modern, high standard rooms and facilities. There is a chapel with new furnishings, a library and a bookshop. The Yorkshire Dales are within easy reach.

Open: All year. Receives men, women, groups.
Rooms: 38 singles, 16 doubles. Mainly en-suite.
Facilities: Disabled. Conferences, garden, library, chapel, guest lounge, TV, payphone.
Spiritual Help: None.
Guests Admitted to: Public rooms and chapel.
Meals: Dining room. Traditional food. Vegetarian and special diets.
Special Activities: None.
Situation: Rather busy.
Maximum Stay: By arrangement.
Bookings: Letter/tel/fax.
Charges: £49-£75 per person per day full board.
Access: Train: 2 miles from main station. Bus: Main bus route. Car: A660 from Leeds.

Mirfield

Community of the Resurrection

Stocksbank Road
Mirfield, W. Yorkshire WF14 0BN

Tel: 01924 494318
Fax: 01924 490489
e-mail: cr@mirfield.org.uk
Website: www.mirfield.org.uk

Anglican

Here is a famous monastery and Community which finds its roots in
the monastic tradition of the Christian Church – a tradition concerned
with the quest for God in prayer and worship in the common life and
in work and service. The church, the chapel, the buildings are splendid and there are lots of them. There is an extensive programme of
courses, retreats and events. **Highly Recommended.**

Open: All year except July. Receives men, women, young people,
groups.
Rooms: 25 singles, 2 doubles. Guest accommodation is in guest house
where silence is the norm.
Facilities: Park, library, guest lounge, payphone.
Spiritual Help: Personal talks. Spiritual direction. Personal retreat
direction. Directed study.
Guests Admitted to: Unrestricted access.
Meals: Everyone eats together. Simple food. Vegetarian.
Special Activities: Planned programme and details of other houses.
Send for the brochures.
Situation: Quiet in countryside.
Maximum Stay: 2 weeks.
Bookings: Letter.
Charges: See brochures.
Access: Train: Wakefield Westgate. Bus: from Leeds or Huddersfield.
Coach: To Dewsbury. Car: M1 Exit 40, M62 Exit 25.

Queensbury

Mountain Hall
Queensbury
W. Yorks. BD13 1LH

Tel: 01274 816258

Mind-Body-Spirit

Mountain Hall is perched 1200 feet up, affording magnificent views
over the city of Bradford, the Dales, and to the distant mountains. Built
by a local mill owner in the last century as a social institution for his
workers, it now functions as a residential centre for rest and theme holidays, special interest courses and guided retreats. What is meant by
the latter is a retreat from ordinary life into a peaceful environment
where complementary therapies will help you heal yourself. What's on

offer can include aromatherapy, Bach Flower Remedies, Chakra balancing, Chi Kung, massage, meditation, reflexology, crystals, and visualisation. There is an annual programme – a mixed choice of offerings here.

Open: All year. Receives men, women, groups, non-retreatants.
Rooms: 5 singles, 5 doubles, some twins.
Facilities: Conferences, guest lounge, TV, payphone. Car parking.
Spiritual Help: Personal talks, meditation, directed study, personal retreat direction. Various relaxation techniques and methods.
Guests Admitted to: All public rooms.
Meals: Everyone eats together in guest dining room. Traditional food. Vegetarian. Special diets (supplementary charge).
Special Activities: Planned programme of events. Send for the brochure.
Situation: Quiet.
Maximum Stay: By arrangement.
Bookings: Letter/telephone.
Charges: Currently £20 B&B per night, 2-night retreat package with therapies and workshop at £135. 2-day courses run about £80 plus accommodation costs.
Access: Train or bus to Bradford or Halifax. Car route via A644.

Todmorden

Losang Dragpa Buddhist Centre
Dobroyd Castle
Pexwood Road
Todmorden, W. Yorks. OL14 7JJ

Tel: 01706 812247
Fax: 01706 818901
e-mail: info@losangdragpa.co.uk
Website: www.losangdragpa.co.uk

Buddhist

A growing Community of over 25 live in this old castle and they offer a very wide range of courses and retreats, some with intriguing titles such as *Free Your Mind*, *Patience*, and *Dancing in the Play of Impermanence*. There are beginners classes. Many projects are in hand here to transform the place and its 24 acres of grounds plus a walled Victorian garden. To help in all this, there are working holidays available which means 35 hours a week work in exchange for food, accommodation and teachings and there is a leaflet available giving you all the details. Sounds a good deal. Losang Dragpa Centre is set in a lovely place and is part of the New Kadampa Tradition of Buddhism, a tradition founded in the West by the Venerable Geshe Kelsang Gyatso, a respected scholar and meditation master from Tibet who has written extensively on Buddhism and founded other centres around the world. **Highly Recommended.**

Open: Most of year except January retreat period but guests can stay over it. Receives men, women, young people.

Rooms: 12 singles, 2 doubles, dormitories.
Facilities: Garden, park, library, guest lounge, payphone. No smoking, silence in public rooms.
Spiritual Help: Meditation, directed study.
Guests Admitted to: Unrestricted. Shrine room, work of Community.
Meals: Everyone eats together. Vegetarian, organic.
Special Activities: Planned programme of events – weekend retreats, residential courses, meditation classes and workshops, day courses, working holidays. Send for the brochure.
Situation: Very quiet near a village but in countryside.
Maximum Stay: By arrangement.
Bookings: Letter, tel/fax – 2-4pm, e-mail.
Charges: For a weekend retreat from about £70 for a single room to £63 per person in a double. Dormitory around £45, bring your own sleeping bag. The programme details charges for the various types of retreats and stays here.
Access: Train or car both good. By train only a 15-minute walk from station – but it is uphill all the way.

Our hearts were made for you, O God, and will not rest until they rest in you.

SAINT AUGUSTINE

WALES

Abergynolwyn

**The Grail Retreat Centre
Tan y Bryn House
Tan y Bryn Street
Abergynolwyn
Near Tywyn, Gwynedd LL36 9YA**

Tel: 01654 782268 or 01686 668502

Inter-Denominational

Situated in the Celtic heartland of Mid-Wales amid mountains and lakes and only seven miles from the sea, The Grail Retreat Centre has its own chapel and is, appropriately, near a lake which translates from the Welsh as Lake of the Peaceful Retreat. The director of the Centre is an Anglican priest and he leads retreats along with others. Some of the retreats include such as those on mystical teaching in world religions, native peoples' spiritualities – Aboriginal, Bushmen and Native American, contemplative circle dancing, sorting out Christian beliefs, the inclusive church and contemplative prayer. Most retreats are 2 days. An expanded programme for the coming years is in development so do write for brochures.

Open: All year for groups except for individuals for the hermitage. Receives men, women, young people, groups.
Rooms: 2 singles, 4 doubles, hermitage available. Additional accommodation in nearby village homes.
Facilities: Library, guest lounge.
Spiritual Help: Personal talks, group sharing, meditation, spiritual direction.
Guests Admitted to: Chapel.
Meals: Taken in room. Traditional/Vegetarian food. Special diets.
Special Activities: Planned programme. Send for brochure.
Situation: Very quiet in countryside.
Maximum Stay: By arrangement or by event.
Bookings: Letter or telephone evenings.
Charges: Suggested rate between £35 and £55 per 24hrs.
Access: Train and Bus No. 30 to Tywyn. Car route A489, then B4405 to village. See map on brochure.

Anglesey

**Tre-ysgawen Hall
Capel Coch, Llangefni
Isle of Anglesey LL77 7UR**

Tel: 01248 750750
Fax: 01248 750035

Mind-Body-Spirit

This is a country house hotel in the heartland of Anglesey with all the facilities you would expect of such a place from the 1882 drawing room and library to an American type bar, four-poster beds and jacuzzi baths. However, do not let the luxury put you off for Tre-ysgawen runs a serious programme of events designed to deepen spiritual awareness and the gaining of self-revelation. The range of courses is wide from meditation practices to healing.

Open: All year. Receives all guests.
Rooms: 1 single, 18 doubles/twins.
Facilities: Disabled, conferences, garden, guest lounge, TV, payphone, direct dialling.
Spiritual Help: Personal talks and group work. Group sharing. Meditation.
Guests Admitted to: Unrestricted access except for staff rooms.
Meals: Restaurant type catering.
Special Activities: A planned programme of courses – send for current brochure.
Situation: Very quiet and tranquil in countryside.
Maximum Stay: Usually for a course.
Bookings: Letter, telephone, fax.
Charges: £285 per course everything included. £21.50 for day which includes morning coffee, lunch and afternoon tea. Other rates on demand.
Access: Ask for brochure which details routes by car.

Bangor

Life Foundation International Course Centre
Nant Ffrancon, Bethesda
Bangor, Gwynedd LL57 2EG   Tel: 01248 602900
                                        Fax: 01248 602004
                          e-mail: enquiries@lifefoundation.org.uk
                          Website: www.lifefoundation.org.uk

Mind-Body-Spirit – Yoga

Situated in the beautiful Welsh mountains of Snowdonia National Park, this Centre is the home base of the World Peace Flame, a peace initiative by peacemakers around the world. The team at the Centre are from a wide range of backgrounds who have come together to provide spiritual awareness, self-empowerment, and self-development courses. Specialities include Dru Yoga, meditation retreats and spiritual development courses. *Tools for transformation* sums it up best.

Open: For retreat and course programme. Receives men, women and groups.
Rooms: 3 singles, 3 doubles. No smoking. No alcohol.
Facilities: See brochure.
Spiritual Help: Inner self-development, self-help tools, yoga, meditation.

Guests Admitted to: Unrestricted access.
Meals: Everyone eats together. All meals are vegetarian.
Special Activities: Programme of events. Brochure available.
Situation: Welsh mountains of Snowdonia National Park.
Maximum Stay: Duration of retreat.
Bookings: Letter/tel 10am-5pm.
Charges: 2-day retreats from £130. 6-day retreats £340.
Access: Bus, coach and car all possible. Ask for travel directions.

Brecon

Coleg Trefeca
Trefeca
Talgarth, Brecon
Powys LD3 OPP

Tel/Fax: 01874 711423
e-mail: feca@surfaid.org
Website: www.ebcpcw.org.uk/pcwtrefeca.htm

Presbyterian Church of Wales

The centre consists of a group of 18th-century buildings and a modern block, standing in five acres of grounds set in the Brecon Beacons National Park. It was once the home of Howell Harris (1714-1773), one of those who led the evangelical revival in Wales. Short retreats, ecumenical activities, holiday weeks for older folk and young people are on offer. There are healing retreats and a children's weekend as well. The programme brochure and retreats are in both Welsh and English. A good place for a stimulating retreat, mixing with other like-minded people. Operates principally on a group booking system but can take individuals on a B&B basis at any time and on a full board basis when a group is in residence.

Open: All year. Receives men, women, young people, families, groups and non-retreatants.
Rooms: 19 twin-bedded doubles.
Facilities: Some for disabled but do enquire. Conferences, garden, library, guest lounge, TV and payphone. Children welcomed. Pets by arrangement.
Spiritual Help: Personal talks if requested. One warden is an ordained minister. Group sharing during annual healing week service. Directed study as part of courses.
Guests Admitted to: Unrestricted access.
Meals: Everyone eats together. Traditional home cooking with provision for vegetarian and special diets by prior arrangement only.
Special Activities: Planned programme, though groups, churches and secular organisations may follow their own programme.
Situation: Very quiet, in an area of outstanding natural beauty. 10 miles from Brecon and an ideal centre for those who wish to walk, climb, pony-trek, or simply admire the views.
Maximum Stay: By arrangement.
Bookings: Letter or telephone but must confirm in writing.
Charges: Reasonable but see brochure.

Access: Train to Abergavenny. Bus to Brecon, then pick-up by prior arrangement. Car route via B4560.

**Llangasty Retreat House
Llangasty, Brecon
Powys LD3 7PJ**

Tel: 01874 658250
Fax: 01874 658328

Church in Wales (Anglican) – Ecumenical

This isolated and large stone house, hidden away from roads and the busy world, is comfortable, cheerful and overlooks a marvellous lake. There are magnificent views to the Black Mountains and superb walking.

Open: All year. Receives men, women, young people, families, groups.
Rooms: 9 singles, 3 doubles – there will be 9 singles plus 6 twin rooms when extensions are completed and better disabled facilities.
Facilities: Conferences, garden, library, guest lounge, payphone, direct dialling. Children welcomed.
Spiritual Help: Personal talks, group sharing, meditation, spiritual direction.
Guests Admitted to: Unrestricted access except for the kitchen. Chapel.
Meals: Everyone eats together. Traditional food, home baking. Vegetarian and special diets by arrangement.
Special Activities: Planned events including quiet days with Benedictine spirituality and an open retreat entirely in Welsh. Send for brochure.
Situation: Very quiet, in the countryside.
Maximum Stay: By arrangement.
Bookings: Telephone but confirm by letter.
Charges: Ask for current rates.
Access: By car via Brecon.

Builth Wells

**The Rowan Tree Centre
The Skreen
Erwood, Builth Wells
Powys LD2 3SJ**

Tel: 01982 560210
Fax: 01982 560470
e-mail: marylewis@btinternet.com

Ecumenical

The Skreen has long enjoyed a reputation for being a place where you may search, explore, share, be silent, worship and be at peace with yourself. This is a centre offering a major programme focused on the study and practice of contemplative and creative theology, spirituality, and liturgy with many outstanding people as leaders and teachers. Some examples of courses are *Seeking Revelation for Today*, *Living Spirituality from the Banks of the Nile*, *Healing Function of the Imagination*, *Cosmic Images*, and *Celtic Desert Retreat*. Many of the leaders, like Victor de Waal, Mary Lewis, and Wendy Robinson, are much admired for their retreat work. Sometimes there are also transpersonal psychology weekends by trained counsellors and psychotherapists. The house is beautifully situated above the River Wye, near a small village. This is one of the most admired and respected retreat centres in Britain. **Highly Recommended.**

Open: For all programmed events. Receives men and women.
Rooms: 2 singles, 5 doubles. 1 hermitage.
Facilities: Chapel, garden, library. Out-going calls only guest telephone.
Spiritual Help: Personal talks. Group sharing. Meditation.
Guests Admitted to: Chapel and to all public areas during the event or course.
Meals: Everyone eats together. Whole food, vegetarian. Special diets.
Special Activities: Planned programme of events. Send for brochure.
Situation: Quiet in beautiful position in Upper Wye Valley.
Maximum Stay: As per programme event.
Bookings: By letter or telephone.
Charges: See programme.
Access: Car-route. Again it is best to see the programme for details of travel instructions.

Corwen

Coleg Y Groes
The College
Corwen
Clwyd LL21 OAU

Tel/Fax: 01490 412169
e-mail: colegygroes@talk21.com

The Church in Wales – Anglican

Two women deacons in the Church of Wales and a pastoral counsellor run this big, comfortable house nestling in a quiet spot between church and mountainside near the River Dee. There are counselling and prayer for healing, and individual needs are catered for in an environment that aims to convey the peace of Christ. It is open to all.

Open: All year except Christmas. Receives men, women, young people, families, small groups and non-retreatants.
Rooms: 6 rooms are available for use as singles or doubles. 1 family room.
Facilities: Garden, quiet room, books to read, guest lounge and TV. Local computer bureau available for guests with fax, computers, e-mail. Parish church adjoining. Children welcomed.
Spiritual Help: Personal talks, individually guided retreats, Ignatian spiritual exercises.

Guests Admitted to: Unrestricted access. Chapel.
Meals: Taken in the guest house or in room. Varied home-cooking.
Vegetarian and special diets.
Special Activities: None.
Situation: Quiet in a small town with countryside around it.
Maximum Stay: By arrangement.
Bookings: Letter or telephone.
Charges: £20 B&B per person per night.
Access: Train or bus from Wrexham.

Vajraloka Buddhist Meditation Centre for Men
Tyn-y-ddol, Treddol
Corwen
Clwyd LL21 OEN
Tel: 01490 460406
e-mail: vajraloka@compuserve.com

Buddhist – Friends of the Western Buddhist Order (FWBO) Tradition

Vajraloka is a men's Buddhist centre with retreats open to those who
have attended a basic meditation course at a Friends of the Western
Buddhist Order (See London section for The London Buddhist Centre).
The centre's purpose is to provide facilities for the practice of meditation and there are retreats suitable for those who have been practising
meditation for at least two months, retreats for experienced meditators,
visualisation retreats, and special retreats for those with particular levels of experience. The Centre is set in the beautiful countryside of North
Wales and it is a very peaceful place. There is a facility for solitary
retreats. Only guests who have attended FWBO meditation classes in
public centres are accepted. Men from other Buddhist traditions may
be received for short retreats of one week if they have about six months
experience of Samatha meditation – mindfulness of Breathing/Metta.
Highly Recommended.

Open: All year. Receives men. Religious who have completed an
FWBO meditation course at a public centre.
Rooms: 3 singles, dormitory, a caravan and retreat cottage.
Facilities: Shrine room, garden, library, direct dialling phone.
Spiritual Help: Meditation. On all retreats the community teaches a
creative approach in meditation workshops. Personal talks. Personal
retreat direction.
Guests Admitted to: Shrine room, gardens, all public and guest des-
ignated areas.
Meals: Guests eat together. Vegetarian/vegan food.
Special Activities: Planned programme of events – send for the
brochure. Some events may be restricted depending on a person's
experience. One of very few single-sex Buddhist meditation centres in
Europe where meditation continues throughout the year.
Situation: Very quiet at the end of a country lane in rolling hills
Maximum Stay: 3 months.
Bookings: By letter or telephone.
Charges: £20 per night for concessions, otherwise £24 for the waged –
full period retreat must be booked.

Access: By car, but ask when you book as the route is a little complicated. Taxi and bus possible.

The Vajrakuta Buddhist Study Centre for Men
Blae-y-ddol, Corwen
Clwyd LL21 OEN   Tel: 01490 460648

Buddhist

The Vajrakuta Buddhist Study Centre for Men is a Dharama study centre of the Friends of the Western Buddhist Order with a community team dedicated to the study of this spiritual practice. It is linked to Vajraloka centre which is about half a mile down the road. Some 8 to 10-week long study seminars are offered each year. Primarily a study centre for members of the Friends of the Western Buddhist Order, there are general study courses for men with some basic Buddhist knowledge. The daily programme includes meditation, group study and ritual. Some retreats are suitable for beginners and you do not have to be a Buddhist to come here – but it is best to have had some contact with another FWBO centre before coming here.

Open: All year, receives men.
Rooms: Mostly in shared quarters, but sometimes a single is available. Hermitages of a caravan with all facilities in grounds and a cottage several miles away are available for solitary retreats.
Facilities: Shrine room, garden, library. 2 solitary retreat facilities.
Spiritual Help: Meditation practice, directed study.
Guests Admitted to: Shrine room.
Meals: Everyone eats together. All meals are vegetarian or vegan.
Special Activities: A short but excellent and formal retreat programme of open seminars for men which may include such topics as the *White Lotus Sutra*, the *Nature of Existence* based on the text of Sangharakshita, and the Bodhisattva's Way of Life.
Situation: Lost in green hills with ample grounds and beautiful surrounding countryside.
Maximum Stay: By arrangement.
Bookings: By letter or telephone.
Charges: From £25 to a concessionary rate of £20 per night. See brochure for other rate information.
Access: Most people come by train and bus – ask for specific directions.

Most of the trouble in the world is caused by people wanting to be important.

T.S. ELLIOT

Dolgellau

Carmelite Monastery
Cader Road, Dolgellau
Gwynedd LL40 1SH   Tel: 01341 422546

Roman Catholic

This monastery of stone buildings with modern additions is a traditional Carmelite Community and offers private retreats only in a guest bungalow near the chapel.

Open: All year. Receives women, men, young people, religious, non-retreatants.
Rooms: 1 double. Facility available to women considering the Carmelite religious life.
Facilities: Garden, TV, books to read, payphone.
Spiritual Help: Personal talks.
Guests Admitted to: Chapel.
Meals: DIY facilities for all.
Special Activities: None.
Situation: Quiet and in the countryside with opportunities for walks in the mountains.
Maximum Stay: 1 week.
Bookings: Letter.
Charges: Donation by agreement.
Access: Bus to nearest town or by car.

Hawarden

St Deiniol's Library
Hawarden
Flintshire CH5 3DF   Tel: 01244 532350
                                              Fax: 01244 520643
                              e-mail: deiniol.visitors@btinternet.com
                              Website: www.st-deiniols.chester.ac.uk

Claimed to be Britain's finest residential library, St Deiniol's is unique, offering an outstanding library that attracts scholars and others from around the world, bed and board in beautiful surroundings and peace and quiet. It seems a dream but it really is there with a programme of courses, seminars, and day conferences on a variety of theological and Victorian study themes with leading scholars. The library also contains Britain's largest private collection of material on St Francis and the early Franciscans. *If you wish to use the library a reference is required in advance as with all specialist libraries.* A relaxed place to study and to have a good rest. It is amazing that in this modern age such traditional civility still exists. This is a particular place but if it seems right for you, then it could be the ideal retreat. **Highly Recommended.**

Open: Open all year. Receives everyone.
Rooms: Both singles and doubles are available.

Facilities: Disabled. Conferences, garden, park, library, guest lounge, TV, guest telephone.
Spiritual Help: None.
Guests Admitted to: Unrestricted access. Chapel.
Meals: Everyone eats together. Traditional food. Vegetarian and special diets.
Special Activities: Planned programme – send for information sheet.
Situation: Quiet in a village.
Maximum Stay: None.
Bookings: Letter/telephone.
Charges: £20 per person B&B. Resident for library use B&B plus dinner £23-£36 per person per night.
Access: Train: Hawarden or Shotton. Bus: from Chester. Car: A55 and A550

Knighton

The Bleddfa Trust
Centre for Caring and the Arts
The Old School
Knighton, Powys LD7 1PA   Tel: 01547 550349

Non-religious

Bleddfa does not offer accommodation but is well worth a day visit or attending one of the workshops. The wide-range of workshops based at the Bleddfa Barn Centre cover many aspects of spirituality, poetry, and meditation in a tranquil setting which is perfect for walking, sitting, painting, thinking and gathering together peacefulness. The Bleddfa Art Gallery which is part of the operation here has gained a national reputation for the quality of its exhibitions. There is a small book-and-gift shop and you may take tea inside or in a charming herb garden.

Open: All year except December to March. Receives everyone.
Rooms: Guests stay in local B&B accommodation.
Facilities: Various meeting rooms, Old School gallery, bookshop, a barn centre for groups and workshops.
Spiritual Help: Quiet days. Personal talks by arrangement.
Guests Admitted to: Everywhere.
Meals: Teas. Food arranged for some events, other times bring your own.
Special Activities: Send for brochure.
Situation: In wonderful countryside with distant views.
Maximum Stay: Only for event.
Bookings: Letter or telephone.
Charges: Depends on workshop or event – see brochure.
Access: By car on A488 between Knighton and Llandrindod Wells.

Llanddoged

Christian Conference, Retreat and Holiday Centre
Pencraig Arthur
Llanddoged, Llanrwst
Gwynedd LL26 0DZ   Tel: 01492 640959

Inter-Denominational

The Reverend John Farrimond, a Methodist minister, who trained in
the Ignatian School of spirituality, offers personal talks on a one-to-one
basis. There will probably be changes in what is on offer here in the
future so do write and ask what the current situation is. The house is
located on the edge of Snowdonia National Park in the Conwy Valley
so there is excellent walking. The famous Bodnant Gardens are only
five miles away.

Open: February to December. Receives men, women, young people,
families, groups and non-retreatants.
Rooms: 2 single, 5 doubles, self-catering flat. No smoking.
Facilities: Garden, library, guest lounge, TV, guest telephone.
Spiritual Help: Personal talks on one-to-one basis.
Guests Admitted to: Unrestricted access.
Meals: Everyone eats together. Traditional food. Vegetarians catered
for. DIY.
Special Activities: Send for brochure.
Situation: Very quiet in the countryside.
Maximum Stay: 2 weeks.
Bookings: Letter or telephone.
Charges: Varied rates. Please contact about current charges.
Access: By car or train.

Llandrindod Wells

Dyffryn Farm
Llanwrthwl, Llandrindod Wells
Powys LD1 GNU   Tel: 01597 811017
                                          Fax: 01597 810609
                                 e-mail: dyffrynfm@cs.com
                     Website: www.rhayader.co.uk/dyffryn

Inter-Denominational

Situated in mid-Wales in a beautiful part of the Wye Valley, this seven-
teenth century house and farm of 20 acreas has pastures, springs, old
stone walls and in the house in winter welcoming warm fires.

Open: All year. Receives everyone.
Rooms: 2 singles, 4 doubles plus self-catering.
Facilities: Garden, guest lounge, TV.
Spiritual Help: Personal talks. Group sharing. Spiritual direction.
Personal/ministry appraisal.
Guests Admitted to: Unrestricted access.

Meals: Everyone eats together. Traditional, wholefood/vegetarian. Special diets.
Special Activities: 3-4 weekend retreats a year.
Situation: Countryside and beautiful.
Maximum Stay: 2 weeks. Otherwise extended by arrangement.
Bookings: Letter/tel/fax.
Charges: Around £30 per person per day full board.
Access: Train: Llandrindod Wells – 8 miles away. Car: Off A470.

Llandudno

Loreto Centre
Abbey Road
Llandudno, Gwynedd, LL30 2EL   Tel: 01492 878031
                                            Fax: 01492 878031
                    e-mail: loreto.centre@llandudno42.freeserve.co.uk

Roman Catholic

The Loreto Centre is run by the Loreto Sisters and is located near the West Shore at the foot of the Great Orme. It is only a ten-minute walk from town, parish church and the East Shore. There are ten en-suite rooms and it is a comfortable place to stay.

Open: All year except Christmas. Receives men, women, young people, groups.
Rooms: Many singles, 10 twin, 2 doubles – 10 en-suite available. DIY facilities.
Facilities: Garden, guest lounge, TV payphone, direct dialling. Children welcomed.
Spiritual Help: Personal talks, directed study.
Guests Admitted to: Unrestricted access. Chapel, work of Community.
Meals: Plain. Vegetarians and special diets by arrangement.
Special Activities: Programme of events including preached retreats. Send for brochure.
Situation: Quiet in countryside by the sea. Spectacular views.
Maximum Stay: 2 weeks.
Bookings: Letter or telephone.
Charges: Wide range from about £20 for students to £200 plus for an 8-day directed retreat.
Access: Train, bus and car all possible. Good directions in the brochure.

Llangunllo

The Samatha Centre
Greenstreete
Llangunllo, Powys LD7 1SP   Tel: 01348 811583

Buddhist (Theravada Tradition)

The Samatha Centre consists of a big farmhouse set in 88 acres of land. The setting is lovely, with views in all directions of green pastures and rising hills. There are streams and woods with secluded places where small huts have been built for use by those meditating who want solitude. Everyone is welcome here to learn this gentle and effective way of meditation. There are regular classes for the more experienced and some for beginners.

Open: During organised weekends and weeks. Receives men, women, young people.
Rooms: 9 singles, 4 in huts.
Facilities: Disabled. Camping, garden, park, library, guest telephone.
Spiritual Help: Individual instruction on Samatha meditation, directed study. There is always an experienced teacher to whom a person can talk on their practice. This is an important aspect of the courses here.
Guests Admitted to: Unrestricted access everywhere. Shrine room, work of Community.
Meals: Everyone eats together. Traditional and wholefood. Provision for vegetarians, and special diets within reason.
Special Activities: Send or telephone for brochure. Beginners can go to occasional introductory weekend courses in meditation practice.
Situation: Deep in the countryside on a green hill and very peaceful.
Maximum Stay: Length of course undertaken, usually a weekend or week.
Bookings: By letter or telephone.
Charges: £100 per week for non members.
Access: Train: to Llangunllo station which is less than a mile away. It is an easy walk down a lane and up a small hill to the Centre. By car from Knighton in Powys to Llangunllo, then through the village and the Centre will be seen on a hill to the left. The entrance is sign-posted.

Llandyssul

Bach y Gwyddel
Cwmpengraig, Drefach Felindre
Llandyssul, SA44 5HX   Tel/Fax: 01559 371427

Mind-Body-Spirit – Eco-spirituality

Run by a couple who offer different but complementary skills to guests. Transpersonal therapy, the creation of personal rituals which assist in moving through life changes, holistic massage, story-telling, group facilitation, instruction in developing low impact alternative energy systems, and guided walks through old sacred sites and wildlife habitats are examples of what is on offer. A cat called Alice may be there to offer excellent *pet therapy* including hugs, cuddles and deep stroking. Simplicity and a search for spiritual paths is important here.

Open: All year. Receives men, women, young people, families, and groups.
Rooms: 2 singles. A Mongolian nomadic dwelling called a *Yurt* and a camping site.

Facilities: Camping, garden, wood supplies, hot showers and toilet facilities, direct dialling phone. Guest area. Children welcomed.
Spiritual Help: Personal talks, group sharing, meditation. Massage. Transpersonal psychotherapy. Acupuncture.
Guests Admitted to: Their own retreat and garden area of an acre and by arrangement to the adjoining 18 acre permaculture farm owned by a trust that includes a pond, woodlands and a wildflower meadow.
Meals: A number of options here from DIY cooking to eating prepared food with the residents. It is up to you, but the cooking is mainly wholefood and fish with some traditional dishes depending on the season.
Special Activities: None but the adjoining permaculture trust sometimes holds courses and camps on country craft skills, organic growing, alternative energy, building and permaculture design.
Situation: Very quiet in the countryside.
Maximum Stay: By arrangement.
Bookings: Letter or telephone.
Charges: By arrangement but from £2.50 per night self-catering, camping and retreat hut. Therapies are extra. A room in the farmhouse is £13 per night.
Access: Train to Carmarthen then bus to Drefach Felindre which is about a mile away.

Llanidloes

Wilderness Trust
Waen Old Farmhouse
Llidiartywaen, Llanidloes
Powys SY18 6JT   Tel: 01686 413842

Interfaith

Open: March to December. Receives everyone.
Rooms: 1 single, 1 double, barn, camping site, 2 caravans, hermitages.
Facilities: Camping, garden, guest lounge, payphone. Children welcomed.
Spiritual Help: Personal talks.
Guests Admitted to: Chapel. Unrestricted access.
Meals: Everyone eats together. Wholefood. Vegetarian and special diets. DIY facilities.
Special Activities: None. Places are offered for smallholding work on a free keep basis.
Situation: Quiet in the countryside – a smallholding with work on restoring buildings, care for animals.
Maximum Stay: Unlimited for paying guests, others by arrangement.
Bookings: Telephone.
Charges: £15 per day full board or free to working guests. £50 per week.
Access: Train: Caersws Bus: Llanidloes. Car: ask for travel details.

Monmouth

Society of the Sacred Cross
Tymawr Convent
Lydart, Monmouth
Gwent NP5 4RN   Tel: 01600 860244

Anglican

Lots of vegetables and fruit are grown by the sisters at this popular
place, so the food is fresh if plain. You will feel well looked after in this
house which has views across a lush valley of green fields in the Wye
Valley. Young men and women are sometimes offered an experience of
one to three months of living alongside the resident Community which
is a contemplative one – hence there is much silence here.

Open: Almost all year – enquire as to closed weeks. Receives men,
women, young people.
Rooms: 9 singles, 3 doubles.
Facilities: Chapel, garden, library, guest telephone.
Spiritual Help: Personal talks by arrangement.
Guests Admitted to: Chapel, choir, work of the Community.
Meals: Traditional food taken in guest dining room. Vegetarian. Self-
catering facilities.
Special Activities: None.
Situation: Very quiet, in the countryside. 65 acres in Wye Valley.
Maximum Stay: By arrangement.
Bookings: By letter or telephone 6.45-7.45pm.
Charges: Guidelines: £20 per person per night full board; £15 self-
catering per day.
Access: By car is easiest. House is 4 miles south of Monmouth.

Pantasaph

Franciscan Retreat Centre
Pantasaph, Holywell
Clwyd CH8 8PE   Tel: 01352 715030
                                              Fax: 01352 715349
                               e-mail: kay.pantasaph@dial.ipex.com
                                    Website: friarypantasaph.org

Roman Catholic

There are preached retreats here as well Padre Pio and Advent weekends.

Open: February to December. Receives men, women, young people,
groups.
Rooms: 24 singles, 2 twins, and a 6-bedroom holiday house.
Facilities: Garden, library, guest lounge, payphone.
Spiritual Help: Personal talks, preached retreats.
Guests Admitted to: Chapel, choir.

Meals: Everyone eats together in guest house. DIY facilities. Traditional food.
Special Activities: Planned programme of retreats.
Situation: Quiet.
Maximum Stay: By arrangement.
Bookings: Letter.
Charges: There are various charges depending on whether it is for the night, the weekend or a 6-day retreat so you need to ask.
Access: By car route – see brochure details. Train to Flint via London-Holyhead Line. There is a national coach stop at Flint. The Centre is 7 miles from Flint. Pick up possible if arranged in advance.

Penmaenmawr

Noddfa Spirituality Centre
Conwy Old Road
Penmaenmawr, Gwyned LL34 6YF

Tel: 01492 623473
Fax: 01492 622517
e-mail: noddfarshm@aol.com

Roman Catholic

Retreats at Noddfa are open to members of all Christian denominations. Encounters with the Bible, and individually guided, preached, holistic, and Celtic retreats are all on offer here.

Open: All year. Receives men, women, groups, and those who care for others in their own homes.
Rooms: 24 singles, 4 doubles.
Facilities: Chapel. Conferences, garden, library, guest lounge, TV, guest telephone.
Spiritual Help: Personal talks. Groups sharing. Spiritual direction. Personal retreat direction. Massage. Reflexology. Short breaks for carers. Counselling. Social group activities.
Guests Admitted to: Unrestricted access.
Meals: Everyone eats in dining room. Traditional food. Vegetarian and special diets.
Special Activities: Planned programme. Send for brochure.
Situation: Quiet, in a village.
Maximum Stay: Open.
Bookings: Letter/tel/fax.
Charges: £25 per day full board. Retreats are priced separately – see brochure.
Access: Train to Penmaenmawr on Holyhead line. National coach from London, Liverpool, Manchester or Birmingham. Boat from Ireland easy. Car route usually via A55.

Porthcawl

St Clare's Prayer Centre
Clevis Lane
Porthcawl, Glamorgan CF36 5NR   Tel/Fax: 01656 783701

Roman Catholic

Open: All year. Receives everyone.
Rooms: 3 singles, 4 doubles. Hermitage. Cottage.
Facilities: Conferences, garden, library, guest lounge, TV.
Spiritual Help: Personal talks. Spiritual direction. Meditation.
Reflexology. Reiki.
Guests Admitted to: Unrestricted access. Chapel.
Meals: DIY facilities. Ask about meals served when you contact them.
Special Activities: Planned events.
Situation: Very quiet.
Maximum Stay: None.
Bookings: Letter/telephone.
Charges: Ask for charge rates.
Access: Best by car.

Tremeirchion

St Beuno's Spiritual Centre
St Asaph
Tremeirchion
Clwyd LL17 OAS   Tel: 01745 583444
                                    Fax: 01745 584151
                                    e-mail StBeunos@aol.com
                         Website: www.home.aol.com/StBeunos

Roman Catholic

This is a leading Jesuit centre of spirituality for the teaching and study
of the spiritual exercises of St Ignatius of Loyola for Christians from all
over the world. These famous exercises are a series of Scripture-based,
Christ-centred meditations and contemplation designed to help each
retreatant to discover his or her 'hidden self'. There are courses
designed to last six or eight days, others which are given in eight-day
periods over three months, and the full course of spiritual exercises
involving a continuous period of some 30 days. The Ignatian exercises
are among the most famous and rigorous of all spiritual retreats. You
should first read up about this form of retreat and perhaps discuss it
with your spiritual adviser or priest before deciding to go. This is a
place for a serious *religious* retreat in seeking God. **Highly
Recommended.**

Open: All year except January. Receives men and women.
Rooms: 50 singles.
Facilities: Limited for disabled, garden, library, payphone, direct
dialling.

Spiritual Help: Meditation, one-to-one retreats, 3-month courses in apostolic spirituality for Christians, 30-day retreats, 2-month training courses.
Guests Admitted to: Unrestricted access.
Meals: Everyone eats together. Traditional food. Vegetarian and special diets catered for.
Special Activities: Send for brochure which explains.
Situation: Very quiet in the countryside.
Maximum Stay: The 3-month course.
Bookings: Letter, telephone, fax, e-mail.
Charges: Invited donations of about £260 and £200 for 8 and 6-day retreats respectively. Weekends around £60.
Access: By rail to Rhyl, otherwise by car or bus.

Welshpool

Abhedashram
Camlad House
Forden, Welshpool
Powys SY21 8NZ   Tel/Fax: 01938 580499

Yoga – Vedanta Traditions

This Ashram and Residential Meditation and Conference-Retreat Centre houses people who have committed their lives to the study and practice of a spiritual life in the methods of Yoga and Vedanta traditions. The ashram has been established in Wales since 1983 under the auspices of the Universal Confluence of Yoga-Vedanta Luminary Trust. It welcomes people interested in this spiritual way which comprises two systems of Indian philosophy. In a new 1997 building, the centre is set in a quiet place with regular day and weekend programmes.

Open: All year. Receives men and women.
Rooms: 1 single, 2 twin rooms. 5 family rooms. Centrally heated. There will be more capacity as dormitories and other rooms are being refurbished. Guest apartment.
Facilities: Increasing facilities here as refurbishment is continuous.
Spiritual Help: Guidance in practice of these two traditions.
Guests Admitted to: All public and guest areas and outside grounds.
Meals: Vegetarian.
Special Activities: Programmes and course – send for information.
Situation: 29 acres in quiet countryside.
Maximum Stay: 1 week in first instance.
Bookings: Letter/telephone.
Charges: £15 per person per night for retreat accommodation. Weekend programmes £65 all-inclusive. Other programmes are free. Donations welcomed.
Access: One hour from M6/M56 and less from the M54. Train: Station ten minutes away. National coach possible – ask for details.

Whitland

Holy Cross Abbey
Velfrey Road
Whitland, Dyfed SA34 OQX   *Not available on telephone.*

Roman Catholic

This Cistercian Community of nuns has only limited accommodation.
However, they do receive guests – but you must write them.

Open: Most of year. Receives men and women.
Rooms: 1 single, 1 double.
Facilities: Chapel, DIY facilities.
Spiritual Help: Personal talks by request sometimes possible.
Guests Admitted to: Chapel.
Meals: DIY plus very plain traditional food.
Special Activities: None.
Situation: Quiet in the countryside.
Maximum Stay: 1 week.
Bookings: *Letter only.*
Charges: Donation according to means.
Access: Car and by train to Whitland station, half a mile away.

*Happiness cannot be found through great effort and willpower, but is
already there, in relaxation and letting go.*
                                        VEN. LAMA GENDUN RINPOCHE

SCOTLAND

By Beauly

Centre of Light
Tighnabruaich Struy
By Beauly, Inverness IV4 7JU

Tel: 01463 761254
e-mail: linda.christie@virgin.net

Mind-Body-Spirit

This is a centre for healing and retreats set in the Highlands. The core direction is on meditation and Light Training which is done on four levels – learning Resonance Kinesiology, opening the heart to the higher self, building better connections between yourself and the Creator Being, and understanding human and planetary progression and your place in the scheme of things. The centre, set in five acres, serves as a base for other practitioners who offer various courses. Situated in a beautiful glen, there are mountains all around, rivers, trees and even a waterfall. Facilities and setting are light, airy and clean. **Highly Recommended.**

Open: All year. Receives everyone.
Rooms: 4 singles. 4 doubles. Dormitories. Hermitage.
Facilities: Garden, park, library, guest phone.
Spiritual Help: Personal talks, group sharing, spiritual direction, meditation. Kinesiology visualisation, colour and breath work.
Guests Admitted to: Unrestricted.
Meals: Everyone eats together or can be taken in your room. Vegetarian food. Special diets.
Special Activities: Planned events. Send for brochure.
Situation: A safe and supportive landscape for a retreat in nature.
Maximum Stay: Most are 3-9 days.
Bookings: Letter/telephone.
Charges: From £70-£170 per day. Concessions available.
Access: Train: Inverness. Bus: Beauly-Struy. Coach: Inverness. Car: A9 from the south to Inverness. They will provide excellent map if you ask.

Crieff

St Ninian's Centre
Conlrie Road
Crieff, Perthshire PH7 4BG

Tel: 01764 653766
Fax: 01764 655824
e-mail: stninians@dial.pipex.com

Church of Scotland

A former church, St Ninian's has been adapted into a modern residential centre, providing a wide range of courses, retreats, renewal weekends and refreshment breaks.The little town of Crieff is situated in pretty countryside and has much to offer in the way of parks and nature trails for walking, and local sports facilities, including fishing.

Open: All year except Christmas period. Receives everyone.
Rooms: 22 singles, 14 doubles, 4 dormitories.
Facilities: Conferences, guest lounge, garden, TV, library, guest telephone.
Spiritual Help: Personal talks. Group sharing.
Guests Admitted to: Unrestricted access.
Meals: Everyone eats together. Traditional food. Vegetarian and special diets.
Special Activities: Planned events. Brochure available.
Situation: Quiet, views across the hills.
Maximum Stay: Open.
Bookings: Letter/tel/fax.
Charges: £28 full board per 24 hours, up to £160 per week full board plus VAT.
Access: By rail, bus or car via Perth and Stirling.

Dalmally

Craig Lodge
Dalmally, Argyll PA33 1AR
Tel: 01838 200216
Fax: 01838 200622
e-mail: mail@craiglodge.org

Roman Catholic

Open: February to end November. Receives everyone.
Rooms: 4 singles, 10 doubles.
Facilities: Disabled. Garden, library, guest lounge, TV, payphone.
Spiritual Help: None.
Guests Admitted to: Unrestricted access. Chapel.
Meals: Wholefood. Vegetarians and special diets.
Special Activities: None, but guided retreats are held at weekends.
Situation: Very quiet surrounded by mountains.
Maximum Stay: Open.
Bookings: : Letter/tel/fax 9–5pm
Charges: £30 per night full board.
Access: Car from Glasgow on A82 to Oban.

Dunblane

Scottish Churches House
Kirk Street
Dunblane, Perthshire FK15 0AJ
Tel: 01786 823588
e-mail: schse@dial.pipex.com

Inter-Denominational

This is a conference centre, belonging to all the mainline churches in Scotland, but daily retreats are organised for individuals. The Centre consists of a row of converted and renovated 18th century cottages and a church along two sides of the Cathedral square. The atmosphere is quiet and homely.

Open: All year except Christmas/New Year period and Easter weekend. Receives everyone.
Rooms: 8 singles. 21 doubles.
Facilities: Conferences, garden, park, library, guest lounge, guest telephone, guest fax.
Spiritual Help: Personal talks. Spiritual direction. Meditation. Directed stuidy during planned retreats.
Guests Admitted to: Unrestricted access.
Meals: Everyone eats together. Wholefood/vegetarian. Special diets.
Special Activities: Planned programme. Send for details.
Situation: Quiet in a Cathedral close.
Maximum Stay: Open.
Bookings: Letter/tel/fax – best time to telephone 9.40am-2.30pm
Charges: Programme ranges from about £15 to £100.
Access: By rail, bus or car.

Edinburgh

House of Prayer
8 Nile Grove
Edinburgh EHIO 4RF

Tel: 0131 4471772
Fax: 0131 4469122
e-mail: nilegrove@rscj.freeserve.co.uk
Website: www.rscj.freeserve.co.uk

Roman Catholic – Inter-Denominational

Located in one of Scotland's few moneyed and middle-class suburban areas, the House of Prayer embraces all denominations and tries to promote a non-sensational Christian spiritualism. Meditation is encouraged and there are two chapels. The Community and the Retreat Team are members of the Society of the Sacred Heart of Jesus, an international congregation for women. Rooms are clean and bright and surrounding the house is a fine garden. There are plenty of courses to chose from in the programme such as 30-day retreats, women in scripture and tradition, Taizé prayer days, work with icons, and a day on the Bhagavad Gita. Individually guided retreats in the tradition of the Ignatian Exercises are available. **Highly Recommended.**

Open: All year except Christmas, Easter, August. Receives men, women, and young people.
Rooms: 5 singles, 1 double.
Facilities: Disabled for day events. Chapel, conferences, garden, library, guest lounge.

Spiritual Help: Personal talks, group sharing, meditation, directed study.
Guests Admitted to: Unrestricted except for Community areas.
Meals: Taken in guest dining room. Home-cooked food. Vegetarian and special diets.
Special Activities: Planned programme. Day events. Brochure available.
Situation: Quiet suburb in a city.
Maximum Stay: 8 days.
Bookings: Lettert/tel/fax/e-mail.
Charges: Range from about £25-£30 full board per day to about £200 for an 8-day event. Concessions possible. See brochure.
Access: By rail or car to Edinburgh. Local buses from Waverley Station.

Elgin

Pluscarden Abbey
Elgin, Moray IV30 8UA

Tel: 01343 890257
Fax: 01343 890258
Website: www.pluscardenabbey.org

Roman Catholic

Pluscarden is unique in being the only mediaeval monastery in Britain still housing a monastic community. The complete Benedictine Divine Office is sung in Latin to Gregorian chant – wonderfully well too. You can buy a CD to take home if you want. The monks do market gardening, stained glass, book binding, and work with the bees. Year by year the reputation of these most excellent men increases in their gifts of hospitality. If you want a retreat that is truly monastic in a far place with great depth in the prayer life, then go to Pluscarden. But if all you want is a rest from a troubled and busy world, then go here too for it *is* a place apart. **Highly Recommended.**

Open: All year. Receives everyone.
Rooms: 26 singles, 2 doubles.
Facilities: Disabled. Garden, library, guest lounge, guest telephone.
Spiritual Help: Personal talks. Spiritual direction.
Guests Admitted to: Chapel. Church.
Meals: Men eat together lunch and supper. Otherwise taken in guest-house. Traditional food. Vegetarian and simple special diets. DIY facilities available.
Special Activities: Some events.
Situation: Very far north and very quiet.
Maximum Stay: 2 weeks.
Bookings: Letter/tel/fax.
Charges: Donations.
Access: Train: to Elgin. Car: A96, B9010, follow signs.

Eskdalemuir

Kagyu Samye Ling Monastery and Tibetan Centre
Eskdalemuir, Langholm
Dumfries DG13 0QL   Tel: 01387 373232
                                                         Fax: 01387 373223
                                              e-mail: samye@rokpa.u-net.com

Buddhist – Tibetan Kagyu Tradition

The Centre was the first British Tibetan monastery to be set up following the Cultural Revolution. Lamas regularly visit in summer and
guests may request interviews. All guests may participate in temple
meditation, prayer and work. The atmosphere is lively and warm. The
full-time community consists mostly of young people. There is a dairy,
farm, foundry, weaving and painting shops, a pottery and printing
press, a medical centre and much more – lots of activities and work go
on here. A stimulating place, there is plenty to do and a wonderful
landscape to explore. There is a new Shrine room and a Tibetan medical centre where Tara Rokpa therapy is offered on different levels. (Ask
for their brochure which explains this therapy.) The Five Golden Rules
of Kagyu Samye Ling Monastery and Tibetan Centre are *to protect life
and refrain from killing, to respect others' property and refrain from stealing,
to speak the truth and refrain from lying, to encourage health and refrain from
all intoxicants,* and *to respect others and refrain from sexual misconduct.* The
three areas of activity here are spirituality, humanitarian aid and
therapy. What this means in reality is that Samye Ling is a place where
there can be many young people in recovery from addiction and many
others who may have found here a lifestyle that is much more positive
and healthy than the one they left behind. This does make for an atmosphere rather different from your usual Christian monastery – not
necessarily one in which older people would feel uncomfortable and
one which is often peaceful and calm. If you remember that the best
slogan for Samye Ling is *Compassion in Action*, then you will find this
retreat and spirituality centre a fine place to visit. Samye Ling is a
centre for preservation of Tibetan culture, an international centre of
Buddhist training and network for international humanitarian activities, therapy, promotion of interfaith understanding, the Tara College of
Tibetan Medicine, and for a Community of over a 100 people, both
monastic and lay. In 1992, Holy Island near Arran in the Firth of Clyde
was purchased by the Samye Ling Centre for the solitude it offered as
an ideal venue for prayer and meditation (see entry below). **Highly
Recommended.**

Open: All year. Receives everyone.
Rooms: Accommodation for 83 people.
Facilities: Conferences, camping, garden, library, guest lounge, guest
telephone.
Spiritual Help: Personal talks. Spiritual direction. Personal retreat
direction. Meditation. Directed study.
Guests Admitted to: Unrestricted access.
Meals: Everyone eats together. Simple vegetarian food only.
Special Activities: A big planned programme of events, courses and

study. Send for the brochure which is among one of the best available from a retreat centre.
Situation: Rather isolated, quiet but busy in summer. There can be lots of poeple visiting here.
Maximum Stay: By arrangement.
Bookings: Letter/tel/fax – 9am-5pm Mon-Fri.
Charges: Rates include meals: £25 per night single, £15 in dormitory, £40 for a twin room, £12.50 per night in a tent camping out. Weekend courses which include accommodation and meals £45 per person.
Access: Train: to Carlisle, then by bus. Bus: to Hawick, then by taxi. Car. via M6, A7.

The Holy Island Project
Kagyu Samye Ling Monastery and Tibetan Centre
Eskdalemuir, Langholm
Dumfries DG13 0QL
Tel: 01387 373232
Fax: 01387 373223
e-mail: samye@rokpa.u-net.com

Interfaith – Tibetan Buddhist Kagyu Tradition

Lama Yeshe Losal, the Abbot of Samye Ling Monastery and director of this project, has said about this place: *May every wonderful and wholesome thing arise here and may its goodness and happiness spread throughout the entire world.* The project to make this ancient holy place open to everyone and to restore the living of holiness on it, has been a project now for over five years. An excellent and interesting brochure in colour is available. There is a programme each year now. The subjects usually covered in it include meditation, interfaith work camp, T'ai Chi – Qi Gong work, and the taking of a holistic view of the island through literature and poetry.

Open: All year – but programme is for May-September. Receives men, women, young people *over 16 years of age*, groups.
Rooms: 4 doubles.
Facilities: Camping. *No smoking. No alcohol. No drugs.*
Spiritual Help: Personal retreat direction. Meditation. *Read the programme brochure.*
Guests Admitted to: Unrestricted access.
Meals: Everyone eats together. Vegetarian food only.
Special Activities: Planned programme. Send for brochure.
Situation: A beautiful sacred Scottish island.
Maximum Stay: Open.
Bookings: Letter/tel/fax.
Charges: Rates per night: Camping £12, twin bedroom per person £22, single occupancy of a twin room in off-season only £25. These rates include full board.
Access: It is necessary to receive instructions from the Monastery when you have booked.

Falkland

**Tabor Retreat Centre
Key House High Street
Falkland Fife KYI5 7BU**   Tel: 01337 857705

Ecumenical

Tabor, an 18th century house, is in the High Street next door to Falkland
Palace, and situated in a garden with views of the Lomond Hills. It is
an ecumenical house welcoming men and women of all traditions or
none. The name of the centre comes from Mount Tabor where Jesus
chose to be apart for a time, the place of change. As the resident
Community is small, an informal atmosphere prevails and there is a
mixture of silence and family style life.

Open: All year. Receives men, women, groups, non-retreatants.
Rooms: 4 doubles but can be booked as singles.
Facilities: Garden, guest lounge, library.
Spiritual Help: Personal talks, group sharing, meditation, personal
retreat direction.
Guests Admitted to: Unrestricted access.
Meals: Everyone eats together – in the kitchen usually. Wholefood,
mainly vegetarian. Special diets.
Special Activities: Planned programme. Send for brochure.
Situation: Quiet in a conservation village.
Maximum Stay: 5 nights.
Bookings: Letter or telephone.
Charges: By donation – suggested as £25 full board.
Access: Train, bus, and car are all possible. See the brochure.

Forres

**The Findhorn Foundation
The Park
Forres, Morayshire IV36 0TZ**

e-mail: reception@findhorn.com
Accomms@finmdhorn.com
Website: www.findhorn.com

Mind-Body-Spirit – Eco-spirituality

This is a well-publicised and famous place and can get very crowded
in the summertime. The Community was founded in 1962 by three
people, who believed in the principles that the source of life or God is
accessible to each person and that nature, including earth, has intelligence and is part of a much greater plan. Nature spirits, or *devas*, are
said to have allowed them to raise vegetables and exotic flowers from
a barren soil of sand and gravel. Today Findhorn is a highly organised
and large operation and one of the largest private communities in
Britain. Enthusiasm, harmony and love are the precepts by which they
all try to work and there is a strong emphasis on meditation. Courses
of all descriptions, length and type run throughout the year. Such is the

popularity of this place that accommodation needs usually to be booked months in advance. It is definitely not a place for a private retreat as understood in the Christian or Buddhist traditions. New Bold House, part of the Community, offers a live-work-meditate lifestyle for those who wish to share it. They have a separate programme and charges. There are also secondary island retreat centres of the Foundation which are included in the brochure information.

Open: All year. Receives men, women, young people, groups, families.
Rooms : Varied so ask what is on offer when you book.
Facilities: Disabled possible. The facilities range from houses, chalets, caravans and camp sites plus all manner of shared things like a Visitors Centre and retail shopping. It is best to ask exactly what accommodation is on offer when you enquire. Children welcomed if supervised.
Spiritual Help: Personal talks, meditation, and certain courses on offer.
Guests Admitted to: Unrestricted access except to private houses and rooms.
Meals: Meals include vegetarian provision.
Special Activities: Planned programme of events. Brochure with information on Findhorn available.
Situation: Quiet but busy and those seeking silence may be out of luck here.
Maximum Stay: According to programme and by arrangement.
Bookings: Letter/telephone.
Charges: These vary and can run over £360 per week full board – but there is a fixed prices system. Credit cards accepted.
Access: Air, rail, coach, car all possible. See brochure for detailed instructions.

Minton House
Findhorn Bay,
Forres, Moray IV36 OTZ   Tel: 01309 690819
                                                   Fax: 01309 691583
                                          e-mail: minton~findhorn.org

The purpose of the Minton Trust which runs the place is to seek through direct experience a deepening of spiritual awareness. Guests are able to share in some of the Findhorn events and facilities as Minton is within the Findhorn Foundation Community, but it has its own agenda. The house is a large pink mansion standing on the shoreline of Findhorn Bay and set in seven acres with lovely views. While individuals are welcome, many find it is better to go as part of a planned event. In the past, some people have found Minton House's accommodation and food rather too simple and sparse and the welcome less than warm – so perhaps it is better to ask exactly what accommodation and meals are on offer, how many will be in your group, and who will be directing the activities.

Open: All Year. Receives everyone.
Rooms: 2 singles, 6 doubles.

Facilities: Disabled – check it out when you enquire. Conferences, camping, garden, park, library, guest lounge, payphone. Sauna and hot tub.
Spiritual Help: Meditation. Therapies as required. Yoga. Taizé singing every Sunday morning.
Guests Admitted to: Unlimited access.
Meals: Everyone eats together. Wholefood/vegetarian.
Special Activities: Planned programme of events. Brochure available.
Situation: Quiet with views of the bay.
Maximum Stay: Open.
Bookings: Letter/tel/e-mail.
Charges: From £22 to £45.
Access: Train, Bus, Car all possible. Ask for details.

Garvald

Sancta Maria Abbey
Nunraw Guest House
Garvald, Haddington East Lothian EH41 4LW   Tel: 01620 830228

Roman Catholic

This is a very popular monastery and the accommodation in a guest house, some distance from the Abbey itself is limited to about 30 people. Sometimes guests may be asked to share a room. The guest house is run in keeping with the contemplative nature of a monastic life. The surrounding countryside is very beautiful and there is a large agricultural establishment. This is a place of silence and deep spirituality where you may truly put aside the burdens of everyday living and open yourself to the benefits of silence and solitude. The purpose in coming here is to seek God.

Open : All year except February and Christmas. Receives men, women, young people, families, groups.
Rooms: 7 singles, 8 doubles, dormitory rooms in the guest house.
Facilities: Park, library, guest lounge, payphone, direct dialling. Children welcomed.
Spiritual Help: Personal talks.
Guests Admitted to: Chapel.
Meals: Traditional food taken in the guest house.
Special Activities: None.
Situation: Very quiet in the countryside. Woodlands, lakes, moorland, farmland.
Maximum Stay. By arrangement.
Bookings: Letter or telephone.
Charges: Donation.
Access: By car.

Glasgow

Ignatian Spirituality Centre
7 Woodside Place
Glasgow G3 7QF

Tel: 0141 3540077
Fax: 0141 3540099

Roman Catholic – Ecumenical

Training courses, retreats and events based on the spiritual exercises of St Ignatius of Loyola for all who seek God in their lives is precisely what this retreat place is about. There are day and evening events as well as longer courses. The centre is in the middle of a major city – but even here you can make a day retreat in peace. *This is a non-residential centre.*

Isle of Cumbrae

College of the Holy Spirit
Millport, Isle of Cumbrae KA28 0HE

Tel: 01475 530353
Fax: 01475 530204
e-mail: tccumbrae@argyll.anglican.org

Scottish Episcopalian (Anglican)

The small but very beautiful island of Cumbrae enjoys wonderful views of the surrounding mountains and islands and is known for its marvellous birdlife and wild flowers. Easily accessible by public transport with only a 10-minute ferry crossing, the College built in 1851 is attached to one of Britain's smallest cathedrals. The programme here is a short one but with some interesting retreats such as *The Promised Help, Painting and Prayer*, and *Marriage Refreshment* – this latter a renewal opportunity for couples in an atmosphere of peace and quiet.

Open: All year except over Christmas period. Receives everyone.
Rooms: 4 singles, 15 doubles.
Facilities: Conferences, garden, library, guest lounge, TV, guest telephone.
Spiritual Help: Personal talks. Spiritual direction. Personal retreat direction by prior arrangement only.
Guests Admitted to: Church, guest areas.
Meals: Taken in guest house. Traditional food. Vegetarian and special diets.
Special Activities: A short programme over the year. Leaflet available.
Situation: During the summer tourist months it can be quite busy here – otherwise quiet.
Maximum Stay: 10 days.
Bookings: Letter/tel/fax. *Note: B&B guests who are not on retreat are received here during the school holidays.*
Charges: B&B £17-£22. Half-board £26-£31.
Access: Train and then ferry. Car: Glasgow/Largs/then ferry.

Isle of Iona

Duncraig
Isle of Iona PA76 6SP Tel: 01681 700202

Inter-Denominational

A plain old house in a simple but historically spiritual setting offering a quiet and relaxing place for a private retreat.

Open: March to October. Receives men and women, groups.
Rooms: 2 singles, 2 doubles.
Facilities: Garden, library, guest lounge.
Spiritual Help: Personal talks, group sharing, meditation.
Opportunity to be quiet. There is silence from 10.30pm until 9.15am the next morning.
Guests Admitted to: Unrestricted access. A chapel, church, oratory is available on the island.
Meals: Everyone eats together. Traditional/vegetarian food. DIY facilities as well.
Special Activities: None.
Situation: Very quiet and somewhat remote.
Maximum Stay: *Minimum* stay 3 days.
Bookings: Letter or telephone.
Charges: £30 to £40 full board.
Access: Train: Glasgow-Oban-ferry to Mull. Car: Reach Oban then ferry.

Iona Community
The Abbey
Isle of Iona, Argyll PA76 6SN Tel: 01681 700404
Fax: 01681 700460
e-mail: ionacomm@iona.org.uk
Website: www.iona.org.uk

Christian Ecumenical

The Iona Community is an ecumenical movement of ordained and lay Christians and welcomes more than 150,000 people to this ancient, holy island every year. It was on Iona that St Columba in 563AD began his mission to bring Christianity to Scotland. The 13th-century Benedictine abbey and church here have been restored and there is an extensive programme of events but retreats are possible in November. This is not a particularly quiet place. It is filled with many visitors and is an active facility which involves everyone in participating in all aspects of the Community life including daily chores. The Iona Community also run the Camas Adventure Centre (see Isle of Mull entry) and the MacLeod Centre (see this section).

Open: April – October. Receives everyone.
Rooms: 3 singles, 16 doubles, 2 dormitories. Total accommodation is for up to 45 people.
Facilities: Library, guest telephone.

Spiritual Help: Group sharing. Meditation. There is no individual support although care for one another is facilitated.
Guests Admitted to: Unrestricted access. Church. Work of Community.
Meals: Everyone eats together. Vegetarian/wholefood mainly. Special diets.
Special Activities: Planned programme. Lots going on here from daily worhsip and Scottish-style social events to a pilgrimage around the island's sacred places.
Situation: Remote historic, sacred island with a small crofting population. A place of outstanding natural beauty.
Maximum Stay: 2 weeks.
Bookings: Letter/telephone weekdays.
Charges: Current weekly rate and daily in brackets: Adult £185 (£33.50), Low Income 16–21 years of age £108 (£19.50), and then there is a special rate for children of different age groups.
Access: Train from Glasgow to Oban, then ferry to Isle of Mull, bus or car 37 miles across Mull, finally a ferry to Iona.

Macleod Centre
Isle of Iona, Argyll PA76 6SN

Tel: 01681 700404
Fax: 01681 700460
e-mail: ionacomm@iona.org.uk
Website: www.iona.org.uk

Christian Ecumenical

Run by the Iona Community (see above entry) which today has over 220 members, 1500 associates and around 1700 Friends. The members who are men and women from many backgrounds and denominations, living throughout Britain, are committed to a Rule involving daily devotional discipline, sharing and accounting for their use of time and money, regular meetings and action for justice and peace. See above entry for a description of this retreat place.

Open: April to October. Receives everyone.
Rooms: 2 singles for group leaders. Dormitories to accommodate up to 50 guests.
Facilities: Disabled. Library, guest lounge, payphone.
Spiritual Help: Group sharing. Meditation. Sharing in community life. Pastoral care where needed from incoming group leaders.
Guests Admitted to: Unrestricted access. Abbey Church. Work of Community.
Meals: Everyone eats together. Mostly vegetarian food. Special diets.
Special Activities: Planned programme. Brochure available.
Situation: Remote historic, sacred island with a small crofting population. A place of outstanding natural beauty.
Maximum Stay: 2 weeks possible.
Bookings: Letter/telephone during office hours.
Charges: See brochure.
Access: Train from Glasgow to Oban, then ferry to Isle of Mull, bus or car 37 miles across Mull, finally a ferry to Iona.

Isle of Mull

Camas Adventure Camp
Ardfenaig, Bunessan
Island of Mull, Strathclyde PA67 6DX

Tel: 01681 700404 (Information)

Ecumenical

Camas is a stone-built salmon fishing station about three miles from
Iona and a short walk over a moor. With no electricity, light comes from
oil lamps, wood fires, sunshine and stars. For many from cities and
towns with their street lamps where it is always light, the true dark
night is a novel experience. Walking, abseiling, canoeing and even the
excitement of a night spent sleeping in a cave are on offer. All activities
are led by experienced trained people. Camas weeks run from May
through September. Ask for the brochure which details the programme
and the charges. The Centre is run by and from the Iona Community
(see this section).

Open: May to September. Receives men, women, young people,
groups.
Rooms: Dormitories.
Facilities: Very simple lifestyle. See the brochure.
Spiritual Help: Group sharing. Meditation. Benefits of a simple
lifestyle.
Guests Admitted to: Shared life and work of the Community.
Meals: Everyone eats together. Vegetarian wholefood.
Special Activities: Planned programme. Brochure available.
Situation: : Remote historic, sacred island with a small crofting popu-
lation. A place of outstanding natural beauty.
Maximum Stay: 6 days.
Bookings: Letter/tel.
Charges: See brochure for the current rates.
Access: Train from Glasgow to Oban, then ferry to Isle of Mull, bus or
car across Mull.

Isle of Skye

Quiraing Lodge
Staffin
Isle of Skye IV51 9JS

Tel: 01470 562330

Mind-Body-Spirit – Interfaith in an Anglican Background

The house is in a lovely setting, surrounded by an acre of garden, slop-
ing down to the shore while behind rise the magnificent hills of the
Quiraing. Good walks all around with bicycles available for those who
want to explore further afield. The programme is varied with an interest in deepening relationships with Gaia and the spiritual forces in
nature as well as renewal of the Christian heritage and the experience
of other faiths such as Buddhism. Some of the events on offer may

range from *Celtic Pilgrimage, Inner Silence to Outer Body, Interfaith Exploration Retreat*, and retreats to Iona celebrating the anniversaries of St Columba and St Augustine and their relevance to our lives today. There are silent weeks in the programme year. Located almost at the top of Skye, the lodge is situated in an area of great earth power, ley-lines, energy points and sacred sites. Many people come here to help recover themselves from a life crisis of health, work or relationships. **Highly Recommended**.

Open: December to October annually. Receives everyone.
Rooms: Singles and doubles – all retreatants have a room to them-selves unless coming as a group.
Facilities: Garden, library, guest lounge, guest telephone.
Spiritual Help: Personal talks, group sharing, spiritual direction. Massage and osteopathy are available nearby. There is counselling in the house.
Guests Admitted to: Unrestricted access.
Meals: Everyone eats together. Wholefood/vegetarian food. Special diets.
Special Activities: Planned events. Send for brochure.
Situation: On the shore of Staffin Bay with hills behind – very quiet and peaceful.
Maximum Stay: As long as necessary.
Bookings: Letter/telephone.
Charges: Donations – suggested range of £15-£35 per person per day.
Access: Ask for travel details when booking.

Kilmuir

Coach House
Kilmuir, North Kessock
Inverness IVI IXG   Tel: 01463 731386

Inter-Denominational

The Coach House is a place where you can rest, reflect, study and recover some inner direction to face the strains of your ordinary life. The work here is to provide the space and guidance for this to happen with individual retreats and workshops. Three types of retreat are usu-ally available: an individually guided retreat based on the St Ignatius Exercises, those based on spiritual or transpersonal counselling with one to one sessions, and a self-guided retreat with guidance help if needed. On the retreat workshop side, there are a good variety of top-ics within the programme, ranging from topics like *Celebrating Easter through Colour* to *Deepening Inner Wisdom*. Many people come here who cannot articulate exactly what it is they are searching for as well as those with a particular faith tradition who wish to stretch the bound-aries of their previous understanding of their beliefs. **Highly Recommended**.

Open: March to December. Receives everyone.
Rooms: 4 singles in house plus 1 single in cottage. 2 doubles.
Facilities: Garden, library, guest lounge.
Spiritual Help: Personal talks. Group sharing. Spiritual direction. Personal retreat direction. Meditation. Directed study. Workshops. Bereavement and transpersonal counselling.
Guests Admitted to: Unrestricted access.
Meals: Everyone eats together. Traditional/vegetarian food. Special diets.
Special Activities: Planned programme. Brochure available.
Situation: Very quiet overlooking the Firth with woods, beach and hill walking at hand.
Maximum Stay: Open.
Bookings: Letter or telephone 9.15am or after 8.30pm.
Charges: Up to £29 full board per day. Workshops run about £72 for the weekend.
Access: Train, bus, air, and car all possible, as collection may be possible from arrival points.

Kinnoull

St Mary's Mission and Renewal Centre
St Mary's Monastery
Kinnoull, Perth PH2 7BP   Tel: 01738 624075

Roman Catholic

This is a large, rather institutional retreat centre overlooking Perth and enjoying peaceful seclusion. There is plenty of accommodation here and retreat and renewal courses are available. Individuals are welcomed throughout the year.

Open: All year except over Christmas season. Receives everyone.
Rooms: 20 singles, 16 doubles.
Facilities: Conferences, garden, library, guest lounge, TV, payphone.
Spiritual Help: Personal talks, group sharing, meditation, directed study.
Guests Admitted to: Unrestricted access.
Meals: Everyone eats together. Traditional food. Vegetarians and special diets.
Special Activities: Planned programme. Send for leaflet.
Situation: Quiet, on edge of town.
Maximum Stay: By arrangement.
Bookings: Letter/telephone.
Charges: Enquire about charges when you book if not given in current programme.
Access: Train: to Perth, bus thereafter. Car: Perth, then via Hatton Road to the monastery.

Musselburgh

Carberry Tower
Musselburgh
Midlothian EH21 8PY   Tel: 0131 6653135/3488
                                                   Fax: 0131 6532930
                                        e-mail: carberry@dial.pipex.com
                              Website: www.dspace.dial.pipex.com/carberry

Inter-Denominational

Carberry Tower is a Scottish country house – big, grey, solid, and granite – but with delightful public rooms, a good library and a complete
new building, Friends House, which has 14 en-suite mostly double
bedrooms. It is owned by the Carberry Trust representing all Scottish
churches. The programme is extensive and includes Alpha courses,
youth weekends, Bible related studies, and open and mid-week
courses. It would be difficult not to find a topic which would be of
retreat interest here. Inspite of more en-suite facilities the camp site is
still open and there has been an improvement in disabled facilities.

Open: All year. Receives everyone.
Rooms: Accommodates more than 80 people and has a number of
new en-suite rooms – modern, comfortable and up-to-date. Camping
site available.
Facilities: Disabled. Chapel. Conferences, garden, camping, park,
guest lounge, TV, payphone. Children welcomed.
Spiritual Help: Personal talks, group sharing, meditation.
Guests Admitted to: Unrestricted to all public areas. Chapel.
Meals: Everyone eats together. Traditional food with vegetarian pro-
vision. Special diets.
Special Activities: Planned programme. Lots of activities – almost
every weekend some event or course is going on here. Two brochures
annually available.
Situation: Very quiet but busy with guests a lot of the time. Set in
some 30 acres of park with fine trees.
Maximum Stay: By arrangement.
Bookings: Letter/tel/fax/e-mail.
Charges: Rates in programme. Concessions usually possible.
Access: Car is easiest. There is a good, map in the brochure. Pick up
from public transport may be possible – discuss it if you can't take the
car.

Orkney

Woodwick House
Evie, Orkney KW17 2PQ   Tel: 01856 751330/0171 5385633
                               e-mail: woodwickhouse@appleonline.net
                                     Website: www.orknet.co.uk/woodwick

Non-Denominational

Woodwick House is a guest house in a particularly lovely situation which makes it a place for a private retreat to get away from it all but not in a religious or a particular spiritual domestic environment. Woodwick House run by a small team of people is a peaceful place set in 12 acres of bluebell woodland with its own burn and bay in the beautiful islands of Orkney. This is a bit unusual in that Orkney is mostly bare of trees so at Woodwick it feels like a self-contained and enclosed space to be. There are 8 rooms for up to 16 guests open all year, open fires and nicely prepared meals using local produce. Bird and seal watching, painting, walking or just sitting in front of the fire and reading a book from the house library are all possible here. A good place for small group retreats as well. Simple brochure available on request.

Roberton

Beshara School of Esoteric Education
Chisholme House
Roberton, Hawick Roxburgh TD9 7PH   Tel: 01450 880215
Fax: 01450 880204
e-mail: beshara~dial.pipex.com
e-mail: secretary@beshara.org
Non-Denominational

Beshara means good news. It is reputed to be the word the angel Gabriel used when he announced the coming of Christ to Mary. The idea of the Beshara School is to strive towards an understanding of the unity of existence. This study of spiritual awareness is quite demanding as it encompasses many mystical traditions, especially sufism and in particular the works of Muhyddin Ibn Arai. Residential courses of differing lengths from a weekend to six months are available. The study consists of periods of meditation, work, study and devotional practices and visitors are always welcome. The house itself is Georgian, the accommodation almost luxuriously comfortable, and the food imaginatively prepared. The staff and students are helpful and relaxed.

Open: All year. Receives everyone.
Rooms: 7 singles, 8 doubles.
Facilities: Disabled. Garden, library, payphone.
Spiritual Help: Personal talks. Meditation. Directed study.
Guests Admitted to: Main building and work of the Community here.
Meals: Everyone eats together. Traditional and vegetarian food. Special diets.
Special Activities: Planned events. Information available.
Situation: Set in 170 acres of moorland and pasture – a very quiet place.
Maximum Stay: By arrangement.
Bookings: Letter/tel/fax/e-mail.
Charges: By donation according to means – suggested rate about £23 a day for adults and special lower rate for children.
Access: Train/bus/car all possible – best to ask specifics of stations, motorways.

Sandilands

Green Pastures
Sandilands
Near Lanark ML I I 9TY   Tel/Fax: 01555 664711
                                              Mobile: 0441 173902

Christian – Inter-denominational

A modern purpose-built retreat and equipping centre set between a
town and a village where the pastoral ministry is to equip Christians to
connect at a deeper level with Christ, themselves and others and to
enable Christians to use their gifts in service to their families, church
and community.

Open: All year. Receives men, women, groups.
Rooms: 5 twin-bedded rooms. Bring a Bible, notebook and towel and
slippers if residential.
Facilities: Conferences, garden, guest lounge, TV.
Spiritual Help: Personal talks, spiritual direction, personal retreat
direction, meditation, directed study. Discipleship counselling for
those in personal and spiritual conflicts.
Guests Admitted to: Chapel. Guest areas.
Meals: Taken in guest house. Traditional food.
Special Activities: Planned programme. Send for information and
leaflet.
Situation: Quiet in countryside.
Maximum Stay: 3-4 days.
Bookings: Letter/telephone.
Charges: On programme from £10 to £46 but check out what this
includes when you are booking. Weekend runs about £46 and about
£20 for B&B and dinner.
Access: Ask for directions when booking.

Tibbermore

The Bield at Blackruthven
Blackruthven House
Tibbermore, Perth PH I I PY   Tel: 01738 583238

Inter-Denominational

Situated on a 370 acre farm of which some 30 acres are parkland and
paddocks, this place offer a large space for retreats and healing. The
farm is organic including how the pigs, cows, and chickens are raised.
A farm project is operating working with people with learning disabilities.

Open: All year. Receives everyone.
Rooms: 4 singles, 5 doubles.
Facilities: Disabled. Conferences, garden, parkland, guest lounge,
payphone. There is swimming here in a heated indoor pool, walking,

tennis, art room facilities and services in the chapel in the morning and evening.
Spiritual Help: Personal talks. Group sharing. Spiritual direction. Personal retreat direction. Meditation. Directed study.
Guests Admitted to: Chapel, grounds and pool.
Meals: Taken in guest house or room.
Wholefood/vegetarian/vegan/organic. DIY tea kitchen. Special diets.
Special Activities: From time to time there are events.
Situation: Very quiet in a beautiful setting some four miles from Perth, a nice country town.
Maximum Stay: 6 nights.
Bookings: Letter/tel/fax – Mon to Wed 10am-4pm.
Charges: This retreat house operates by donations but the rate suggested is as follows. Inclusive of all facilities: Full Board £35. Half-Board £30 Full day £15. Half-day £8,
Access: Car: A85 from Perth to Crieff.

Silence of the heart practised with wisdom will see a lofty depth and the ear of the silent mind will hear untold wonders.

HESYCHIUS OF JERUSALEM

IRELAND

May the road rise to meet you,
May the wind be always at your back,
May the sun shine warm upon your face,
The rains fall soft upon your field
And until we meet again
May God hold you in the hollow of His hand.

Irish Blessing

As you might expect in one of the world's most deeply religious countries, Ireland offers an amazing choice of retreat centres and programmes. It is difficult to go to any of them without being in some of the most beautiful scenery in Europe. Most places are Roman Catholic but ecumenical in outlook, offering a warm welcome to all who seek to increase their spiritual awareness. The famed Irish hospitality and conviviality include the religious communities in all these places and they are keen to develop retreat programmes that appeal to all ages and temperaments from deeply traditional spirituality retreats to novel ones involving animals. From Donegal to the lakes of Killarney, the only problem will be which retreat place to choose.

ANTRIM

Belfast

Columbanus Community of Reconciliation
683 Antrim Road
Belfast BT15 4EG   Tel/Fax: 028 90778009
                              e-mail: columbanus@cinni.org

Ecumenical

Most of the guests at Columbanus are interested in the religious and social political situation in Northern Ireland. They use this place as a base from which to explore such implications and as a means of informing themselves on a personal basis. Using these experiences they hope to create change in their own cultural and church environments. Programmes can be arranged for groups. This is very much an ecumenical community, comprising Roman Catholics, Anglican and Presbyterian members, all of whom share the aims and ministry of reconciliation. The Community wishes to share in every way possible its vision of unity, justice, and peace. To this end it helps to service the works of other agencies, both secular and religious.

Open: All year. Receives men, women, young people, groups, and non-retreatants.

Rooms: 5 singles, 2 doubles.
Facilities: Conferences, garden, library, guest lounge, communal TV, guest telephone. Direct dialling. Children welcomed.
Spiritual Help: Community prayers – morning, lunch time, evening
Guests Admitted to: Chapel, unrestricted access everywhere, work of Community.
Meals: Main meal eaten together. Traditional food. Vegetarian.
Special Activities: Wide-ranging programme from guided reflections through music to group exploration of Bible-linked beliefs and themes using movement and self-expression. Monday night series addresses Northern Ireland issues such as healing of memories, a view from prison, and what is acceptable policing for all. Send for brochure.
Situation: Large gardens and situated beside Cavehill Country Park.
Maximum Stay: Unlimited by arrangement.
Bookings: Letter or telephone.
Charges: B&B IR£10 per night, full board IR£80 per week.
Access: Buses: Nos. 1, 2, 3, 4, 5, 6, 45 from City Hall.

Larne

Drumalis Retreat Centre
Sisters of the Cross and Passion
Glenarm Road, Larne
Co. Antrim BT40 1DT

Tel: 028 28272196
Fax: 028 28277999
e-mail: drumalis@dial.pipex.com

Roman Catholic- Ecumenical – Inter-Faith

The Drumalis Vision Statement says it all: *Drumalis is a place of welcome, an oasis on the journey of life. A living community where all experience the power of God's love and compassion. Discover and value their gifts. Seek to be healers in a divided world. Grow in their relationship with God and all Creation. We draw our life and strength from sharing and prayer.* The house itself is a rambling late Victorian mansion with a view across Larne Harbour which has been called awe-inspiring. The programme here includes, for example, *Healing Touch Workshop, Yoga, Prayer and Painting,* and a *Dream Retreat* and a *Transformation Retreat.*

Open: All year except Christmas and Easter. Receives men, women, young people, groups. Non-retreatants in a self-catering cottage only.
Rooms: Many singles and doubles here.
Facilities: Conferences, garden, library, guest lounge, TV, payphone.
Spiritual Help: Personal talks, group sharing, meditation, personal retreat direction, spiritual direction.
Guests Admitted to: Almost unrestricted access. Chapel, choir.
Meals: Everyone eats together. Traditional food. Vegetarian and special diets.
Special Activities: Retreats for lay people, parishes, religious. Renewal courses. Folk and prayer groups. Inter-church work. Christian fellowship groups. Celtic spirituality. Cursillo weekends. Send for brochures.

Situation: Quiet in town but with spacious grounds near sea and harbour.
Maximum Stay: Depends on retreat or course undertaken.
Bookings: Letter, telephone or fax.
Charges: See brochures for course rates but suggested offerings of IR£30 per day full board.
Access: From Belfast take M2, leave at Exit A8. By train, bus and harbour follow signs for the Coast Road. Drumalis is on right before Bankhands Lane just before leaving the town.

Portglenone

Our Lady of Bethleham Abbey
11 Ballymena Road
Portglenone, Ballymena
Co. Antrim BT44 8BL

Tel: 028 25821211
Fax: 028 25822795

Roman Catholic

There are a large number of day visitors here so it can be a busy place even though it is in the countryside.

Open: All year except Christmas and Easter. Receives men, women, young people, families, groups, and non-retreatants.
Rooms: 5 singles, 3 doubles.
Facilities: There is a room available for conferences, guest lounge, TV payphone. Direct dialling on request. Children welcomed.
Spiritual Help: Personal talks and priests available every day.
Guests Admitted to: Guest chapel.
Meals: Taken in guest house. Traditional food. Vegetarians and special diets catered for.
Special Activities: None.
Situation: Rather busy in countryside.
Maximum Stay: 6 days.
Bookings: Letter or telephone.
Charges: None fixed so by donation or other arrangement.
Access: Car and bus routes. Ask for bus directions.

CORK

Castlemartyr

Carmel College
Castlemartyr, Cork

Roman Catholic

Until recently a school, this grand country house of 1720, enjoys wonderful views over vast lawns running down to waterways – just part of the 140 acres of lakes, pasture, forest, and garden that surround the house. The chapel, full of light, is in the old ballroom and has magnificent plaster work ceilings. Now used as a prayer centre for those wanting a restful and reflective day retreat. It is a good place to pause, recollect, and reflect for a while.

Garranes Allihies

Dzogchen Beara
Garranes Allihies
West Cork

Tel: 00 353 27 73032
Fax: 00 353 27 73177
Website: www.rigpa.org/dzbeara.htm

Buddhist – Tibetan Tradition

This meditation and retreat centre for Buddhist study and practice is 400 feet up on the cliffs above Bantry Bay, with a vast panorama of the Atlantic Ocean. The Centre is under the spiritual direction of Sogyal Rinpoche, and is affiliated to the Rigpa Fellowship. Sogyal Rinpoche was born in Tibet and raised as a son by one of the most revered spiritual teachers of this century, Jamyang Khyentse Choki Lodro. Rinpoche studied at university in Delhi and Cambridge and has been teaching in the West since 1974. He is the author of *The Tibetan Book of Living and Dying* and founder and spiritual director of RIGPA, an international network of centres and groups that follow the teachings of the Buddha under his guidance. Sogyal Rinpoche and other Tibetan masters lead retreats at Dzogchen Beara several times a year. The Centre also offers a range of retreats and courses on various aspects of Buddhism such as meditation, compassion, and spiritual care for the dying, most of which are open to beginners. Visitors are also welcome at other times and attend daily meditation classes or simply relax in the beautiful and peaceful environment of the place. **Highly Recommended.**

Open: All year. Receives men, women, young people, families, groups and non-retreatants.
Rooms: Hostel, dormitories, self-catering cottages.
Facilities: Conferences, garden, book and gift shop, payphone. Children welcomed.
Spiritual Help: Meditation, directed study for students following the Rigpa Study and Practice Programme.
Guests Admitted to: Shrine room.
Meals: Self-catering, DIY.
Special Activities: Programme of planned events – send for brochure. Daily meditation classes to which beginners are welcome. Good walking with sporting facilities in vicinity.
Situation: Very quiet in countryside with dramatic and beautiful views.
Maximum Stay: By arrangement.
Bookings: Letter, fax or telephone.
Charges: From IR£7.50 per night for hostel accommodation.
Access: By bus from Cork City.

Cobh

St Benedict's Priory
The Mount
Cobh, Co. Cork   Telephone: 00 353 21 811354

Roman Catholic

This Community aims at providing a place of silence and solitude where guests may be able to recollect and dwell within themselves at peace.

Open: All year. Receives men, women, young people and small groups up to 8.
Rooms: 6 singles, 1 double.
Facilities: Garden, Bible garden in 1½ acres with pool and stream, library, guest lounge, direct dialling. No rooms on ground floor.
Spiritual Help: Personal talks. Daily Mass and Exposition of Blessed Sacrament. Share in the liturgy of the Community.
Guests Admitted to: Chapel. Helping in garden possible.
Meals: Everyone eats together. DIY facilities for breakfast. Traditional food, some grown in own garden. Provision for vegetarians possible but no special diets.
Special Activities: None.
Situation: Very quiet, in a picturesque town on an island in Cork harbour so the sea is at hand. All rooms have view of harbour, some have balconies.
Maximum Stay: 1 week.
Bookings: By letter or telephone.
Charges: Suggested donation IR£20 per day
Access: Train, road or ferry to Cobh. Rail from Cork City. Air to Cork Airport. Boat from France or England to Cork.

Montenotte

St Dominic's Priory and Retreat Centre
Ennismore
Montenotte, Co. Cork   Telephone: 00 353 21 4502520
                                    e-mail: ennismore@eircom.net

Roman Catholic – Inter-Denominational

Although located in an urban area of Cork, St Dominic's offers an oasis of green lawns and quiet views with much peace and quiet. A friendly old dog may be the first to greet you and the warm welcome is continued inside by the housekeeping staff or a member of the community. The excellent food is prepared in an old-fashioned kitchen – the homemade chicken soup and bread are delicious. The gardens surrounding this ambling large house have plenty of benches and there is a charming old walled garden with box-hedge paths. All in all, a perfect place for a stroll and a good think. The facilities here are numerous and include an 1824 stable block converted into The Meditation House with two buildings of bunks for youth retreats which is modern and comfortable. Next to that a separate Hermitage is available to sleep up to six people and nearby a Pottery plus a specially designed Meditation Room, a lounge, and large conference area. Altogether a nice group of stone buildings around a pretty courtyard down the drive away from the main house. For the disabled there is a modern lift and other special arrangements. As to the retreat programme on offer, these lines of Scripture are good to bear in mind if you find a weekend course entitled 'pottery meditations' too unusual an approach for a retreat: *Get up and make your way to the potter's house: there I shall let you hear what I have to say* (Jeremiah 18:2). Other stimulating courses on offer here from the resident Dominican Community may include bio-spirituality focusing, Celtic spirituality, Meister Eckhart, Myers-Briggs, integrating sexuality, and celebrating creativity.

Open: All year. Receives men, women, young people, families, groups and non-retreatants.
Rooms: 38 singles, 2 doubles, hermitage, hostel.
Facilities: Disabled, simple chapel with lots of light, conferences, garden, library, TV, guest lounge and payphone.
Spiritual Help: Personal talks, group sharing, meditation, community prayers, personal retreat direction.
Guests Admitted to: Unrestricted access. Chapel
Meals: Taken in the guest house. Traditional/wholefood. Vegetarian and special diets. DIY available.
Special Activities: Planned programme of events – *Bio-spirituality Focusing, Christian Meditation, Enneagram, Myers-Briggs,* and *Celtic Spiritual Heritage* are examples of what is on offer. Send for brochure.
Situation: Quiet in a countryside town so can be rather busy. With 30 acres of grounds and spectacularly situated gardens, the Centre feels as though it is in open countryside, but is only 3 miles from the city centre.
Maximum Stay: 1–2 weeks.
Bookings: Letter or telephone.
Charges: Retreat House IR£30 per day full board. 6-day retreat IR£165–IR£175. 5-day retreat IR£150.
Access: By train to Cork. Bus from city centre. Car: see map in brochure.

DONEGAL

Creeslough

Capuchin Retreat Centre
Ard Mhuire, Creeslough
Letterkenny, Co. Donegal

Tel: 00 353 74 38005/38031
Fax: 00 353 74 38371

Roman Catholic

The Capuchin Friary offers quietness on the shore of Sheephaven Bay, adjacent to Ards Forest Park. The programme here places great emphasis on Scripture-based retreats.

Open: February to December. Receives men, women, young people, groups, non-retreatants.
Rooms: 25 singles, 25 doubles.
Facilities: Conferences, garden, park, guest lounge, TV, payphone, direct dialling.
Spiritual Help: Personal talks, group sharing, meditation, directed study.
Guests Admitted to: Chapel.
Meals: Everyone eats together. Traditional food. Vegetarians catered for.
Special Activities: Special programme. Write for details.
Situation: Very quiet in the countryside near seaside with forest walks.
Maximum Stay: By arrangement.
Bookings: Letter.
Charges: About IR£22 per day.
Access: On bus and car routes.

Pettigo

St Patrick's Purgatory
Lough Derg, Pettigo
Co. Donegal   Tel/ Fax: 00 353 72 61518

Roman Catholic but open to all.

St Patrick's Purgatory has been a place of prayer and pilgrimage for at least 1000 years. The pilgrimage to this holy place is one of the toughest in the Christian world. This island sanctuary located on Lough Derg challenges human frailty but may bring a deep and richly rewarding experience of spirituality, enabling participants to find peace of mind and giving them new strengths for continuing their life's journey. A historic centre of Celtic spirituality, St Patrick's Purgatory remains a unique place of prayer and penance. The traditional pilgrimage is a 3-day undertaking of fasting and incorporates a 24-hour vigil which means you do not go to bed for that period – it is meant to be penitential. The fast means just that too – a simple meal of dry toast and black tea each day. You must be in normal health, at least 15 years old and be able to walk (including barefoot) and to kneel unaided. You fast from mid-night prior to leaving the next day by boat to the island. This type of pilgrimage, deeply Christian and Catholic in nature and also highly ritualistic, is not to be undertaken without great seriousness of purpose in the seeking of God. There is a less arduous 1-day retreat which does not require fasting or walking barefoot. As in all great places of spiritual pilgrimage, demand is great and prior booking is essential.

Open: April to October. receives men, women and those over 15. *Not suitable for children.*
Rooms: 750 singles.
Spiritual Help: Personal talks, group sharing, meditation, Way of the Cross, Healing of Memories, Eucharist.
Guests Admitted to: Unrestricted access.
Meals: Whole food, very plain.

Special Activities: Brochure available in English, French, German explaining what is offered and details of pilgrimage retreats.
Situation: Isolated, very quiet on an island.
Maximum Stay: Depends on time of year.
Bookings: Letter or telephone – but well in advance for over 20,000 pilgrims come here every year.
Charges: Ask for 3-day rate.
Access: By boat.

Rossnowlagh

Franciscan Friary and La Verna House
Rossnowlagh
Co. Donegal

Tel: 00 353 72 51342/52035
Fax: 00 353 72 52206
e-mail: frbern@gofree-indigo.ie

Roman Catholic

This is a centre of peace and reconciliation with the emphasis on a *Franciscan presence*. The Friary tries to offer a quiet time *to people burnt out and needing a listening ear.* The buildings are modern with all necessary facilities and close to the sea. If you go on a retreat here, bring your own Bible. **Highly Recommended.**

Open: All year except for Christmas to first week January. Receives men, women, supervised young adults, groups, and small seminar groups of non-retreatants.
Rooms: 17 double rooms.
Facilities: Garden, park, bookshop, library, guest lounge, TV guest payphone, direct dialling.
Spiritual Help: Daily Mass, RC Church, chapel, personal talks, group sharing, meditation, Sacrament of Reconciliation, inter-denominational Bible sharing and prayer, healing and counselling services.
Guests Admitted to: Everywhere except Community living quarters. Chapel, Choir, Shrine room, Repository.
Meals: Taken in guest house. DIY facilities. Traditional, plain food but with variety of dishes. Vegetarian and special diets.
Special Activities: Planned programme. For example, *Dances of Universal Peace, One God, One Humanity, One Me, Peace and Reconciliation, and Thinking and Praying with St Francis of Assisi* and *The Role of Spirituality in Addiction Recovery.*
Situation: Very quiet in the countryside with nearby swimming and surfing. Summer can be busy.
Maximum Stay: A week to 10 days.
Bookings: Letter or telephone, then in writing.
Charges: 1-day retreat about IR£15, 6–8 day retreats donation to about IR£200. B&B about IR£22 per person. Smaller donations possible.
Access: Coast road between Donegal Town and Ballyshannon. About 5 miles from Ballyshannon. No public transport but pick-up possible by prior notice.

DOWN

Newry

Society of African Missions
Dromantine, Newry
Co. Down BT34 1RH　　　　　　　　　Tel: 028 30821224

Roman Catholic

Only 70 miles from Dublin or 30 from Belfast, this large centre is situated in beautiful countryside with good walks at hand. While groups with their own programme usually come here, it is open for a private retreat.

Open: All year except Christmas. Receives men, women, young people, groups, and non-retreatants.
Rooms: 96 singles.
Facilities: Disabled. Conferences, payphone.
Spiritual Help: Only by arrangement.
Guests Admitted to: Chapel.
Meals: Meals taken in guest house. Plain good food with vegetarians and special diets catered for.
Special Activities: No special programme or events.
Situation: Quiet in countryside about six miles from nearest town.
Maximum Stay: By arrangement.
Bookings: Letter or telephone.
Charges: Depends on number of group and length of stay.
Access: Car route easiest from either Dublin or Belfast.

Rostrevor

Christian Renewal Centre
44 Shore Road, Rostrevor
Newry, Co. Down
BT34 3ET　　　　　　　　　　Tel: 028 41738492
　　　　　　　　　　　　　　　　Fax: 028 41738996
　　　　　　　　　　e-mail: crc-rostrevor@lineone.net

Inter-Denominational

The Community here was founded in 1974 as a group of Christians drawn together from different churches to seek to demonstrate and proclaim the uniting love of Christ. The centre is a large place, part of it old but modernised and the other new attached buildings. Renewal weekends and 3-day break retreats are a speciality.

Open: All year. Receives all.
Rooms: 6 singles, 6 doubles.
Facilities: Disabled. Garden, library, guest lounge, TV, payphone. Children welcomed.

Spiritual Help: Personal talks, group sharing, directed study.
Guests Admitted to: Gardens, prayer room, quiet room, communal kitchen.
Meals: Everyone eats together. Traditional food. Vegetarian and special diets.
Special Activities: Special programme. Send for brochure.
Situation: Very quiet in a village beside Carlingford Lough at the foot of the Mourne mountains.
Maximum Stay: 1 week.
Bookings: Letter or telephone.
Charges: IR£17.50 per day full board. IR£9 B&B.
Access: Bus from Belfast or Dublin airport to Newry Courthouse, then by bus to Rostrevor. Train from Belfast or Dublin to Newry station, then by bus. Car: follow signs from Newry for Warrenpoint.

DUBLIN

Catholic Youth Council
20/23 Arran Quay
Dublin 7

Tel: 00 353 18725055
Fax: 00 353 18725010
e-mail: info@cyc.ie

Roman Catholic

The Catholic Youth Council offers a number of holiday centres for youth groups, some with disabled facilities. The centres are primarily used by groups for holidays and training as well as for retreat purposes. The centres in **Glendasan, Teach Chaoimhin** and **Teach Lorcain** are designed particularly for prayer and religious retreats. Groups make their own programmes. There are no resident staff except at **Coolure House**, Co. Westmeath which is a fully staffed centre located near Lough Derraghvara with a wide range of services for retreats plus extensive indoor and outdoor facilities plus an equestrian centre. Most centres are in beautiful rural and coastal areas and some have planned activities in July.

Open: All year. Receives young people.
Rooms: Dormitories.
Facilities: See above.
Spiritual Help: Self-directed.
Guests Admitted to: Unrestricted on site usually.
Meals: Self-catering.
Special Activities: None.
Situation: See above.
Maximum Stay: None.
Bookings: Booking form.
Charges: These vary depending on centre and how long the stay will be – send for rate sheet.
Access: Ask for directions for centre booked.

**Dominican Retreat and Pastoral Centre
and St Joseph's Retreat Centre
Tallaght
Dublin 24**   Tel: 00 353 14048123/00 353 14048191
                                        Fax: 00 353 14596080

Roman Catholic

Square in the middle of Ireland's fourth most populated area and surrounded by endless urban sprawl, St Joseph's is a surprisingly first-rate
place for anyone going on retreat. The guest house is very comfortable
with its own big reading room, tea and coffee bar, bookshop and all the
other facilities one could want from hair dryers to TV room. But the real
delight are the gardens with ancient walkways and many fine old trees.
The Community is fairly large and, unusual today in the religious life,
it is composed of all ages from young to old. They are very hospitable
and friendly in their welcome but mostly receive individuals who come
in a group because of their catering set-up – but sometimes it is possible for a person to visit on their own. Their combined voices rise up
strong in choir and fill the large church which was designed by one of
Pugin's star pupils. The Friars run a number of educational and retreat
programmes as well as caring for some 7000 parishioners in this
densely populated area. As this is a major priory of the Dominican
Friars, it is a place of prayer and contemplation.

Open: September to May inclusive. Receives men, women, small
groups.
Rooms: 30 rooms plus a hermitage.
Facilities: Disabled for one person only. Conferences, chapel, garden,
payphone, direct dialling. TV outside retreat times only.
Spiritual Help: Personal talks group sharing, meditation, directed
study. 1-day, 6-day retreats.
Guests Admitted to: Chapel, choir, garden.
Meals: Everyone eats together. Traditional food. Vegetarian and
special diets possible.
Special Activities: Planned programme. Send for brochure.
Situation: In busy urban area, but a quiet and peaceful oasis.
Maximum Stay: 1 week.
Bookings: Letter only.
Charges: Ask for rates.
Access: Bus: No. 77 or 77a from Eden Quay in Dublin. Easy access by
local bus. Car route from M50.

**Friends of the Western Buddhist Order – Ireland
23 South Frederick Street
Dublin 2**   Tel: 00 353 16713187

Buddhist. They will provide information on the activities of the
organisation in Ireland.

GALWAY

Athenry

Esker Retreat House and Youth Village
Athenry, Co. Galway

Tel: 00 353 91 844549
Fax: 00 353 91 84569
e-mail: eskerret@indigo.ie

Roman Catholic

As you leave Athenry, you drive into a flat and unattractive valley dotted with houses and the stone walls so common in this part of Galway. Soon, Esker Monastery looms in the distance, the only sizeable structure in sight. As you approach this formidable looking building, yet another suddenly appears – a nearby cement works. But do not be put off for as you enter Esker's drive, the trees surround you and soon you are in a different world of rich greenery and grassy pastures. Close up the monastery now seems friendly if institutional. Rooms are old-fashioned but comfortably furnished. Many members of the Community are retired after many years of work but one may join you in the lounge or for a meal. It is a friendly, old-fashioned place with active retreat programmes including those for the young. Here, wisdom has prevailed and a completely separate Youth Village has been created and set aside only for younger groups. Food is plentiful but traditional. There are Stations of the Cross in the garden along a bluebell walk through trees where violets and primroses glow in the shade. The Stations are in an Italian and elegant style. It is a prayerful place.

Open: All year. receives men, women, young people, families, groups, and non-retreatants.
Rooms: 17 singles, 28 doubles, camping site, carvan site.
Facilities: Disabled. Conferences, camping, gardens, woodland park, pitch and put course, lots of walks in grounds and in surrounding area, guest lounge, TV, payphone. Children welcomed.
Spiritual Help: Personal talks. Group sharing. Spiritual direction, Personal retreat direction. Meditation. Religious services. Other activities include: inner healing, AA Groups, therapeutic massage, craft and art classes, Celtic spirituality.
Guests Admitted to: Unrestricted access everywhere.
Meals: Everyone eats together. Traditional food with provision for vegetarians and special diets within reason.
Special Activities: There is a planned programme of retreats and events both in the main facilities and in the Youth Village. Send for information.
Situation: Very quiet in countryside.
Maximum Stay: 2-3 weeks or by arrangement.
Bookings: Letter.
Charges: IR£30 per day full board. Youth Village charges by arrangement as a group possible
Access: Train and bus possible. Ask for details of places. People can be met if prior notice given. Car route easy.

Newcastle

An Diseart
Le Retraite Sisters
2 Distillery Road
Newcastle, Co. Galway   Tel: 00 353 91 524548
                                             Fax: 00 353 91 581312

Roman Catholic

This is a small community and usually only one person is received on
retreat at a time. There is space and time for silence in a self-catering
hermitage. A small oratory links this with the main house.

Open: All year. Receives women only.
Rooms: 2 bedrooms. Self-contained Hermitage.
Facilities: None except rooms and chapel.
Spiritual Help: Personal talks. Retreat direction if requested.
Guests Admitted to: Chapel.
Meals: Self-catering.
Special Activities: None.
Situation: Town.
Maximum Stay: 8 days.
Bookings: Letter.
Charges: Donation – suggested IR£10 per 24 hours.
Access: By road. Ask for bus directions.

KERRY

Ardfert

Ardfert Retreat Centre
Ardfert
Co. Kerry   Tel: 00 353 667134276

Roman Catholic

The Centre is staffed by Presentation Sisters and a priest director, and
serves many parishes. While this is a place for group bookings, individuals wishing to join any Saturday or Sunday parish-group retreat
are welcome to do so by prior arrangement with the secretary of
the Centre. There is a library service for books and videos on Christian
topics.

Open: Most of the year but check as they are closed for four weeks in
summer. Receives men, women, young people, and groups.
Rooms: 30 singles.
Facilities: A diocesan retreat centre in constant use by parish groups
and schools.

Guests Admitted to: Almost unrestricted access.
Spiritual Help: Personal talks, spiritual direction, group sharing and meditation.
Meals: Available for groups but not for individual visitors. Traditional food.
Special Activities: These range from residential weekends of prayer and Enneagram workshops to days of support and prayer for dependants of those suffering from alcoholism. Send for brochure.
Situation: Very quiet, in the countryside.
Maximum Stay: According to the programme.
Bookings: By letter.
Charges: Offering about IR£40 per person or IR£75 per couple. Preached retreats and Directed Retreats day rate available.
Access: Train and bus to Tralee. Car: Centre is 5 miles north of Tralee.

Inch

Lios Dána
The Natural Living Centre
Inch, Annascaul
Co. Kerry

Tel: 00 353 6658189
Fax: 00 353 6658223

Mind-Body-Spirit

Claiming to be Ireland's leading holistic holiday centre for rest and renewal and the practice of a new apporoach to life, Lios Dana is set in a wonderful location on the southern shoreline of the Dingle peninsula in the southwest of Ireland. There are three-day programmes which include yoga and shiatsu massage, group courses from March to October in a variety of holistic disciplines or you can come for a simple holiday break and use the centre's facilities. Country walks, sea and mountains and early Christian sites are all possible here.

Open: All year. Receives everyone.
Rooms: 8 bedrooms. Self-catering chalets
Facilities: Large exercise room, library, guest lounge, conservatories, hot and cool pool.
Spiritual Help: Creative and healing exercises and therapies.
Guests Admitted to: Unrestricted in guest areas.
Meals: Vegetarian.
Special Activities: See above. Send for brochure.
Situation: Quiet by sea and shore.
Maximum Stay: By arrangement.
Bookings: Letter/telephone.
Charges: Tariff sheet available, but rates run from a single room for one person IR£40 per day full board to IR£7.50 day use of centre only.
Access: Rail: to Tralee and then bus. Car: 2 hours from Cork or Limerick. Air: 20 miles from Kerry County airport.

Killarney

Franciscan Prayer Centre
Killarney, Co. Kerry

Tel: 00 353 6431066
Fax: 00 353 6435345

Roman Catholic

Killarney is one of the most beautiful places in the world and no one can resist the beauty of its lakes, forests and mountains. The Franciscan Prayer Centre in the heart of this wondrous place of nature, seems ideally placed for the search for God. It is also in the heart of the town of Killarney but sits up from the road above the noise. The rear of the buildings open out into large grassed gardens but unfortunately there are not many places to sit comfortably. However, the inside of the place makes up for these drawbacks with a large guest lounge with TV/video, a real fire which you can light if you feel like it. There is a quiet room where Divine Office takes place and a peaceful prayer room near the guest rooms. There are 3 libraries and meals are taken with the resident Community. While the rooms are clean and comfortable, they are plainly furnished but the beds are very good. Central heating plus extra room heaters makes it snug in winter. You can go directly into the attached church from the guest accommodation. The church is loaded with wall and ceiling decorations combined with a stunning old-fashioned altar loaded with various ornamentation and mosaics circa 1917. A special feature is the sound of running water which does move one to think at first of *the living waters of faith*. This may help some with their contemplation – for others it will be a distraction. Overall, an atmosphere of friendly but somewhat impersonal caring. It is only a few minutes to some of the glorious lakes of Killarney – not to be missed for true inspiration of the wonder of creation. You can take a cart and pony just near the Centre and be driven to see it all.

Open: All year. Receives men, women, young people, groups.
Rooms: 15 singles, 3 doubles.
Facilities: Church, garden, park, library, small bookshop, guest lounge, TV, payphone.
Spiritual Help: Group prayer, Friday evening Divine Office together with Community in church.
Guests Admitted to: Chapel, choir. Unrestricted access. Work of community.
Meals: Everyone eats together. Traditional food. Vegetarians catered for.
Special Activities: Planned directed retreats. Send for information. Private retreats with spiritual direction if wanted.
Situation: Quiet in a village.
Maximum Stay: By arrangement.
Bookings: Letter
Charges: By offering but around IR£20–IR£25 full board per day is suggested.
Access: Train, bus and car route all easy.

LIMERICK

Murroe

Glenstal Abbey
Murroe
Co. Limerick   Telephone: 00 353 61386103

Roman Catholic

A long, elegant drive leads up to this great abbey of stone but the large castle-like building houses the school run by the monks here. Their monastery and the guest area is much more modest – in fact it is fashioned from the old stable block. Rest assured, however, the monks are not deprived for their place quietly surrounds a pretty cloister away from noise and visitors. The church standing to one side by itself is a stunner inside. The decorations of ceiling and altar are in vibrant colours of geometric designs. Somehow this modernity combined with plain walls and simple furnishings works well. The gardens are large and have long walks through woods and by water with azaleas blooming in the late spring. There is a walled and terraced early 18th century garden which is usually locked but ask if you can go inside. The monks are very hospitable and although accommodation is simple, it is adequate and in keeping with a monastic retreat. A new guest house is planned for the near future. Glenstal, founded in 1927 on the site of a medieval abbey, has a tradition of involvement in arts and crafts, especially in the areas of sculpture, metalwork, wood-turning and pottery. This is a large, active and growing religious community.

Open: All year except Christmas. Receives men and women.
Rooms: Both singles and doubles.
Facilities: Conferences by arrangement, park and gardens, small library and payphone.
Spiritual Help: Personal talks if requested.
Guests Admitted to: Chapel.
Meals: Everyone eats together. Traditional food. Vegetarians. Tea/coffee facilities.
Special Activities: No planned programme of events.
Situation: Quiet and in the countryside.
Maximum Stay: 3 to 7 days.
Bookings: By letter.
Charges: Donation. Average IR£22–IR£25 per day
Access: Rail from Dublin. Car: 12 miles from Limerick, off the Dublin Road.

God is beauty.

SAINT FRANCIS OF ASSISI

MEATH

Navan

Bellinter Retreat House
Bellinter, Navan
Co. Meath   Tel: 00 353 4621241
                                        e-mail: bellinter@eircom.ie

Roman Catholic

Bellinter House is a splendid stone Palladian mansion set in 14 acres of
parkland on the banks of the river Boyne which has been successfully
adapted to meet the needs of a retreat and conference centre. It actively
promotes an atmosphere of reconciliation where people of all races,
creeds and denominations can meet in peace. Among the directed and
preached retreats is a special one, *From Experience to Wisdom and Wonder*,
held in the spring and again in the summer for retiring religious and
lay people 55 or over. There are plans in operation now for increasing
the lecture and meeting facilities at Bellinter.

Open: All year. Receives everyone except families.
Rooms: 23 singles, 8 doubles, 16 twin-doubles.
Facilities: Conferences, gardens, library, guest lounge, TV, payphone,
direct dialling.
Spiritual Help: Directed and preached retreats.
Guests Admitted to: Unrestricted except for private Community area.
Meals: Taken in Guest House. Whole food with provision for vegetar-
ians and special diets.
Special Activities: Planned programme. Interfaith Evenings, Celtic
Spirituality, Restoring Blessedness, and Christian-Jewish Bible Course
are examples of what is on offer. Send for brochure.
Situation: Quiet in countryside.
Maximum Stay: No maximum.
Bookings: Letter or telephone.
Charges: Daily IR£40 full board. Weekend IR£74 full board. Non-
resident rates IR£25 per day with meals.
Access: Car is easiest but bus is possible. Send for map details.

MONAGHAN

Monaghan

Montfort House of Prayer
Monaghan   Tel: 00 353 4781709

Roman Catholic

Open: All year except July, August, Christmas and Easter. Receives
men, women, young people, families, groups, religious.
Rooms: 3 singles, 9 doubles

Facilities: Conferences, garden
Spiritual Help: Personal talks, groups sharing, meditation, directed study, prayers for healing.
Guests Admitted to: Chapel.
Meals: Taken in guest house. DIY facilities. Traditional food.
Special Activities: None.
Situation: Quiet in a town.
Maximum Stay: 4 days.
Bookings: Letter.
Charges: IR£24 per day.
Access: Car easiest way.

TIPPERARY

Kilsheelan

Rosminian House of Prayer
Glencomeragh
Kilsheelan, Clonmel
Co. Tipperary

Tel: 00 353 52 33181
Fax: 00 353 52 33636
e-mail: thegeln@rosminians.iol.ie

Roman Catholic

The House of Prayer sits at the foot of the Comeragh Mountains looking out over the valley of the River Suir. This splendid refurbished 19th century house has new and attractive rooms, tastefully decorated like a small, elegant country hotel with pretty wallpaper and curtains. The bathrooms are sparkling clean and generously equipped. The community went for professional advice on the decorating and it is a great success. With such outstanding attention to comfort and detail (even down to writing stationery in the desks) plus central heating, large dining room, library, church hall, spacious gardens, ornamental ponds, streams, and hens, ducks, and a peacock wandering around adding a dash of colour, Rosminian House must be one of the best retreat houses in Europe. For exercise, there are a variety of forest walks, countryside rambles and mountain hills, all easily available. In addition to the main house, there is Glen Lodge, a separate modern and well furnished self-catering house which is ideal for private retreats, groups and workshops. The small community of five make everyone feel at home. There is a daily Mass with a Taizé one the last Saturday of each month and both a Medjugorje evening as well as a Maranatha Rosary Group each week. This neat-as-a-pin place is just the base for a spirituality and retreat programme that combines deep religious traditions with new thinking – for example the Eucharist may be celebrated outdoors by a waterfall in the hills and there are Creation Retreats using animals such as horses and riding. As to the food, it is honest and plain with home-made pies and other good dishes. As the song says, it may well be a long, long way to Tipperary but if you're headed to the Rosminian House of Prayer, the journey is worth it. **Highly Recommended.**

Open: All year except four days at Christmas. Receives men, women, groups and religious.
Rooms: 15 singles, doubles. Approved by Irish Tourist Board under specialist accommodation.
Facilities: Disabled – on ground level. Conferences, garden with water ponds, library, TV payphone, direct dialling.
Spiritual Help: Personal talks, personal retreat direction, spiritual direction. Daily Mass with a Taizé Mass monthly. Sacrament of Reconciliation. Massage. Reflexology.
Guests Admitted to: Chapel. Residential guests have freedom of the house.
Meals: Everyone eats together. Wholefood and traditional. Vegetarian and special diets.
Special Activities: Special programme including a Step Spirituality programme, De Mello Weekend courses and preached retreats. Creation Retreats. Planned programme. Brochure available.
Situation: Very quiet in the countryside.
Maximum Stay: By arrangement.
Bookings: Letter or telephone.
Charges: Full board IR£30 daily. Self-catering IR£18 daily. Massage therapy IR£20. Reflexology IR£15.
Access: Car route easy. Bus possible – ask for directions.

Roscrea

Mount St Joseph Cistercian Abbey
Roscrea
Co. Tipperary   Tel: 00 353 505 21711

Roman Catholic – Ecumenical

The monastery guest house is a large one with wide cool hallways and much silence. The Community members are rather elderly and the singing in the choir perhaps diminished in volume now but not in the quality of praise – especially at Compline in the huge, grey stone, vaulted monastic church. The liturgy is deeply rich and inspiring. Almost 300 boys attend secondary school here but they are not intrusive. The Abbey is set in quiet countryside and is conducive to prayer and relaxation. In this monastic splendour combined with simplicity, the atmosphere is friendly and warm from a Community still busy seeking God and living full lives.

Open: All year except Christmas. Receives men, women, young people, groups, religious and non-retreatants.
Rooms: 9 singles, 11 doubles.
Facilities: Prayer room in guest house with Blessed Sacrament reserved. Conferences, guest lounge and payphone, direct dialling.
Spiritual Help: Personal talks. Spiritual direction. Personal retreat direction. Mass daily, Divine Office, Sacrament of Confession available.
Guests Admitted to: Chapel, Blessed Sacrament room.
Meals: Everyone eats together in the guest house. Traditional food. Vegetarians catered for.

Special Activities: No planned programme but there is a brochure available.
Situation: In quiet countryside.
Maximum Stay: 1 week.
Bookings: By letter or telephone.
Charges: On application.
Access: By rail or car from Dublin. Good bus services to Roscrea town – guest house 2½ miles away. Taxi services from Roscrea.

WATERFORD

Waterford

Grace Dieu Retreat Centre
Sacred Heart Missionaries
Tramore Road, Waterford
Co. Waterford   Tel: 00 353 51374417/51373372
                              Fax: 00 353 51874536
                          e-mail: gracedieu@ireland.com
              Website: www. Homepage.eircom.net/^gracedieu.

Roman Catholic

A large and very busy place offering a wide variety of retreats from Scripture study weekends to *Exploring The Inner Child* and extending the opportunity in retreats for a person to develop more profound insights, such as retreats which explore male and female energies. The old house which is the retreat centre was built about 1810 but has an equally large modern addition. All the rooms are up to date and all but two out of some 34 are en-suite with showers. The grounds are not extensive but offer mature trees, private sitting areas and a pleasant walk among trees and nearby pastures of almost a mile. All ages and all kinds of retreat programmes are catered for here with a chapel, simple in design and into which light pours from all sides. The resident community are friendly and have a wide range of interests. There are good facilities for the disabled – recently 16 disabled people with their own helpers were accommodated on a retreat.

Open: Open all year. receives men, women, young people, groups.
Rooms: 3 singles, 4 doubles plus 26 twin rooms.
Facilities: Conferences, guest lounge, payphone
Spiritual Help: Spiritual direction. Personal retreat direction. Aromatherapy massage in summer months. Guided meditation group.
Guests Admitted to: Chapel, work of Community.
Meals: Guest dining room. Traditional food. Vegetarian and special diets.
Special Activities: Programme of retreats. Send for brochure.
Situation: Quiet.
Maximum Stay: 7 days.
Bookings: Letter.
Charges: Charges vary from IR£34 to IR£39 per person per day. See brochure.

Access: Bus possible – ask for information when you book. Car route easy.

Ballymore Eustace

Avelin Retreat
Poulaphouca, Bishopland
Ballymore Eustace, Co. Wicklow

Tel: 00 353 45864524
Fax: 00 353 45864823
e-mail: begg@iol.ie
Website: www.avelin.hitsplc.com

Christian – Ecumenical

Avelin is a member of the Retreat Association (see Helpful Addresses) and the Methodist Retreat Group. The place is a warm and comfortable modern bungalow with four bedrooms en-suite. There are Celtic retreat programmes availabe with the Methodist minister and his wife who run Avelin. This retreat involves some walking – sometimes in the Irish mist. Some lovely places to see on such a retreat and some beautiful works of art to contemplate.

Open: All year.
Rooms: 4 doubles en-suite.
Facilities: Garden, guest lounge, TV. Guests may use e-mail and fax facilities.
Spiritual Help: Personal talks. Group sharing. Spiritual direction. Directed study.
Guests Admitted to: Unrestricted access. Quiet Room.
Meals: Everyone eats together. Traditional/vegetarian food. Special diets.
Special Activities: Programme. Send for information.
Situation: Quiet near lakes and mountains.
Maximum Stay: For the retreat or by arrangement.
Bookings: Letter/tel/fax/e-mail.
Charges: 6-day Celtic Pilgrimage Retreat IR£400. IR£21 per person sharing per night B&B.
Access: Train: They will collect you from Dublin. Bus: No.65 from Dublin. Car: N81.

There is no thought, feeling or desire within us which cannot become the substance of prayer.

GERARD W. HUGHES

Donard

**Chrysalis
Donard, Co. Wicklow**

Tel and Fax: 00 353 45404713
e-mail: peace@chrysalis.ie
Website: www.chrysalis.ie

Mind-Body-Spirit

A holistic centre for renewal and growth in a former rectory dating
from 1711 now restored, specialising in residential courses in personal
growth and spirituality. While the main concern here is with Mind-
Body-Spirit spirituality approaches, there are Christian traditions within the workshop programme such as de Mello exercises. This quiet
sanctuary offers space for diverse spiritual traditions with an extensive
programme of residential and one-day courses. These include *De Mello
Retreats, Touch and Relaxation, Facing Co-dependency, Searching for Inner
Freedom, Journal Writing,* and *Healing and Transformation, Inner Yoga and
Imagery* workshops. Vegetarian food and two hermitages add to the
attractions of this place. **Highly Recommended.**

Open: All year except Christmas. Receives everyone.
Rooms: 3 singles, 4 twin doubles, 2 dormitories, 2 hermitages.
Facilities: Conferences, garden, park, library.
Spiritual Help: Personal talks, group sharing, meditation, directed
study.
Guests Admitted to: Guest areas.
Meals: Everyone eats together. DIY facilities. *Vegetarian food only.*
Special Activities: Planned programme. Brochure available.
Situation: Very quiet in the countryside.
Maximum Stay: Usually 5 days, but longer possible for self-catering.
Bookings: Letter. Telephone.
Charges: See current brochure but workshops range from about
IR£145 to IR£295.
Access: Bus or car.

FRANCE

Le mesure de l'amour c'est d'aimer sans mesure.

SAINT AUGUSTINE

While the majority of retreat places in France are Roman Catholic monasteries and convents, there has been a rapid increase recently in the number of Buddhist and Alternative Spirituality places. Buddhism is the most rapidly expanding religion in France today with some five million people claiming interest in this spiritual path. Some Buddhist retreat places are in old buildings but many are modern and purpose-built. Many of the Christian religious communities and the lay people associated with them have modern guest house facilities too which are often striking in design and concept and very comfortable. On the other hand, the oldest monasteries are huge buildings orginally built to house big communities of men or women and, consequently, such places can strike you as very institutional. But many of these rambling places have refurbished guest rooms which are reasonably comfort-able. Many French monasteries will expect your stay to be a spiritual one and not just for relaxation. In other words, if you are not there to be quiet and pray, why have you come? The response to changes in the religious life in France have been different than those in Britain so the choice of retreats and courses on offer in France is narrower although the individual retreat and group pilgrimage remain widely popular, with retreat programmes increasing in breadth and scope every year. Buddhist centres expect you to be there for spiritual intentions and, while you often need or should have some previous experience of med-itation, it is not always mandatory.

Alternative Spirituality facilities and programmes have increased in France by leaps and bounds with a great expansion of courses, work-shops, training and retreats. A quick look in any French magazine shop will confirm the wide range of interests the French have in holistic and alternative spirituality and health approaches. These centres and their programmes are often exciting, enabling, and positive in terms of de-stressing, exploration of new horizons, self-improvement, and for discovering the inner person. Yoga is taught all over France and almost as popular is T'ai-Chi, Circle and African dancing, and other forms of mind-body-spirit endeavours.

For those interested in Buddhist teachings and retreats, the selec-tion is also wide ranging from Tibetan establishments to new teaching approaches to traditional Buddhism. Obviously if you speak some French, it helps when going on retreat in France, but today many peo-ple, especially the young in France, know some English. In any case, most French people are tolerant and polite in accepting any attempt, no matter how inadequate, to speak their beautiful language. There are some programmes in English so it is worth sending for information if you spot a place that appeals to you. (To phone France dial 00 33, then omit the first 0 of the area code.) Some of the retreat centres in Britain also run courses in France, often in lovely settings. From time to time, major Buddhist events are held in which English is available in instantaneous translation. For example, His Holiness The Dalai-Lama recently undertook a five-day programme of teaching on the theme of the road to awakening in the south west in which French, English and German translations were all available.

While there are sure to be one or two pleasant culinary surprises when you stay on retreat in France (even if it is only the freshness of the food), do not expect the meals in monastic France necessarily to reflect the fame of that nation's reputation for cooking. By and large monks and nuns everywhere in the world cook simple, plain food. Vegetarians on retreat in France are in for a difficult time as provision for them is at a minimum unless they stay in Buddhist or Alternative Spirituality centres. This has nothing to do with lack of Christian hospitality but everything to do with cultural differences.

As to costs for your retreat in France, the charges are usually in the range 180 to 350FF full board per day in a monastery. It can be lower but usually not higher. Sometimes too, it is by donation. The same applies to Buddhist places but Alternative Spirituality centres offer programmes, treatments and room and board rates that correspond to those you would expect in Britain.

The following retreat places are listed by the departments of France. Bonne chance!

AIN (01)

Bourg en Bresse
Auris
6, rue Viala
01000 Bourg en Bresse   Tel: 04 74 22 48 86
Alternative Spirituality. Yoga, de-stressing, meditation, chanting, voice workshops, and personal therapies are all on offer here. Send for brochure.

Le Plantay
Abbaye Notre-Dame-des-Dombes
Le Plantay
01330 Villars-les-Dombes   Tel: 04 74 98 14 40
                                                            Fax: 04 74 98 16 70
Roman Catholic. Trappist monks. Receives men, women, groups who desire a retreat of silence and prayer. Accommodation for 40. Camping, woods, domitory and barn. Disabled facility for one. 1-hr video on the monastery which was founded in 1863 is available. Monks make various products including dried fruits, petits fours and have a small shop.

Miribel
Centre Alain de Boismenu
Rue de La Chanal, B.P. 236
01702 Miribel   Tel: 04 78 55 31 47
                                                            Fax: 04 78 55 00 59
Roman Catholic. Welcomes men, women and groups who want a retreat of reflection, recollection, and prayer. Close to the town, the guest house has a private garden and offers peace and a spiritual atmosphere. Accommodation for up to 100 guests with a number of meeting rooms and equipment. Must book in advance of arrival.

AISNE (02)

Brumetz
Maison de la Trinité
02810 Cerfroid, Brumetz   Tel: 03 23 71 41 85
Fax: 03 23 71 23 04
Roman Catholic. The Community of sisters receive up to thirty men
and women guests. 30 singles, 1 double, guest lounges. Chapel, choir.
Personal talks with a sister if requested.

ALLIER (03)

Chantelle
Abbaye Bénédictine Saint-Vincent
Rue Anne de Beauzier
03140 Chantelle   Tel: 04 70 56 62 55
Fax: 04 70 56 62 69
Roman Catholic. Benedictine Community, receives men, women,
accompanied disabled. 27 rooms, 5 conferences rooms, library, chapel,
choir. Personal talks, meditation. 8 days maximum stay.

Dompierre-sur-Besbre
Abbaye Notre Dame de Sept-Fons
03290 Dompierre-sur-Besbre   Tel: 04 70 48 14 90
Roman Catholic. Men, religious, for religious retreats only. Personal
talks possible.

Moulins
Monastère de la Visitation
65, rue des Tanneries
03000 Moulins   Tel: 04 70 44 27 43
Roman Catholic. Visitation nuns. 2 rooms for women with enclosure
for a silent retreat.

ALLIER (04)

Ganagobie
Monastère Notre-Dame
04310 Ganagobie   Tel: 04 92 68 00 04
Fax: 04 92 68 11 49
Christian. This monastery has been restored to create an enterprise
centre which organises seminars on such things as management and
ethics. Information available on courses.

Faucon de Barcelonnette
Couvent Saint-Jean de Matha
04400 Faucon de Barcelonnette   Tel: 04 92 81 09 17
Roman Catholic. The Community of religious men welcome individuals
or groups for stays of not more than 21 days. There are 14 single rooms,
9 doubles, about 200FF full board per day.

ALPES-HAUTE (05)

Laragne
Terre Nouvelle
B.P. 52
05300 Laragne   Tel: 04 92 65 24 25
Alternative Spirituality. A place like Findhorn Community (see entry).
Many workshops in the summer. Send for course information and
event charges.

Saint Etienne de Laus
Hôtellerie Notre-Dame du Laus
05130 Saint Etienne de Laus   Tel: 04 92 50 30 73
                                                       Fax: 04 92 50 90 77
Roman Catholic. This is a very large establishment with accommodation
for upwards of 400. It is also very popular and bookings for summer
need to be made at least four months in advance. With a view of the
mountains, this retreat house offers disabled facilities, library, lounges,
personal talks, conferences, chapel, choir, masses, and courses. Full
board rates vary but are in 190 to 300FF range. Send for information.

ALPES-MARITIMES (06)

Carros
Communauté des Carmélites
06510 Carros-Village   Tel: 04 93 29 10 71
Roman Catholic. Carmelite nuns. Receives men, women, young people
in rather isolated and very peaceful situation. 7 rooms for retreats of 10
days maximum. Personal talks, prayers in chapel with Community.

La Trinité
Sanctuaire de Notre-Dame de Laghet
06340 La Trinité   Tel: 04 93 41 09 60
                                                       Fax: 04 93 41 21 78
Roman Catholic. The sisters of the Sacred Heart receive men and women
retreatants and pilgrims. Some 60 rooms, guest lounges, library, personal talks, conferences. Rates about 225FF full board per day.

ARDÈCHE (07)

Rochessauve
Aleph
07210 Rochessauve   Tel: 04 75 65 10 99
                                                       Fax: 04 75 65 08 02
Alternative Spirituality. It is claimed that this centre is like no other. It
is certainly true that it is in a magical place in the Ardèche. Here is a setting of gorges, mountains, prehistoric sites, and sacred places. What
happens at Aleph is aimed at helping you to make contact with nature
and, in turn, with your own nature. Send for information on their philosophy and courses.

Saint-Étienne-de-Lugdarès
La Père Hotelier
Abbaye Notre-Dame-des-Neiges
07590 Saint Laurent les Bains　　　　　　Tel: 04 66 46 00 68
Roman Catholic. Open Easter to All Saints Day. Receives all, young
people in annexe. Group conferences. Setting up high in mountains.
Much silence and an austere life. Send for their brochure.

Vanosc
Maison Saint-Joseph
07690 Vanosc　　　　　　　　　　　　　Tel: 04 75 34 62 95
Roman Catholic. Receives men and women. 40 singles, 8 doubles,
library, guest lounge, personal talks, chapel, choir. It is possible here to
attend an Ignatian retreat. Send for information.

AUDE (11)

Capendu
Monastère Sainte-Claire
Azille
11700 Capendu　　　　　　　　　　　　Tel: 04 68 91 40 24
Roman Catholic. Open to men and women for retreats or just a short
period of reflection. Limited number of rooms. 8 days maximum stay.

Fanjeaux
Belvedere Saint Dominique
Rue de la Porte en Rivière
Prouilhe
11270 Fanjeaux　　　　　　　　　　　　Tel: 04 68 24 72 36
Roman Catholic. This is an international cultural and retreat centre in a
village 360 metres up with a panoramic view of the plain of Lauragais.
It is run in conjunction with the Dominicans with a programme of
events and courses. Receives men, women, groups. 10 rooms several
guest lounges, library, personal talks, meeting rooms, chapel.

AVEYRON (12)

Espalion
Abbaye Notre-Dame-de-Bonneval
Le Cayrol
12500 Espalion　　　　　　　　　　　　Tel: 05 65 44 01 22
Roman Catholic. Cistercian nuns. Open to all for spiritual retreats. 32
single rooms.

Mur-de-Barrez
Monastère Sainte-Claire
2, rue de la Berque
12600 Mur-de-Barrez　　　　　　　　　Tel: 05 65 66 00 46
Roman Catholic. A Community of Poor Clares welcoming women and
families with children. Much peace and solitude. Chapel, personal talks
and spiritual direction possible, library, TV, meeting rooms. 13 singles,
17 doubles, 3 triples. About 180FF full board per day or self-catering.

Saint-Sernin-sur-Rance
Monastère Notre-Dame-d'Orient
12380 Saint-Sernin-sur-Rance   Tel: 05 65 99 60 88
Roman Catholic. Receives young and not so young, laymen and lay-
women, priests, monks, nuns.

BOUCHES-DU-RHÔNE (13)

Aix-en-Provence
Carmel de Notre Dame de l'Assomption
4 Montée Saint-Joseph, Route du Tholonet
13090 Aix-en-Provence   Tel: 04 42 21 40 58
Roman Catholic. Women and young women – two or three at a time –
are received here by the Carmelite nuns.

Grans
Domaine de Petite
Union Culture et Promotion
Route de Saint-Chamas
13450 Grans   Tel: 04 90 55 93 60
                                                  Fax: 04 90 55 87 74
Roman Catholic. Receives everyone for spiritual retreats, seminars and
courses. It is an isolated house with a very large woodland park. 20 singles, 16 doubles, 4 domitories, 7 meeting rooms, TV, pilgrims way,
chapel, library. Rates about 225FF full board and 160FF demi-pension.

Jouques
Abbaye Notre-Dame-de-Fidélité
13490 Jouques   Tel: 04 42 57 80 17
                                                  Fax: 04 42 67 05 21
Roman Catholic. Receives individuals and groups for Benedictine hospitality who are searching for peace and silence. Choir in Gregorian
chant.

Simiane-Collongue
Communautés Bénédictines de Sainte Lioba
Quartier Saint-Germain
13109 Simiane-Collongue   Tel: 04 42 22 60 60
Roman Catholic. Open all year to everyone. Receives either those for a
silent retreat in the convent or all others in guest housing. Hill walking
nearby.

Tarascon
Abbaye Saint-Michel-de-Frigolet
13150 Tarascon-sur-Rhône   Tel: 04 90 90 52 70
                                                  Fax 04 90 95 75 22
Roman Catholic. A magical place of herbs set in the summer beauty of
Provence. Open to all including pilgrims. 36 rooms, a restaurant which
is also open to day visitors, meeting rooms, TV chapel, choir, personal
talks possible. About 260FF full board. Can sometimes be busy in summer with lots of people coming and going – but it is well worth a visit
even for the day.

CALVADOS (14)

Bayeux
Monastère des Bénédictines
48, rue Saint-Loup – BP 219
14402 Bayeux Cedex   Tel: 02 31 92 02 99
                                          Fax: 02 31 21 59 91
Roman Catholic. Receives women and families. Open all year. Maximum
stay 2 weeks. Accommodation for 35. Chapel. Personal talks possible.
Quiet location and much silence.

Caen
Monastère de Carmélites
51, avenue Clemenceau
14000 Caen   Tel: 02 31 93 66 63
Roman Catholic. Welcomes all for private individual retreats. Longer
stays for those considering a vocation.

Juaye-Mondaye
Abbaye St Martin de Mondaye
14250 Juaye-Mondaye   Tel: 02 31 92 58 11
                                          Fax: 02 31 92 08 05
Roman Catholic. Open all year. Receives mostly men. Disabled. Special
Open Door retreats in summer. Participation in Divine Office warmly
welcomed. Accommodation for 60, 3 lounges and 2 workshops, library,
chapel, personal talks possible. A popular place – you need to book several months in advance.

LISIEUX

Lisieux is another international Christian place of pilgrimage located in
France. Sainte Thérèse de l'Enfant Jésus (1873-97) or *The Little Flower* as
she is often called, was the daughter of a watchmaker. At the early age
of 15, she obtained permission to enter the Carmelite convent at
Lisieux. She wrote about twenty prayers and an autobiography,
L'Histoire d'une âme (The Story of a Soul), which has been translated into
fifty languages and is the biggest spirituality bestseller after the Bible.
She had little education, suffered grave and painful illnesses from
which she eventually died in agony, and sometimes faltered in her
beliefs. Yet, she is one of the most famous and beloved saints in the
world. Her popularity lies in her appeal to ordinary people. She
believed, among other things, in a return to the word of God, a priority for all Christians of the virtues of faith, hope and charity in everyday
life, the call of each baptised person to sanctity, and the need for broth-
erly affection for those of different beliefs and for those who do not
believe in God. She rose above the religious thinking of her time and
she showed with inspired insight a new way to God based on the central message of the Gospels, which is love.

Accueil Providence
17 chemin de Rocques
14100 Lisieux

Tel: 02 31 48 56 62
Fax: 02 31 48 56 76

Roman Catholic. This is a very large place where a lot of groups and school groups come. Individual retreats are possible. All the facilities you would expect of such a large modern complex.

Ermitage Sainte-Thérèse
23 rue du Carmel
14100 Lisieux

Tel: 02 31 48 55 10
Fax: 02 31 48 55 27

Roman Catholic. This is a centre for pilgrims open all year except 15 December to 15 January. There is a calendar of retreats and both individuals and groups are received.

CHARENTE (16)

Montmoreau-Saint-Cybard
Abbaye Sainte-Marie-de-Maumont
Juignac
16190 Montmoreau-Saint-Cybard

Tel: 05 45 60 34 38

Roman Catholic. Open to individuals or groups for stays of up to 8 days. Personal talks by arrangement. Chapel, choir. 23 rooms. Need to book 15 days in advance.

A partir de notre vécu, se découvre une voie d'éveil du coeur et de l'esprit, simple et universelle. Elle constitue le fond commun de tout cheminement authentique.

Lama Denys

CHARENTE-MARITIME (17)

La Rochelle
Carmel
1 rue Saint-Dominique
17000 La Rochelle

Tel: 05 46 41 47 02

Roman Catholic. Open to all women religious and young women. 3 rooms.

Saint Palais sur Mer
Béthanie
Monastère des Dominicaines
67 avenue de Courlay
17420 Saint Palais sur Mer

Tel: 05 46 23 12 19

Roman Catholic. Receives all as individuals or in groups up to 20 persons. 13 rooms, guest lounge, TV, meeting room. Personal talks possible. Chapel. Help is usually asked of guests for setting the tables, washing up and redoing the beds when they leave. If you want to come here in July or August you need to book at least 3 months in advance.

CHER (18)

Saint-Doulchard
Monastère de Saint-Doulchard
115 route de Vouzeron
18230 Saint-Doulchard   Tel: 02 48 65 57 65
Roman Catholic. Receives individuals and groups for retreats. Maximum stay 8 days. About 20 rooms available. Chapel services in French. Mass everyday.

CORRÈZE (19)

Aubazine
Monastère de la Théophanie
Le Ladeix
19190 Aubazine   Tel: 05 55 25 75 67
Byzantine Catholic nuns. Religious services in French. Receives men, women, young people, very small groups. One of the nuns speaks English. Great hospitality from this Community. The monastery is an old farmhouse, high up in the Massif Central. Courses on Byzantine spirituality and on the art and theology of Icons are sometimes offered. Vegetarian food on request. 11 singles, 3 doubles, central heating in winter, guest lounge, library, chapel, personal talks possible. A busy place – Easter and summer time you need to book at least a month in advance.

CORSE (20)

Vico
Couvent Saint-François
20160 Vico   Tel: 04 95 26 83 83
                        Fax: 04 95 26 64 09
Roman Catholic. The Community receives everyone for an individual or group retreat. You may come for a few days or a weekend for reflection and prayer. The convent is high up on the mountain with views. About 40 beds. About 250FF full board. Guest lounge, chapel, choir, meeting rooms, library, personal talks possible.

COTE-D'ÔR (21)

Flavigny-sur-Ozerain
Abbaye Saint-Joseph-de-Clairval
21150 Flavigny-sur-Ozerain   Tel: 03 80 96 22 31
                                        Fax 03 80 96 25 29
Roman Catholic. Open only to men for spiritual retreats of 5 days or for a maximum stay of 1 week. 17 single rooms, library, chapel, choir, personal talks possible.

Saint Nicholas Les Citeaux
Abbaye de Citeaux
21700 Saint Nicholas les Citeaux　　　　Tel: 03 80 61 11 53
　　　　　　　　　　　　　　　　　　　　Fax: 03 80 62 36 79
Roman Catholic. Founded in 1098, this is the mother house of the order
of Cistercians where some 40 monks live a life of simplicity and austerity. The abbey is in a great park about 200 metres up and the monks
welcome individuals who want to make a retreat of up to 8 days. 25 singles, 12 doubles, 5 family rooms, 2 guest lounges, chapel, choir, personal talks possible.

CÔTES-DU-NORD (22)

Saint-Brieuc
Carmel
55, rue Pinot-Duclos
22000 Saint-Brieuc　　　　　　　　　　Tel: 02 96 94 22 95
Roman Catholic. Receives women for individual retreats.

Saint Jacut de la Mer
L'Abbaye
B.P. I
22750 Saint Jacut de la Mer　　　　　Tel: 02 96 27 71 19
　　　　　　　　　　　　　　　　　　　　Fax: 02 96 27 79 45
Roman Catholic. Managed by the association La Providence, this
retreat house is open from September to the end of June for both individuals and groups who wish to make a retreat. They run a programme
of courses, retreats, and events. Send for brochure. The atmosphere is
good for silence and time to reflect. Disabled. 45 singles, 40 doubles, 7
family bedrooms, meeting rooms, guest lounges, tennis, library, TV,
chapel, choir.

CREUSE (23)

La Cellette
Le Blé en Herbe (The Ripening Seed)　　　　
Puissetier
23350 La Cellette　　　　　　　　　　　Tel: 05 55 80 62 83

Alternative Spirituality – Eco-spirituality. Holistic retreats. Open from
March to November. Receives men, women, children, groups. Set in the
rolling foothills of the Massif Central, this well-established place has an
eight acre organic garden with wild flower fields and is surrounded by
unspoiled countryside. The lifestyle here is one of simplicity and close-
ness to Nature. A variety of options for *a get-away from it all retreat* are
on offer. Programmes may include *Holistic Massage, African Dancing,
Meditation of Dance, Shiatsu and Healing, Sacred Space for Women,* and
Herbal Medicine. Facilities include personal talks, group sharing. 2 singles, 4 doubles, camping and caravan site, a barn. Vegetarian food.
Costs about 170FF per day full board camping but 25FF per night.
Highly Recommended.

Bergerac
Carmel du Sacré-Coeur
79, rue Valette
24100 Bergerac   Tel: 05 53 57 15 33
Roman Catholic. Open only to those who are making a retreat or families of the religious. Open May and June. 5 singles.

Echourgnac
Abbaye Notre-Dame-de-Bonne-Espérance
Echourgnac
24410 Saint-Aulaye   Tel: 05 53 80 36 43
                                                      Fax: 05 53 80 08 36
Roman Catholic. Trappist nuns. Open all year to all for spiritual retreats of up to 10 days. A very peaceful place with 25 rooms, 2 guest lounges, chapel.

Monestier
Centre d'études et de prière
Sainte Crois
24240 Monestier   Tel: 05 53 63 37 70
Christian. A study and prayer centre run by an Orthodox priest and his wife. There are some workshops organised by different people, Send for brochure.

Montignac
Dhagpo Kagyu Ling
Saint-Léon-sur-Vézère
24290 Montignac   Tel: 05 53 50 70 75
                                                      Fax: 05 53 50 80 54
                           e-mail: Dhagpo.Kagyu.Ling@Wanadoo.fr
Buddhist. Karma Kagyu Tibetan. This is one of three international centres, the others being in Sikkim and America. The property was given by Bernard Benson in 1977 and is a place of silence near the famed Lascaux caves. Practice is in Tibetan but information available in English. Three-year, three-month and three-day retreats are all on offer. Day membership is possible. Accommodation ranges from dormitories at about 40FF a night to singles and doubles 50-120FF a night. Meals from 30-40FF.

Saint-Léon-sur-Vézère
La Bicanderie
24290 Saint-Léon-sur-Vézère   Tel/fax: 05 53 50 75 24
                           e-mail: chanteloube@wanadoo.fr
Buddhist. Vajrayana Tibetan. Situated in a green valley, not far from Brive in the direction of Bordeaux. Spiritual practices are in Tibetan but information is available in English and French. Three-year guided retreats are possible here and various programmes of study which cost about 100FF a day. Single and double rooms cost 120FF a day and food 140FF a day.

St Crépin Carlucet
Centre Eviel
Les Granges
24590 StCrépin Carlucet   Tel: 05 53 28 93 27
Fax: 05 53 28 81 17
Alternative Spirituality. This is a centre for personal development and awakening the spiritual in yourself. Courses on offer may include workshops with titles like *Opening the Heart, the Inner Clown, Truth through Painting, Intuitive Massage, Relaxation Techniques,* and *Bio-Dance.* Send for information on current year's programme and the rates.

DOUBS (25)

Besançon
La Roche D'Or
25042 Besancon   Tel: 03 81 51 42 44
Roman Catholic. This place has become quite famous for giving retreats and it is worth sending for their annual programme.

Nans-sous-Sainte-Anne
Prieuré Saint-Benoît
Nans-sous-Sainte-Anne
25330 Amancey   Tel: 03 81 86 61 79
Roman Catholic. The nuns receive women, religious, priests and couples for private retreats and to take part in the Community prayers. 3 singles, 5 doubles, 1 work room, chapel, choir, personal talks possible.

DRÔME (26)

Aiguebelle
Abbaye Notre-Dame d'Aiguebelle
Montjoyer
26230 Grignan   Tel: 04 75 98 52 33
Roman Catholic. Trappists monastery. Guest house for retreats.

Chateauneuf de Galaure
Foyer de Charité
B.P. 11
26330 Chateaneuf de Galaure   Tel: 04 75 68 79 00
Fax: 04 75 68 66 91
Christian. A place for individual and group retreats. Send for brochure.

Crest
Monastère de Sainte-Claire
53, rue des Auberts
26400 Crest   Tel: 04 75 25 49 13
Fax: 04 75 25 28 80
Roman Catholic. Receives all for retreats of up to 8 days. Disabled. 25 rooms, garden, library, chapel, choir, personal talks possible. Book at least 15 days before you want to go.

Grignan
Prieuré de l'Emmanuel
26230 Grignan   Tel: 04 75 46 50 37
Roman Catholic. Receives everyone looking for peace and reflection.
Retreats and courses on biblical subjects. Brochure available. 8 rooms,
dormitories, guest lounge, possibility of camping. Woods and lavender
fields all around.

Saint-Bonnet de Valclérieux
Chateau de Valclérieux
Saint-Bonnet de Valclérieux
26350 Crépol   Tel: 04 75 71 70 67
Alternative Spirituality. A beautiful and popular place which organises
yoga and various health therapy courses and workshops for both individuals and groups. Send for information and charges on year's current programme.

Saint Jean en Royans
Atelier Saint-Jean Damascene
Centre d'Enseignement Icone-Fresque-Mosaique
La Prade
26190 Saint Jean en Royans   Tel: 04 75 48 66 75
                                                  Fax: 04 75 47 70 77
Christian. An information centre on icons, frescos, and mosaics which
welcomes all for a spiritual stay to study these three disciplines from an
artistic and religious viewpoint. There is a park and swimming pool
nearby and a number of other local attractions worth a visit. 4 doubles,
chapel, TV, personal talks possible. About 65FF a night.

Triors
Monastère Notre-Dame de Triors
Triors B.P.1
26750 Chatillon St Jean   Tel: 04 75 71 43 39
Roman Catholic. Receives everyone for retreats but respect must be
maintained for silence. Simplicity and austerity of place and life here. 9
singles, 9 doubles, dormitory. Men eat in refectory. Others DIY for
meals.

EURE (27)

Le Bec-Hellouin
Abbaye Notre-Dame-du-Bec
Le Bec-Hellouin
27800 Le Bec-Hellouin   Tel: 02 32 44 86 09
                                                  Fax: 02 32 44 96 69
Roman Catholic. This is a grand monastery of the Benedictine Olivetan
Order in France. Set in green pastures and near to the Channel ports, Le
Bec is open to all. Men stay with the monks individually or in groups
and take meals in the refectory. There are about 30 rooms available in
two areas – one is inside the monastery for guests who wish to join the
Community in their silence and prayer while the other accommodation
is outside and reserved for groups and young people on retreat and for

study and various courses. The Divine Office is sung in Gregorian chant and in French. Women guests stay in the nearby convent, **Monastère Sainte-Françoise-Romaine** (Tel: 02 32 44 81 18 Fax: 02 32 45 90 53) and may join the religious services such as Vespers and Mass in the abbey which is only 2 km away. If you think you would like to go on retreat in France and want something not too far from home, then these two Communities will warmly welcome you and you will find peace and sanctuary here. For either the abbey or the convent, write and ask what their charges will be and, for the convent, what accommodation is available when you want to stay. Car is easy and train is possible on the Paris Saint-Lazare/Évreaux line, stopping at Bec-Hellouin. **Highly Recommended.**

FINISTÈRE (29)

Plounéventer
Monastère de Kerbenéat
29400 Plounéventer   Tel: 02 98 20 47 43
                                                              Fax: 02 98 20 43 03
Roman Catholic. Receives everyone. A tree-lined lane leads to the church reflecting a setting for this monastery which is near woods with fields on most sides. A quiet place with the possibility of visiting a hermitage nearby. 10 singles, 2 family rooms, meeting room, 2 guest lounges, library, chapel, choir, personal talks possible. From about 150FF to 2000FF full board per person. Write well in advance to book.

Le Relecq-Kerhuon
Carmel de Brest
88 bis, boulevard Clemenceau
29219 Le Relecq-Kerhuon   Tel: 02 98 28 27 93
Roman Catholic. 3 rooms for women only for private retreat. DIY for meals.

GARD (30)

Uzès
Carmel
7, avenue Louis-Alteirac
30700 Uzès   Tel: 04 66 22 10 62
Roman Catholic. Open only for individual retreats. Uzès is a wonderfully restored small town with graceful arches around the market square. Full of tourists in the summer with many foreigners owning local holiday homes, this small town is, nevertheless, a gem of a place.

GARONNE (HAUTE) (31)

Blagnac
Monastère Notre-Dame-des-Sept-Douleurs
et de Sainte-Catherine-de-Sienne
60, avenue Général-Compans
31700 Blagnac   Tel: 05 61 71 46 48

Roman Catholic. Dominican nuns. Open to all. Guest accommodation is separate from the monastery. Long or short stays. Guest lounges, library, chapel, choir. Individual or groups retreats with own leaders for reflection and prayer. Beautiful setting in a quiet place by the Garronne river.

Bellegarde-Sainte-Marie
Abbaye Sainte-Marie-du-Désert
31530 Bellegarde-Sainte-Marie   Tel: 05 61 85 61 32
                                                     Fax: 05 61 85 04 32
Roman Catholic. Cistercian monks. 25 rooms for retreatants for up to 8 days. There is an annual pilgrimage in September for the Nativity of the Virgin Mary.

Muret
Carmel
La Combe-Sainte-Marie
67, chemin Lacombe
31600 Muret   Tel: 05 61 51 03 67
Roman Catholic. Carmelite nuns who receive guests for individual retreats in solitude.

GERS (32)

Auch
Soeurs Dominicaines d'Auch
10, rue de la Somme
32000 Auch   Tel: 05 62 05 07 37
                                                     Fax: 05 62 63 67 25
Roman Catholic. Welcomes young women to join them for a private retreat of prayer and life with the Community. If you do go, take time to see the remarkable carved wood choir stalls in Auch Cathedral which are one of the great heritages of France. Information is available in English about them.

Saramon
Monastère Cistercien de Sainte-Marie-de-Boulaur
32450 Boulaur   Tel: 05 62 65 40 07
                                                     Fax: 05 62 65 49 37
Roman Catholic. Receives women, young people, groups and families only. Open May – September. Groups only in winter. 53 beds.

GIRONDE (33)

Auros
Abbaye de Sainte-Marie-du-Rivet
33124 Auros   Tel: 05 56 65 40 10
Roman Catholic. Cistercian nuns. One of the oldest monasteries in France with a 13th century church surrounded by 9th century fortifications. Guest accommodation for individuals in search of calm and repose. 26 rooms, guest lounge, personal talks possible, large park, nice garden, much peace. Choir offices in French and Gregorian chant.

Bordeaux
Centre Louis-Beaulieu
145, rue de Saint-Genés
33082 Bordeaux Cedex

Tel: 05 56 96 57 37
Fax: 05 56 96 88 12

Roman Catholic. Retreat House which welcomes individuals and groups. It is on the Lourdes – Compostelle route so it is also a centre for pilgrims on route. Situated in the town, there are 30 rooms, 6 rooms with 4 beds each, guest lounge, meeting rooms, library, park, sports facilities. About 200FF full board per day.

Monastère de la Visitation
47, cours Marc-Nouaux
33000 Bordeaux

Tel: 05 56 44 25 72

Roman Catholic. Receives women only. Try to write in the first instance.

Rions
Monastère du Broussey
33410 Rions

Tel: 05 56 62 60 90
Fax: 05 56 62 60 79

Roman Catholic, Receives everyone for silence and prayer. Guests may join the Community in their life of prayer. 18 rooms, guest lounge, garden, chapel, library, personal talks possible. Write in first instance and include a SAE. Suggested donation about 175FF per day.

HÉRAULT (34)

Le Bousquet-d'Orb
Monastère Orthodoxe Saint-Nicolas
La Dalmerie
34260 Le Bousquet-d'Orb

Telephone: 04 67 23 41 10

Orthodox – Eastern Rite. Receives men and women. Open Easter to October for spiritual retreats only of up to 7-day stay. 8 beds, camping. Guest dining room. Orthodox only for holy sacraments.

Montpellier
Espace Manrèse – Centre de Spiritualité Ignatienne
21 bis/23 rue de la Garenne
34090 Montpellier

Tel: 04 67 04 38 60
Fax: 04 67 04 38 79

Roman Catholic. Jesuit run guest house attached to their Community building where individual retreats are possible for a few days or longer stay for undertaking the spiritual exercises of St Ignatius. Disabled possible, but always ask about exactly what is on offer. 7 rooms, library, chapel, choir, personal talks and spiritual direction possible, pilgrims welcomed. About 200FF full board per day.

Roqueredonde
La Borie Noble
38650 Roqueredonde

Tel: 04 67 44 09 89

Ecumenical Christian. The main house of the charitable organisation *La Communauté de l'Arche*. It is high up in the mountains and not easy to find or get to. The Community here live an austere life based on Gandhian principles. About 100 live a simple life here – for example, without electricity. Open all year round. Receives men, women, young people, families and groups. Visitors join in the Community work and routines. If you do not know about the work of *l'Arche* which has houses in Britain and elsewhere, you may find it rewarding to find out, especially if you are young and want to help other people less fortunate than yourself within a community life context even if only for a short time.

Saint-Mathieu-de-Tréviers
Communauté Dominicaine
34270 Saint-Mathieu-de-Tréviers   Tel: 04 67 55 20 62
Roman Catholic. Open to men, women, families, groups. 40 rooms, some doubles, many en-suite, library, guest lounges, personal talks possible. Situated between sea and mountains among trees. A place of deep silence and prayer.

ILLE-ET-VILAINE (35)

Plerguer
Notre-Dame-de-Beaufort
35540 Plerguer   Tel: 02 99 48 07 57
Roman Catholic. Dominican nuns. Open to all for the purposes of a retreat. 20 rooms plus annexe and dormitory. Maximum stay 10 days. 20 rooms, 2 guest lounges, library, chapel, personal talks possible. Write for your booking to the Guest Sister at least 8 days in advance. The monastery is among trees, near a lake.

INDRE (36)

Fontgombault
Abbaye Notre-Dame-de-Fontgombault
36220 Fontgombault   Tel: 02 54 37 12 03
                                          Fax: 02 54 37 12 56
Roman Catholic. Benedictine monks. Receives guests in an 11th century abbey where retreats are in silence and austerity. Retreatants are expected to be present at the principal Divine Offices. Simplicity and silence are the key notes to going on retreat here. If you are thinking about trying a religious life and want a place for a retreat of silent and contemplative reflection, try this place.

Pellevoisin
Monastère des Dominicaines
3 rue Notre Dame
36180 Pellevoisin   Tel: 02 54 39 00 46
                                          Fax: 02 54 39 04 66
Roman Catholic. Open to all. Accommodation for 8 for religious retreats, guest lounge, meeting room, chapel, choir, personal talks possible. Pellevoisin has been a place of pilgrimage since 1815 when there were apparitions of the Virgin Mary here.

ISÈRE (38)

Biviers
Centre Saint Hugues
38330 Biviers
Tel: 04 76 90 35 97
Fax: 04 76 90 35 78
Roman Catholic. At the entrance to Grenoble and near the mountains, this Jesuit Community offers a place for silence and reflection.

Voiron
Monastère de la Visitation
Notre-Dame-du-May
38500 Voiron
Tel: 04 76 05 26 29
Roman Catholic. Visitation nuns. Receives individuals and groups for silent retreats and participation in prayer. Women may make a retreat within the enclosure for deep silence, meditation, and prayer. Spiritual guidance in the tradition of St Francis de Sales is available if desired.

Voreppe
Monastère des Clarisses
94 chemin Sante-Claire
38340 Voreppe
Tel: 04 76 50 26 03
Fax: 04 76 50 03 44
Roman Catholic. The Community of sisters welcome individuals and groups for 8 to 10-day retreats. Chapel choir, personal talks possible. A small monastery and guest house in a setting of trees and mountains.

JURA (39)

Vitreux
Abbaye D'Acey
Vitreux
39350 Gendrey
Tel: 03 84 81 04 11
Roman Catholic. Cistercian monks. Open to all. 15 rooms. Groups do their own catering. A popular place so book several months in advance.

LANDES (40)

Mugron
Abbaye Notre-Dame de Maylis
40250 Mugron
Tel: 05 58 97 72 81
Fax: 05 58 97 72 58
Roman Catholic. Benedictine monks of the Olivetan Order as at *Le Bec* (see above). The monastery is situated in lovely country in the midst of this vast department of France which has millions of trees. The Community organises retreats usually for groups but individuals who want a retreat for spiritual reasons are welcomed. Many ancient churches in the area. Nearby at the hilltop town of St Sever there is an annual summer exhibition with demonstrations of the work of outstanding artisans, including bookbinding, wood-turning, and weaving.

Saint Vincent de Paul
Oeuvre du Berceau de Saint-Vincent de Paul
40990 Saint Vincent de Paul   Tel: 05 58 89 90 01
                                                   Fax: 05 58 89 97 77
Roman Catholic. Here in the birthplace of St Vincent de Paul, the
founder of an Order who serve the poor throughout the world. There
is a retreat guest house which welcomes individuals and groups for
retreats and courses. There are a number of tourist sites in the area.
Disabled possible. Accommodation for 50 with meeting rooms, guest
lounge, library, TV, chapel. Personal talks possible, pilgrims welcomed.

LOIRE (42)

Pradines
Abbaye Saint-Joseph-et-Saint-Pierre de Pradines
42630 Pradines   Tel: 04 77 64 80 06
Roman Catholic. Receives individuals or groups for retreats in silence.
Maximum stay 7 days. Disabled. 2 dining rooms, 2 guest lounges,
meeting room, library, chapel, choir, personal talks possible. Donations
toward cost of board and room.

HAUTE- LOIRE (43)

Langeac
Monastère de Sainte-Catherine de Sienne
2, rue de Pont
43300 Langeac   Tel: 04 71 77 01 50
                                                   Fax: 04 71 77 27 61
Roman Catholic. Dominican nuns. Receives individuals and groups for
retreats. Maximum stay 2 weeks. 13 rooms, central heating, chapel, personal talks possible. Write the guest sister at least one week in advance.

Le Puy en Velay
Saint-Georges Retreat House
4, rue Saint Georges
43000 Le Puy en Velay   Tel: 04 71 09 93 10
                                                   Fax: 04 71 09 93 17
Roman Catholic. Receives everyone. This is a place of pilgrimage and
Saint Georges is a very large complex and grand seminary building
where people are welcomed all year as individuals or in groups.
Massive amount of accommodation, park, gardens, disabled facilities,
library, TV, chapel choir, personal talks possible, pilgrims welcomed. If
you want to stay in Le Puy and can not stay here, then ask about other
places because there are a number in the vicinity.

LOIRE-ATLANTIQUE (44)

La Meilleraye-de-Bretagne
Abbaye Notre-Dame-de-Melleray
44520 La Meilleraye-de-Bretagne   Tel: 02 40 55 20 01
Roman Catholic. Cistercian Trappist monks. Receives men for spiritual
retreats and visits for peace and reflection. Retreats are in silence.

LOIRET (45)

Saint-Jean-de-Braye
Monastère des Bénédictines de Notre-Dame-du-Calvaire
65, avenue de Verdun
45801 Saint-Jean-de-Braye   Tel: 02 38 61 43 05
Roman Catholic. Benedictine nuns. Religious retreats only. Receives
women and young women. Weekends for young women within cloister for those considering a religious life. Not particularly a quiet situation as it is in a busy town.

LOT (46)

Montcuq
Le Chartrou
Belmonet
46800 Montcuq   Tel: 05 65 31 90 23
Alternative Spirituality. A Naturopathy retreat for de-stressing and
increasing your energies by means of diet, nutrition and revitalisation
which maximise the natural biological forces of your body. Brochure
with events and courses plus charges available. If treatments are on
offer always make certain you understand how much is being charged
for what.

Rocamadour
Centre d'Accueil Notre-Dame
Le Chateau
46500 Rocamadour   Tel: 05 65 33 23 23
                                                Fax: 05 65 33 23 24
Roman Catholic – Ecumenical. This centre is run by the Diocese of
Cahors and is open all year for individuals or groups on retreat.
Rocamadour possesses a church of the Middle Ages in which there is a
sanctuary. This sanctuary is considered by Christian pilgrims to be a
holy place and it is, indeed, a mysterious and spiritual place set in a
rugged and equally mysterious countryside. In the sanctuary is an
ancient wooden statue of Mary holding the Child Jesus which is simple
yet deeply dramatic and possibly a great work of art. 46 rooms, guest
and meeting rooms, library, TV, chapel choir, disabled facilities (the
sanctuary has steps and the place itself is steep and not very easy of
access). Personal talks possible. Rates of charges on demand. If you can
stay here, then try to stop and visit the sanctuary. There are lots of
tourists about in the summer but the atmosphere inside is peaceful.

LOT-ET-GARONNE (47)

Agen
Foyer Valpré Le Lido
500 avenue Léon Blum
Route de Cahors
4700 Agen   Tel: 05 53 47 47 73
Fax: 05 53 66 59 72
Roman Catholic – Ecumenical. Located 170 km from Lourdes and only 100 km from Toulouse, this centre welcomes everyone as individuals or in groups for days of reflection and rest, and retreats of prayer. 20 rooms, 4 family rooms, disabled facilities, library, TV, chapel, choir, personal talks possible, conferences.

Loubes-Bernac
Le Village des Pruniers (Plum Village)
Buddhist. School of Mahayana Vietnamese, Unified Buddhist Church. Plum Village is a group of several rural retreat places over three departments of France – the Dordogne, Gironde and the Lot-et-Garonne. The latter is set among grape vines and the celebrated plum trees of the Agen area. **Hameau du Bas, Meyrac, 47120 Loubès-Bernac** (Tel: 05 53 94 75 40) is a Community which receives men and women and married couples. **Hameau du Haut, Le Pey, 24240 Thénac** (Tel/Fax: 05 53 58 48 58 is a monastery receiving men only. **Hammeau Nouveau, 13 Matineau**, 33580 Dieulivol (Tel: 05 56 61 66 88) is a convent receiving women. More than 400 people a year attend these places for meditation. This is a big, busy and serious place with at least three major retreats organised each year. About 1200-1500FF a week and meals are vegetarian. Send for information which is available in English as Buddhist places have different requirements as to meditation technique experience and other aspects of Buddhism. You will need to book three months in advance.

MAINE-ET-LOIRE (49)

Angers
Prieuré de Notre-Dame-du-Calvaire
8, rue Vauvert
49100 Angers   Tel: 02 41 87 76 28
Roman Catholic. Benedictine nuns. Individuals or in small groups for retreats or possibility within the enclosure for women religious and young women who want to participate more fully in the community's life of prayer.

Bégrolles-en-Mauges
Abbaye de Bellefontaine
49122 Bégrolles-en-Mauges   Tel: 02 41 63 81 60
Fax: 02 41 75 60 46
Roman Catholic. Cistercians. Receives men and mixed groups for retreats only. 50 singles, 15 doubles, guest lounge disabled facilities, library, chapel, personal talks possible. Men may be able to help with some work of community.

MANCHE (50)

Avranches
Monastère du Carmel
59, boulevard du Luxembourg
50300 Avranches Tel: 02 33 58 23 66
Roman Catholic. Receives men and women retreatants. 4 rooms. A place for a prayer and reflection retreat. Set between a busy road and quiet countryside.

Le Mont-Saint-Michel
Communauté de l'Abbaye
B.P. 3
50170 Le Mont-Saint-Michel Tel: 02 33 60 14 47
Fax: 02 33 60 31 02
Roman Catholic. Benedictine monks. Receives men and women for spiritual retreats *only*. 12 beds. Guests must attend all Divine Offices. A famous setting and place which is still one of the greatest tourist attractions of Europe. However, a stay with the Community here does not guarantee you a visit to the monument. Visit it before or after your retreat. A magnificent site.

Saint-James
Prieuré Saint-Jacques
50240 Saint-James Tel: 02 33 48 31 39
Roman Catholic. This Community of nuns receives women individuals and religious who want a private retreat and perhaps to participate in the Community's life of prayer. 9 rooms, chapel, pilgrims welcomed, personal talks sometimes possible.

Saint-Pair-sur-Mer
Carmel
213, route de Lézeaux
50380 Saint-Pair-sur-Mer Tel: 02 33 50 12 00
Roman Catholic. Receives individuals for religious retreats.

MARNE (51)

Arcis-le-Ponsart
Abbaye Notre-Dame-d'Igny
51170 Arcis-le-Ponsart Tel: 03 26 78 08 40
Roman Catholic. Open for spiritual retreats only for stays of up to a week. Participation in the Divine Office with help from one of the Community in this Cistercian abbey. Brochure available.

Reims
Monastère Sainte-Claire
11 bis, avenue Roger-Salengro
51430 Tinqueux Tel: 03 26 08 23 15
Roman Catholic. St Claire nuns. Open to women, religious, priests, and married couples. 55 beds including annexe, barn, and dormitory. Closes last two weeks of July.

Saint-Thierry
Monastère des Bénédictines
51220 Saint-Thierry　　　　　　　Tel: 03 26 03 10 72
　　　　　　　　　　　　　　　　　Fax: 03 26 03 15 49
Roman Catholic. Receives individuals and groups for retreats. 22
rooms, 3 guest lounges, library, chapel, choir, personal talks possible.
Maximum stay 8 days. Write 15 days in advance to the Guest Sister.

MAYENNE (53)

Craon
Monastère des Bénédictines du Saint-Sacrement
15, rue de la Libération
53400 Craon　　　　　　　　　Tel: 02 43 06 13 38
　　　　　　　　　　　　　　　　　Fax: 02 43 06 03 80
Roman Catholic. Receives women, young women, families, and group
retreatants. 14 rooms plus other accommodation, library. Some rooms
are on the road, some facing the garden. Divine Office in Latin
Gregorian chant. Women may apply to make a retreat within the enclosure.

MEURTRE-ET-MOSELLE (54)

Art sur Meurthe
Villa Chaminade
1, rue du Chateau
54510 Art sur Meurthe　　　　　Tel: 03 83 56 97 44
Roman Catholic. A Marianist Community who welcome all persons,
groups, and families for stays of 1 to 8 days. Spiritual direction for a
retreat on request. Accommodation for 25 persons, library, guest
lounge, chapel. Personal talks possible.

MORBIHAN (56)

Bréhan
Abbaye Notre-Dame-de-Timadeuc
Bréhan
56580 Rohan　　　　　　　　　Tel: 02 97 51 50 29
　　　　　　　　　　　　　　　　　Fax: 02 97 51 59 20
Roman Catholic. Cistercians. Receives men and women for stays of up
to 8 days. Near the monastery are two further guest centres for young
people. The atmosphere is peaceful and you join the Community in
much silence. 41 rooms. Full board available – charges on request. 2
guest lounges, disabled facilities, library, chapel, choir, personal talks
possible.

Tout comprendre, c'est tout pardonner.

VOLTAIRE

Campénéac
Abbaye la Joie Notre-Dame
Campénéac 56800
Tel: 02 97 93 42 07
Fax: 02 97 93 11 23

Roman Catholic. Cistercian nuns. Receives men and women, groups for conferences. 30 rooms, 2 dormitories, camping, library, chapel, choir, meeting room, guest lounges, personal talks possible. Very quiet, in the heart of Brittany and close to the Forest of Broceliande. The nuns have a visual exhibition on the monastic life.

Plouharnel
Abbaye Sainte-Anne de Kergonan
56340 Plouharnel
Tel: 02 97 52 30 75

Roman Catholic. Benedictine monks. Receives men individually for retreats or study. 15 singles. Meals in refectory. Divine Office in Gregorian chant. Quiet location close to the sea.

MOSELLE (57)

Gorze
Béthanie
Prieuré Saint-Thiébault
57680 Gorze
Tel: 03 87 52 02 28
Fax: 03 87 69 91 79

Christian. Centre of meditation run by an Orthodox priest. Individual retreats possible. Write and ask what can be arranged for you, explaining what you are looking for.

NORD (59)

Le Mont-des-Cats
Abbaye Sainte-Marie-du-Mont
Le Mont-des-Cats
59270 Godewaersvelde
Tel: 03 28 42 52 50
Guest House: 03 28 42 58 22

Roman Catholic. Open to all. 30 rooms. Meals taken in silence. Countryside location.

Moustier-en-Fagne
Prieuré Saint-Dodon
59132 Moustier-en-Fagne
Tel: 03 27 61 81 28

Roman Catholic. This is a Benedictine Olivetan Community of nuns so you will be assured of a warm welcome in a very homely and peaceful atmosphere. Closed September and October. Receives men, women, young people, groups. 5 rooms plus separate DIY annexe for groups with own leader. Stays up to 15 days. There is a Byzantine chapel and icon painting is a speciality of the community. Byzantine liturgy once a week. A very quiet setting near a small river with lots of trees and much peace. It is possible to walk into Belgium from here.

Mouvaux
Centre Spirituel du Hautmont
31, rue Mirabeau B.P. 19
59420 Mouvaux   Tel: 03 20 26 09 61
                                                  Fax: 03 20 11 26 59
Roman Catholic. A centre run by the Jesuits open all year for individuals and groups. Set in a large park, 46 rooms, 2 meeting rooms, 10 guest and course rooms, 8 work rooms, disabled, chapel, choir, personal talks possible. Full board 175 to 200FF a day.

ORNE (61)

Alençon
Monastère Sainte-Claire
7, rue de la Demi-Lune
61000 Alençon   Tel: 02 33 26 14 58
Roman Catholic. St Claire nuns. Receives men and women. 12 rooms for retreatants. A fairly noisy location in town – but within the life is peaceful.

Soligny-la-Trappe
Abbaye Notre Dame de la Trappe
61380 Soligny-la-Trappe   Tel: 02 33 34 50 44
                                                  Fax: 02 33 34 98 57
Roman Catholic. Trappist monks. Receives men only – individually or in groups for retreats of up to 8 days. 30 beds, library, personal talks possible, chapel, choir. Full board available. Retreats in silence. A very quiet location in a forest.

PAS-DE-CALAIS (62)

Boulogne-sur-Mer
Monastère de la Visitation
9, rue Maquétra
62220 Saint-Martin-Boulogne   Tel: 03 21 31 35 88
Roman Catholic. Receives religious and women. Retreats in silence. Participation in Divine Office.

Wisques
Abbaye Saint-Paul
Wisques
62219 Longuenesse   Tel: 03 21 95 11 04
Roman Catholic. Benedictine monks. Receives men individually or in groups for retreats. Spiritual direction and personal talks possible. 23 rooms and camping available for young people. Brochure available.

PUY-DE-DÔME (63)

Chamalières
Monastère des Clarisses-Capucines
11, avenue de Villars
63407 Chamalières Cedex   Tel: 04 73 37 73 11
Roman Catholic. One of only three Capuchin monasteries remaining in
France. The nuns are enclosed. Franciscan spirituality. Receives everyone for individual retreats. 8 rooms. Brochure available.

Randol
Abbaye Notre-Dame-de-Randol
63450 Saint-Amant-Tallende   Tel: 04 73 39 31 00
Roman Catholic. Benedictine monks. Receives men. A new monastery
opened in 1971 of very modern architectural design, dramatically set
on the very edge of a steep gorge in an isolated position. A similar looking place as Prinknash Abbey in England, but much grander and
imposing. 5 days maximum stay. Retreatants must respect the silence
and attend services if possible. Library, chapel, personal talks possible.
No preached retreats but spiritual direction is sometimes possible.

PYRÉNÉES-ATLANTIQUES (64)

Anglet
Convent des Bernardines Notre Dame de Refuge
Avenue de Montbrun
64600 Anglet   Tel: 05 59 63 84 34
Roman Catholic. Bernardine nuns. Receives women only for silent
retreat. 5 single rooms, meals with community. The food is from their
own fields and gardens.

Orthez
Monastère Sainte-Claire
35, rue Saint-Gilles
64300 Orthez   Tel: 05 59 69 46 55
Roman Catholic. The nuns have a few rooms for self-catering stays.
Participation in prayers of the community.

Urt
Abbaye Notre-Dame-de-Belloc
64240 Urt   Tel: 05 59 29 65 55
                                                      Fax: 05 59 29 44 08
Roman Catholic. Benedictine monks. Receives men, married couples,
small groups of men for day retreats and retreat stays up to 1 week in
an isolated monastery in one of the loveliest parts of France with
mountains and valleys lush with wildflowers and trees. Sheep abound
as do tiny villages where life seems to continue much as it has for centuries inspite of everything. It is possible here to imagine that indeed all
is well with the world. This has not always been so – the abbot and his
prior were sent to Buchenwald and to Dachau concentration camps
during the Second World War because of the help given to refugees and
resistance fighters. After the war, the Abbey Community was awarded
the honour of the Cross of War. Today the Abbey continues to offer hos-

pitality to all in accordance with the Rule of Saint Benedict that all guests should be received as if Christ himself. There are18 singles, 10 doubles, 4 dormitories, guest lounges, library, personal talks possible, chapel choir. Conferences possible. Programme of activities sometimes available – ask for brochure. The monks are attentive to the needs of busy modern people who are looking for a time and situation in which to find peace and silence for seeking the spiritual. Also there are Benedictine sisters nearby at the **Monastère Sainte-Scholastique, 64240 Urt**, Tel: 05 59 70 20 28) so write them for details of their hospitality.

PYRÉNÉES -HAUTE (65)

Laslades
La Seve
40 Route de Tarbes
653560 Laslades   Tel: 05 62 35 08 34
Mind-Body-Spirit. A programme of healing courses and experience of self, including discovering your relationship in the Zodiac signs, essential oil therapies, and rediscovery of the senses of taste, sight, hearing, touching and smelling.

LOURDES

Lourdes is one of the greatest places of religious pilgrimage in the world. It is visited by millions of people every year so it is always very crowded. The history of this great Christian shrine is a simple one. A fourteen year old poor peasant girl, Marie-Bernarde Soubirous (1844-79) received 18 apparitions of the Blessed Virgin Mary at the Massabielle Rock in Lourdes over a period of months. During this time, a spring appeared in the grotto of the rock, the waters of which are believed to be miraculous. Almost from the beginning people visited the grotto to seek cures for their illnesses and fulfilment of their prayers. The girl later became a nun and is known today as Saint Bernadette. The Catholic church is medically and ethically extremely rigorous in deciding if any claim of a cure is authentic. There have been a small but impressive number of cases declared so over the years and you may read about these in detail. The grotto itself is filled with candles and has remained relatively simple. People here are quite silent and all attention is on spiritual intentions – the atmosphere is unique and conducive to prayer inspite of the number of people gathered together. However, an enormous church has been built on the site with religious chapels and sanctuaries plus a museum and all the various facilities related to handling millions of visitors each year. Many of these are ill, infirm, in wheelchairs or on stretchers. Indeed, those suffering from illnesses and handicaps come by the coach and plane load each year. At all times, there are visitors who may not be Christians or who have doubts about the existence of God but have been attracted to Lourdes by its global fame. Along with many Christians, they may be appalled by the commercial aspects of Lourdes like the streets lined with shops and tables selling religious trinkets like rosaries, statues, and bottles of holy water from the grotto spring, the distress of ill pilgrims, and the harsh realities of how men and women may behave when driven by their religious yearnings. But all great religious shrines and places of pilgrimage through the ages, whether Christian or not, suffer this kind of commerce and Lourdes is no exception. A visitor, who is not a pilgrim or believer, needs to put to one side all this human economic foible and think about the spiritual awareness that draws pilgrims here by the millions. All have taken time to devote a few days to prayer and God. And too, is it such a bad thing that some hope, no matter how faint, may be given to the sick and the incurable when nothing else has given it ? So, the Shrine at Lourdes and its huge church are well worth a visit. Forget the streets lined with tourist religious trinkets and concentrate on the prayerful atmosphere of the Shrine with its many candles of inspiring light. Afterwards you might take a picnic lunch to Lourdes Lake nearby and drift in a pedal-boat – it is a kind of day retreat that lifts the heart.

There are many hotels and guest houses in all price ranges in Lourdes and, of course, a number of religious houses some of which take guests. The Lourdes tourist information office that will help you find accommodation. Lourdes website **http://www.lourdes-France.com** gives details about the place and some good photos.

Lourdes
Carmel Notre-Dame-de-Lourdes
17, route de Pau
65100 Lourdes   Tel: 05 62 94 26 67
Roman Catholic. Receives men and women for day retreats and in the summer months for longer stays.

Lourdes
Foyer Familial
2 avenue Saint-Joseph
65100 Lourdes
                                                    Tel: 05 62 94 07 51
                                                    Fax: 05 62 94 57 14
Roman Catholic. Run by the Dominican sisters. The house with a garden is situated in town not far from the shrine and sanctuary area. 12 singles, 9 doubles, 5 family rooms.

Lourdes
Le Bosquet
Maison Familiale
Le Grange Juloa
65100 Lourdes
                                                    Tel: 05 62 94 29 72
                                                    Fax: 05 62 42 09 80
Non-Religious. Situated about 3 kilometres from Lourdes, this large establishment is open all year for seminars or retreats. Situated in a village on the mountain with beautiful views of the Pyrénées.

Lourdes
Résidence de la Pastourelle
34 rue de Langelle
65100 Lourdes
                                                    Tel: 05 62 94 26 55
                                                    Fax: 05 62 42 00 95
Ecumenical. This large residence is in the centre of Lourdes and has all services, especially for the disabled with physical care services possible and all facilities. Although near the shrine, it is a peaceful place.

Lourdes
Maison Sainte-Thérèse
32-34 rue du Sacré-Coeur
65100 Lourdes   Tel: 05 62 94 35 16
                                                    Fax: 05 62 94 70 13
Roman Catholic. The Community of Emmanuel receive guests for up
to seven days who may participate in the life of the Community. It is
about quarter of an hour's walk from the shrine. Accommodation for
up to 60. Full board about 130FF per night. Languages spoken include
English.

Lourdes
Monastère des Dominicaines
Route de Pontacq
65100 Lourdes   Tel: 05 62 94 12 43
                                                    Fax: 05 62 94 89 76
Roman Catholic. The sisters here offer monastic hospitality to all
whether as individuals or in groups. Maximum stay is 15 days. It is
open for private retreats. 22 rooms, full board about 160FF day.
Languages spoken include English.

Maubourguet
Église Protestante Évangélique
138 Place Libération
65700 Maubourguet   Tel: 05 62 96 32 22
Evangelical Christian. For those travelling to the increasingly popular
Southwest, there is a welcome for all Christians on Sundays at 10.15am
at the Evangelical church in Maubourguet. Just park in the central market square and walk in. The first Sunday of the month service usually
makes provision for English language speakers.

Tourney   ✳
Abbaye Notre-Dame
65190 Tourney   Tel: 05 62 35 70 21
Roman Catholic. Benedictine monks. Receives men and women.
Services in French. 30 singles for men plus dormitories. 12 rooms for
women. Men take meals in refectory. Women guests eat separately.
Quiet location, close to a river. Lovely area of south-west France and
regularly visited by local people. **Highly Recommended.**

PYRÉNÉES-ORIENT (66)

Prades
Star of Light Mountain Retreat Centre
Maison Bird, Conat
66500 Prades   Tel/fax: 04 68 96 04 80
                                            e-mail: bird.conat@easynet.fr
Mind-Body-Spirit. Course and workshop programmnes including
Hatha Yoga, Reiki Healing, and workshops with titles such as *Men,
Stress, Health and Well-being* and *The Zodiac of Your Soul*. Charges run
from £100 per person for the course plus shared accommodation at
£210 per person per week.

RHIN-BAS (67)

Kuttolsheim
Sakya Tsechem Ling
Institut Euopéen de Bouddhisme Tibétain
5 rond-point du Vignoble
67520 Kuttolsheim
Tel: 03 88 87 73 80
Fax: 03 88 60 74 52

Buddhist. Vajrayana Tibétain. About 20 minutes drive from Strasbourg. Daily practice. Languages used include French, English, German and Tibetan. There are courses and a library. Accommodation about 40FF per night and food taken together 35FF a meal.

Rosheim
Monastère Notre Dame du Sacré Coeur
Hotellerie Notre Dame de la Source
3 rue Saint-Benoît
67560 Rosheim
Tel: 03 88 50 41 67
Fax: 03 88 50 42 71

Roman Catholic. Benedictine nuns who receive men and women all year round and organise retreat programmes. 15 rooms plus dormitories. Very modern in newly converted farm buildings. Divine Office in Gregorian chant. Courses are available during the year in Gregorian chant. Walks in forest and countryside. Brochure available.

Strasbourg
Centre Zen de Strasbourg
21 rue des Magasins
6700 Strasbourg
Tel: 03 88 75 06 50

Buddhist Japanese. Soto Zen. This centre was created in 1970 by a number of groups in France and southern Germany. Three weekends a year are organised including a beginners session. Send for programme. There is regular practice of *Zazen*, using English, German and French.

RHIN-HAUT (68)

Landser
Monastère Saint-Alphonse
68440 Landser
Tel: 03 89 81 30 10

Roman Catholic. The nuns receive everyone for retreats. 8 days maximum. Located in the heart of the village high up in the mountains with a large park. 6 rooms, guest lounge, TV, meeting room, chapel, choir, personal talks possible. Full board about 150FF. Write a month in advance.

Oelenberg
Abbaye de Notre-Dame d'Oelenberg
Oelenberg
68950 Reiningue
Tel: 03 89 81 91 23

Roman Catholic. Receives men and women individually or in groups for retreats. 26 rooms.

Sigolsheim
Monastère des Clarisses-Capucines
5, rue Oberhof
68240 Sigolsheim   Tel: 03 89 78 23 24
Roman Catholic. Receives women only. 3 rooms available all year for
religious and women. Maximum stay is 8-10 days. Guest lounge for the
daytime.

RHONE (69)

L'Arbresle
Centre Thomas More
La Tourette
B.P.105
69591 L'Arbresle   Tel: 04 74 01 01 03
Roman Catholic. Designed by Le Corbusier, the centre is in the
Dominican convent of La Tourette for weekend retreats of reflection on
religion and society.

Lyon
Terre du Ciel
B.P. 2050
69227 Lyon cedex 02   Tel: 04 72 41 07 51
Alternative Spirituality. The Terre du Ciel organisation have a centre,
L'Espace, 8 rue Henri IV 69002 Lyon, where a large number of events
are run. These cover a wide section of practices like *Sadhana* yoga, oriental dance, finding the inner self, and *Ayurveda* massage. The leaders
of the courses and workshops are usually well known and established
leaders in the mind-body-spirit field. They also organise courses and
retreats at other venues outside Lyon. Send for information.

SAÔNE-ET-LOIRE (71)

La Boulaye
Kagyu Ling
Centre Bouddhique Vajrayana
Chateau de Plaige
71320 La Boulaye   Tel: 03 85 79 43 41
                                                             Fax: 03 85 79 43 09
Buddhist. The monastery is known as *The Temple of a Thousand Buddhas*
and was founded in 1974 by the Tibetan master Kalou Rinpoché. There
are a number of courses held here and in other places on Tibetan meditation, spirituality, yoga, philosophy and language. Send for annual
programme of what is on offer and the charges.

Mazille
Carmel de la Paix
71250 Mazille B.P. 10   Tel: 03 85 50 80 54
                                                             Fax: 03 85 50 83 83
Roman Catholic. Carmelite nuns. Open to both men and women.
Accommodation in small chalets and hermitages. Couples may come

on retreat here with the possibility of organising someone in the monastery to care for the children some of the time. Participation in Divine Office. Help welcomed with farming chores. A good place for a deeply peaceful retreat.

Mazille
Maison sur Le Monde
Centre Jacques Vidal
71250 Mazille   Tel: 03 85 50 82 89
Ecumenical. Situated about seven kilometres from Cluny in an old presbytery. This is the place to seek prayer in a Christian ambience.

Taizé
Communauté de Taizé
71250 Taizé   Tel: 03 85 50 30 30
                                                              Fax: 03 85 50 30 16
Ecumenical. In founding the Taizé Community, Brother Roger opened ways to heal the divisions between Christians and through reconciliation of Christians to overcome certain conflicts in humanity. In his own words he felt that *the Church can be a leaven of community and peace in the entire family*. Today the Community includes some 80 brothers, both Protestant and Catholic, from over twenty countries. This is one of the most popular retreat places in the Western world – in some years there may be over 6000 visitors in a single week. Taizé receives men, women and especially young people for whom it is a very popular place. 30 rooms plus dormitories, camping, and caravans. While all activities take place in Taizé itself, most adult accommodation is in villages nearby. Accepts disabled and families with children. Personal talks, meditation, and group discussions. There are special meetings for different age groups – for example, special activities for younger people and other events for the over-60s. Everyone eats together and the food is very simple. No provision for vegetarians or special diets. Send for information which lists the various meetings and gives important details which you need to know before deciding to go there. You must write at least two months before your intended stay and wait for a reply before making any firm arrangements. It is so crowded in summer that older people are advised to come before or after that period. In spite of all these crowds and popularity, Taizé remains a place where you may find inner peace and the joy. **Highly Recommended.**

SARTHE (72)

Solesmes
Abbaye Saint-Pierre de Solesmes
72300 Sablé-sur-Sarthe   Tel: 02 43 95 03 08
Roman Catholic. Founded in 1010 and occupied until 1790, it was again opened in 1833 and later refurbished and rebuilt. The guest house is in the enclosure and receives men only for retreats of a few days to a maximum of 1 week. The work of the monks here is divided between prayer, manual work and intellectual endeavour and study. It is a silent place. There is an outstanding collection of Gregorian music.

SAVOIE (73)

Albertville
Abbaye Notre-Dame de Tamié
Plancherine
73200 Albertville   Tel: 04 79 32 42 01
                                               Fax: 04 79 37 05 24
Roman Catholic. The monks receive men and women. Accommodation
for about 30 guests. Families are also welcome but stay in a separate
chalet. Disabled, library, chapel, choir, conferences possible, personal
talks and directed retreats possible. You may participate in the Divine
Office and help with the work of the community is appreciated.
Beautiful location in the mountains. Peaceful and calm setting.

Arvillard
Institut Karma Ling
Ancienne Chartreuse de Saint-Hugon
73110 Arvillard   Tel: 04 79 65 64 62
                                               Fax: 04 79 25 78 08
Buddhist. This is a centre for Buddhist study and meditation. Men,
women, and families are welcome. High up in Savoie, the centre is a
place for awakening the heart of your spirit and to experience authentic living. There is a college of studies and retreats for individuals may
be from 10 days to 6 months' duration. Variety of accommodation from
single rooms to dormitories. Vegetarian food. Send for information and
brochure about the centre.

Saint Pierre de Curtille
Hautecombe Abbey
73310 Saint-Pierre de Curtille   Tel: 04 79 54 22 14
Christian. A Charismatic Community now lives here and they receive
guests. Monastic communities change slowly and have fair stability,
but other groups can change quickly and radically so it always a good
idea to write in the first instance and ask what is on offer at the time
you are thinking of going there.

Saint-Pierre-d'Albigny
Monastère de la Visitation
Clos Minjoud
73250 Saint-Pierre-d'Albigny   Telephone: 04 79 28 50 12
Roman Catholic. The sisters receive up to three women *only* within the
enclosure where there is a large park. Individual retreats outside the
enclosure are for both men and women – one person or a couple at a
time. There is a small garden with mountain walking near at hand.

SAVOIE-HAUTE (74)

Saint Gervais les Bains
Fleur des Neiges
287, chemin des Granges d'Orsin
74170 Saint Gervais les Bains   Tel: 04 50 93 41 96
                                               Fax: 05 50 93 49 56

Roman Catholic. Beautifully situated in the mountains with Mont Blanc only 2 km away. Welcomes all to join in the Community's life of prayer and the monastic offices. 20 singles, 5 doubles, library, guest area, TV, chapel, personal talks and directed retreats possible, small conferences, camping by arrangement. Full board from about 200FF to 300FF per person

SEINE (PARIS) (75)

Paris
Abbaye Sainte-Marie
3, rue de la Source
75016 Paris Tel: 01 45 25 30 07
Roman Catholic. Benedictine monks. It has a well-known library which is open by arrangement for study purposes. Receives men only for spiritual retreats who want silence and solitude – not for tourist stays. Personal talks possible, sometimes courses. Men and women together accepted for a few hours of silence and reflection or for a day retreat. Everyone eats together. This is a sanctuary of peace in the midst of a rushing, noisy and beautiful city.

Paris
Centre International Sivanda de Yoga Vedanta
123 boulevard de Sébastopol
75002 Paris Tel: 01 40 26 77 49
Fax: 01 42 33 51 97
Yoga. With centres and ashrams around the world, this organisation has trained over 8000 yoga teachers. Send for information on courses and study available in France.

Paris
Monastère de Bethléem
Notre-Dame de la Présence de Dieu
2, rue Mesnil
75116 Paris Tel: 01 45 01 24 48
Roman Catholic. The sisters receive men and women who want to participate in silent prayer or in the liturgy of the community. There is no guest accommodation at the monastery. The community lives as much as possible in the spirit of the desert in the middle of this great city. From Sunday night to Monday noon they try to live out this special spiritual practice and the church is closed during this period.

Paris
Monastère de l'Adoration-Réparatrice
39, rue Gay-Lussac
75005 Paris Tel: 01 43 26 75 75
Roman Catholic. Receives men and women for individual retreats except during July and August.

Paris
Monastère de la Visitation
68, avenue Denfert-Rochereau
74014 Paris Tel: 01 43 27 12 90

Roman Catholic. Receives up to 5 women at a time only who are welcomed to the enclosure to join the nuns in silence, solitude, and Divine
Offices.

Paris
Mont Thabor – Myriam-Salomé
c/o Léonore Gottwald, Secrétariat
105 rue de la Convention
75015 Paris   Tel: 01 45 58 00 11
Christian – Alternative Spirituality. An association formed by the
Marianist priest Bernard Rérolle. Christian and Eastern spirituality,
meditation, *T'ai Chi*, sacred rituals, body in spirit exercises are on offer.
There is a good programme of weekends. Prayer groups. Send for season's brochure.

SEINE-MARITIME (76)

Rogerville
Fraternité du Père Arson
14, rue du Père Arson
76700 Rogerville   Tel: 02 35 20 42 57
Roman Catholic. Franciscan sisters and friars welcome all to this retreat
house which is open all year. There are 15 rooms, conference rooms,
guest lounge, TV, chapel, personal talks possible. Full board about
200FF.

Saint-Wandrille-Rançon
Abbaye Saint-Wandrille
76490 Saint-Wandrille   Tel: 02 35 96 23 11
Roman Catholic. The monks receive men, women, young people and
groups. Up to 8-day stays. 35 rooms. Men eat with the community.
Women and couples eat separately. Personal talks, group discussion. A
quiet location in a village. Must book one month in advance.

SEINE-ET-MARNE (77)

Brou-sur-Chantereine
Prieuré St Joseph
1, avenue Victor-Thiébaut
77177 Brou-sur-Chantereine   Tel: 01 60 20 11 20
                                                     Fax: 01 60 20 43 52
Roman Catholic. Receives women, religious, and couples in guest
house for individual or group retreats in silence and prayer. 9 singles,
3 doubles, 2 family room, guest lounge, disabled facilities, library,
chapel, choir, personal talks possible. Write in the first instance to the
guest sister.

Faremoutiers
Abbaye Notre-Dame-et-Saint-Pierre
1 rue Fenelon Desfourneaux
77515 Faremoutiers   Tel: 01 64 04 20 37
                                                     Fax: 01 64 20 04 69

Roman Catholic. Benedictine contemplative nuns. Receive women and groups of up to 15 in self-catering accommodation. Chapel, choir, garden, library, personal talks possible. Some liturgy is in Gregorian chant but the psalms are in French usually. Brochure available. Approximately 55 km from Paris.

Jouarre
Abbaye Notre-Dame-de-Jouarre
6, rue Montmorin
77640 Jouarre   Tel: 01 60 22 06 11
                                                    Fax: 01 60 22 31 25
Roman Catholic. The sisters receive women, families, and small groups. 40 singles, 9 doubles, library, chapel, choir, personal talks possible, meeting room. Guests eat evening meal in silence. There is a Merovingian crypt of special interest. Brochure available. Quiet village setting.

YVELINES (78)

Bonnelles
Monastère des Orantes-de-l'Assomption
Chemin de Noncienne
78830 Bonnelles   Tel: 01 30 41 32 76
Roman Catholic. Receives men and women individually or in groups for retreats. 32 rooms, guest lounge, library, disabled facilities, TV, chapel, personal talks possible, meeting room.

SEVRES-DEUX (79)

Niort
Monastère du Carmel
157, rue de Strasbourg
79000 Niort   Tel: 05 49 24 18 72
                                                    Fax: 05 49 33 59 39
Roman Catholic. Carmelite nuns who receive women only. 3 beds. Retreats in silence and prayer. Participation in Divine Office. Chapel open to the public. A town location.

TARN (81)

Montredon
Labessonnie
Castelfranc
81360 Montredon   Tel: 05 63 75 62 84
                                                    Fax: 05 63 75 63 14
Alternative Spirituality. Provides space and encouragement for the stressed and weary – all in need of rest and recuperation. B&B available. Cultural events and concerts. Contact in UK on Tel: 01715 385633 as to what is on offer and charges this season.

Dourgne
Guest House
Abbaye Saint-Benoît-d'en-Calcat
81110 Dourgne   Tel: 05 63 50 32 37
Roman Catholic. Open to men in the monastery, others in the guest
house. 26 singles, 39 doubles, library, guest lounge, TV, chapel, choir,
meeting rooms. Guest house visitors eat separately from the
Community. Full board 180FF or 85FF B&B. A quiet location in the
countryside.

TARN-ET-GARONNE (82)

Mas-Grenier
Abbaye Saint-Pierre
82600 Mas-Grenier   Tel: 05 63 02 51 22
Roman Catholic. Benedictine nuns who receive all individuals and
groups in their guest house next door in the Acceuil St Pierre for silent
day retreats or longer retreats. 35 rooms.

VAR (83)

Cogolin
Trimurti
Chemin du Val Périer
83310 Cogolin   Tel: 04 94 54 44 11
                                               Fax: 04 94 54 63 31
Alternative Spirituality. Trimurti is a centre for courses, workshops,
resources for knowing yourself and for personal development. Situated
in the south of France in the countryside back of St Tropez, there is
much on offer here with good facilities for guests. Send for information
on the current year's programme.

Cotignac
Monastère La Font Saint-Joseph du Bessillon
83570 Cotignac   Tel: 04 94 04 63 44
Roman Catholic. A place of peace on a hillside with distant views only
90 kilometres from Marseille. An enclosed Community, the nuns
receive women only for retreats. 6 singles, central heating.

VAUCLUSE (84)

Avignon
Centre Atma
50, rue des Liuces
84000 Avignon   Tel: 04 90 27 35 14
Alternative Spirituality – Yoga. The centre is open all year for courses
and workshops in yoga and massage. They also organise a group expe-
dition to India each year. Write for brochure.

Le Thor
Le Petit Trentin
84250 Le Thor   Tel: 04 90 33 85 04
Roman Catholic. Run by the Companions of Trentin, retreats are offered to all for 5 to 12 days' duration. Accommodation for 12. 2 guest lounges, library, TV, chapel, choir, personal talks possible, pilgrims welcomed.

Montfavet
Monastère Sainte-Claire-de-Notre-Dame-des-Miracles
La Verdière
B.P. 28 84141 Cedex Montfavet   Tel: 04 90 31 01 55
Roman Catholic. 5 km from Avignon. Receives men and women in a very peaceful atmosphere for retreats of up to 8 days.

VENDEE (85)

Chavagnes en Paillers
Centre spirituel Ursulines de Jésus
Rue de la Petite Maine B.P. 8
85250 Chavagnes en Paillers   Tel: 02 51 42 36 38
                                                          Fax: 02 51 42 32 78
Roman Catholic. The Community offers retreats, weekend retreats of prayer and other events. Welcomes men and women in a climate of prayer and peace. 60 singles, 23 doubles, park, guest lounge, disabled facilities, TV, chapel, choir, personal talks and directed retreats possible, meeting rooms. Full board about 200FF per day.

VIENNE (86)

Ligugé
Abbaye Saint-Martin
86240 Ligugé   Tel: 05 49 55 21 12
                                                          Fax: 05 49 55 10 98
Roman Catholic. Benedictine monks. Open to all. Guest house near monastery of about 20 single rooms, 15 doubles, dormitories and camping. Gregorian chant in Divine Office.

Poitiers
Abbaye Sainte-Croix
Saint-Benoît
86280 Poitiers   Tel: 05 49 88 57 33
Roman Catholic. Benedictine nuns who receive women, young people, families, and groups for spiritual retreat and prayer only. 30 rooms, 2 guest lounges.

Saint-Julien l'Ars
Monastère de l'Annonciation
11 rue du Parc
86800 Saint-Julien l'Ars   Tel: 05 49 56 71 01
Roman Catholic. Benedictine nuns. Receives women for retreats of up to 8 days. Young women may participate in life of Community. Chapel,

personal talks and group discussions, pilgrims welcomed. Quiet in a country village.

VOSGES (88)

Ubexy
Abbaye Notre-Dame de Saint-Joseph
88130 Ubexy　　　　　　　　　　　　　　Tel: 03 29 38 25 70
Roman Catholic. Cistercian nuns. Receives men and women for retreats of up to 8 days. 15 rooms, dormitory, 3 guest lounges, library, chapel, choir, personal talks possible.

YONNE (89)

Saint-Léger-Vauban
Abbaye Sainte-Marie de la Pierre-Qui-Vire
89630 Saint-Léger-Vauban　　　　　　　Tel: 03 86 32 24 06
　　　　　　　　　　　　　　　　　　　　　Fax: 03 86 32 24 06
Roman Catholic. Open all year except January to men and women, groups for individual retreats of up to 1 week. 7 single rooms, 12 doubles plus dormitories. Participation in Divine Office and guests may help with work of the Community. There is a library, a church and two oratories for private prayer. Personal talks possible. Guests eat separately with some meals taken in silence. A very peaceful location in the woods. Write Guest Brother 2 weeks in advance.

Sens
Monastère de la Nativité
105, rue Victor-Guichard
89100 Sens　　　　　　　　　　　　　　　Tel: 03 86 65 13 41
Roman Catholic. Dominican nuns. Receives men and women for retreats. Situated in town near the cathedral, there is accommodation for 80. Charges for room and board do vary so ask when you contact the guest sister. Vegetarian food sometimes possible. Library, chapel, choir, personal talks possible, meeting rooms. Brochure available.

TERRITOIRE DE BELFORT (90)

Lepuix-Gy
Prieuré Saint-Benoît de Chauveroche
90200 Lepuix-Gy　　　　　　　　　　　Tel: 03 84 29 01 57
　　　　　　　　　　　　　　　　　　　　　Fax: 03 84 29 56 80
Roman Catholic. Receives men, women, and groups for individual retreats in a small guest house of 7 rooms. Meals taken with the Community in silence. There is also a chalet for groups close by the priory with accommodation for 25 in 6 rooms.

ESSONNE (91)

Évry
Maison Sainte Geneviève
Notre Dame de Sion
2m, avenue Ratisbonne
91000 Évry
Tel: 01 60 77 31 45
Fax: 01 69 36 49 90

Roman Catholic. This guest house of the Sisters of Our Lady is only 30 km from Paris. They welcome individuals and large and small groups for retreats. The guest house is situated in a park near the Seine. 24 rooms, lots of lounges and other rooms, library, TV, chapel. Camping possible for young people. Write to the Director.

Vauhallan
Abbaye Saint-Louis-du-Temple
Limon
91430 Vauhallan
Tel: 01 69 85 21 00

Roman Catholic. Benedictine nuns. The Abbey was founded in memory of the French royal family who were imprisoned in the temple tower during the revolution. Glass windows designed by Marie Geneviève Gallois (1888 – 1962). Receives men and women in small groups or as individuals under guidance of one of the sisters. Accommodation for 40 in a number of buildings, dormitory, conference rooms, library, chapel, choir, personal talks possible. Library. Peaceful village location.

HAUTS-DE-SEINE (92)

Fontenay aux Roses
Résidence Universitaire Lanteri
7, rue Gentil Bernard
92260 Fontenay aux Roses
Tel: 01 41 13 36 00
Fax: 01 43 50 88 45

Roman Catholic. This retreat and guest centre is open from the beginning of July until mid-September to everyone who wants to be alone. Groups are also received for an unlimited period who organise their own retreats. Accommodation for 160 in singles, doubles, family rooms, 2 guest lounges, parking, library, TV, church, chapel, personal talks possible, meeting rooms. Full board 260FF and it is possible to stay without taking meals in the centre. Reduction in charges for groups. Enquire in writing a month in advance.

Vanves
Prieuré Sainte-Bathilde
7, rue d'Issy
92170 Vanves
Tel: 01 46 42 46 20

Roman Catholic. Benedictine nuns receive women only. Closed July and August. 10 single rooms. Personal talks possible. Library and book shop. Quiet location but in a city.

EVANGELICAL CHURCHES IN FRANCE
(Églises Évangéliques en France)

There are a number of evangelical fellowships throughout France. *The Fédération Évangélique de France* will provide information.

Fédération Évangélique de France
40 rue des Réservoirs
91330 Yerres, France   Tel: 04 69 49 06 21
                                             Fax: 04 69 48 17 89

EVANGELICAL CENTRES FOR HOLIDAYS
(Centres Évangéliques de Vacances).

The Federation given above also runs the Centres Évangéliques de Vacances. Write to them for details of these centres.

Arles
L'Étoile du Matin
Centre Évangélique de l'Espérou
5, rue de la Madeleine
13200 Arles   Tel/Fax: 04 90 93 55 77

St Jean de Vedas
La Maison des Cédres
36, rue de la Cadorque
34430 St Jean de Vedas   Tel: 04 67 27 54 67
                                             Fax: 04 67 27 24 05

Chamrousse
Centre Évangélique Le Belledonne
38410 Chamrousse   Tel: 04 76 89 90 17
                                             Fax: 04 76 89 94 27

Bourg d'Oisans
Le Camp des Cimes
La Rivoire
38520 Bourg d'Oisans   Tel: 04 76 80 07 20

Le Champ près Froges
Centre de Vacances Champfleuri
38190 Le Champ près Froges   Tel: 04 76 71 41 07
                                             Fax: 04 76 71 38 44

Sondernach
Centre de vacances 'Landersen'
68380 Sondernach   Tel: 03 89 77 60 69
                                             Fax: 03 89 77 74 31

Munster
Centre Évangélique Chrischona
13, chemin de la foret Hohrodberg
68140 Munster   Tel: 03 89 77 31 35
                                             Fax: 03 89 77 05 37

Houlgate
Maison Évangélique
4, passage Évangélique
B.P. 30 - 14510 Houlgate

Tel: 02 31 28 70 80
Fax: 02 31 24 60 46

St Lunaire
Centre des Jeunes
Le Pont St Lunaire
35800 St Lunaire

Tel: 02 99 46 33 94

St Albain
Château de St Albain
71260 St Albain

Tel: 03 85 33 12 95 / 03 85 33 14 28

L'homme debout est la gloire de Dieu.

IRÉNÉÉ DE LYON

CREATION SPIRITUALITY IN FRANCE
(Mouvement creation spirituality)

Followers of Mathew Fox's *Creation Spirituality* theology may find courses, seminars, and workshops in France by writing to the correspondent who can provide information. (See London section for the Creation Spirituality Centre in England.)

Francis Gohard
Mouvement Creation Spirituality
76 rue de Margnolles
69300 Caluire

Tel: 04 72 27 01 63

HERMITAGE RETREATS (L'expérience de poustinia)

It is possible to have a hermit experience of silence and being alone in a poustinia (see Glossary) in France. These self-catering places are hermitages in the heart of the town but so situated and arranged that you can have the kind of retreat offered by such solitude. There are a number also located in various monasteries and Communities in France and you will have to enquire whether they have a single accommodation isolated from others. But here are two places offering hermitages, one in Paris and one in Lyon. The big monasteries often also have special hermitages for guests so it is worth asking if you are writing and want to try this spiritual adventure for your retreat.

Madonna House
1 rue de l'Abbé Migne
75004 Paris

Tel: Myriam 01 42 72 16 04 for Paris
Tel: Jacqueline 04 72 34 61 81 for Lyon

BUDDHIST FACILITIES AND PROGRAMMES

Association Zen en Mouvement
55 bd Stalingrad
06300 Nice

Association Un Pas vers les Tibétains
26 Chaussée de l'Etang
94160 Saint Mandé   Tel/fax: 01 43 28 47 24

Friends of the Western Buddhist Order – France
c/o 21 Place de la Republic
11300 Limoux   Tel: 04 68 31 78 02
Buddhist. Information available on centres and activities in France.

Institut Karmappa
35 chemin rural de la Ferrière
06750 Valderoure   Tel: 04 93 60 90 16
Fax: 04 93 60 48 75

Nyima Dzong
Institut Européen de Bouddhisme Tibétain
Château de Soleils
04120 Castellanne   Tel: 04 94 76 90 88
Fax: 04 94 85 68 27
e-mail: nyima@wanadoo.fr

FURTHER INFORMATION ON FRANCE

The following publications cover houses of retreat, places that receive pilgrims, retreat programmes of courses and workshops, and monastic hospitality in France. They may prove helpful to those who are enthusiastic to explore their spirituality in that country. These books are in French and published there, but they can usually be ordered from larger British book shops or you can obtain them from **The English Language Bookshop, 5 rue du Bourg, 65100 Lourdes,** Tel/fax 05 62 42 27 94 who speak English and will order and post them to you. Regrettably, many of the great number of books published in France on spiritual subjects are never translated into English.

Centre d'Information et de Documentation Religieuses (CIDR), 6 place du parvis de Notre Dame, 75004 Paris, Tel 01 46 33 01 01. This is an organisation which publishes a monthly brochure, Calendrier des retraites spirituelles, listing retreat programmes including courses and workshops which are on offer at various monasteries and retreat houses in France.

Des outils pour un changement, **Éditions Terre du Ciel, B.P. 2050, 13 rue Henri IV, 69227 Lyon cedex 02**, Tel 04 72 41 07 51, Fax 04 78 37 65 44. The organisation Terre du Ciel is one of the best sources in France for information about aspects of Christian, Judaic, Buddhist, and Sufi spirituality, yoga, holistic health methods, and many of the leading as well as the somewhat obscure mind-body-spirit approaches to self awareness and harmony with others and with planet earth. The aim of Terre du Ciel is to create and bring together invitations for change and renewal of self. They publish a bi-monthly journal with articles and listings of workshops and courses which reflect this aim.

Bouddhisme – Actualités, **Nice Premier, 455 Promenade des Anglais, 06199 Nice cedex 3**. A monthly magazine with information about what is happening in the various places of Buddhist practice in France with lots of addresses for forthcoming programmes and ads for courses and visiting teachers. It is on sale in most larger newspaper and magazine shops.

Guide des monastères, **Maurice Colinon, Pierre Horay Éditeur, Paris**. In addition to listing various monasteries in France, Belgium, Switzerland and Luxembourg, this guide gives a short history about monasticism, a directory of the Catholic religious orders in France and those monasteries which make and sell artisan products. It is usually possible to stop and buy such products without staying as a guest. They also publish a guide to monasteries in Europe for those interested beyond French speaking countries.

Guide des Pélerinages de France, **Bernard Iselin, Dervy, Paris**. There have been Christian pilgrims almost since the beginning of Christianity itself. The tradition of walking along a sacred way, stopping to pray at holy sites, and finally arriving at a great and famous holy place is, of course, not unique to Christians. In Europe, the pilgrimage of the way of Saint Jacques de Compostelle has been famous for centuries. It takes the pilgrim through France and Spain from sacred place to sacred place on a specific route. Today, it is an increasingly popular spiritual journey whether you do it by walking, which is the traditional and authentic way, or by bicycle, motorcycle, car or horse. This guide is an excellent reference, giving the history of Christian pilgrimages, route directions, discussion of holy and sacred sites, and the places of sanctuary and welcome for pilgrims along the way. An illustrated book, Les Chemins de Saint-Jacques de Compostelle, B.P. 20, 65502 Vic-en-Bigorre is also very good.

Guide Saint-Christophe, **Association Saint-Christophe, Paris Cedex 05**. This guide covers many retreat houses in France and some other European countries – it is particularly good on places in Belgium and Italy but Hungary, Switzerland, Spain, and Portugal are also included. In addition there is information on the pilgrim way of Saint Jacques de Compostelle (see above) and on places for peaceful holidays.

Guide des Centres Bouddhistes en France, **Philippe Ronce, Éditions Noesis 12 rue de Savoie Vie Paris**. This guide lists centres all over France, many with illustrations of the sites and lamas and gives good details of facilities, practices and spiritual schools which are also grouped in a helpful index.

SPAIN

Spain is a treasure house of peaceful and welcoming monasteries gradually becoming known to tourists and those seeking a retreat. The Spanish tourist offices now supply details of those offering hospitality. (See below.) Many of these only receive guests of one gender and the accommodation can be simple and the food plain. They are not hotels and the monks and nuns are inspired by values of simplicity, silence and seclusion. While you will be expected to respect their way of life, your personal religious beliefs will not normally pose any problem. Such places would not normally expect to accommodate unmarried couples in the same room. Charges are usually very nominal, likely to range between 1200 and 2000 pesetas a day. Hundreds of people still follow the Pilgrims Way through France and across Spain to Santiago de Compostela, staying along the way at such monasteries which are often located in some of Spain's most lovely countryside. Many contain great works of art. Given the limited number of rooms do try to write in advance to book. If like a pilgrim along the way you just happen to stop at a monastery, you will probably find a bed for the night and a meal.

For those wanting an organised retreat in Spain, there are travel operators who specialise in such programmes (see Travel Organisations section.) Such retreats in recent years have included a Holy Week retreat in Valladoid, north of Madrid, which is famous for its Holy Week processions, with group leaders which included several well-known British retreat facilitators. Another is a retreat to Poio, a Mercedarian monastery south of Santiago, with excursions to Santiago de Compostela and the Trappist monasteries of Galicia.

You could try combining hotel accommodation with monastery visits, staying at one of Spain's hotel type paradores like the **Parador de Santo Domingo de la Calzada, Plaza del Santo No. 3, Santo Domingo de la Calzada (Tel: 0034-941 340 300)** and venturing out from there to visit famous but peaceful monasteries like the **Monastery of Santo Domingo de Silos**, south of Burgos, and the **Monastery of San Millan de la Cogolla** which is east of Burgos and a place that those interested in art and architecture should greatly enjoy. These places are in or near Spain's wine growing area of La Rioja.

In recent years, there has been an increase in the number of alternative spirituality and Buddhist centres in Spain. The warm weather and the relaxed atmosphere of Spain providing restful settings for many healing and renewal programmes including de-stressing courses, yoga, relaxation techniques, complementary health methods, and development of new inner values for self-realisation. The programmes are much the same as you would find in such places in Britain. Often set in sunny holiday sites like Granada, the core aim is to get you to relax and be renewed in a holistic approach. One of the most successful in recent years has been **Cortijo Romero** (see below). Among the Buddhist places is one called **Guyaloka**, hidden away in the mountains of Valencia (see below). It is owned and run by the Friends of the

Western Buddhist Order (FWBO) and all booking and information must be sought through the Padmaloka Buddhist Retreat Centre for Men in Britain (see British section). **Tara Samye Dzong** organised with the Kagyu Samye Ling Tibetan Centre in Scotland. Write them direct either in Spain or in Scotland.

Spanish Tourist Office
22/23 Manchester Square
London W1M 5AP   Tel: UK Brochure Request Line 09001 669920.
                                      Calls cost about 60p per minute.

Barcelona
Abadia de Montserrat
Montserrat, Barcelona   Tel: 0034 938 350 251
Roman Catholic. A Benedictine community receiving men, women and children in a guest house situated in a marvellous and high up mountain setting. There is lots to discover here – a wonderful view, a library and a museum rich in treasures including paintings by El Greco. Many day visitors come here. There are concerts and various cultural events during the year. 48 singles and 4 doubles available and a place to eat. Charges about 2500 pesetas per person per day room and board.

Barcelona
Karma Lodro Gyamtso Ling
Pau Claris No. 74
2-008010, Barcelona   Tel/fax: 0034 933 015 472
Buddhist. A place organised with the Kagyu Samye Ling Tibetan Centre in Scotland. Write either to Barcelona or to Scotland (see Scotland section for information).

Burgos
Abadia de Santo Domingo de Silos
Santo Domingo de Silos
Burgos   Tel: 0034 947 390 049
Roman Catholic. Benedictine abbey receiving men only. 21 rooms which are much above the average in comfort with individual bathrooms and central heating. There is a peaceful and serious atmosphere here with the Divine Office in Gregorian chant. The Holy Week religious services are impressive and justly famous.

Burgos
Abadia de San Pedro de Cardena
Burgos   Tel: 0034 947 290 003
Roman Catholic. This was the first Benedictine monastery in Spain. Founded in AD899, it has a long and colourful history, surviving through invasions and wars. A Cistercian abbey, receives men only for a stay of up to eight days who wish to share in the spiritual life of the Community. 24 rooms within the monastery and full board is offered. Much silence and an atmosphere of contemplation prevail here.

Burgos
Monasterio de Las Huelgas
Burgos　　　　　　　　　　　　　Tel: 0034 947 206 045
Roman Catholic. Receives women in an annexe guest house.

Burgos
Monasterio de Palacios de Benaver
Palacios de Benaver, Burgos　　　　　Tel: 0034 947 451 009
Roman Catholic. Receives both men and women. A convent with four
guest rooms with Gregorian chant at the services.

Caceros
Monasterio de Yusto
Cuacos, Caceros　　　　　　　　　Tel: 0034 927 480 530
Roman Catholic. Receives men for stays of up to a week.

Cantabria
Abadia de Via Celis
Corbreces, Cantabria　　　　　　　Tel: 0034 942 725 017
Roman Catholic. Cistercian community receiving men only for stays
of up to one week. This is a place to stay if you are going on a serious
religious retreat and not just to rest and relax. The atmosphere is
strict, silent, and deeply spiritual.

Estercuel
Monasterio de Nuestra Senora del Olivar
44558 Estercuel, Teruel　　　　　　Tel: 0034 974 753 144
Roman Catholic. Founded in 1627 and situated at 700 metres, you can
take the train to Alcaniz and get a bus from there. There are 23 rooms
and men, women, groups and children with their parents are welcomed. Costs about 2500 pesetas a day per person full board. Camping
is possible.

Ibiza
El Jardin de Luz - The Garden of Light
Apdo 1126
07800 Ibiza　　　　　Tel: 0034 971 334 644　Fax: 0034 971 391 086
Alternative spirituality. Open June to October. A spacious place without much luxury but lots of beauty with the emphasis on creativity and
simplicity. Accommodation for 34 in dormitories. Meals are taken
together. Food is international cuisine and vegetarians can be catered.
Nice garden. In a forest about 2 km from the beach. Open to groups
who arrange their own programme. About 5000 - 6000 pesetas a day all
included.

Javea Port
Javea Port
Costa Blanca
Ecumenical. A retreat apartment owned and run by the Grace and
Compassion Benedictine sisters in Britain (see England section). The
self-catering apartment is in a little fishing port near the harbour,
church, and a number of restaurants. Three bedrooms accommodating
six people. Central heating, well equipped and open all year round.

Write to the Superior, St Benedict's, 1 Manor Road, Kemp Town, Brighton BN2 5EA.

La Coruna
Monasterio de Santa Maria de Sobrado
Sobrado, La Coruna　　　　　　　　　Tel: 0034 981 787 509
Roman Catholic. Receives men only.

La Vid de Aranda
Monasterio de Santa Maria de la Vid
09491 La Vid de Aranda, Burgos　　　Tel: 0034 947 530 510
　　　　　　　　　　　　　　　　　　Fax: 0034 947 530 429
Roman Catholic. With many styles of architecture ranging from Roman to Baroque, this monastery founded in 1162 is in an imposing position above the village among trees. Men, women and children with parents are received. 54 single and double rooms with meals taken with the Community. About 3000 pesetas per day per person full board and room.

Leon
Monasterio Santa Maria de Carrizo
Carrizo de Ribera, Leon　　　　　　　Tel: 0034 987 357 055
Roman Catholic. Cistercian nuns. Receives men and women. 4 rooms for a maximum stay of eight days. The convent closes early in the evening and guests are expected to respect the religious timetable.

Leon
Monasterio de San Pedro de las Duenas
Sahagun, Leon　　　　　　　　　　　Tel: 0034 987 780 150
Roman Catholic. Benedictine nuns who receive both men and women in a guest house. Visitors may come here just to relax and rest or for a retreat for which the charges are lower.

Leyre
Abadia de San Salvador de Leyre
31410 Leyre, Yesa　　　　　　　　　　Tel: 0034 948 884 011
Roman Catholic. High in the mountains, the abbey looks down on the plain. Mass and religious offices in Gregorian chant. Men only are received – but fathers may bring their children if over seven years. Stays of 3-10 days. 8 rooms within the monastery with charges with meals about 2500 pesetas. There is a 3-star guest hotel outside the monastery itself which is charming and very comfortable. A double room about 11000 pesetas.

Madrid
Abadia de Santa Cruz del Valle de los Caidos
28029 Valle de los Caidos, Madrid　　Tel: 0034 91 890 5411
　　　　　　　　　　　　　　　　　　Fax: 0034 91 890 5594
Roman Catholic. Situated near the huge monument to the Civil War which was built by General Franco, the monks have made this abbey a prayerful place of welcome. Men and woman are received in two different facilities. One is in the monastery itself and this is reserved for men wishing to join in the spiritual life of the Community. Full room

and board per person per day here is about 2200 pesetas. The other accommodation is outside the monastery and can receive many guests with 110 rooms with bathrooms. Full room and board if from 4400-5500 pesetas per day per person. **To communicate direct telephone 0034 91 890 5492.**

Madrid
Monasterio de El Paular
Rascafria, Madrid   Tel: 0034 918 691 4 25
Roman Catholic. Receives men for stays of up to ten days.

Manresa
Taras Samye Dzong
Place Major No.6-1
08240 Manresa   Tel: 0034 938 720 254
Buddhist. A place organised with the Kagyu Samye Ling Tibetan Centre in Scotland. Write direct or to Scotland (see Scotland section) for information.

Navarre
Monasterio de La Oliva
Cascastillo, Navarre   Tel: 0034 948 725 0065
Roman Catholic. Receives both men and women in a place which is a wonderful example of Cistercian architecture. Peaceful but busy and hard working atmosphere.

Órgiva
Cortijo Romero
18400 Órgiva, Granada   Tel: 0034 958 784 252
Alternative spirituality. Receives everyone over 16. Groups and individuals welcome. Cortijo Romero has been established for some years now and is located in an inspiring location in a wonderful climate. The courses there are designed for personal rest and renewal and the enrichment and discovery of self. Examples of what is offered are: *Movement and Stillness* for learning to be grounded in who you are, *Yoga for Form and Feeling*, and *Forgiveness, Gratitude and Grace* for dealing with issues of human development. Facilities include swimming pool, orchard, 3 singles, 11 doubles, guest lounge, and guest telephone. Personal talks, group sharing, meditation, and directed study, all take place. Costs from about £325 to £375 per week including courses, excursions, accommodation and meals. **Information and Bookings Tel: UK 01494 782720. Fax: 01494 776066.** (See England section.)

Palencia
Monasterio de San Isidro de Duenas
Venta de Banos, Palencia   Tel: 0034 988 770 701
Roman Catholic. A Trappist monastery open to men, women and married couples seeking a retreat.

Salamanca
Convent de Carmel Dascatros
Las Mostas, La Alberca
Salamanca   Tel: 0034 923 437 133

Roman Catholic. A strictly religious place where men only may go for spiritual retreat and then only by prior request and permission. *It is not open to tourists.* The film director, Luis Bunuel, stayed here once and fell in love with the beautiful Las Batuecas valley where the monastery is situated. He called it *a paradise on earth.* Remember that you must write first to this monastery to make arrangements to stay.

Segovia
Monasterio de Santa Maria del Parral
El Parral, Segovia   Tel: 0034 911 431 298
Roman Catholic. Receives men in 3 en-suite rooms for stays of up to a week for those seeking a spiritual retreat. Guests can either follow the monks' routine and take meals with them or be independent.

Segovia
Monasterio San Juan de la Cruz
Alameda de la Fuencisla
40003 Segovia   Tel: 0034 921 431 349
                                                   Fax: 0034 921 431 650
Roman Catholic. In a Renaissance style, the monastery receives men and women in a retreat centre of 40 rooms. There are gardens and a large library.

Soria
Monasterio de Santa Maria de la Huerta
Santa Maria de la Huerta, Soria   Tel: 0034 975 327 002
Roman Catholic. Cistercian monks receiving men only in eight rooms. Best to write first and not just show up.

Tarragona
Abadia de Santa Maria de Poblet
Espluga de Francoli
Tarragona   Tel: 0034 977 870 089
Roman Catholic. Receives men only within the abbey itself and guests are expected to keep to the community's monastic timetable. Everyone eats together in the refectory.

Valencia
Centro Budhista de Valencia
Calle Ciscar 5, pta 3a
46005 Valencia   Tel: 0034 963 740 564
Buddhist. Run by the Friends of the Western Buddhist Order (see London section). They will provide information on this place and others in Spain.

Valencia
Guyaloka
c/o Padmaloka Buddhist Centre
Surlingham
Norwich NR14 7AL   Tel: 01508 538112
Buddhist. Guyaloka is a magical place of peace and austere simplicity for men. It is set high in a remote and secret place in the Spanish mountains. The deep silence here offers a chance for you to deepen your

meditation experience. The full time Community are committed to creating a monastic Vihara devoted to study, meditation and work in this place. You can enjoy a summer retreat here, a solitary retreat in one of the little chalets dotted around the valley nearby, a winter semi-working retreat, or a working retreat led by Yashodeva and members of the Guyaloka Community. This working retreat gives you a chance to spend an extended period away from the ordinary busy life of towns and cities. There is ample time for exploring the valleys and mountains around the centre. Prices for accommodation and board range from £12 per night for a solitary chalet to £30 per week working retreat up to £77 for the semi-working retreat.

YOGA CENTRES

There are many local yoga classes as well as clubs and groups through-out Britain and across Europe. Most of these do not own a meeting centre of their own, so they meet in various venues from halls to community and local leisure centres. In many cases the area or region-al organisation is run by a volunteer and all correspondence is done from home. Educational authorities now commonly include yoga classes in their adult and evening education programmes. Most of the yoga teachers' associations will provide you with a list of the teachers, courses, and classes in your area. The following national organisation is the information centre for yoga in Britain.

British Wheel of Yoga
1 Hamilton Place
Boston Road
Sleaford, Lincs. NG34 7ES   Tel: 01529 306851

Founded in 1965 and affiliated to the European Union of Federations of Yoga, the British Wheel of Yoga has a nation-wide network of teachers and representatives who are available to help you at a local level. It has been recognised by the British Sports Council as the governing body for yoga in Great Britain and is a non-profit making charity run by vol-untary support. Information is available on yoga practices and they can provide a list of representatives of the organisation and teachers in your immediate area. There is an excellent directory of what events are scheduled with addresses and general and course information. In addi-tion, there is a journal, *Spectrum*, with interesting articles on yoga and related subjects. If you need information about yoga or do not know where or how to start, then the British Wheel of Yoga will help you.

ENGLAND

Bedfordshire
Bedfordshire Yoga Association, Contact: Ann Davenport,
Tel: 01234 852756.
Yoga for Health Foundation, Contact Claire Hayler, Tel: 01767 627271.

Bristol and North Somerset
Centre for Yoga Studies, Bristol, Contact: Marian Miles,
Tel: 0117 9525612.
Lansdown Yoga, Bath, Contact: Janet White, Tel: 01225 447498.
Viniyoga Britain, Bath, Contact: P. Harvey, Tel: 01225 426327.
Yogaliving, Bath, Contact: Derek Thorne, Tel: 01761 470819.

Buckinghamshire
North Bucks Yoga Teachers' Association, Contact: Shirley Brogan,
Tel: 01604 58909.

Yoga with Danielle, Marlow, Contact: Danielle Arin, Tel: 01628 486698.

Cambridgeshire
Yoga Biomedical Trust, Cambridge, Contact: Dr Robin Monro,
Tel: 01223 36730.

Cheshire
Cheshire Yoga Teachers' Association, Contact: Christine Royle,
Tel: 0161 9738319.
Wilmslow Circle of Yoga, Contact: Joan Thomson, Tel: 0161 4325517.
The Yoga Circle, Contact: M. Priestner, Tel: 0161 9040588.

Cleveland
Cleveland Yoga and Well-Being Group, Contact: Mavis Fielding,
Tel: 01642 816055.
Numthorpe Yoga Group, Middlesboroiugh, Contact: Yvonne Muir,
Tel: 01642 817196.

Cornwall
Amrit Centre, Truro, Contact: Shivani, Tel: 01726 883811.
Ananda Yoga Centre, Truro, Contact: Nandini Devi, Tel: 01872 530317.

Cumbria
Awakenings, Contact: Christine Pickering, Tel: 01539 531672.
Barrow Yoga Group, Contact: Eileen Williams, Tel: 01229 82371
Southlakes Yoga Teachers Club, Ulverston, Contact: Betina Mitchell,
Tel: 01229 861134.
Yoga Quests, Lancaster, Contact: Phillip Xerri, Tel: 01524 381154.
You and Me Yoga Centre, Burton-in-Kendal, Contact: Maria
Gunstone, Tel: 01524 782103.

Derbyshire
Derbyshire Yoga Teachers' Association, Chesterfield, Contact:
Margaret Love, Tel: 01246 569084. 274 Smedley St., Matlock, DE4.
Tel: 0629 56381.

Devon
Devon School of Yoga, Sidmouth, Contact: Duncan Hulin,
Tel: 01395 512355.
Devon Yoga Teachers' Federation, Contact: Angela Blezard,
Tel: 01837 54880.
Maitri Centre, Dartmouth, Contact: Eddie Shapiro, Tel: 01803 833695.
South Devon Classical Yoga, Newton Abbot, Contact: Mike Rowe,
Tel: 01803 812746.
Viniyoga Southwest, Exeter, Contact: Liz Murtha, Tel: 01392 438615.

Dorset
St Ronan's House, Contact: Maureen Tobias, Tel: 01308 23194.
Viniyoga South West, Dorchester, Contact: Domenica Lopane,
Tel: 01305 268639

Durham
Darlington Yoga Group, Contact: Vera Oates, Tel: 01325 730092.

Essex
Dharma Yoga Centre, Bassingbourn, Contact: Mary Demetriou,
Tel: 01763 249957.
Iyengar Yoga Centre for Essex, Chelmsford, Contact: Susan Long,
Tel: 01224 5421496.
Satyananda Yoga Centre, Colchester, Contact: Swami Yogaprakash,
Tel: 01206 823383.
School for Living Yoga, Loughton, Contact: Ernest Coates,
Tel: 0208 5024270.
Shanti Bhakti Sangha, Contact Vera 0208 5492754.

Gloucestershire
Forge House Centre, Kemble, Contact: Michael Lawlor,
Tel: 01285 770635.
Gloucestershire Integral Yoga, Redmarley, Contact: Brenda Judge,
Tel: 01531 820354.
Viniyoga Cotswolds, Cirencester, Contact: Mary Harris,
Tel: 01285 750293.

Hampshire
Sukha Yoga Club, Basingstoke, Contact: Jill Cossins,
Tel: 01256 762417.
Karuna Yoga School, Southampton, Contact: Fiona Ashdown,
Tel: 023 80632881.
Satchidananda Wholistic Trust, Alton, Contact: Swami
Satchidananda Ma, Tel: 01420 561054.
Southampton Yoga Association, Contact: Dr A.K. Shahani,
60 Radway Rd, Shirley, Southampton SO1 2PJ.

Hertfordshire
Herts Yoga Workshop, St Albans, Contact: Kerstin Elliot,
Tel: 01727 760067.
Kundalini Yoga and Meditation, St Albans, Contact: Valerie
Crawford, Tel: 01727 826183.
Yoga Classes, Watford, Contact: Gillian Ellis, Tel: 01923 856285.

Kent
Radha House, Canterbury, Contact: Jayne Boys, Tel: 01227 768813.
South East Yoga Teachers' Association, Tunbridge Wells,
Contact: Audrienne Handcock, Tel: 01892 521855.
Viniyoga in Kent, Deal, Contact: Pamela Tyson, Tel: 01732 353804.

Lancashire
Lancashire Yoga Teachers' Association, Oswaldtwistle, Contact: Irene
O'Meara, Tel: 01254 381325.
Oswaldtwistle Yoga Group, Contact: Irenme O'Meara,
Tel: 01254 381325.

Leicestershire
Leicestershire Yoga Circle, Contact: Brenda Kirby, Tel: 0116 2793594.
Viniyoga East Midlands, Melton Mowbray, Contact: Sheila Baker,
Tel: 01664 464852.

London

Art of Health and Yoga Centre, Contact Robert Lindsell,
Tel: 020 86821800.
British Wheel of Yoga Centre, Leicester Square, London.
Tel: 020 89502266 on Mondays.
British Wheel of Yoga County Representatives: N. London -
P. Griffin, 26 Parkfield Gardens, N. Harrow HA2 6JB,
Tel: 020 84276597, **South London** - P. Dob, 1 Longfield Dr, East Sheen
SW14 7AU, Tel: 020 88763928.
City Yoga Centre, Contact Paul Lurenson, Tel: 020 72533000
Dharma Yoga Centre, Oxford Circus, Contact: Julie Friedeberger
Tel: 020 8857286.
Hatha Yoga for Body-Mind Awareness, Contact: Maro Stoyanuidou,
Tel: 020 73722203.
Kishmir Yoga Group, 35 Nassington Rd, London NW3 2TY
Tel: 020 77940773.
Life Centre, London W.8 Contact: Godfrey Devereaux,
Tel: 020 72214602.
Maida Vale Yoga Institute, Iyengar Yoga, Contact: Rosanne Seal,
Tel: 020 76243080.
Nataraja Yoga Centre, 46 Crouch Hall Rd, London N8 8HJ,
Tel: 020 83405279.
North East London Iyengar Yoga Institute, Contact: Brigid Philip,
Tel: 020 725649137.
Practical Ayurveda, Middlesex, Contact: Dr Anne Roden, 27 Lankers
Drive, N. Harrow, HA2 7PA.
Relaxation Centre, 7-11 Kensington High St, London W8 5NP,
Tel: 020 79383409.
Satyananda Yoga Centre, 70 Thurleigh Rd, SW12, Tel: 020 86734869.
School of Yoga, Westminster and Croydon, Tel: 020 86573258.
Shared Experience Yoga Group, Oxford Circus,
Contact: J. Friedeberger, Tel: 020 88587286.
Sivananda Yoga Vendanta Centre, 51 Felsham Rd, SW15 1AZ,
Tel: 020 87800160.
Toynbee Hall, Contact: Peter Ballard, Tel: 01255 551443.
Viniyoga South London, Contact: Geoff Farrer, Tel: 020 77085636.
Viniyoga, Contact: Pamela Tyson, Tel: 01304 367166.
Yoga-Dham, Middlesex, Contact: Tara Patel, Tel: 020 84286691.
Yoga Therapy Centre, Royal London Homeopathic Hospital Trust,
60 Great Ormond St., London, WC1N 3HR, Tel: 020 78337267.
Yoga 2000, Contact: Antonia Boyle, Tel: 01959 56888.

Manchester

Manchester and District Instutute of Iyengar Yoga,
Contact: Janice Yates, Tel: 0161 3683614.
Whitefield Yoga Group, Manchester, Contact: Pauline O'Gara,
Tel: 0161 7662305.

Merseyside

Comprehensive Yoga Fellowship, New Brighton,
Contact: Gordon Smith, Tel: 0151 6399402.
Merseyside Yoga Association, Contact: Janet Irlam, Tel: 0151 6526343.

Norfolk
Norfolk Yoga Group, Contact: Bob Camp, Tel: 01603 36659.
Aylsham Meditation Group, Aylsham, Contact: Cherry Cooke,
Tel: 01263 732426.

Northamptonshire
Body Mind. Inc, Raunds, Contact: Annette Sykes,Tel: 01933 623706.
Northamptonshire Yoga Association, Rushden,
Contact: Sheila Robinson, Tel: 01933 312599.
Northamptonshire Meditation Group, Contact: Margaret Gill,
Tel: 01604 781761.

Northumberland
Northumberland Yoga Group, Felton, Contact: Betty Websell,
Tel: 01670 787423.

Nottingamshire
Friends of Yoga Society, Contact: Pauline Mainland,
Tel: 0115 97335435.

Oxfordshire
Banbury Yoga Group, Contact: Janice Pearse, Tel: 01295 262412.
Chinese Wu Hsing Buddhist Yoga, Oxford, Contact: Christopher
Jones, Tel: 01865 245095.
Oxford Yoga Group, Contact: Gillian Webster, Tel: 01865 841018.
Stillness in Action, Beckley, Contact: Maarten Vermaage,
Tel: 01865 351650.

Shropshire
The Bodylife Centre of Massage and Yoga, Broseley,
Contact: Derek Osborn, Tel: 01952 883135.

Somerset
Self Realisation Meditation Healing Centre, Queen Camel,
Contact: Christy Casley, Tel: 01935 850266.
Viniyoga Southwest, Taunton, Contact: Ranju Roy, Tel: 01823 322826.

Staffordshire
Staffordshire Yoga Fellowship, Stoke-on-Trent,
Contact: Mary Myatt, Tel: 01782 657730.
Stafford Yoga Group, Irene Yates, Tel: 01785 662207.

Surrey
Farnham Sports Centre Yoga Group, Witley,
Contact: Sarah Ball, Tel: 01483 422655.
Godalming Students' Association, Contact: Mrs J. Milner,
Tel: 01483 417428.
Maybury Centre, Woking, Contact: Riny van Akkeren,
Tel: 01483 724065.
Satya Yoga, Godalming, Contact: Sandra Billinge, Tel: 01483 419601.
School of Yoga, Croydon, See School of Yoga in London section.
Surrey Iyengar Yoga Centre, Cheam, Contact: Ruth White,
Tel: 020 86440309.
Witley Yoga Group, Witley, Contact: Sarah Ball, Tel: 01448 3422655.

Woking and District Yoga Club, Chobham, Contact: Ralph Gabriel,
Tel: 01276 858884.
Woking Leisure Centre Yoga Club, Woking, Contact: Brenda Brown,
Tel: 01483 747519.

Sussex
Bihar School of Yoga, Worthing, Worthing, Contact: Swami
Ramdevananda, Tel: 01903 820525.
Hastings and District Yoga Association, Contact: Ken Bennett,
Tel: 01424 434400.
Hourne Farm Centre for Yoga, Crowborough, Contact: Peter Randel,
Tel: 01892 661093.
Patanjali Yoga Centre and Ashram, Battle, Contact: Sri Indar Nath,
Tel: 01424 870538.
Viniyoga in Sussex, Contact: Gill Lloyd, Tel: 01293 536664.

Tyne and Wear
North East Institute of Iyengar Yoga, Seaburn Dene,
Contact: Gordon Austin, Tel: 0191 5487457.
Kripalu Yoga Support Group, North Shields,
Contact: Muriel McLacland, Tel: 0191 2570988.

West Midlands
Birmingham and District Institute of Iyengar Yoga,
Contact: Jayne Orton, Tel: 0121 7438143.
Life Foundation School for Therapeutics (UK), Bilston,
Contact: Paulette Agnew, Tel: 01902 409164.
Satyananda Yoga Centre, Birmingham, Contact: Ann Fletcher,
Tel: 0121 4445976.
Shirley Community Association Yoga Class, Shirley,
Contact: Evelyn Hewett, Tel: 0121 7446330.

Wiltshire
Ashtanga Yoga, Westbury, Contact: Allan Oakman, Tel: 01373 859313.
The European Shiatsu School, Marlborough, Contact: Chris Jarmey,
Tel: 01672 86362.
Swindown and District Yoga Association, Swindon,
Contact: Connie Pearce, Tel: 01793 721230.

Worcestershire
Malvern Hills Yoga Centre, Contact: Gail Reeves, Tel: 01684 310884.

Yorkshire
Charmony Yoga Circle, Huddersfield, Contact: June Morella,
Tel: 01484 535298.
Crayke Yoga Club, Easingwold, Contact: Jane Cluley, Tel: 01347 23004.
Yoga for All, York, Contact: Jane Reed, Tel: 01904 423340.

SCOTLAND

Brahma Kumaris, Glasgow, Contact: Rose Goddenough,
Tel: 0141 4235141.

Edinburgh and Lothians Yoga Association, Edinburgh,
Contact: Pat Lines, Tel: 0131 4452947.
Friends of L.I.F.E.- Lendrick Lodge, Trossachs,
Contact: Sadie Mulvanny, Tel: 01877 376263.
Scottish Yoga Teachers' Association, Contact: Frances Corr,
Tel: 0131 3433553.
West of Scotland Yoga Teachers' Association, Glasgow,
Contact: Pearl Slane, Tel: 0141 9430597.

WALES

Classical Yoga for the New Age, Llandeilo, Contact: Sue Armour,
Tel: 01558 823842.
Life Foundation School of Therapeutics (UK), Bangor,
Contact: Gordon Sweeney, Tel: 01248 370076.
Mandala Yoga Ashram, Llandeilo, Contact: The Secretary,
Tel: 01558 685358.
Natural Healing Centre, Llanelli, Contact: Margaret Howells,
Tel: 01554 757194.
North Wales Yoga and Natural Therapy Centre,
Contact: Helen Humphreys, Tel: 01492 533961.
Padmasambhava, Llandeilo, Contact: Sue Armour, Tel: 01558 823842.
Support Group for Yoga Teachers and Serious Students, Harlech,
Contact: Margaret Ellis, Tel: 01766 780365.

IRELAND

An Sanctoir, Cork, Contact: Charlie Stevens, Tel: 02835444.
Viniyoga Ireland, Dublin, Contact: Hanna Gillespie,
Tel: 00 353 12889012.
Yoga Fellowship of Northern Ireland, Rathfriland,
Contact: Marie Quail, Tel: 028 40631138.

FRANCE

La Fédération Nationale des Enseignants de Yoga (F.N.E.Y.), Contact:
Yse Masquelier, 3 rue Aubriot, F-75004 Paris, Tel: (00 33) 01 42 70 03 05.

Centre Atma, 50 rue des Lices, 8400 Avignon, Tel: 0490273514.
Centre de Yoga Iyengar de Lyon, Clos de Fourviere II, 40 rue Roger
Radisson, 69005 Lyon, Tel: 0478360384.
École Française de Yoga du Sud-Est, 18 rue Victor Leydet, 13100 Aix-
en-Provence, Tel: 0442279220.
Fédération Inter-Régionale de Hatha-Yoga, 322 rue Saint Honoré,
75001 Paris, Tel: 0442603210.
Kaivalyadhama-France, Lozeron, 26400 Gigors-et-Lozeron,
Tel: 0475764295.
L'assocation provençale de Hatha Yoga, 12 rue J. Daret, Aix-en-
Provence, Tel: 0542641854.
La Fédération Tantra Kundalini Yoga, Chateau Laroque, 33890
Juillas.

La Fédération des Yogas Traditionnels, Andr´Riehl, 65 rue des Cedres, 84120 Pertuis, Tel: 0490096527.
La Val Dieu, Pyrenees, Contact: Annette Tolson, Tel: 01225311826.
La Yoga Thérapie, Christine Campagnac-Morette, 5 place du Général Beuret, 75015 Paris.

SPAIN

Associacion Espangnola de Praticantes de Yoga, Mrs Manuel Morata, 10 Casa Jimenes, 50004 Zaragoza. Tel: (00 34) 97621956016.

Cortijo Romero Holidays, Granada, Tel: 01494782720 (see entry under Spain retreat section).
Hugo Acuna, c/Damas 11a, 08003, Barcelona, Tel: 933192086.
Windfire Yoga Retreat, Ibiza, Windfire Yoga, 36 Stanbridge Road, London SW15 1DX, Tel: 020 87803050.
Yoga and Meditation Seminars, Majorca, Derina Newell, 125 High St., Hedleigh, Suffolk, IP7 5EJ, Tel: 01473 822761.

OPEN CENTRES

Open Centres are various groups who are concerned with meditation, movement, healing, spirituality awareness, and interfaith work. They include but are not limited to yoga centres, meditation groups, and private houses. They are, in essence, centred in spiritualities and healing within the context of mind-body-spirit but not to the exclusion of other spiritualities and religions. The organisation which helps to link them together in common interest is Open Centres.

Open Centres
Avrils Farm
Lower Stanton St Quintin
Chippenham
Wiltshire SN14 6PA   Tel: 01249 720202

Open Centres publish a bi-annual non-profit making newsletter which links all the centres and people who share the same mind-body-spirit aims. The newsletter includes a directory listing meditation groups around the country, Julian meetings which are devoted to the practice of Christ-centered contemplative meditation, the list of Open Centres and regional addresses for the National Federation of Spiritual Healers. Some of the open centres are detailed in this guide and these are marked with an asterisk.

*The Abbey, Sutton Courtney, Abingdon, Oxon OX14 4AF,
  Tel: 01235 847401
  Amrit Hermitage, Helland Cottage, Ladock, Cornwall TR2 4QE,
  Tel: 01726 883811
*The Barn, Lower Sharpham, Ashprington, Devon, TQ9 7DX,
  Tel: 01803 732661
*Beacon Centre, Cutteridge Farm, Whitestone, Exeter EX4 2HL,
  Tel: 01392 81203
  Beech Lawn, Beech Grove, Mayford, Woking, Surrey GU22 OSX,
  Tel: 01483 747519
  Bournemouth Centre C.M., 26 Sea Rd, Boscombe, Bournemouth,
  Tel:01202 36354
  Bridge Trust, Back Cottage, W. Williamston, Kilgetty SA68 OTL
*Caer, Rosemerryn, Lamorna, Penzance, Cornwall TR19 6EN,
  Tel: 01773 672530
*Centre of New Directions, White Lodge, Stockland Green Rd,
  Speldnurst, Kent TN3 OTT
  Centre of Unity, 6 Kings Grange, 46 W. Cliff Rd, Bournemouth,
  Dorset BH4 8BB
  The Coach House, Kilmuir, N. Kessock, Inverness IV1 1XG
  Centre of Truth, Suite 4, Carlton Chambers, 5 Station Rd,
  Shortlands, Kent BR2 OEY
  Coombe Quarry, Coombe Hill, Keinton Mandeville,
  Somerset TA1 1DQ, Tel: 01458 223215

Croydon Healing Centre, Kesborough, 16 Bisdenden Rd, Croydon,
Surrey CRO 6UN, Tel: 020 86881856
Easter Centre, 16 Bury Rd, Hengrave, Bury St Edmunds,
Suffolk IP28 6LR, Tel: 01798 704881
Ellbridge, Broadhempston, Totnes, Devon TQ9 6BZ, Tel: 01803813015
***Flint House**, 41 High St., Lewes, E. Sussex BN7 2LU,
Tel: 01273 473388
***Gaia House**, Woodland Rd, Denbury, Devon, TQ12 6DY,
Tel: 01803 813188
***Grail Centre**, 125 Waxwell Lane, Pinner, HA5 3ER, Tel: 020 88662195
***Grail Retreat Centre**,Tan-y-Bryn St, Abergynolwyn,
Gwynedd LL36 9WA Tel: 01694 7822268
***The Grange**, Ellesmere, Shropshire SY1 9DE, Tel: 01691 623495
Fellowship of Meditation, 8 Prince of Wales Rd. Dorchester
Tel: 01305 251396
***Hawkwood College**, Painswick Old Rd, Stroud, Glos. GL6 7QW,
Tel: 01453 759034
Herts Holistic Health Ctre, Tel: 01707 24631
Home Farm Workshops, Burley on Hill, Oakham,
Rutland LEA15 7SX, Tel: 01572 757333
***Kirkby Fleetham Hall**, Kirkby Fleetham, N. Yorks GL7 OSU
Tel: 01609 748711
Lifeways, 30 Albany Rd, Stratford on Avon, Warks, CV37 6PG,
Tel: 01789 292052
Living Centre, 12a Durham Road, Raynes Park, London SW20 OTW
Tel: 020 89462331
Middle Piccadilly, Holwell, Sherbourne, Dorset, Tel: 01963 23468
***Minton House**, Forres, Moray IV36 OYY, Tel: 01309 690819
Newbold House, St Leonard's Road, Forres, Moray IV36 ORE
Tel: 01309 72659

Associated with these Open Centres are a number of regional members
of the National Federation of Spiritual Healers. You can obtain a list
from them of the names and address of each of their 15 regional associations and a brochure of their annual courses.

National Association of Spiritual Healers
Old Manor Farm Studio
Church Street, Sunbury-on-Thames
Middlessex TW16 6RG   Tel: 01932 783164

HELPFUL ADDRESSES

Organisations and Associations

Retreat Association
The Central Hall
256 Bermondsey Street
London SE1 3UJ   Tel: 020 73577736

Christian - Ecumenical

The Retreat Association is a very important national organisation which makes available the programmes of many of the Christian retreat houses in Britain. It has grown in scope and excellence of work over the last few years and comprises these Christian retreat groups: the **Association for Promoting Retreats** (mainly Anglican), the **National Retreat Movement** (mainly Roman Catholic), the **Methodist Retreat Group**, the **Baptist Union Retreat Group**, the **United Reformed Church Silence and Retreat Group**, and the **Quaker Retreats and One-to-One Ministry (Q-ROOM)**.

The Retreat Association aims to foster and develop the rich and diverse expressions of Christian spirituality. There are no individual members. It provides information and resources, maintains networks and co-ordinates new initiatives and publishes an annual journal *Retreats*.

Retreats lists retreat houses and their programmes in Britain and Ireland. There are articles about retreats and the journal is available by post from the Association or from Christian book shops. Do ask also in your local book and magazine shop as it may be available there. You may send an SAE for a list of courses.

If you are looking for a spiritual director, the Retreat Association can help by putting you in touch with a contact person in your area.

Amaravati Buddhist Centre
Great Gaddesden
Hemel Hempstead
Herts. HP1 3BZ   Tel: 01442 842455
                                                       Fax: 01442 843721

Creative Arts Retreat Movement
182 High Street
Street, Somerset BA16 0NH

Bahá'í Community of the UK
27 Rutland Gate
London SW7 1PD   Tel: 020 75842566

Brahma Kumaris World Spirituality University
Global Co-operation House
65 Pound Lane, London NW10 2HH   Tel: 020 84591400
                                            Fax: 020 84516480
                              e-mail:bk@bkwsugch.demon.co.uk

British Buddhist Association
11 Biddulph Road
London W9 1JA   Tel: 020 72865575
                                            Fax: 020 72865575

Buddhist Society
58 Ecclestone Square
London SW1 1PH   Tel: 020 78345858
                                            Fax: 020 79765238

Council of Churches for Britain and Ireland
Inter-Church House
35-41 Lower Marsh
London SE1 7RL   Tel: 020 76204444
                                            Fax: 020 79280010

Evangelical Alliance UK
Whitefield House
186 Kennington Park Road
London SE11 4BT   Tel: 020 72072100
                                            Fax: 020 72072150

Fellowship of Contemplative Prayer
202 Ralph Road
Solihull, West Midlands B90 3LE   Tel/Fax: 0121 7456522

Friends of the Western Buddhist Order
London Buddhist Centre
51 Roman Road
Bethnal Green, London E2 OHU   Tel: 020 79811225
                                            Fax: 020 89801968
                              e-mail lbc@alanlbc.demon.uk

Hindu Cultural Trust Centre
55 Manor Road
Hounslow, Middlesex TW4 7JN   Tel: 020 82300571

Inter Faith Network for the United Kingdom
5-7 Tavistock Place
London WC1H 9SN   Tel: 020 73870008
                                            Fax: 020 73877968

Inter Faith Resource Centre
91 Mantilla Drive
Styvechale, Conventry CV3 6LG   Tel: 024 76415531

Islamic Centre England
140 Maida Vale
London W9 1QB

e-mail: ice@ic-el.org
Website: www.ic-el.org

Iyengar Yoga Institute
223a Randolph Avenue
London W9 1NL

Tel/Fax: 020 76243080

Lesbian and Gay Christian Movement
Oxford House
Derbyshire Street
London E2 6HG

Tel/Fax: 0171 7391249
e-mail: lgcm@churchnet.ucsm.uk
Website: www.members.aol.com/lgcm
Counselling Helpline: 020 77398134

The Open Centre
Third Floor
188 Old Street
London EC1 9FR

Tel: 020 72511504

Mind-Body-Spirit

Now running for over twenty years, The Open Centre offers a programme to increase your awareness of yourself and others and to help you take a look at your relationships, your assumptions and your decisions about life and work. The key ideas are centred in therapy, movement, healing and growth. Courses on offer may include primal integration, bio-energetics, and transactional analysis. There is a brochure available on request and, as a guide, prices range from £30-£35 per hour for individual sessions to intensives and residential courses at £110-£305.

Pagan Federation
BM Box 7097
London WC1N 3XX

Tel/Fax: 01691 671066

Quaker Retreats and One-to-One Ministry
80 Lock Street
Abercynon, Glamorgan CF45 4HU

Roman Catholic Church in England and Wales
Catholic Communications Centre
39 Eccleston Square
London SW1V 1BX

Tel: 020 72338196
Fax: 020 79337497
e-mail: 101454.103@compuserve.com

Salvation Army
101 Queen Victoria Street
London EC4P 4EP

Tel: 020 72365222
Fax: 020 72366272

Vedanta Movement (Hindu)
13 Elsenham Street
Southfields, London SW18 5UN   Tel: 020 88746100

World Congress of Faiths
2 Market Square
Oxford, Oxon OX1 3EF   Tel: 01865 202751
                                            Fax: 01865 202746

World Sikh Foundation
88 Mollison Way
Edgware, Middlesex HA8 5QW   Tel: 020 82570359

HELPFUL PUBLICATIONS

Christian (Ecumenical)
Retreats
Retreat Association
The Central Hall
256 Bermondsey Street
London SE1 3UJ   Tel: 020 73577736

Christian (Baptist)
Baptist Times
PO Box 54
129 The Broadway
Didcot, Oxon11 8XB

Christian (Anglican)
Church Times
33 Upper Street
London N1 OPN   Tel: 020 73594570
                                                      Fax: 020 72263073

Christian (Evangelical)
Evangelism Today
320 Ashley Down Road
Bristol B57 9BQ   Tel/Fax: 0117 9241679

Christian (Roman Catholic)
The Tablet
Great Peter Street
London SW1P 2HB

Buddhist
Tricycle: **The Buddhist Review**
Sharpham Coach Yard
Ashprington
Totnes, Devon TQ9 7UT   Tel: 01803 732082
                                                      Fax: 01803 732037
                        e-mail: buddhist.publishing@dial.pipex.com

Buddhist
Middle Way and The Buddhist Directory of Buddhist Groups and
Centres in the UK
The Buddhist Society
58 Eccleston Square
London SW1V 1PH

Hindu
Hinduism Today
1b Claverton Street
London SW1V 3AY

Tel: 020 76308688
e-mail: 100700.513@compuserve.com

Jewish
Jewish Chronicle
25 Furnival Street
London EC4A 1JT

Tel: 020 74151500
Fax: 020 74059040
e-mail: jacdmin@chron.co.uk

Mind-Body-Spirit
Kindred Spirit Quarterly
Foxhole
Dartington
Totnes, Devon TQ9 6EB

Tel: 01803 866686
Fax: 01803 866591
e-mail: kindred@spirit.co.uk

Mind-Body-Spirit
Parabola
PO Box 3000
Denville, New Jersey 07834
USA

Internet: http://www.parabola.org

Muslim
Islamic Times
Raza Academy
138 Northgate Road
Edgeley, Stockport SK3 9NL

Tel: 01614 771595

Retreats in the USA
Sanctuaries by J and M. Kelly
Bell Tower, N.Y. ISBN 0-517-88517-4

Yoga
Spectrum
The Journal of the British Wheel of Yoga
123 Bear Road
Brighton, East Sussex BN2 4DB

Tel: (Editorial) 01273 698560

TRAVEL ORGANISATIONS

Retreats Abroad
Retreats Beyond Dover
St Etheldreda's Church
14 Ely Place
London EC1N 6RY   Tel/Fax: 020 78312388

Pilgrimages
Tangney Tours
Pilgrim House
Station Court
Borough Green, Kent TN15 8AF   Tel: 01732 886666
                                          Fax: 01732 886885

SELECTED READING

People often wonder what to take on a retreat for reading outside the material which may be provided. A religious retreat place will usually have available literature centred around their beliefs. Other places may leave you to browse in their library or bookshop. Guest house libraries with so many books often make choice difficult. Regardless of whether you follow a particular spiritual path or not, reading which may widen your understanding of spirituality and the inner self can often prove helpful. It may bring reflection on your lifestyle and your present values while you are taking time out from ordinary living – or even give you a greater vision of humanity and God than you might have had before. It is for this reason that this very short list is not organised according to any particular religion or spiritual path.

A Thirst for God: Daily Readings with St Francis de Sales, DLT, London 1985.

Bhagavad-Gita: Chapters 1-6, Maharishi Mahesh Yogi, Penguin, London 1969

Confessions of Saint Augustine, Trans. R.S. Pine-Coffin, Penguin Books, London 1961

Essential Rumi, Translated by Coleman Barks, Harper, San Francisco, USA 1995

Golden Age of Zen, C. H. Wu, Image Books, Doubleday, New York 1996

Good News Bible, The Bible Society, HarperCollins, London 1994

In Search of Nature, Edward O. Wilson, Island Press, Washington DC, USA 1996

Interior Prayer: Carthusian Novice Conferences, Darton, Longman and Todd, London 1996

Introducing The New Testament, John Drane, Lion Books, Oxford, 1986

Introducing the Old Testament, John Drane, Lion Books, Oxford, 1987

Koran, Translated by N.J. Dawood, Allen Lane 1978

Living the Sacred, Stafford Whiteaker, Rider Books 2000

Meister Eckhart, The Essential Sermons, Paulist Press, New York, 1981

Muhammad: A Short Biography, Martin Forward, Oneworld, Oxford 1998

Native American Spirituality, Dennis Renault and Tomothy Freke, Thorsons, London 1996

New Jerusalem Bible, Darton, Longman and Todd, London 1990

New Seeds of Contemplation, Thomas Merton, A New Directions Books, 1972

Path of Life, Cyprian Smith, Gracewing, 1995

Paths in Solitude, Eve Baker, St Pauls, 1995

Practice of the Presence of God, Brother Lawrence, Mowbray, London, 1980

Souls on Fire, Elie Wiesel, Touchstone, USA

Teachings from the Silent Mind, Ven. Ajahn Sumedho, Aamaravati Buddhist Centre, 1987

Way of the Shaman, Michael Harner, HarperCollins, New York, 1990

Western Buddhism, Kulananda, HarperCollins, 1997

GLOSSARY

Alexander Technique: Gentle manipulation which guides the body into a more natural posture and relaxed state, bringing awareness of how to help you to do the same by yourself. It is of particular help to those with back and postural problems and tension-related ones.

Aromatherapy: This is a holistic treatment which enhances well-being, relieves stress and helps the body restore energies. Many conditions can be helped. Essential oils are selected for each person's needs and gently massaged into the skin.

Baha'i': This Faith began in Persia in 1844 as a new religion. Bahá'í members believe their scriptures to be the revealed word of God. Key beliefs are belief in one God, the unity of mankind, independent investigation of truth, the common foundation of all religions, the harmony of science and religion, equality of opportunity for men and women, elimination of all prejudices, universal education, abolition of the extremes of poverty and wealth, establishment of world peace, and the concept of progressive revelation.

Buddhism, Buddha: Buddhism does not believe in a personal deity. It makes no claim to have a divinely inspired book and it has no central organising authority. The teachings of Buddhism are an inheritance from Siddhartha Gautama's own search for truth. He was believed to be *enlightened*, that is to be a Buddha. Thus, the emphasis for Buddhists is on a tradition of teachings. While they begin by learning about these teachings, in the end each individual must discover their own experience of truth and what it has taught them. The *Noble Eightfold Path* in Buddhist teachings is concerned with wisdom, morality, concentration and meditation. Central in its role in Buddhism is meditation of which there are various methods.

Charismatic retreat: Christian healing retreat which usually involves praying in tongues and prophecy.

Choir: A body of singers assisting at Divine Office. Lay singers are usually the choir at church services, but the choir in a monastery consists of the religious of that Community who come together to pray the Divine Office and guests who they may or may not invite to join them.

Christianity, Christian life: The common focus of Christianity is on the person of Jesus of Nazareth. He is seen as the criterion by which all of life is to be evaluated. The universal significance of Jesus is always asserted. The name *Christians* was originally given to early followers of Jesus who believed him to be the *Christ* or Messiah. Christian life is the living out of the command by Jesus to *love one another as I have loved you*, so Christians try to base their lives on the pattern of his life which was characterised by sacrificial and self-giving love.

Community: In the Christian sense, a group of people who live together under a common rule, usually but not always with obedience to one person, who worship together and whose lives are devoted to seeking God. It is traditional for Communities to be of men or women, but this is not always the case (see Burford Priory). Sometime men and women religious in separate communities will work and worship together (see Turvey Abbey). Buddhist monks and nuns also live in Communities working and sharing a life devoted to Buddhist practices. There are lay people (see Omega Order) who also live together with much the same purpose.

Compline: The last prayer at night in the Catholic and Anglican liturgy of the hours (see *Divine Office).*

Contemplative: A person devoted to religious meditation and who gives his or her life to seeking God as the primary purpose and aim of life.

Contemplative prayer: The prayer of stillness or contemplative prayer, has been a recognised way of praying for thousands of years. It is silent and based not on knowing about God, but on knowing God. The message of Psalm 46 may best sum it up: *Be still and know that I am God.*

Counselling: A form of helping people with various personal or relationship problems through understanding, empathic and uncritical listening. This approach is combined with helping the person to clarify the problem and decide what action to take. It gives people a chance to *get things off their chest.*

Cursillo: A renewal weekend retreat for Christians to try to experience their religion from new perspectives.

De Mello retreats: Anthony de Mello S.J. was born in Bombay and died in New York in 1987. He was a popular spiritual guide who wrote a number of books on methods and practices for increasing prayer, meditation and deepening the inner self through various exercises and stories for reflection. He drew heavily on the Ignatian Exercises (see that entry) and his work is very Scripture orientated.

Dharma: Dharma means the intrinsic property of something, the thing which holds it together, that which sustains it, thus, the essential, final character of something including a person. For example, the Dharma of water is its wetness. Used in both Hindu and Buddhist traditions to represent the truth or spiritual teachings.

Directed retreat: A six to eight-day retreat which consists of silent prayer, deep inner reflection and includes a daily meeting with a spiritual director. An Ignatian retreat is usually a directed one.

Divine Office, Canonical Hours, Liturgy of the Hours, Offices: All these terms are used to describe the official daily prayer cycle of the Catholic Church which is an adaptation of the liturgy of the synagogue evolved over the centuries. The *hours* consist of seven periods of prayer which may be chanted, sung, or spoken together in a group or individually. These are called Virgils, Lauds, Terce, Sext, None, Vespers, and Compline. A version is used by the Anglican church, usually referred to as Morning Prayer and Evensong. The liturgy is built around the psalms and songs and words from Scripture. The Divine Office provides the prayer structure for monastic life.

Eco-spirituality: A spirituality based on relating our inner self and the way we live to earth, the natural world and all other creatures. Through realising our connection to earth, we may deepen the universality of our spirituality. Eco-spirituality, while essentially a mind-body-spirit spirituality approach, can also be found mirrored in Christian retreats and in Celtic spirituality. For example, Nature Retreats where use may be made of walks in woods, wildflowers, fields, mountains or sea to enhance inner awareness.

Ecumenical, Ecumenical Movement: The movement in the Christian church towards the visible union of all believers in Christ. This aspiration for unity is an old one and widely popular today. A retreat house or retreat programme which is *ecumenical* means it is open to all of Christian faith no matter to which church they belong.

Enclosure: The practice of separating a part of a religious house to the exclusion of the opposite sex. Today some Communities are semi-enclosed, that is the members do not leave the convent or monastery except rarely and for specific necessary purposes like visits to the dentist.

Enneagram: A very ancient method, using a circular diagram with nine points, for insight into discerning a person's spiritual disposition and activity (see *Introduction*).

Eucharist: The word means thanksgiving and is the term applied to the central act of Christian worship, instituted by Christ who *gave thanks*, and because the service is the supreme act of Christian thanksgiving to God. Other names used are *Holy Communion*, *The Lord's Supper*, and the *Mass*. Bread and wine are used in an act of sacred consecration and prayer to form the service of thanksgiving.

Evangelical: Evangelicals are Christians who try to live according to the Christian scriptures viewed as the supreme authority for Christian life. They feel strongly called upon to help bring others into the Christian church by means of **evangelism** (meaning *Good News*) by sharing what Christians believe God has done in and through Jesus Christ.

Guided retreat: A retreat which is guided from time to time by a spiritual director but not on a daily basis as for a directed retreat (see above).

Hermitage Retreats, Poustinia, Poustinia Experience: *Poustinia* is a Russian word meaning a hermitage. These were originally little isolated huts, located deep in the forests of Russia. What they offered were total silence, solitude, and the uninterrupted time to seek God. Today, there are a few of these in Britain and Ireland, usually in the form of a self-catering cottage or a small caravan parked outside the monastery in a field.

Hinduism, Hindus: The Hindu tradition allows the use of various symbols, names, terms and images which may help people to discover the divine. Within the religion there are both those who believe in one God and for whom there is a distinction between God and the world, and those who believe that God is simultaneously both one and many. A number of central values are shared by most Hindus although in practice they may differ in interpretation. These key ideals and values include respect for parents and elders, reverence for teachers, regard for guests, vegetarianism, non-violence, tolerance of other races and religions, the sanctity of marriage, the discouragement of all pre-marital and extra-marital sexual relationships, the sacredness of the cow, and an appreciation of the equality and sanctity of all living beings.

Icon: A painting or enamel which represents a saint or other sacred person. Icon painting retreats use the painting of the icon as a structure and centring for prayer.

Inter-denominational: Common to several religious denominations.

Inter-faith: Common to several different religions. An Inter-faith retreat would be one held with members of two or more faiths.

Ignatian Exercises, Saint Ignatius of Loyola: St Ignatius (1491–1556) was founder of the Society of Jesuits. He wrote *Spiritual Exercises* which has remained one of the great Christian spirituality practices for deepening faith and inner awareness of God. Ignatian retreats are usually 8, 10, or 30 days in duration and have recently regained much of their popularity. A spiritual director is assigned to guide you through it. There is much solitude and silence so that time and space is given over to meditation and reflection.

Islam, Muslim: Islam is monotheistic and God is all merciful, all powerful and all present. He controls and sustains the universe and, although humans may choose which path of life to follow, all eventually return to God to whom they are accountable. Islam rests on seven basic beliefs: the oneness of God, the books revealed by God, belief in the prophets, the angels, a Day of Judgement, life after death, and that all power belongs alone to God. Muslim practice is based on the *Five Pillars of Islam*. The first is the declaration of Faith or *Shahadah* which is that there is no God except God and Muhammad is his messenger.

Laity, Lay man or Lay woman: Members of the Christian church who do not belong to the clergy.

Massage: Massage counteracts stress by bringing deep relaxation of the body and person. As the muscles relax, the breathing improves and circulation strengthens. It helps restore harmony and balance to the mind and body. It also strengthens the body itself.

Meditation: In Christian meditation, the term denotes mental prayer. its method is the devout reflection on a chosen, often biblical, theme to deepen spiritual insight. In Buddhist and Hindu practice, meditation is a way toward personal development by directly working on the mind to transform it. Although there are hundreds of approaches to meditation, these divide into two main streams of practice. One is to calm and refresh the mind, relax the body and psychological tensions so a deeply contented state is achieved. The other meditation practice aims at developing wisdom in the context of self, others, and the nature of all things. Breathing techniques are often part of the meditation method.

Monks, Nuns, Religious: Monks are men, and nuns or sisters are women, who have undertaken to live a life, usually together in a Community, devoted to seeking God or enlightenment. They may be Christian, for example, and may make promises of poverty, chastity and obedience. Buddhists also have monks and nuns living in Communities.

Non-religious: Belonging to no established religion or faith.

Non-retreatant: A description often used by those running retreat houses and the term is used in this guide. It refers to a person who is staying at a retreat centre for rest and relaxation during a short, quiet holiday and is not planning to attempt anything of a spiritual nature. Many places do not want visitors who only desire a holiday and this is understandable. Other places actively encourage this type of guest.

Order: Monks, nuns and religious belong to Orders which dictates the type of life they lead. Among the best known Orders in Western Christianity are the **Society of Jesus** noted for teaching and missionary work, the **Benedictines** with an emphasis on prayer, work and study of Scripture and holy books, the **Dominicans** who are known for intellectual study, the **Carmelites** who have a life centred on silent prayer and meditation, and the **Franciscans** who follow the rule of St Francis of Assisi.

Pilgrim, pilgrimage: Journeys to holy places motivated by personal devotion with the aim of obtaining supernatural help or as an act of penance or thanksgiving. Lourdes has acquired world fame as a place of pilgrimage (see France section). Pilgrims are those who are in the process of a pilgrimage.

Preached retreat: A group retreat in which a speaker or facilitator gives talks each day, usually on a particular theme which has Scripture as its core.

Private retreat: A retreat period of solitude and usually much silence without guidance or direction from anyone.

Reflexology: This ancient healing therapy originated in China centuries ago. It is a form of compression massage of the feet and hands in which energy pathways in the body are activated, benefiting self-healing and a feeling of well-being. It is used as well to treat specific areas of complaint or blocked energy.

Refectory: Monastery dining room.

Reiki: An Asian healing technique in which an energy transfer occurs between the therapist and the patient by the laying on of hands. This may promote healing, a sense of well-being and the reduction of stress.

Sacrament: A sacrament is an outward and visible sign of an inward and spiritual grace given to Christians by Christ. In Christian theology the term has wide variations. Three sacraments, Baptism, Confirmation, and Orders are held to be non-repeatable. The Eucharist (see entry above) is a sacrament.

Scripture, Holy Scripture: The sacred writings of the Old and New Testament, together known as the Bible.

Shamanism, Shaman: One of the primitive religions in which all the good and evil of life are thought to be brought about by spirits which can be influenced only by Shamans. Some Shaman religions are those of the Native American Indians and people of the Ural region in Siberia. A Shaman is a priest or medicine-man, a *master of ecstasy* in touch with the realm of experience or reality that exists outside the limited, narrow state of our normal waking consciousness. By performing certain acts and rituals a Shaman is able to influence good and evil spirits and change consciousness to bring about a greater state of wholeness. It is widely used for the discovery of the inner person and for healing. Shamanism, particularly that of the Indians of the Americas, has greatly increased its popularity in the West, especially in Britain and France (see Eagle's Wing Centre for Contemporary Shamanism in London section). Programmes of many mind-body-spirit places often include courses and workshops with shaman themes or practices, e.g. sweat lodges, chanting, drumming, dancing.

Shiatsu: This is a powerful Japanese healing therapy. Shiatsu means finger pressure and is applied on specific areas, blocked energies are released with increased circulation and general flexibility resulting.

Sufism: Sufism is a commitment to the practical and accessible aspects of Islam but emphasises the inner or mystical aspects of the faith. The members of Sufi Orders may use various aids for their spiritual development including meditation, chanting or ritual dancing.

T'ai Chi chuan: Ancient Chinese method to achieve meditation through movement in a series of flowing, extremely graceful, slow and gentle movements or exercises intended to quiet the inner self, the mind and the body. The movements also actively exercise most of the muscles of the body. They can be done by people of any age.

Vipassana meditation: Insight meditation, originating in Southeast Asia and now popular in Europe, practised to attain mindfulness and understanding of the nature of self and others. It assumes that kindness, compassion and generosity of spirit may be cultivated by a person.

Virgin Mary, the Blessed Virgin Mary, Mary: The mother of Jesus Christ. In the Bible, Mary figures prominently in the stories of Jesus' birth. Belief in Mary's intercessions through direct prayer to her is probably a very old Christian belief dating from the 3rd to early 4th centuries. While there are others in the world, the most famous shrines to Mary are at Lourdes (see section on France) and Fatima where there were apparitions of her. Mary's presence in the New Testament stories is marked by her obedience to God and her humility.

Zen: A transliteration of the Sanskrit word *Dhyana* meaning meditation.

REPORT FORM

To: The Good Retreat Guide
        Rider Books
        Random House
        20 Vauxhall Road
        London SW1V 2SA

I have visited the following retreat on.................................20...........

Establishment name...

Address...

....

Post code................................Telephone...

In the space below, please describe what the retreat was like and give
any other details you feel to be relevant. For example, include what
you thought of the rooms and meals, the situation, atmosphere, spiritual help offered, special activities and charges. (Please continue on
the reverse of this sheet if necessary.)

From my personal experience I recommend this retreat centre for
inclusion in/exclusion from future editions of *The Good Retreat Guide*.

I am not connected in any way with this retreat centre other than as a
guest.

Name and address (BLOCK CAPITALS, PLEASE)

....

....

....

Signed...

*(Alternatively, please e-mail the above information to
113364.3521@compuserve.com)*

REPORT FORM

To: The Good Retreat Guide
        Rider Books
        Random House
        20 Vauxhall Road
        London SW1V 2SA

I have visited the following retreat on.................................20..........

Establishment name...

Address...

....

Post code...............................Telephone..

In the space below, please describe what the retreat was like and give any other details you feel to be relevant. For example, include what you thought of the rooms and meals, the situation, atmosphere, spiritual help offered, special activities and charges. (Please continue on the reverse of this sheet if necessary.)

From my personal experience I recommend this retreat centre for inclusion in/exclusion from future editions of *The Good Retreat Guide*.

I am not connected in any way with this retreat centre other than as a guest.

Name and address (BLOCK CAPITALS, PLEASE)

....

....

....

Signed..

(Alternatively, please e-mail the above information to
113364.3521@compuserve.com)

LIVING THE SACRED

Ten Gateways to Open Your Heart

Stafford Whiteaker
Author of *The Good Retreat Guide*

Getting in touch with our spiritual and practising the sacred in our everyday lives are essential for our physical, mental and emotional health. However, few of us know where to look or how it will help us if we do manage to catch a glimpse of the true self at the heart of our being. Here is a book especially written to guide you in this great spiritual adventure.

In *Living in the Sacred*, Stafford Whiteaker offers ten gateways to letting spirituality flower in your life.

- Stillness – the way of connecting to the sacred
- Mindfulness – the way of being in the present to the moment
- Listening – the way of hearing with the heart.
- Meditation – the way of opening the spiritual realm
- Loving – the way of seeking reality
- Celebrating – the way of belonging to Creation
- Dreaming – the way of rediscovering unity
- Affirmation – the way of taking stock
- Prayer – the way of talking to God
- Creativity – the way of grounding the new vision

'Unpretentious, human and thoroughly helpful. Buy it' *Daily Express*

'Teaches you to use your inner energy to improve your physical and emotional health' *Here's Health*

'Challenging practical suggestions liberally sprinkled through a text which contains a great deal of spiritual wisdom'
Benedict Barker, *Fellowship of Solitaries*

'This is a book whose intended purpose is to help anyone live a life that is truly sacred, in touch with God, however he or she might define that concept. A work designed for people of our times, people who have questions based on a perception of emptiness in their lives'
The Month

THE LITTLE BOOK OF INNER SPACE

Your Guide to Finding Personal Peace

Stafford Whiteaker

Do you sometimes feel swamped? Or ask, 'Where's the real me?'

Such eternal questions can be answered deep inside us in the sanctuary of our essential spirit. This indispensable little book shows how to find this place of retreat from the hectic world – and how to emerge from it fresh and renewed.

People have always hungered for peace and inner well-being. And today these have become essential requirements if we want to maintain healthy lives and balanced relationships. The way to meet such needs has always been through development of our interior life, the place where our spirits dwell. It is right that we should want to spend time in this inner world, which can renew and refresh our lives.

'Learn how to retreat from too many demands and to trust the still-ness you find within yourself. Become effective at making space in this life for who and what you are. In this way you may fill your life with hope, love and peace because you are truly yourself. When you want to shout, 'Give me space!' When you feel squeezed, rattled, crowded and pressured, open this little book. Let it help you to take the peace you need and deserve. Learn to live in this world but not to let the world live too much in you.'

Stafford Whiteaker

ORDER FORM

Living the Sacred by Stafford Whiteaker   £9.99

The Little Book of Inner Space by Stafford Whiteaker   £1.99

ALL RIDER BOOKS ARE AVAILABLE THROUGH MAIL
ORDER OR FROM YOUR LOCAL BOOKSHOP.

PAYMENT MAY BE MADE USING ACCESS, VISA,
MASTERCARD, DINERS CLUB, SWITCH AND AMEX, OR
CHEQUE, EUROCHEQUE AND POSTAL ORDER (STERLING
ONLY).

EXPIRY DATE.................................SWITCH ISSUE NO.

PLEASE ALLOW £2.50 FOR POST AND PACKING FOR THE
FIRST BOOK AND £1.00 PER BOOK THEREAFTER.

ORDER TOTAL: £...........................(INCLUDING P&P)

ALL ORDERS TO:
RIDER BOOKS, BOOKS BY POST, TBS LIMITED, THE BOOK
SERVICE, COLCHESTER ROAD, FRATING GREEN,
COLCHESTER, ESSEX, CO7 7DW, UK.

TELEPHONE: (01206) 256 000
FAX: (01206) 255 914

NAME...

ADDRESS...

....

....

Please allow 28 days for delivery. Please tick box if you do not wish to
receive any additional information.

Prices and availibility subject to change without notice.